The
Blanchot R

The
Blandford Reader

The Blanchot Reader

Maurice Blanchot

Edited by

Michael Holland

BLACKWELL
Oxford UK & Cambridge USA

First published in English 1995
Original publication of material by Maurice Blanchot copyright © Maurice Blanchot.
See individual essays for dates of publication.

Blackwell Publishers Ltd
108 Cowley Road
Oxford OX4 1JF, UK

Blackwell Publishers Inc.
238 Main Street
Cambridge, Massachusetts 02142, USA

British Library Cataloguing in Publication Data

A CIP catalogue record for this book is available from the British Library.

Library of Congress Cataloging-in-Publication Data

The Blanchot reader, Maurice Blanchot / edited by Michael Holland.
   p. cm.
Includes bibliographical references and index.
ISBN 0-631-19083-X (alk. paper). – ISBN 0-631-19084-8 (pbk.)
   1. Literature – Philosophy. 2. Blanchot, Maurice – Criticism and interpretation.
I. Holland, Michael, 1950–.
PN49.B54   1995
801' 95'092–dc20 94-45210   CIP

Typeset by Pure Tech Corporation, Pondicherry, India
Printed in Great Britain by
T.J. Press Ltd, Padstow, Cornwall.

This book is printed on acid-free paper.

Contents

Preface

When Peter Hoy first introduced me to Maurice Blanchot's work in 1970, his name was almost unknown in the English-speaking world, except as that of the author of brilliant occasional pieces about other authors. Ten years later he was already beginning to be translated in America and, as the 1980s progressed, more and more of his books, both fiction and non-fiction, began to appear in English. Today that process is virtually complete. Not before time, the availability of Blanchot's work in English is today commensurate with the interest being shown in his work on both sides of the Atlantic. It is deeply sad that Peter Hoy, who died in 1993, will not see the fruits of his generous contribution to the *Reader* of a comprehensive bibliography of Blanchot in English. My thanks go to Joan Head, Alysoun Stewart and Tyler Jo Smith for enabling me to include it posthumously.

This *Reader* is not the first selection of Blanchot's writings to appear in translation. What distinguishes it, however, is a desire to situate its author squarely in his time. Precisely because the translation of his works is nearing completion, it is more than ever necessary to counter what has proved a powerful temptation for Blanchot's readers, in France and elsewhere: to respond to the peculiar importance of his writing, in its relation to time and to history, as if it took place outside time and took no account of history. As Michel Surya wrote in 1990: 'what is not generally known is that, throughout his life, Maurice Blanchot displayed intense *public* presence' (see *Lignes*, 11 (September 1990), p. 161). If no account is taken of this, his work will simply appear esoteric and its substance will be impoverished. Too much of what has been written about Blanchot has contributed to such an impoverishment. In short, therefore, the purpose of the *Blanchot Reader* is to serve as a *vade mecum* for Blanchot's readers, providing points of orientation for them within the fifty-year period from 1940 to 1990, during which the main body of his writing was produced – a period which was, both historically and personally, one of enormous change.

First of all, I should like to thank Maurice Blanchot for the positive support he has given to the project; may he see the *Reader* as a token of my respect. I should also like to thank Stephan Chambers, as well as Steve Smith and then Andrew McNeillie of Blackwells for the unstinting encouragement they provided during what turned out to be a long, slow gestation period for this *Reader*. In the final stages, Sandra Raphael proved a patient and supportive guide. My thanks go, too, to the translators who worked with me: Susan Hanson, Leslie Hill, Roland-François Lack, Ian Maclachlan, Ann Smock, Chris Stevens and Michael Syrotinski. Their skill and resourcefulness was matched only by the spirit of cooperation with which they approached this collective undertaking. Finally, Ann Jefferson was a constant source of strength, a dear and loving helpmeet.

Michael Holland
April 1995

Acknowledgements

The editor and publisher would like to thank the following for permission to include the material collected in this edition: 'The Recent Novel', 'Mallarmé and the Art of the Novel', copyright © 1943 and 1971, Editions Gallimard; 'Artaud', 'The Disappearance of Literature', 'The Pursuit of the Zero Point', 'The Death of the Last Writer', copyright © 1959, Editions Gallimard; 'How is Literature Possible?', Editions José Corti; 'Sade's Reason', copyright © 1949 and 1963, Les Editions de Minuit; 'Madness *par excellence*', copyright © 1953 and 1971, Les Editions de Minuit; 'The Ease of Dying', copyright © 1994, the University of Nebraska Press; articles originally published in Jean Paulhan, *Progress of Love on the Slow Side*, translated by Michael Syrotinski and Christine Laennec; 'On a Change of Epoch', 'The Indestructible', 'The Exigency of Return (1969)', copyright © 1993, the Regents of the University of Minnesota; 'The Right to Insubordination', Mme Madeleine Chapsal; Bernard Wall's translation of 'La raison de Sade' appeared in *Horizon*, vol. XX (December 1949–January 1950), pp. 423–51, under the title 'The Marquis de Sade'; also Mme Françoise Laye and MM. Jean Piel, Pierre Nora, Yvon Bres.

Introduction

*Ordonner, en fragments intelligibles
et probables pour la traduire, la vie
d'autrui, est tout juste, impertinent.*
Stéphane Mallarmé[1]

Maurice Blanchot's work is becoming available in English in a way which
will illuminate the thinking of the last thirty years at what is a critical
time. It is a time when the crisis which this thinking has precipitated in
thought has reached its own crisis, the point at which it is in search of its
own validation by seeking to be of its time, a time of its own making.
Blanchot's thinking will illuminate this crisis, not by casting fresh light
upon it, but through a sort of phosphorescence, affecting its light with a
seemingly apocalyptic gleam, inhabiting it and becoming visible within it
as its origin, an origin locatable in history, but in history experienced as
a loss of origin and as the end of history.

'Who?'

Throughout his life Maurice Blanchot has kept his identity shrouded in
uncertainty. No writer can ever have been such a presence in his time and
yet remained so impossible to place. In the last twenty years, as his reputa-
tion has spread to the English-speaking world, this anomaly has become
acute, particularly since it is predominantly with reference to other names –
those of Derrida, Foucault, Levinas and recently Nancy – that Blanchot's
own has become significant. Almost all of his works are now available in
English translation or soon will be. Yet undermining their signature,
echoing in the name it names, there still remains a resounding 'Who?'

This is not simply a question of biography. Blanchot's life and career
have, it is true, been governed consistently (and until recently, absolutely)
by the rule he receives, via Jean-Luc Nancy, from Kant and Bacon, and
applies in evoking his friendship with Levinas: *de nobis ipsis silemus*.[2] This
silence surrounding the simple facts of his existence has, moreover,
gradually generated an inordinate curiosity about it. Yet while the line
between what is legitimate about this interest and what is not has still to

be drawn (and it is not ultimately Blanchot's to draw: *silemus* cannot become *sile*), the question 'Who?' arises from somewhere lying totally outside the field of biographical accountability, in the experience to which his life as a writer has led him.

Responding in his own name to the question *Who Comes After the Subject?*, put by Jean-Luc Nancy in 1989, Blanchot replied: ' "Who", without claiming once again to put *the ego* in question, does not find its proper site, does not let itself be assumed by Me.'[3] And later in the volume, in dialogue with Nancy, Jacques Derrida quotes some lines written earlier by Blanchot, in 1962, on the death of his friend Georges Bataille, the author of *The Inner Experience*:

> And when we ask the question: 'who was the subject of that experience?', this question is perhaps already an answer, if, for the one who conducted it, it is in this interrogative form that it found utterance in him, substituting for the closed and unique 'I' the openness of a 'Who?' without answer. Not that this means that he had simply to ask himself: 'What is this me that I am?', but much more radically, he had to seize hold of himself, unremittingly, no longer as an 'I' but as a 'Who?', the unknown and shifting being of an indefinite 'Who?'[4]

Moreover, that Bataille's experience was not merely something Blanchot could comprehend, but something that corresponded closely to his own experience as a writer, can be seen in what the narrator of *The Last Man* (1957) says: 'But slowly – suddenly – it dawned on me that this story [*histoire*] was without a witness: I was there – the "I" was already no more than a Who?, an infinity of Who? – so that no one should come between him and his destiny.'[5]

In bringing together a selection of Blanchot's writings covering a period of fifty years, I have sought to strike a meaningful balance between the need to ground today what goes under the name Blanchot in history and the exigency[6] of encountering the 'unknown and shifting being' of 'a "Who?" without answer', 'an infinity of Who?', an encounter which is the singular experience of any reader of his work. I have thus, in effect, taken him at his own word when he writes in 'The Ease of Dying' (1969) (see p. 301):

> since what is not seen is the only important thing, in the end, it remains true that great historical changes are also destined, because of their burden of absolute visibility, and because they allow nothing but these changes themselves to be seen, to free up the possibility of being understood or misunderstood intimately, and

without having to spell things out, the private falling silent so that the public can speak, thus finding its voice.

The historical changes he is referring to – the Occupation, the Algerian War and its aftermath, then May 1968 – clearly mark out the path this *Reader* will follow, not spelling things out, but rather staging a version of the dialogue between speech and silence which makes up Blanchot's writing, a dialogue unfolding through time and enfolding time, until it opens on to that 'step (not) beyond' whose *in-junction*, where voice can only falter, abolishes both speech and silence, public and private, and founds the absolute contemporaneity of a community in writing, to which, as writing, it is an endless appeal.

An Absent Signature

Maurice Blanchot was born in 1907. After studying at the University of Strasbourg, where his friendship with Emmanuel Levinas began, he continued his studies in Paris, before embarking on a career as a journalist on the foreign desk of the *Journal des Débats*. He remained with this paper until it folded in 1944, after almost 150 years of existence. In 1940, with the fall of France and the German Occupation, he withdrew from his established position with the *Débats*, which moved to Clermont and supported the Vichy regime, and confined his activities to the publication of a weekly column of literary criticism, which he sent to Clermont from the Occupied Zone, where he spent the war.

In parallel with this career with the *Débats*, a strait-laced paper styling itself 'le journal de l'élite',[7] Blanchot pursued a more adventurous, not to say precarious course, which took him, via a number of young and idealistic Catholic Nationalist reviews such as *Réaction* and *La Revue du Siècle* in the early 1930s, towards intense involvement with writers and journals at a new extreme of Nationalist sentiment, beginning with Paul Lévy's daily *Le Rempart* in 1933 and culminating with *Combat* from 1936 and *L'Insurgé* in 1937.[8] For these journals, as the 1930s progressed, the rise of Hitler posed a threat not only from without but also from within, owing to the constitutive incapacity of the institutions of the Third Republic to maintain the integrity and status of the French nation.

In the years between Hitler's rise and the *débâcle* of 1940, but particularly with the victory of the Front Populaire in 1936, these two parallel courses in Blanchot's career began to converge. The *Débats* itself gradually abandoned its more moderate stance and, under the pen of men who would soon side with Vichy, fell into line with the other more extreme, and now increasingly vociferous journals in denouncing those within

France whom they held responsible for a defeat that seemed more and more inevitable.

It is during these years that Blanchot's career as a journalist began to follow a third and more occult path, one which led him, along obscure and solitary byways, entirely outside the world of catastrophe and revenge which his world had become, indeed outside the world altogether. From the outset, his journalism was predominantly anonymous: he never became a 'signature' on the *Débats*. Indeed, as he became established, the number of articles bearing his signature dwindled to nought. With the founding of *Le Rempart* by Lévy in 1933, he seemed to find a niche, signing a daily editorial throughout most of that year. Mysteriously, however, this ceased at the beginning of September. And when *Le Rempart* became *Aujourd'hui* in 1934, despite signing a declaration of support for Lévy, caught up in the Stavisky affair,[9] Blanchot did not write for the paper. Indeed, there is to my knowledge no trace of his signature anywhere in 1934.[10]

Were that the end of it, the practical impossibility (to date) of distinguishing between anonymity and absence in the case of Blanchot's involvement with these newspapers would mean that increasing uncertainty surrounded his career as a journalist between late 1933 and his reemergence in 1936 and 1937 in *Combat* and *L'Insurgé*. That in itself, despite the disappearance of almost all trace of him from late 1937 onwards, would in turn make it difficult to view his career independently of that of his associates, both on the *Débats* and outside. This has been a powerful tendency since Jeffrey Mehlman began to explore certain areas of Blanchot's pre-war and wartime activity,[11] a tendency encouraged by the Heidegger and de Man affairs.[12] From that perspective, the fact that he confined himself to book-reviewing in the *Débats* during the Occupation cannot dispel the suspicion that he remained in tacit sympathy with the views upon which the *Débats* and its more extreme contemporaries converged, in short, that he was a passive supporter of Pétain and the Vichy regime.

But that is not the end of it. Though it is still difficult to establish precisely when it happened, Blanchot's relationship with Lévy, thanks to which he briefly acquired a consistent signature as a journalist, led to the very opposite: the post of editor-in-chief of a high-circulation weekly, founded by Lévy in 1928, namely *Aux Ecoutes*, a prime characteristic of which was that all of its articles, with the exception of Lévy's editorials, were unsigned. During the 1930s Blanchot's writing thus displayed two sorts of anonymity: one, because it is indistinguishable from absence, makes it impossible to establish his precise position during those years, and so renders him for some people, given his opinions, essentially *suspect*. The other points to something very different: the choice, from a point in time as yet to be determined, but more significantly up to a crucial date (1940), of *anonymity* as a mode of political response (and of political responsibility); a retreat from the posture required of a signature (or simply an absent signature); but above all an eschewal of the violence – the verbal, doctrinal but also potentially real violence – emanating from that signature in the later 1930s. At a clearly determined point (December 1937) Blanchot abandoned his signature. But at some point before this he had already adopted a stance which undermined his posture radically. In ceasing to be a signature, therefore, Blanchot was not simply going underground: he was emerging fully on to new ground, which, as we shall see, proved absolutely uncertain, but which ensured one thing, for him then and also for us now: his honour, despite being jeopardized at the time by the logic according to which it sought to act, and however open to question it therefore is in certain quarters today, remains fundamentally intact. For close though Lévy himself may have been, throughout the 1930s, to the ideology of national revolution that culminated in Vichy, one thing stood decisively in the way of him or his publications ever going the way of those who eventually converged in collaborating with the Pétain regime: his consciousness of being a Jew. In 1933, when he founded *Le Rempart*, he saluted the display of solidarity with German Jews by the likes of François Mauriac in the following terms:

> Let us read and ponder these splendid texts. Let us compare them to the odious texts coming to us from Germany. Let us compare the two peoples, the two souls, the two civilizations, and draw our own conclusions.[13]

In other words, whatever reservations one may have in retrospect about Lévy's ideological position, he was a Nationalist but before that he was a Jew. By becoming his associate on *Aux Ecoutes*, in the anonymity of what prided itself on being a collective venture, Blanchot can be said to have willingly tempered the violent logic and exacerbated individualism of his own Nationalist extremism with an ethic, or at least an exigency, which remained utterly alien to it, and for which he was denounced in 1942 in no uncertain terms:

> Maurice Blanchot, who used to be the editor-in-chief of the Jew Lévy, has made his debut in what he calls the novel, just as he made his debut in what he no doubt used to call a political newspaper. In exactly the way he once refused to see reality, preferring to submit to the ethic of those who employed him, today he refuses to recognize what the art of story-telling and the art of writing are . . . On

top of his other charms, [his Thomas] possesses that of being as outmoded as the Jewish art he is identified with.[14]

From one angle, it could be argued, the deviation being denounced here, however integral it was to Blanchot's perceived position in the 1930s (as Diane Rubinstein has revealed),[15] leaves him nevertheless a prisoner of an ideology he can neither act upon nor repudiate: merely deprived of the courage of his convictions by his adherence to a principle that others close to him will soon abominably betray. Though exonerated entirely of any charge of anti-Semitism, and free of that imprescriptible guilt attaching to those who collaborated with Vichy and shared its racist ideology, he might appear simply to have withdrawn anonymously into a moral limbo, from where, *aux écoutes*, he could wait and see. Adopting this perspective, the most his readers could do today would be to draw a veil over that period in his life, considering it of no relevance to what the name Blanchot has come to signify in the post-war period. Yet while the position in which he found himself as disaster approached was essentially an ambivalent one, poised between two irreconcilable exigencies, something other had entered his life by then and made what, as anonymity, could be no more than a deviation, if a morally decisive one, into a radical turn for the better. This, as the review in *Je Suis Partout* indicates, was literature.

'To have done with it'

From about 1935 onwards, literature – or something going by that name – provided Blanchot with a means of coming to terms with what seemed increasingly like the imminence of the end. Far earlier than other commentators, he had pessimistically prophesied the downfall of France. From 1933, events both abroad and at home rapidly appeared to him to be obeying a logic which posed the direst threat to the nation. In response, his articles repeatedly and relentlessly denounced that logic and deduced from it, with increasing frenzy, the necessity for violent counteraction if France was to survive. By the time his first novel, *Thomas the Obscure*, appeared in 1941, the end that had for so long seemed imminent had really come.

But to consider Maurice Blanchot therefore simply as a novelist of catastrophe, writing after the event a disaster that is historically locatable, would be entirely to misunderstand the relationship between literature and the end which he began to explore from 1935 onwards. By the time the fall of France really happened, Blanchot had already become indifferent to it. For him the disaster had already happened by that stage, the end had already come. He did not wait for the end to experience the end, because he could not wait. In a manner which has still to be elucidated, and which raises fundamental questions about the nature of nationalist sentiment, Maurice Blanchot saw (slowly? suddenly?) that all his fears were quite imaginary. This was, however, no cause for comfort. The reality in which his fears originated did not disappear or change its nature: on the contrary, it conformed increasingly to his increasingly fearful predictions. It truly became dangerous and fearful. But as such, it completely escaped human control, making all relation to it impossible, and so opening the way for the imaginary to take its place. Blanchot's fears turned out to be totally imaginary, in other words, because the reality he feared had gone off the scale of the human mind's ability to accommodate it.

The discovery that, politically, reality had gone out of control could of course have prompted a withdrawal into literature, considered as an impregnable bastion within which to preserve the nation's identity and safeguard its values. In the literary journalism that Blanchot began to produce alongside the most virulent of his political journalism in 1937, this tendency is not absent.[16] Nevertheless, it would be as erroneous to see Blanchot as a novelist of salvation as it would be to see him as a novelist of catastrophe, writing so as to ride out disaster rather than in its aftermath. His turn to literature no more comes *before* the end, in simple historical terms, than it comes after it. If, by the time it comes, Blanchot had already become indifferent to the catastrophic end he long denounced as imminent, this is because, along with the entire rationale of the Nationalist position, foundering on the contradictions of its own response to events,[17] the Nationalist Subject (from which Blanchot's identity at the time can be said entirely to derive) has been set adrift from its anchorage in the real world, lost all its bearings and been engulfed by the uncontrollable course of events.

This is because that Subject – the 'I' speaking in the name of the nation – defined itself, in both thought and action, exclusively in terms of control. Since the late nineteenth century, Nationalists had been seeking to counter the effects of the French Revolution by projecting a mode of simultaneous being and doing, called 'Revolution' in its turn, which would sweep away the imperfect reality of the Republic and allow order to be restored to the nation. This attempt to control what was often referred to in the 1930s as 'the established disorder' (*le désordre établi*) was by then coming to seem resolutely utopian. The new order, the 'France of tomorrow'[18] as it was termed in 1934 (after the riots of 6 February), came to appear increasingly remote as the decade wore on. As the logic of the threat from both without and within became more and more inexorable, 'Revolution' ceased to be conceivable as a transitional *sursaut* or burst of liberating energy, aimed at restoring an order capable of exercising its own beneficent control. It became, if not an end in itself, the horizon to everything: the only conceivable alternative to the world as it had become. Such was the decline of France, both within and without, that to restore it in its integrity now meant unleashing revolution as a blind leap of faith. To be a Nationalist ceased to be a state of innocent, youthful zeal, an appeal for a better world and to what is better in people, and became a sombre and sectarian way of being in the world when the world is falling apart. Paul Lévy reflected this development exactly in 1937 when he wrote:

> Are there not in the land, in the whole of France, a few thousand Frenchmen capable of grouping together, not with a view to any electoral manoeuvres, but in order to conspire out in the open? To conspire in the cause of national recovery? . . . Where are the saviours?[19]

Henceforth, because the Nationalist Subject had no nation, either real or projected, to which to belong, all he could belong to was revolution. Revolution, that process of taking control so as to hand control on, becomes permanent at this time, because there is nowhere to hand control on to any more. Consequently, the violence or Terror which is an indispensable moment in the revolutionary hand-over of control, becomes the permanent reality of revolution. Revolution, being henceforth the only world remaining for the Nationalist, thus turns his existence into pure Terror. He is caught in a protracted moment of absolute transition, in which being and doing coincide as violent Terror, and where the only world is that formed by the violent community to which he belongs.

This precarious world can exist and provide existence for the Nationalist for as long as it appears capable of imposing its own control on events. No longer a path between one world and another, its sole remaining aim is violently to enter and dominate a 'world' that has gone out of control. By the later 1930s this was a desperate gamble. For those ready to wait and see, it paid off: the National Revolution installed by Pétain reconciled these two worlds, by instituting violence and terror as the basis on which the new French State was founded. Blanchot did not wait and see. This is because he could not. The titles of his last two political articles say it all: 'France, a Nation to Come', 'Dissidents wanted.'[20] Not only had there ceased to be a link between the current state of things and what was once the nation; more significantly, the community of revolutionary activists upon whose intervention everything hinged was an essentially dispersed one: dissidence is a solitary move, and the opposite of sectarianism. At or around this point, it would seem plausible to argue, Blanchot saw events plunging so far into disorder and out of control that revolution appeared futile, and the violent community in Terror it offers a terrible utopia. At the same time, his commitment to the Nationalist cause meant that this community in violence had become the only world in which, potentially, to be and act. He was in an impossible position. The gamble won by those willing to wait was lost by him, and the price he paid was considerable. Deprived of a world, either potential or real (or even the borderline between them), in which to exist as a revolutionary subject, he was, at a stroke, also deprived of any subjectivity other than that state of violence and Terror in which being and doing were inseparable. For as long as revolution remained an imminent event, that pent-up quantum of violence remained under control, a control guaranteed by language in anticipation of the control it would restore to the nation. At that time, in other words, Blanchot existed, as a subject in the world, purely as and purely in the *language* through which his own violence was projected as a simultaneous mode of being and doing in company with others called revolution. With the frustration of that project, the language which made him a subject and offered him a world was reduced to silence, while his violence, no longer focused outward into a real world that his language can no longer refer to, was left to invade the silent, dispersed space that had opened up within him, a space deprived of the twin poles of self and world, and hence of all stable difference between inside and out, real and imaginary, conscious and unconscious – in short, a hiatus in being whose only contour and confine was violence.

This condition, which is that of a subject exposed to the unmediated effect of its own violence because what mediated it, namely language, has become redundant, with the disappearance of a world in which violence could have a real effect, is the real imaginary condition in which Maurice Blanchot found himself and his fears by the late 1930s. It is, I would argue, the condition underlying the anonymity of *Aux Ecoutes*, into which he withdrew completely until 1940. If he was the 'backbone' of the journal according to Lévy,[21] in its turn it provided him with a head, with a substitute for an identity he no longer had, a collective ear in the absence of a personal voice. In addition, however, it is a condition for which the language of literature, to which he turned in the 1930s, offered real though painful relief. On two occasions, in 1973 and 1983, Blanchot looked back to this moment in terms which, by the way they differ, throw light on the situation I am seeking to describe. Referring to the opening sentence of *Thomas the Obscure*: 'Thomas sat down and looked at the sea,' he wrote at the beginning of *Le pas au-delà*:

It is certainly satisfying (too satisfying) to think that, solely because
something like these words '*he – the sea*', with the exigency that
results from them and whence also they result, are written, somewhere there is inscribed the possibility of a radical transformation,
even if only for a single person, that is to say his suppression as a
personal existence. The possibility: no more.[22]

Those opening words, which he described as 'without future, without
pretension', contained within them '[a] wrenching force, a power of
destruction or a power for change' which in retrospect he defines as 'the
exigency of writing' (*l'exigence d'écrire*) in which his career as a writer
originates. In the 1930s however, as I have argued, that force had also
erupted into his existence as a revolutionary, destructive violence, cut off
from reality and totally deprived of language. The suppression of his
personal existence, as well as appearing a real possibility in the language
of fiction, was also and more decisively to be the terrifying imaginary
condition into which he would really be plunged with the loss of the
language of politics. He would really lose touch with all reality save that
of the voiceless violence within him. Language, deprived of a referent
with the withdrawal of a real world gone out of control, would remain as
no more than the mute signifier of his violent, fractured (non-) being.
And ten years after *Le pas au-delà*, in *After the Fact*, Blanchot described
his very first piece of fiction, *The Last Word* (1935), in terms which differ
significantly from those in which he looked back to *Thomas the Obscure*:

> Undoubtedly, to begin writing only to come so quickly to the end
> (which would have been the encounter with the last word), meant
> at last that there was the hope of not making a career, of finding the
> quickest way to have done with it right at the start.[23]

In other words, his turn to literature, which is to say the language of the
imaginary, was apparently first and foremost simply an attempt to assume in language, the space of an instant (according to a temporality that
revolution also seemed to offer), the purely imaginary state into which
language and therefore subjectivity in the world would silently collapse.
It was to be no less than an act of intellectual suicide, destined to confine
him once and for all in the impersonality and indifference of a voiceless
anonymity by stilling the turmoil to which he had been reduced. Things
are less straightforward however. As he admits in *After the Fact*:

> it would be dishonest to forget that, at the same time or in the
> meantime, I was writing *Thomas the Obscure*, which was perhaps
> about the same thing, but precisely did not have done with it and,

on the contrary, encountered in the search for annihilation (absence) the impossibility of escaping being (presence) – which was not even a contradiction in fact, but the demand of an unhappy perpetuity in dying itself.[24]

In other words, for a time during the 1930s, literature remained a totally separate sphere for Blanchot, containing, in parallel, two separate projects (*The Last Word* and *Thomas the Obscure*). Between them, they formed the site, in language, of an absolutely self-sufficient relation between subjectivity and the end, providing Blanchot in advance with a means of acting out, in the imaginary language of fiction, an experience of the endlessness of the end which will soon become all that remains of reality for him:

> the story [*The Last Word*] was an attempt to short-circuit the other book that was being written [*Thomas the Obscure*], in order to overcome that endlessness and reach a silent decision, reach it through a more linear narrative that was nevertheless painfully complex: which is perhaps why (I don't know) there is the sudden convocation of language, the strange resolution to deprive language of its support, the *watchword* [*le mot d'ordre*] (no more restraining or affirmative language – but no: there is still a speech with which to say this and not to say this), the renunciation of the roles of Teacher and Judge – a renunciation that is itself futile –, the Apocalypse finally, the discovery of nothing other than universal ruin.[25]

With the innocence of imagination when it is confined to fiction, *The Last Word* recounts the uttering of the last word or *mot d'ordre* which will put an end to language and hence to everything. Reflecting the absurdity to which revolutionary violence has been reduced, it will establish an order based on annihilation. However, being both the word that imposes order and the word 'order', it therefore both puts an end to language and ensures its endless perpetuation. At the time, however, what Blanchot describes as the impossibility or absurdity of this story (since in addition it evokes 'the absolute disaster [*naufrage*] as having taken place, so that the story itself could not have survived either')[26] was so with reference not to the world, but to another story. Language lives on endlessly in *Thomas the Obscure*. The Apocalypse that silences both Teacher and Judge, while drawing its signifiers from what is about to happen in the real world, is an image for the voicelessness that Blanchot is exploring through the language of fiction by writing *Thomas the Obscure*. 'Unless,' he adds, '[*The Last Word*] claims to be a prophetic work, announcing in the past tense a future that has already arrived.'[27] At some point, I would argue, the purely fictional time-scale of *The Last Word* ceases to exist independently of that of the world and finds itself coterminous with reality in the way Blanchot suggests: for him, the apocalyptic prospect it projects into the past becomes the imminent future in reality. Reality, living on endlessly beyond its end, now becomes totally imaginary. Henceforth, the relationship existing in language between the *The Last Word* and *Thomas the Obscure* will escape the innocent confines of fiction, shifting to become one between literature in the form (initially) of *Thomas the Obscure* and the voicelessness of the real.[28] The absurd impossibility of a narrative seeking to put an end to narrative by narrating the last word will give way to a narrative which has assumed that absurdity and now offers, through its own interminable existence, the only remaining means of confronting, in language, the absurd impossibility of an existence for which language has fallen silent because the world has ceased to exist. When this occurs – some time between 1935 and 1940 – Blanchot's existence is entirely taken over by literature. Literature becomes the language of a reality that consists solely of language reduced to silence and adrift in the imaginary. That is to say, the only reality left to language is that provided by literature, which, as the world careers into an unimaginable abyss, leaving the self a prey to delirious images of what the abyss will be, becomes the language of the silence that language has become, now the subject of language is nothing but the anticipatory phantasm of what is about to become real.

Literature for Blanchot is thus neither a retreat from the real nor a bulwark against it. It is rather the only remaining mode of subjectivity in language open to him in the face of what the real has become. As such, it steals a march on history by virtue of its essentially prophetic or anticipatory nature: for the subject of literature fears are now purely imaginary, disaster has already happened. In the anonymity of everyday existence, be it that of a journalist or, when that freedom was lost,[29] that of the simple citizen (whether a resistant or not) literature constituted a mode of indifference to events for Blanchot by turning the subject living them into an absentee. It is, I would argue, that indifference alone that made Maurice Blanchot into a writer: it is in its margin that what bears his name is inscribed. Because he is now a writer, his life and writings prior to that moment are of significance. But whereas in themselves they seem at best to display a moral ambivalence, inviting those so inclined to investigate and speculate with hindsight, the turn to literature, in which writing and life coincide, means that no examination of Blanchot's life before or after that turn can hope to be meaningful if it does not identify and situate the margin which that turn placed between his life and life itself.

This is not to say that literature, at a stroke, redeemed a life that otherwise would appear compromised. However suspect he continues to be in the eyes of some, no suspicion hangs over Maurice Blanchot's life, as there are those well placed to attest. But literature, in revealing Maurice Blanchot, also reveals a writer to whose existence literature put an end. The question that then legitimately arises is: in placing a margin of indifference between writing and life, did literature as writing life carry over into itself any trace of what, in Blanchot's life, could well have proved absolutely compromising? Did the turn to literature merely offer salvation to one man, by neutralizing what in others led to the worst? Or did that one man's turn to literature offer an example for others? The answer to that cannot be found simply by examining the turn at the point where it happened. Such a fixation is merely the obverse of the fascination with Blanchot's 'past'. The turn, in opening up the margin I have referred to, can only be approached as something which, once in motion, stayed in motion: as the founding trope or *tour d'écriture* whereby writing, as life, unfurled a margin in life. That process now has a history: for over fifty years Maurice Blanchot has lived the writing life to which he turned as history appeared about to end, and by which he lived on beyond the experience of its end. No assessment of the originality of either his writing or his influence can convincingly be made unless they are examined in the ahistorical historicity which they manifest, and seen in the light of an Apocalypse beyond which we all, in our world, live on as survivors. It is such an examination that this *Reader* proposes to encourage.

Notes

1 Stéphane Mallarmé, letter to H. Rhodes, April 1896.
2 'Our Clandestine Companion', in *Face to Face with Levinas*, ed. Richard A. Cohen (New York, SUNY Press, 1986), pp. 41–52 (41).
3 'Who?' in *Who Comes After the Subject?*, ed. Eduardo Cadava, Peter Connor and Jean-Luc Nancy (New York and London, Routledge, 1991), pp. 58–60 (59).
4 Jacques Derrida, ' "Eating Well": An Interview', translated by Peter Connor and Avital Ronell, ibid., pp. 96–119 (110). The text by Blanchot from which Derrida quotes is 'L'amitié', in *L'Amitié* (Paris, Gallimard, 1971), pp. 326–30 (328). I have modified the translation somewhat.
5 *Le Dernier homme* (Paris, Gallimard, 1957), pp. 23–4. The text between the dashes was added in 1957 to the first version of this section of the *récit*, which appeared in the *Nouvelle Revue Française* in November 1956.
6 The term 'exigency' will be a recurrent one throughout the *Reader*, as a translation of the French word *exigence*, which is one frequently used by Blanchot. The meaning of the French shifts between *demand*, *requirement* and *necessity*, without ever corresponding to what is the dominant idea in the English term: namely urgency, not to say emergency. The estrangement which thus affects the English term does not render it inoperative. Occasionally another term will be used to translate *exigence*; this will usually be indicated in the text.

7 Writing in 1943, Robert Manévy described the *Débats* in the 1930s as follows:

> In the shadow of Saint-Germain-l'Auxerrois, just round the corner from the In-
> stitute, the *Journal des Débats*, turned in on itself like an old and sceptical *Académi-
> cien*, confined its energies to polishing the sentences it proposed to its readers, who
> were becoming fewer and fewer. The major political role it had played at the
> beginning of the Third Republic had now been taken over by *Le Temps*. As for
> turning back the clock, it was too experienced and too refined to present the world
> with the spectacle of an old man attempting an impossible feat. It was content to let
> things tick over, saving its strength, its only remaining ambition being to maintain its
> reputation as a well-written paper among the professors at the University and the
> members of the *Académie des Inscriptions et des Belles-Lettres*. (Robert Manévy, *Histoire
> de la presse, 1914–1939* (Paris, Correâ, 1945 [1943]), p. 126)

8 For a details of Blanchot's writing in the 1930s, see my 'Bibliographie I' and 'Bibliographie II', in *Gramma*, 3/4 and 5 (1976), pp. 223–45 and 124–32.

9 *Aujourd'hui*, 22 March 1934, p. 3:

> We the undersigned, journalists with *Le Rempart* and *Aujourd'hui*, hereby declare that
> they have always enjoyed total freedom of expression on these newpapers, a freedom
> all too often unknown in other places. Never has this freedom of expression been
> limited, either directly or indirectly. Their director, Paul Lévy, has always accepted
> *all* of their opinions, *all* of their personal positions, never seeking to give special
> treatment to either an interest group or an individual. Twelve months of collabor-
> ative effort have attached them to a director who has always acted towards them with
> sensitivity, loyalty and independence of mind. They wish here to express to him their
> respectful affection and their attachment.

10 Diane Rubinstein claims, in *What's Left? The Ecole Normale Supérieure and the Right*
(Madison, University of Wisconsin Press, 1990, p. 113), that Blanchot contributed in
1934 to the newly founded journal *La Lutte des Jeunes*. There is, however, nothing signed
by him there.

11 Jeffrey Mehlman, 'Of Literature and Terror: Blanchot at *Combat*', *Modern Languages
Notes*, 95 (1980), pp. 808–29. Several years before Mehlman, Patrick Rousseau and I
sought to confront, without *parti pris*, the issues raised by Blanchot's political writing
between the wars. See 'Topographie-parcours d'une (contre)revolution', *Gramma*, 5
(Winter 1976), pp. 8–43.

12 In *Literature and its Theorists. A Personal View of Twentieth-Century Criticism*, trans.
Catherine Porter (Ithaca, Cornell University Press, 1987). Tzvetan Todorov accuses
Blanchot of a tolerance towards totalitarianism, both political and philosophical, which
sits ill in someone who was 'a spokesman for a certain anti-Semitism' before the war (p.
6). He repeats this stricture in 'Critique et éthique: à propos de Maurice Blanchot', in
Cross-References, ed. David Kelley and Isabelle Llassera (Leeds, Society for French
Studies, 1986), pp. 168–75 (p. 174).

13 Paul Lévy, *Au Temps des grimaces* (Paris, Nagel, 1948), p. 98 (the piece dates from 15
April 1933).

14 *Je Suis Partout*, 534, 18 October 1941, p. 8. This review is signed 'R.' (possibly Lucien
Rebatet). In 1942, the collaborationist weekly *L'Appel* published a piece in the same
spirit entitled 'Videz Thomas [Kick Thomas Out]', in reaction to the news that Blanchot
might be given the directorship of the *Nouvelle Revue Française* (*L'Appel*, 28 May 1942,
p. 4). I am grateful to Keri Bentz for showing me this article.

15 She quotes a letter to her from Blanchot, dated 20 August 1983: 'I remember little about *Combat*. I do recall however that, as I was utterly opposed to Brasillach, who was completely committed to Fascism and anti-Semitism, I made it a condition of my participation on the journal that there was no possibility that he would also be a contributor. Moreover, things were reciprocal. Brasillach detested *Combat*, because I had been involved with it. Opposition to Brasillach and what he represented was a constant for me at that time.' (Diane Rubinstein, *What's Left?* p. 187, n. 72.) [My translation.]

  In *Notre avant-guerre* (Paris, Grasset, 1941), Brasillach writes of *Combat*: 'On *Combat* there were one or two liberal intellectuals whose presence spoilt things in my view, and soon we were obliged to cease our involvement with an organ that openly condemned some of the positions which we had defended elsewhere' (p. 240 of the Livre de Poche edition).

16 See in particular the first of his literary articles in *L'Insurgé*, entitled 'De la Révolution à la littérature' (*L'Insurgé*, 13 January 1937, p. 3).

17 One of Blanchot's political editorials in *L'Insurgé* is entitled 'Notre première ennemie, la France' (3 February, 1937, p. 4).

18 See Robert Francis, Jean Maxence and Thierry Maulnier, *Demain la France* (Paris, Grasset, 1934).

19 Paul Lévy, *Au Temps des grimaces*, pp. 149–50. The piece was written on 4 December 1937.

20 'La France, nation à venir', *Combat*, 19, November 1937, pp. 131–2; 'On demande des dissidents', ibid., 20, December 1937, pp. 156–7.

21 Quoted in the *prière d'insérer* of the most recent edition of *Thomas l'obscur*, which came out in the Gallimard series 'L'Imaginaire' in 1992.

22 *Le pas au-delà* (Paris, Gallimard, 1973), p. 8.

23 'After the Fact', in *Vicious Circles. Two fictions and 'After the fact'*, translated by Paul Auster (Barrytown, New York, Station Hill Press, 1985), p. 64 (translation modified).

24 Ibid., p. 64 (translation modified).

25 Ibid., pp. 64 – 5.

26 Ibid.

27 Ibid. (translation modified).

28 *The Last Word* would not be published until 1947.

29 Though their anonymity prevents any certain comment, editorials in both the *Journal des Débats* and *Aux Ecoutes* (both by then lodged in the same building in Clermont-Ferrand) assert the need for continuing freedom of the press under the new regime being established in Vichy.

PART I

How is Literature Possible?

Between 1941 and 1944 Blanchot wrote about 170 'Chronicles of Intellectual Life' in the *Journal des Débats*. A selection of these appeared in his first volume of criticism, *Faux pas*, in 1943.[1] The first two pieces in Part I, **The Silence of Writers** and **The Search for Tradition**, are among the earliest of these chronicles and, though not included in *Faux pas*, they set the tone and establish the field for what is to come. On one level they reflect the uncertainties to which events, however much they were anticipated, exposed the Blanchot whose outer existence had been reduced to anonymity. With the establishment of the Vichy regime, the political silence resulting from his turn to literature was invaded by a call to the writer to serve the political cause that he had given up for lost. Briefly, Blanchot heeded that call. The allusion, in **The Silence of Writers**, to 'various projects being undertaken by young men' (p. 27), recalls his involvement with the *Jeune France* movement immediately following the establishment of the Vichy regime. The history of this idealistic and short-lived attempt to preserve the cultural values of France has still to be written.[2] By the time he had begun to write his column in the *Débats*, however, Blanchot had pulled out of what, both politically and personally, could never have been other than an ambivalent undertaking for him.[3] Politically, henceforth, he will revert to the silence of indifference, withdrawing entirely into the world offered him by literature now that *Thomas the Obscure* has appeared, a 'world' in which, as he says in 1993, he worked 'totally without security [*à fonds perdu*]'.[4]

But this return to the position he adopted prior to the Occupation has none of the ambivalence it displayed then. It is now clearer than ever that literature offers him a solitary and self-sufficient 'world' in which language alone has reality. But whereas before the war this had deprived him of the identity and the voice he had acquired as a Nationalist, making of him an almost clandestine figure, now the very opposite is the case. The silence which closed around him after 1937 is something he forbids the writer under the Occupation. In the real silence that has descended politically upon France, his silence acquires a voice: the voice of art, primarily, and one which is audible therefore only within the world of art, for the writer and for the reader, where for Blanchot the novelist it remains endlessly broken by silence. But it is now a voice capable of resounding outside art, in the domain where, beneath the political silence that the Occupation imposed on France, attempts are being made to salvage a cultural identity for the nation by enlisting in its cause the solitude of the artist and the silence of art. This voice, which had already been heard within *Jeune France*, as Pierre Schaeffer ruefully recalls,[5] here inaugurates the *Débats* series of 'Chronicles of Intellectual Life' with a rigorous and sometimes caustic critique of the cultural politics of the new

regime. In terms that could leave no one in any doubt about where he
stood politically (even if the place he occupied, namely literature, offered
no firm footing), Blanchot denounces both the orthodoxies and the
attempts at unorthodoxy that are currently vying, theoretically and practically, for the artist's soul. In the process, however, he is not just
deepening the gulf that opened up for him before the war between the
world of the political and the 'world' of literature. Had that been so, the
ambivalence of his political silence before the war would have intensified,
now that Vichy was proposing precisely the National Revolution he had
once called for: his only grounds for refusing it would be the ungrounding
experience of literature by which he had disabled himself politically.
His refusal would not amount to a rejection of the new order. But in fact
his defence of art against the cultural politics of Vichy goes much further,
taking him totally outside the political frame within which he originally
fell silent. For now, the history and the traditions of French art, in whose
name he refuses all enlistment, include the period following the First
World War, which Blanchot twice alludes to in the pieces included here,
and which, from the standpoint of Nationalist politics before and after
1940, appeared as the products of foreign decadence, and the signs of
French decline. It is hardly surprising that Drieu la Rochelle should have
found some of the contributors to Thierry-Maulnier's new journal, the
Revue Française des Idées et des Œuvres (1940) too 'Surrealist'.[6] Blanchot's
contribution, on the subject of Lautréamont, places him squarely in the
avant-garde tradition which he defended consistently in the *Débats*
throughout the Occupation, primarily with reference to his own chosen
art form: the novel.

As well as three pieces on the novel, written for the *Débats* in between
1941 and 1943, I have included the brief review of Jean-Paul Sartre's
Nausea, **The Beginnings of a Novel**, which appeared in *Aux Ecoutes* in
1938, and which marks the only exception to the rule of silence that
Blanchot imposed on himself after 1937. The reasons for this seem clear:
in advance of Blanchot, whose *Thomas the Obscure* was not completed
until 1940, Sartre has taken the novel into the field of existence itself,
revealing the possibility that it alone can make existence livable. Yet from
Blanchot's perspective, both the experience depicted through Antoine
Roquentin, and the role given to language in expressing it, provide no
more than a partial and imperfect version of what Sartre claims to be
exploring. This is because the contingency and superfluousness experienced by Sartre's hero, and explored in his philosophy, never display the
degree of absoluteness they attain in Blanchot's experience and in his
fiction. In a way it could never be for Sartre, either existentially or
ideologically, the novel has become for Blanchot not just a 'world' but a
mode of subjectivity in that 'world'. The experience he explores through

Thomas displays a contingency that is more absolute than that to be found in Roquentin or Sartre, in that both the world and the self in the world have ceased to exist with any certainty for Blanchot, so that all that is real for him henceforth is the language of literature. With the publication of *Thomas the Obscure*, followed by *Aminadab* in 1942,[7] Blanchot is in a position to assert more confidently the originality of his own novel of existence. In the three pieces included here, **The Recent Novel, The Pure Novel** and **Mallarmé and the Art of the Novel**, he implicitly refers to his own work, both to bring out the limitations of prevailing theories of the novel and to provide a bold and provocative description of what the novel should be. As well as raising the artistic status of the genre to a level hitherto reserved for poetry (that of Mallarmé, but also, in a significantly allusive way, that of Hölderlin), these pieces display a critical complexity and a level of theoretical development which are considerably ahead of their time.

With **How is Literature Possible?** the angle of Blanchot's attention shifts. Published as a small volume in 1942, this essay on Jean Paulhan's *The Flowers of Tarbes, or Terror in Literature* is made up of three of the *Débats* chronicles, published in October, November and December of 1941. It is a sign of how seriously Blanchot took the issue which provides his title that he should have embarked upon such a protracted examination of Paulhan's book. The reason is not hard to find: here at last is not just a theoretical account of literature that Blanchot can accept, at least partly (it is, in a way, 'The Beginnings of a Theory' just as *Nausea* was 'The Beginnings of a Novel'); it is an account that focuses directly on that impossible condition into which Blanchot withdrew on falling silent politically, namely *literature* experienced not as the opportunity to propose a version of the world, but as the only 'world' that can accommodate subjectivity when terror (both fear and violence) has deprived it of both a world and a language in which to express it, hence of all personal consistency.[8] Paulhan's book does no less than map out the itinerary that Blanchot had followed since 1937: the abyss over which it leads its unsuspecting reader, as it questions 'not only all of literature, but also the mind, its power and means' (p. 49), is the abyss opened up by the imminent defeat of France in Blanchot's existence, which literature and the indifference it provides allowed him to cross unawares. Now, from within the reality of that abyss of unreality, he looks back, but indirectly, finding in Paulhan an account of what is going on within literature, according to its time-scale and its reality, during the historical events to which he has become indifferent. And though the thinking to be found in this piece is only just emerging in these years (so unthinkable does the experience it refers to remain), it announces what will become for Blanchot a mode of enquiry as important to him as literary criticism or theory, indeed more important eventually, since in enquiring into the possibility of literature, he is enquiring into the possibility of existence itself.

With the Liberation, the vogue of existentialism and its call for a committed literature, Blanchot finds himself in a curious position. Established thanks to *Faux pas* as an original critical thinker, he begins to publish full-length chronicles and articles in a variety of journals. Their reception is consistently admiring, and they eventually provide the material for a second book of criticism, *La Part du feu*, in 1949. Yet because of the predominance and political correctness of the Sartrean orthodoxy, his own position remains uncertain. On the one hand this is appropriate: literature continues to be his 'world', and nothing about events would appear henceforth to make his indifference to them at all questionable. During these years he is writing his last novel, *Le Très-Haut* (*The Most High*) and his first *récit*, *Death Sentence*. Their simultaneous publication in 1948 forms a hinge in his literary writing, moving it onto a new and original experimental level which will absorb him throughout the 1950s. On the other hand, this uncertainty can only provoke a certain malaise. It is clear from as early as 1938, that Sartre's conception of literature is so close to Blanchot's own as to pose a serious challenge to it. In 1938 their proximity lay solely within the field of literature, to which their respective political silences confined them. After 1945, however, it is not only Sartre's conception of the novel that poses a challenge to Blanchot: it is the new relationship between literature and politics that Sartre is proposing. 'Committed literature' does not simply impose a dimension on the writer's existence that Blanchot refuses in the name of art: it defines a relationship between the two dimensions of that existence, art and politics, which Blanchot, in defining the novel both practically and theoretically, has also defined, but in terms of radical separation, not committed involvement. For him literature, its language and the 'world' it offers its subject exist, since late 1937, *in place of* a world that has gone to ruin. In other words, there is literally no place, from Blanchot's perspective, for any meaningful form of artistic 'commitment'. Directly and indirectly, therefore, over a ten-year period, Blanchot challenges and criticizes the Sartrean project. Occasionally he does it in an article in Sartre's journal, *Les Temps Modernes*. I include one of those pieces here, **The Novel is a Work of Bad Faith** (1947), which appeared while the publication of the 'manifesto' of committed literature, *What is Literature?*, was in full stream in the journal. Undoubtedly because of the directness with which it challenges Sartre, through one of his associates but with reference to one of his principal categories, bad faith (*la mauvaise foi*), this article was not included in *La Part du feu*.[9] Nevertheless it provides a very clear perspective on Blanchot's position in the post-war period and a more extensive description of the novel than he has so far undertaken. Furthermore, as well as revealing the extraordinary degree to which the novel is equivalent to the 'world' for him, it once again attests to a level of theoretical investigation into literature that is considerably in advance of its time, and which only Roland Barthes, beginning to write in *Combat*, came near to matching in those years.

The final piece in Part I, **Sade's Reason**, also appeared in *Les Temps Modernes*, and can on the surface be read as a gesture of defiance towards the political and ethical 'correctness' being promoted by the journal.[10] At the same time it offers an original and penetrating analysis of the function and status of unreason, sacrificing nothing of the excess and exorbitance this displays in Sade, while locating it within reason at a hiatus-point of indifference and apathy which both separates logical extremes and leads outside them onto the margins of reason. Like the essay on Paulhan, but more resolutely, it thus provides an indirect perspective on the position Blanchot adopted prior to the war: Sade's fantasies are inscribed within the same space, relative to the world (of reason), as Blanchot's are within the 'world' of literature. At one and the same time, therefore, Blanchot is here both theorizing, in a way he has not done so far, the relationship between literature as a 'world' and the rationale of a world which has ceased to exist for him; and also acknowledging the presence and the role of *violence* in this relationship, and the precarious reality of the borderline between the two worlds. In the post-war period, when he was obliged to confront the fact that a world which for him really died, somehow lived on, **Sade's Reason** reveals a Blanchot poised between a pre-war retreat into literature and a post-war return to the world, which, when it happened, established a relationship between the writer and politics which differed radically from that proposed by Sartre.

Notes

1 For an account by Blanchot of the way *Faux pas* came into being, see 'Pour l'amitié [For Friendship]', 'Pré-texte' to Dionys Mascolo, *A la recherche d'un communisme de pensée* (Paris, Fourbis, 1993), pp. 5–16 (pp. 5–6).

2 For a brief account, see Aline Courtot, 'Quelques aspects de la politique de la jeunesse', in *Le Gouvernement de Vichy, 1940–1942* (Paris, Fondation Nationale des Sciences Politiques / Armand Colin, 1976), pp. 265–90: 'This association ['Jeune France'] was run by men of considerable quality, such as Albert Ollivier, Pierre Schaeffer, Paul Flamant, Maurice Jacquemont (the director of the Théâtre des Quatre-Saisons), Claude Roy, etc. It placed itself at the disposal of groups already in existence . . . It represented an extremely interesting experiment in a popular education of quality, the influence of which was considerably restricted by the circumstances, but which constituted a testing ground for young men who went on, after the Liberation, to pursue their task of artistic promotion and research in a variety of ways' (p. 269).

3 For an account of Blanchot's involvement with the movement, see 'Pour l'amitié', pp. 6–7. At the end of the 'manifesto' published in the name of 'Jeune France' in 1941, the movement is presented as 'a rallying cry to those who are not interested solely in the solitary destiny of their work, but in the presence of art in the life of every man'. 'Jeune France' therefore 'refuses to choose between two fundamental though often conflicting exigencies: that of the community uniting people and artists, that of the exacting vocation of the artist' (*Jeune France. Principes. Direction. Esprit* (Paris, Bordeaux, Lyon, Vichy, Toulouse, Marseille, [undated]), p. 18). If Blanchot withdrew in advance of the dissolution of the movement by the Vichy authorities, it was because its 'refusal to choose' ran counter to a refusal on his part emanating from several years earlier.

4 'Pour l'amitié', p. 6.

5 Pierre Schaeffer, *Les Antennes de Jericho* (Paris, Stock, 1978), p. 278: 'Paul Flamant took a disapproving view [of my popularism and my desire for efficiency], without, however, leaving me entirely at the mercy of Maurice Blanchot, Xavier de Lignac and Maurice Jacquemont, ruthless critics of my ideas, intransigent defenders of the integrity of the artist.'

6 He wrote in his *Journal*, on 3 May 1940: 'Thierry's review will fail because it will not take up a clear position. Kléber Haedens and Blanchot are riddled with Surrealism. Maulnier with Radical and Jewish Moderatism.' See Pierre Drieu la Rochelle, *Journal 1939–1945* (Paris, Gallimard, 1992), p. 180.

7 Sartre provides a rigorous if sceptical account of Blanchot's second novel in '*Aminadab*, or the Fantastic Considered as a Language', in *Literary and Philosophical Essays*, trans. Annette Michelson (London, Radius Books, 1968), pp. 56–72.

8 Jeffrey Mehlman opened up this issue, pertinently if provocatively, in 'Of Literature and Terror: Blanchot at *Combat*', *Modern Language Notes*, 95 (May 1980), pp. 808–29. His perspective is restricted unnecessarily, in my view, by his assumption that in turning to literature Blanchot sought simply to liquidate his political past. As I have tried to show, the political silence which Blanchot imposed upon himself dates from before the war, not during or after it. The voice that arises subsequently is not a political one. Far from imposing silence on the political, however, it begins almost at once to put pressure on that silence. As the *Reader* will subsequently show, the silence will break on two occasions in the post-war era: in 1958 and in 1968. It will only do so once and for all, however, from 1970 onwards, when the literary, the political and the 'ethical' are brought together in a mode of fragmentary writing which extends the scope of enquiry into their inter-relation and into the responsibility, both past and present, that they entail. For an examination of the slow and difficult nature of this process, at one of its stages (1958), see my ' "A Wound to Thought" ', in *Maurice Blanchot: Literature, Philosophy, Ethics*, edited by Carolyn Bailey Gill (London, Routledge, 1995) (forthcoming).

9 Two or three sentences from it can be found in two chapters of *La Part du feu*, 'Le langage de la fiction [The Language of Fiction]' (pp. 79–89), and 'Les romans de Sartre' [The Novels of Sartre] (pp. 188–203).

10 In December 1951 and January 1952, Simone de Beauvoir published a study in *Les Temps Modernes* entitled 'Faut-il brûler Sade?' which appeared, along with other essays such as 'La pensée de droite aujourd'hui [Right-wing Thought Today]' in a volume entitled *Privilèges* in 1953 (see *Must We Burn Sade?* (London, Peter Nevil, 1953)). Both in the essay, where she contests Blanchot's reading of Sade for ignoring 'the aristocratic vision of humanity' which his writing safeguards, and in the preface to *Privilèges*, where she condemns Sade for failing to overcome 'the contradictions of solipsism', it is clear that for her Sade's writing cannot offer any model for the human condition, other than in its most alienated state.

1

The Silence of Writers (1941)*

It is certainly far from easy to define the doubts that have been experienced by certain writers during the months we have just lived through. Why is it that a number of intellectuals have abandoned everything, even mental labour? What thinking or what absence of thinking has led them to such an arid ordeal, in which publishing, writing and contemplation appear as immoral acts that must be harshly forbidden? How did they end up in this strange state of repose, which is both an enigma and a purgatory inflicted upon themselves? To look for the causes of such a state of mind at present can only be utterly pointless. The reasons that come to mind are too obvious, in that they account for everything. War followed by defeat, defeat followed by war; how can one withstand such overwhelming reasons which, on every subject, provide their imperious answers? One can see why even as an explanation for silence, silence has its virtues. Is it not better to put off until later the explanation of a crisis whose true meaning is that we can probably never know its meaning?

Nevertheless, it is a fact that a number of books are appearing, that some of them deserve to be read and reflected upon, and that one cannot read them properly without thinking of the enormous mass of all those that have not been written and normally should have been, that immense library of absent and abolished books. The feeling that this inspires is one of the strangest that someone who has been accustomed to reading can currently experience. When a work appears – and all in all a lot are appearing – it is impossible not to see something miraculous and exceptional in the fact, so natural would it seem were no-one to write again, were the notion of an author to have disappeared in the catastrophe, carried off, far off, along with so many other surface appearances. This is the sign of a considerable malaise. All have not experienced it, but all those who have felt its impact know that this is the most remarkable intellectual phenomenon of these times, when books have appeared as no more than the fringe of a laborious silence.

---

* Originally published as 'Le Silence des écrivains', *Journal des Débats*, 19 April 1941, p. 3.

Where does this malaise come from? First and most obviously, from a certain uncertainty as to the fate of literature and the arts. It is as if several of those who write, not knowing what will be dead tomorrow and what living in the realm of the aesthetic, and ignorant as to what mode of writing will be condemned and what saved, have become lost in rather cruel doubts from which only a number of certain prospects could have extricated them. Such uncertainty is characteristic of those times when art receives from the world more enigmas than the world receives from it. At such times the most extraordinary confusions occur. Crude theoreticians can be heard to maintain that, given that there has been a war, everything by way of daring works and original authors that immediately preceded it must be rejected and trampled down. Denial becomes the critical method *par excellence*. There is repentance for what one once took pleasure in. There is shame at former pride. A distant, comfortable past becomes a refuge from risks it is no longer thought desirable to run. But in great upheavals classicism is no more than a dismal asylum, and the minds that rest there simply find excuses for their fatigue rather than reasons for genuine fidelity.

Other theoreticians, inspired at times by dangerous and alluring ideas, advise both artist and writer not merely to break with the last twenty or thirty years, despite the masterpieces which illustrate them and perhaps because of these, but to devote themselves to a new collective ideal, to enlist in the service of a social order which culture must both express and construct.

This task is not an unworthy one. Writers, in particular young writers, can see the danger of an isolation for which they have so often been criticized. Their minds turn to that public which is made up of their entire nation, in whose service they are ready to sacrifice a great deal, even their intellectual honour. They contemplate that citizenship without which they are nothing. What should they do to atone for their misdeeds? What mission will be entrusted to them in this immense society of misfortune? To write, even if it be only masterpieces? An improper suggestion! They blush at having made it and despise themselves for simply being themselves, with the feeling that the persistence and the excellence of their vocation amount to a flaw.

We are of the view that many artists are experiencing a deep crisis of conscience and seeking with tragic sincerity by what means, outside their art, they can involve themselves personally in the collective undertaking they see before them. How can they enable the people to participate in a culture which is a priceless treasure? In what way can art be transformed so that it becomes common property? By dint of what discipline can thoughts of pure and utter solitude be enlisted in the service of public order? These problems are not new. The artist has always tended in the direction of what he alone loves and only rarely has he succeeded in thinking or painting for mankind as a whole. But it is no less true that, whenever times have been difficult, he has suffered doubts about himself which have driven him to reveal his impotence.

These doubts have never been stronger. We know of various projects being undertaken by young men, who are seeking, in the midst of the general catastrophe, to save art by restoring to it a public or to save artists by turning them into educators of youth. We know of others who have embarked on a critique of excessive individualism and will now admit only works conceived in praise of the homeland, the earth and traditional values. There are others, finally, who are seeking revenge against the gratuitousness of art by bidding the artist serve, enlist, compromise himself – not through the exercise of his talent, which would be perfectly natural, but through adhering to political ideas or principles which he is quite incapable of judging. These calls come in various guises. They are often accompanied by very serious truths, but these they abuse, so as to instil into unsteady minds reasons which they cannot overcome. As a result, it appears to many that the thinking to be found in great books or great canvases is heretical and in conflict with the wisdom of these times, given up to disaster and to tempest.

The war and current misfortunes are not entirely responsible for creating a malaise that a few of yesterday's critics already had an inkling of. An artist, Jean Bazaine, one of the best of his generation, wrote recently in the *Nouvelle Revue Française*:

> For a few years already we had been witnessing a grand onslaught by mediocrity, bedecked in the fine names it has a predilection for: tradition or classicism . . . There was already much talk then about 'returns': a return to line, a return not only to subjects but to 'great subjects', and so on and so forth. 'French art,' as one art weekly put it more or less, 'cannot remain any longer an art of experiment and absence,' and that was said at a time when painting, isolated in a world of decay, had just rediscovered once again the fresh and living source of French art. Who would believe it?[1]

Literature was the target of similar exhortations and had unfortunately begun to follow them. On the pretext of condemning the fine, fortuitous revolt of the post-First World War writers, minds had been drawn towards a perfectly empty humanism, offering neither memories nor promise. Young writers, with a few exceptions, were wary of all inventive originality, and sought merely to express in pale language the banal images of life. They did not know what it is to create. They had neither the talent nor the taste for it. They had almost lost sight of the fact that every man who is jealously and powerfully a person steps into a superb world in which he gives his thoughts and his nightmares, through the necessity of expression, the force of an obligatory existence.

Today, these errors of yesterday, combined with a variety of scruples, make up a strange climate, in which writing is no longer anything but a rather suspect activity. Every author who remains silent gives an icy look to the author who, obeying what are inevitable reflexes, continues to involve himself in producing something. When, even more to his disgrace, an author is true to himself, and if the work he publishes resembles his previous works, astonishment becomes scorn, as if it were unbearable that a writer should continue naïvely to live and speak in the silence of what is a spiritual Pompeii. Fortunately, readers are not dead. On the contrary, it would appear that they are seeking to relive for a few moments everything they have learned over the centuries – dogmas, masterpieces and history – and gathering together, in the register of their memories, everything in the past that gave them a reason for being, and everything that can, for the future, give them reason to hope.

Translator's Note

1 Jean Bazaine, 'Guerres et évasions', *Nouvelle Revue Française*, 326 (April 1941), pp. 617–23 (pp. 621–2).

Translated by Michael Holland

2

The Search for Tradition (1941)*

The books that have appeared over the last few months have fortunately not taken much account of events. We have drawn attention here to one or two works that have been inspired by current circumstances, which were not without their merits. But otherwise there have been very few whose sole justification lay in their topicality. Among all the novels, the poems and the essays, works which must, almost of necessity, remain oblivious to external hopes and fears, almost none have attempted to adjust to the needs of the present. The great temptation that lies in seeking to please the historian has so far affected only the authors of articles and pamphlets.

Nevertheless it is impossible to ignore the preoccupations of a number of critics, whose passion is expressed not only in opinions drawn from everyday convention, but also through hasty and superficial theories, which are the vacuous mirrors of their own disarray. They are unstinting in their warnings and their advice. They aim, with that fine zeal which comes of living for the moment, to reform genres, impose subjects and mould the whole of intellectual life according to the dictates of their current preferences. What do they want? Must writers and artists become the illustrators of whatever happens to be the theory of the day? Theirs are the precepts of fragile minds, eager to imitate rather than be.

These commands are perfectly natural, and in fact quite unimportant. A young writer called Francis Ambrière, currently a prisoner of war who, in the camp where he is being held, manages every month to publish a remarkable newspaper, quotes the following lines, sent by a friend in Paris, in a recent article: 'Yes, publishers are becoming uneasy and establishing their own censorship, but there are few writers who avoid being prophetic and peremptory. Why must the true values of our generation be vilified?' These remarks are of course pertinent, but as Francis Ambrière says, after every social upheaval, short-sighted saviours are two a penny, their loud professions of faith expressing merely their own vain desire to be saved. When all is said and done, it is easy not to hear them. 'We prisoners,' Francis Ambrière says in his conclusion, 'are protected

* Originally published as 'Recherche de la tradition', *Journal des Débats*, 16–17 June 1941, p. 3.

by our isolation from this discordant chorus, which reaches us only as a muffled echo. When we return, let us not add our own noise to it, but rather impose our silence upon it.'

In a similar spirit, forming the preface to a recent novel by Mr Robert Francis, we find a number of remarks in defence of the writer's right to continue with his work as if nothing had happened. 'The intellectual life of a nation such as France,' he writes, 'cannot fall into line, to order, with some moral code hastily derived from recent events. I would even add that I don't even find that desirable, for such an operation would probably lead to the worst possible misunderstanding and the worst possible error, merely allowing a few works and a few people, hastily repainted in the colours of the day, to deceive the public yet again.' Mr Robert Francis goes on to recall the story of St Aloysius of Gonzaga which Péguy so delighted in. 'What would you do,' Louis of Gonzaga was asked while still only a child, 'if you were told that you were going to die in a few moments?' 'Well,' the child said, 'I'd go on playing with my ball.' Mr Robert Francis claims the right for writers to resume their labours where they were interrupted by the war. And he himself sets an example, by publishing a novel entitled *Imaginary Memories* (Gallimard), containing all the brilliant qualities that made his previous works so pleasing, and which have scarcely diminished with use.

What these reactions show is that the frenzied nature of current circumstances has had little effect on people's minds. Minds defend themselves by dreaming, and that provides them with a perfectly sufficient solitude. However, one is forced to acknowledge that a peril must really exist, in so far as one or two people feel the need to guard against it. It is after all astonishing that Mr Robert Francis should have felt it necessary to provide his far from topical novel with this topical preface and to give an explanation for the perfectly natural continuity of his dreams. Is it because he caught himself thinking like the sort of reader or critic who would reproach him with being true to himself, with writing books too similar to those of yesterday? Did he examine himself anxiously because his talent had not been affected by the war? He quotes the following words by Mr Jean Vignaud: 'I expect novelists now to abandon the overgrown children's rules that were fashionable before the war, which moreover bore witness to our exhaustion and our decadence, and at long last to paint the great social frescos of our rebirth.' Such observations recall the hopes of the first Bolshevik leaders, when they called on authors to write totally new masterpieces in honour of their regime. Clearly, nothing is more naïve; but nothing comes more naturally to the way of thinking of the reformer.

Other signs reveal the growing impairment being inflicted by events on the critical mind. A few days ago, twenty young painters exhibited their most recent works together in a Paris gallery, under the title 'Painters in the French Tradition'. Since most of them show signs of that spirit of invention whose demands have been reflected in French painting since the nineteenth century, they quite rightly made a point of appealing to tradition, while emphasizing that fidelity to tradition does not consist in being faithful to certain forms, but in searching for a genuine creativity without which nothing can be transmitted and nothing endures.

Despite the banality of these remarks, the critics responded to them with extraordinary surprise and confusion. Apparently they found themselves incapable of understanding that artists, wishing to blaze new trails in regions already traced out by Picasso, Matisse or Bonnard, could possibly lay claim to a lineage within the history of French art. In their view, these people could call themselves avant-garde painters, or the painters of tomorrow, but not artists with a concern for tradition. What they held against them was thus not so much their desire to re-create works by giving themselves new rules as their ambition to remain, by means of these works, in harmony with the great models of the past.

Such thinking reveals a strange fatigue of the mind. When one sees those critics who talk endlessly of a return to classicism reserving their praise for the most mediocre and insipid efforts, the product of unstudied imitation, one wonders what weakness of imagination, what banality of form is to be found, for them, in the works of the great creative periods, which were all great periods of rupture. What on earth, to their minds, are these classics that they admire and wish to imitate? And what can this imitation be, if they conceive of it as sterile observance, as the preservation of a form whose justification has vanished? Whereas it is crystal clear that classical works only found themselves in harmony with an almost interminable duration because they appeared to come from somewhere higher than their time, tearing through it and burning it up with an extreme concentration that united in itself the past, the present and the future.

To this the reply from some quarters is that there are many weaknesses in these novice works, and that there is even an element of imitation in their experiments. That is quite possible and also perfectly natural. How can one expect a serene and definitive perfection from artists who set themselves formidably difficult problems, in an effort for which they deprive themselves of all of the facilities of realism? In addition to the fact that they are not all equally talented and that some of them, incapable of creating forms, are content to borrow those that recent models place at their disposal, it goes without saying that their endeavours lay them open to all sorts of failure, error and even unconscious repetition. The ambition they are confronting threatens to destroy them at every instant. They are to some extent belittled by the difficulty of their task. They appear less than they are because they would need to be more than themselves.

These dangers are undeniable, but it is all the more necessary to seek them out so as to learn how to master them. What counts is a certain attitude of mind in the face of art, an attitude which is in no way inspired by a taste for novelty, as is sometimes thought, but by an inner demand [*exigence*] and by the necessity of creating a world which gives expression to everything one can be. This method is entirely one of invention and effort. It claims to imitate only by creating. It does not simply use the successes of the past, it asks them for the secret of success, by showing itself as capable as they were of daring, of rigour and of pride. After acknowledging its failures, it says without it ever being possible to contradict it: 'My experiments may well count for next to nothing alongside the works of the great masters, but the superiority of their style over mine can in no way permit me to abandon the search for a style of my own.' And it adds: 'What I have inherited from tradition, over and above the knowledge it provides, is precisely the need for a style, that is to say the idea of a form in which rules appropriately chosen preserve the values I express from the effects of time.'

It is possible to claim that this spirit of creative adventure has been lacking only in periods of decadence. We owe to it the richness and vitality of the period known as the *après-guerre*, following the 14–18 War, which is unjustly maligned by certain young critics. Today it would be very serious if, under the guise of wisdom and a return to humanism, circumstances were used as a reason for recommending some sort of idle vocation and discrediting creation to the advantage of imitation in literary and artistic works. It may well be that the absurd and the fantastic, arbitrariness and vague confusion, threaten all artistic experiment for a while, turning it into a sort of subject for scandal. But there can be no doubt that periods which do not want to take this risk, preferring to live as parasites on the great centuries of creation, are condemned to a spiritual degradation which renders them unworthy of the models they have adopted. They wish to inherit the past and keep it in the past, and are thus incapable of passing it on. They are not even capable of admiring it.

Translated by Michael Holland

3

The Beginnings of a Novel (1938)*

The novel which Jean-Paul Sartre has just published under the title *Nausea* has met with a welcome consisting of astonishment, curiosity and incomprehension. 'Is it a novel?' say the critics as they ponder this work, in which the creation of types, the representation of life, attention to circumstances count for little. And some of them try to see in it a philosophical essay; while others go in search of the usual elements to be found in novel fiction, eventually find them, and are content.

Jean-Paul Sartre can hardly complain about the metamorphoses he is undergoing. The ambition he had is a magnificent one. Amid so many novelists who are content to excel in a genre that has become exhausted, his project was to forge a myth, not with chance and the accidents of human life, but with the very source of all myths. His concern was with the drama of what is fundamental. With no incidents, no adventure, no passion, no fantasy, he has extracted from existence in its unity the most powerful of tragedies. He has based himself in the most intimate heart of being and there set about generating the pleasures of a pure novel.

This is such a rare, important and necessary undertaking that, even though it is imperfect, it deserves the highest praise, and even the false praise of inattentive readers is to its advantage. Mr Sartre accustoms the mind to thinking that there can be artistic creation outside any desire for real events, outside those make-believe existences we call characters which are usually the object of a novelist's ambitions. He takes the novel to a place where there are no longer any incidents, any plot, any particular person; to that site where the mind sustains itself only by beguiling itself with philosophical notions like existence and being, notions that appear indigestible to art and which are are only refractory to it as a result of the arbitrary workings of thought: essential myths which, having been struck by myriad blows, have disappeared in a cloud of dust.

Habits must, however, be very powerful for Mr Sartre, having set out with so conscious a project, to end up mixing in to his powerful subject a number of realistic adventures and expressing this novel of existence by means of conventional psychology. He ends up with the story of a man

* Originally published as 'L'Ebauche d'un roman', *Aux Ecoutes*, 30 July 1938, p. 31.

struck dumb before the fact of existence and seeking to go beyond it to a deeper world. Nausea is the distressing experience that reveals to him what it is to exist without being, the pathetic illumination which puts him in contact, in the midst of things that exist, not with those things but with their existence. This is an original and authentic sentiment, which could, in a more rigorous work, have opened the way, from symbol to symbol, towards essences, and produced a sort of novel of being which would have been a masterpiece on a par with the greatest. But it is a sentiment which, in Mr Sartre's book, simply proliferates, analyses itself and becomes enfeebled in a story which, while remaining very interesting, is almost always inferior to its substance.

This novel is visibly inspired by a philosophical movement that is little known in France, but is of the utmost importance: that of Edmund Husserl and especially Martin Heidegger. Some extracts from Heidegger's work have just been translated into French for the first time. They reveal the power and the creative will behind this thinking which, in the infinite debate between laws, intelligence and chance, offers art a new point of view from which to contemplate its necessity.

Translated by Michael Holland

4

The Recent Novel (1941)*

It is only too clear that the French novel is in some kind of crisis. Despite often stimulating work by highly gifted authors, the last few years have not witnessed a renaissance to compare with what has been attempted in the literature of certain other countries. With a few exceptions, novels of the recent past have been remarkably faithful to an untroubled, mediocre tradition that itself expressed nothing more than the congenial survival of certain ineffectual errors. Nothing perturbed these authors who aspired to little more than the imitation of their forebears. There was nothing wayward in such books, asked only to shoulder the light burden of connecting with ordinary society and the everyday world of things. Every budding novelist thought himself obliged to tell his own story or that of some character drawn from everyday life. They have been uninventive, unadventurous, and not even conventionally original. The question arose whether the novel, so exhaustive of talent and so dominant within the world of letters, was no longer a literary genre but merely an often futile endeavour to keep a few readers entertained.

This decadence has too many causes to be investigated or even alluded to here. Suffice it to say that the novel seems to have lost its way through a puerile attachment to realism, an exclusive preoccupation with external observation and the pursuit of superficial and facile means of analysis. It is easy to understand how the French novel has become the carbon copy of a social and psychological reality that is itself mere convention. First, false notions of a supposed novelistic tradition, a tradition devoted to the portrayal of manners or the description of human strife, have encouraged the novelist to sacrifice whatever extravagant powers of imagination or creative will he might possess. We gladly sacrifice those qualities we sadly lack. Second, the imitation of society or, as they say, of 'life', was an excellent way for the novelist to bring a degree of necessity into a work of fiction. How is a work to be saved from mere contingency when its sentences succeed each other without discipline, when almost every word could be replaced by another without loss, when the work is no more

---

* Originally published as 'Le Jeune roman', *Journal des Débats*, 14 May 1941, p. 3. Reprinted in *Faux pas* (Paris, Gallimard, 1943), pp. 217–20.

than a haphazard assortment of details and episodes? A writer will, only too naturally, answer: though it be nothing more than an aleatory succession of words and a problematic sequence of deeds, in which, accordingly, nothing seems justified, my novel none the less has the justification afforded by the image of life; it enjoys a degree of necessity in so far as it appears to narrate events that have or might have taken place. It borrows from external truth a verisimilitude that gives it coherence and consequence.

Many novelists might give this answer. The inherent dangers are obvious. The solution proposed is to make the necessity of a work depend on its object rather than on itself. It asks nothing of art and everything of art's vague and formless matter. The reader then finds in the book an approximation of life as he has observed it, and this crude and random impression upon him suffices to bestow complete unity and legitimacy upon a collection of otherwise unmotivated and unconnected phrases. It is strange to believe that the reproduction of events confers necessity upon a novel when such events themselves lack necessity, when they are no more than a confused and obscure complex of accident and chance. Whereas the business of the true work is the creation of a world in which what we are and what constitutes us acquire a degree of necessity, of determinism even, that life does not generally accord them, the claim is that the necessity of the realist, psychological novel derives from its faithful expression of life's little contingencies. The novel is justified by being credited with an imitative faculty that deprives it of any genuine causality. It becomes a mere *trompe-l'oeil*, more or less consistent with tangible reality.

The consequences of such a conception of the novel can be deduced without citing concrete examples. It is obvious that these imitations of life can only be approximate and arbitrary. If some degree of attention to form and a continuity of language and plot would appear to be indispensable, how can a work seek to imitate the texture of a reality that has no rhythm, symmetry or shape, nor anything that might suggest literary principles? Traditionalist conventions have thus evolved upon which novelists have drawn relentlessly for their characters, plots and notions of society, halfway between the external world of observation and the closed, pure world of letters. They have been content with mediocre approximations. They have subsisted on obvious routines that the more daring of them have only avoided through a more painstaking or more disorderly willingness to imitate. Almost all have retained from the basic conception of the French novel the need to refer to something external; to look outside, in the name of verisimilitude, for the unity that should have been secured by the internal organization of the work. They have cast the novel in more or less the usual mould: a well-constructed narrative with a reasonably clear plot, meaningful characters and a realistic picture of society. And they have more or less observed the requirement to be imitative and realistic by the use of certain observable traits, actual details and illusionistic elements, sometimes introducing an air of disorder, a modest incoherence that, it is suggested, is lifelike. Most works of fiction are made from just two ingredients: a narrative form derived from an ill-received tradition and constituting the literary part of the novel, and a content derived from necessarily superficial and arbitrary observations of life, constituting the novel's external justification. These ingredients are themselves two sides of the same convention, since life as represented in the novel is and can only be a literary idea of life, the kind of life, precisely, best framed by the traditionally chosen literary form.

That a number of works appear to have broken with this habit and tried to find a new frame is, of course, undeniable. It is, then, all the more curious to find in such works, produced by forceful and adventurous young talents, the same spirit of imitation, the same fondness for external verisimilitude, the same fear of getting too far from life. It is as if these authors have been held back from their secret creative intentions by a traditionalist spirit, claiming to speak for the French soul, inciting them not to bring forth monsters. They occasionally seem to have conceived within themselves works of which they have then become afraid. Rather than extend themselves to become capable of imagining entirely new forms, they have preferred to direct their energies at not being so rich or so daring. They have used up as much energy trying to conform to novelistic conventions as they would have creating new ones. They have done violence to themselves and, having wished for far less then they were capable of, have traded themselves in for authors of a more modest kind.

Obviously, an inventive spirit and a will to break with tradition call for an exacting pursuit of necessity, the rejection of the arbitrary, and resolute concentration, so that any unjustified image or creation can be repudiated; it demands, in a word, the utmost discipline and authority. This may be the true lesson of our tradition. It allows us to dream of a writer, a symbol of purity and pride, who would be for the novel what Mallarmé was for poetry, and to envisage that work with which Mallarmé sought to match the absolute. Yet how are we to sustain such a dream? The value of a book lies in that superior book it helps us imagine. However far books produced today are from realizing this ideal novel, one feels drawn to ask how close they come and to number the opportune pleasures they hold in store for us.

Translated by Roland-François Lack

5

The Pure Novel (1943)*

The journal *Confluences* has published a special issue on 'problems of the novel', covering everything the reader's curiosity or the critic's interest might ask of such a question. It cannot be said that this collective text lends itself to clear thinking, nor does it give coherent expression to any specific conception of the novel. It is obvious that the many different authors who have contributed to this investigation rarely agree about the problems raised. Some follow traditional lines of thought, a few others are more daring. Most use rather vague definitions to endorse the precise preferences they find in themselves or in their own predilections as readers or novelists. Such confusion is not without its charm. It may even be interesting in itself since, behind the anarchy of opinions and the imprecision of vocabulary, the attentive reader may discern those fixed points around which the fate of the genre is being played out.

Edmond Jaloux believes that between the nineteenth and the twentieth centuries an essential difference becomes apparent. Nineteenth-century novels do not call into question what is generally understood by reality. The world represented resembles the world in which everyone usually lives. Men are shown more or less as they can be perceived through everyday imagination and observation. In this respect the work of Balzac and Stendhal finds its continuation in Roger Martin du Gard, Jules Romains and Georges Duhamel. They belong to the same tradition in so far as they aim to respect the traditional structure of the world. In certain contemporary novels the situation changes. The novelist's vision becomes separated from ordinary vision. The author takes the suggestions of his own sensibility as a point of departure and no longer seeks to connect with the appearance of common reality. On the contrary, he distances himself from a world where anyone can see themselves reflected. Novelistic invention, it is suggested, should not be tied to the world of known things: it should harmonize with what is not known, with what cannot be known.

Jaloux is right to find this important. It neatly defines two distinct paths that the novel may take. We can discount the fact that these two tenden-

---

* Originally published as 'Le Roman pur', *Journal des Débats*, 4–5 December 1943, p. 2.

cies distinguish only imperfectly between nineteenth- and twentieth-century novelists, in that the best-known novels of today belong to yesterday's tradition, and while *Maldoror*, the work most clearly opposed to that tradition, was written in 1867. None the less, the simplicity of the definition can be deceptive. The difference between Balzac–Stendhal and Lautréamont does not rest on the greater or lesser display of personal sensibility, a greater or lesser abandon to an irreducible interior vision. It is more likely that the great novelists of the nineteenth-century tradition depend on personal reactions as extraordinary and on dictates of the imagination as peculiar as those of any Surrealist writer, however strange. With a certain sense of paradox, we could well find common points of departure in Stendhal and Lautréamont: they have the same explosive sense of time, both are intoxicated with the will's metamorphic power, both revere the supreme capacity for effortless transgression. The only difference is that Stendhal expresses this fundamental sense through a world of appearances that matches exactly the society of his time, where-as Lautréamont creates from it a world opposed to everyday experience, where *trompe-l'oeil* effects are rejected, images and impressions over-turned.

The Balzac-type novel (to give it, rather arbitrarily, a name), however large the share accorded the imagination, introduces enough recogniz-able elements into its fictional system for the real existence of the reader to find its place therein, if necessary. To an inner world, conceived by an imagination and sensibility far removed from the common model, corres-ponds an outside world that is perfectly adapted to that model. In the Lautréamont-type novel (to give it, too, a name), the inner world no longer claims to produce a likeness; it disdains the verisimilitude that everyday existence presupposes; regardless of habit and custom, it seeks to fashion, to mould the form in which it will become manifest. The exterior should correspond to the interior, not to those conventional practices, those common but arbitrary beliefs that are the basis of social life: this new ambition differentiates the twentieth-century tradition from the nineteenth. Consequently, since the rule of verisimilitude has no value, the novel is free to transform reality; not just colour it differently but change its structure, overturn its laws and extinguish the light of understanding. It secretes its own world. It is master of its own appear-ances. It arranges its figures and incidents into a new ensemble, around a unity of its own choosing and with no need to justify its frame of reference. This freedom can seem absolute, but it is none the less bound by a fundamental necessity to harmonize, without *trompe-l'oeil* effects, the inside and outside of the novel's creation.

This strict correspondence clarifies the meaning given to the term 'pure novel'. It is generally attributed to André Gide who, in the 'diary' of *The Counterfeiters*, sought out the meaning of this expression. If we look at the definitions put to the test by Gide's hero, Edouard, we see similar notions at work, most significantly in this remark:

> I am beginning to perceive [says the novelist, referring to Edouard] what I would call the 'deep subject' of my book. It is, it will be, undoubtedly, the rivalry between the real world and how we represent it to ourselves. The way in which the world of appearances imposes itself upon us and in which we try to impose our particular interpretation onto the world is what constitutes our life's drama.

Elsewhere he proposes a slightly different prescription:

> This will be the subject: the struggle between the facts presented by reality and an ideal reality.

He finds these definitions far from satisfying and indeed they remain equivocal: phrases like 'ideal reality' and 'particular interpretation' adapt well to the habits of everyday realism. None the less this line of research does lead to the pure novel. That which, according to Gide, constitutes our life's drama is also the novel's particular drama: the art of the novel cannot always bear conforming to the 'world of appearances'; the novel is in competition with the reality lived by everybody else; it wants its own appearances, derived from the novelist's own rhythm and interior vision, not those imposed by the vision and day-to-day habits of the reader. What is a pure art? An art that will obey aesthetic necessity alone, an art that, rather than combine the representation of things with certain laws of sensibility, renounces imitation and even the conventions of meaning. The novel thus has serious pretensions to purity, since it claims to create, where necessary, a system that is absolute, comprehensive and indifferent to the ordinary circumstances of things, a system constituted by intrinsic relations and able to sustain itself without support from outside.

Naturally, expressions like pure art and pure novel are themselves rich in ambiguity. Paul Valéry has always accepted that the verbal arts, unlike music for example, cannot create a separate universe, a strange kingdom, sufficient unto itself, existing only for itself and signifying only itself. The purity of poetry does not lie in destroying language as a system of signs, but in producing, from the complexity of signs and sounds, an order that, though meaningful, can only be justified as an ordered ensemble of rhythms and sounds. Similarly, the pure novel can combine sensibility and verisimilitude or sensibility and the comprehensible in the same work, but it will impose order on verisimilitude and on common values according to the inner suggestion that these are meant to translate, so as to translate it exactly. The purity of the novel does not, as Gide's Edouard writes, lie in stripping away all elements that do not belong specifically to the novel, in excluding exterior events, accidents and traumas, or even in suppressing character descriptions or characters themselves. It consists in making all these elements depend on the personal idea of order that they are intended to manifest, in their strict submission to the purpose that they are to project in time, as its shadow in the world. It is easy to see that novels quite indifferent to exterior verisimilitude will still make room for many details furnished by everyday observation; to take *Maldoror* once again as an example, that work is packed with everyday images, recognizable figures and commonplace information. This is self-evident. The pure novel is not concerned with creating a world whose materials are foreign to the world in which we usually live, nor even systematically different from this world; what matters is the imposing of order, the composition of appearances and the references that, in line with particular perspectives, give direction to the ensemble of known images.

It is noticeable that the novel is hardly spoken of without mention of the word 'world'. Partisans of objective narrative and those who seek the truth of their fictions in the imaginary happily agree on this term: 'novelists,' they say, 'do not seek to write a novel but to create a world.' The widespread use of this word is due partly to the preoccupations of contemporary philosophy. A serious study of the novel, and even of the pure novel, would have to investigate the exigencies hiding behind a notion that seems both clear and confused. It would discover, surely, that if every novel has a horizon of being that expresses it, this does not mean that the novel must always take place in the world we know or in a world like it, nor that it depends on the circumstances of 'life', nor that it must feature characters whose simulated existence can be identified with that of the reader. The reality is that, if the novel always has an outside, it is because what we call its inside, the interior pole that is the author's vision, the explicit or implicit sentiment by which he is led, is itself inseparable from the concrete organization in which it develops. It is genuinely a pole, a direction from which run lines of force, spread out and unfolded by the passage of time, giving the impression of an ensemble, of a figure, of man's own situation, always encircled by a horizon. In other words, the world of the novel seems tied to two essential elements: it is an ordering, a system of relations organized in the image of man's situation to express its meaning; and it is not a static order, since it reveals itself through time, it endures, it realizes duration.

We might wonder what reasoning motivates the search for a pure novel, a search that has not, perhaps, as Edmond Jaloux points out, brought forth any exemplary works, but is still the contemporary novel's

most significant contribution. The question, like the problem of the pure
novel as a whole, would require endless commentary. Two brief remarks
are possible. First, such a conception is related to a certain type of
creative mind. If, following Friedrich Gundolf's distinction between
attractive and expansive creation, we take the first to be the mind that
shapes the universe in terms of its self, seeking by attraction to accord the
universe with that self, which then becomes its centre, in the manner of
Dante, and if we take the second form of creation to describe the mind
that pours itself into the world, frees itself of its excessive plenitude to
vitalize and take possession of the world, in the manner of Shakespeare,
clearly the author of the pure novel belongs to the first type. He too seeks
to make of his self the symbol of the world. He draws it towards him in
order to remake it in the light of his own vision. He accepts its data only
as the materials he must reconstitute and order. Conversely, an author
such as Balzac has an expansive genius; he communicates life and
strength to a reality that is sufficient for his needs; he extends himself,
overflowing into the demarcated frame of the universe. Having made this
distinction, the question remains why, in the pure novel, the attractive
mind draws the world to itself, not to give it the harmony of a centre but
to do it violence, to annihilate it and replace it with its own pale illusions.
One reason is that this creative mind lacks power: Gundolf says that
'what is missing from the attractive mind, when it is not on a par with
Dante's, is the world.' The other reason is that the world, which should
provide the creative self with raw material, today seems itself to be
exhausted; it has lost its originality and its objective truth, it imposes
itself only as an inconsistent and impure system whose appearance the
mind feels tempted, even obliged to reject in order to re-establish its own
interpretation of it and to express its own original experience. In this
respect the pure novel, whatever its failings, may deserve more attention
than the accomplished works of objective narrative. It is in search of the
unknown. It demands the inaccessible. We can apply to it Edouard's
remark from. *The Counterfeiters*:

> I've often thought that in art, and in literature in particular, the only
> ones who count are those who set off for the unknown. You don't
> discover new worlds without consenting to lose sight of the shore,
> from the outset and for a long time. But our writers fear the open
> sea; they are mere coasters.

Translated by Roland–François Lack

6

Mallarmé and the Art of the Novel (1943)*

Henri Mondor's books on Mallarmé have given us an opportunity to reread that admirable letter expressing the hopes of the poet as he prepares *Un Coup de dés*. Whenever, by some chance, we recollect this famous letter, so often studied by commentators, so often dreamed of and sometimes secretly rewritten by finer minds, it still seems entirely new, making the reader come to know it as if it had been preserved, untouched by any meditation. We shall read it then, naïvely. The pleasure it gives derives from pride of the purest kind, the kind from which some insight can always be derived. What is Mallarmé's dream?

> It is difficult to say [he writes]: a book, simply, in many volumes, a book that would really be a book, architectural and premeditated, not an anthology of random inspirations, however marvellous they might be ... I'd go further, I'd say: the Book, persuaded as I am that in the end there is only one, unwittingly attempted by anyone who has written, even writers of genius. The orphic explanation of the Earth, the sole duty of the poet and the literary game *par excellence*: for then the rhythm of the book, impersonal and living, even in its pagination, is juxtaposed with the equations of this dream, or Ode.

This passage is, of course, followed by another where Mallarmé resigns himself

> not to making this work in its entirety (it would take I don't know who to do that), but to showing a completed fragment of it, and, through one of its surfaces, making its glorious authenticity shine, indicating thereby all that remained to do, which would take more than a lifetime. Proving by the portions made that this book does exist, and that I have known what I could not accomplish.

* Originally published as 'Mallarmé et l'art du roman', *Journal des Débats*, 27 October 1943, p. 3. Reprinted in *Faux pas* (Paris, Gallimard, 1943), pp. 197–204.

This text has inspired many excellent meditations upon language in the pristine, hitherto untarnished use made of it by Mallarmé: language conceived through a meticulous study of words and their relations, a determined experimentation on the figures and secret soul of syllables and an all-powerful will to expansion and illumination. Yet a text such as this is admirable not only for the purity and the necessity that, in a genuinely delectable union, it imposes on poetry, henceforward removed from the effects of chance; it displays far greater audacity, playing, unmysteriously, with mystery *par excellence*, penetrating it with a few simple, entirely accessible, even enchanting words. A simplicity and clarity whose innocence begins, in the end, to look like a trap. What are we to think of this hand that offers, as if in passing, the key to all creation? Might it not be taking back what it gives, by giving in its reserve infinitely more than it promises? So we come to believe that this text, so mysterious and so clear, is like an unapproachable revelation, destined to efface by its radiant simplicity the importance of what it reveals.

Curiously, no novelist has found in Mallarmé's remarks a definition of the art of the novel and a suggestion of glorious prospects for the novelist's mission. And yet in this text there is so profound a conception of language, so broad a view of the vocation of words, so universal an elucidation of literature that no form of creation could feel excluded. The writer whose troubling mission makes him feel obliged to use the facilities of prose in constructing the rigour of fiction is no less directly addressed than the poet. Clearly, the two can be separated only if one of them – which, it is true, is commonly the case with the novelist – separates himself from what he is. With means at his disposal that are at once identical and different, exercising the same virtues and yet a totally dissimilar discipline, at the same time united and opposed in an extenuating rivalry, the same man produces the work that definitively divides him: a poet who loses everything if he is touched by prose, a prose-writer who is nothing if he cannot match the poem with an art that has borrowed nothing from the poem.

It may be arbitrary to evoke the art of the novel when thinking about the book dreamed of by Mallarmé; none the less the novelist can rightly be thought of as a potential author of this book and rightly asked to contemplate, if he would, the admirable conditions it imposes. His task will be easy if he is prepared to break with most of his habits and agree for a moment to follow Mallarmé to the very foundations of language. What, indeed, was language for Mallarmé, and how is it that language could have appeared to him, not only as the basis of poetry (which, in some sense, would not have been very meaningful), but as the essence of the world? Clearly such a question can only be asked because its very breadth dispenses us, in the space of a brief note, from giving an ambitious answer. In the first place we need not recall the obvious fact that Mallarmé, more deeply than any other, conceived of language not as a system of expression, a useful and convenient intermediary for the mind that seeks to understand and to make itself understood, but as a force for transformation and creation, made to create enigmas rather than to elucidate them. Mallarmé was led very far by the consequences of this idea. Language founds human experience and the universe. The nature and dignity of language are expressed both by man, who reveals himself in a dialogue in which he discovers the event that is his foundation, and by the world, putting itself into words in an act that is its deep origin. The error would be to think of language as an instrument whereby man acts or manifests himself in the world; in reality, it is language that positions man, by guaranteeing the existence of the world and his existence within it. To name the gods, to make the world become discourse, this alone founds the authentic dialogue that is human reality, and it is this naming that provides the discourse with its thread, its brilliant and mysterious figure, its form, its constellation, far from the sounds and rules in use in practical life.

It must be absolutely clear that this way of thinking has nothing to do with the notion that the essence of our nature, or of nature itself, in being discernible, can ultimately be expressed. The poet sets out on quite a different path. He affirms that our human reality is in essence poetic, that this reality is itself the discourse by which it is laid bare; but this means that, far from being subordinate instruments, noble but subjugated functions, poetry and discourse are in their own right an absolute of which ordinary language cannot even see the originality. That language is an absolute, the very form of transcendence, and that it can none the less find its way into a human work, is the idea to which Mallarmé gave calm consideration, in order immediately to pursue its literary consequences. We know that he dreamed of and sketched out a book that was as loaded with the real and the secret, as impenetrable and as clear as the world itself; subject to an order as visible and as ironically hidden as the order of the world. He envisaged a work that could take the place of the universe and of the man who would give birth to it. He saw and gave form to the page that, by means of an ensemble of considered correlations and with words that on the whole had meaning, was destined to create for man the equivalent of a fatal riddle and a despair-inducing silence. Mallarmé the obscure gave brilliance, as if it were something tangible and clear, to what could only be expressed in the total absence of expression. If it had been right to think of him as scandalous, it should have been for the too great clarity of his work, where clarity could only be a supreme defiance and the reflection of an excessive and yet satisfied ambition.

The dangerous nature of such an enterprise is easily sensed. But this danger is its principal *raison d'être*, and it is part of its aim to take what Mallarmé calls the 'literary game' (the expression is to be found in Mallarmé's letter), that is to say, an activity that in some respects may be ineffective, and make it seem like the most dangerous enterprise possible, a tragedy by the end of which the mind can do no more than succumb under the futility of its triumph. The extreme danger inherent in the innocence of a frivolous game is revealed, a revelation perfectly figured by certain poems where the subject seems to be nothing, where there is no subject. It is fundamental to all of Mallarmé's work, to any work. The poem, like any product of the mind, can only denounce the peril that language represents for man; it is the ultimate danger, the lightning bolt that reveals to him, at the risk of being blinded and struck down, that he is lost in the banality of everyday words, in the community of social language, in the quiescence of tame metaphors. Essential language suddenly gleams from within the cloud, and its brilliance attacks, consumes, and devours historicized language, which is compromised, though not replaced. Herein lies the supreme danger, the danger that, by the exercise of an intelligence caught up in infinite labours and by the rigour of mind that ceaselessly rediscovers chance, leads the creator into silence, that is if he knows himself well enough to control his imaginings, if he is conscious enough of his wants to reject any impure or inauthentic form, and determined enough in this prodigious pursuit, to confront in the form of an admirable nothingness, the destiny of which he is worthy. Such silence has a seemingly perfect beauty. Images are abolished. Metaphors have dissipated. Words are broken open. There is only, deep in the mind, a henceforward incorruptible poem that a complete necessity seems to have reduced to absence and which, none the less, recognizes itself in this absence as the image – the final image – of plenitude and of the absolute.

Such dreams, painful to any creator, can only seem mad, even unthinkable, to a novelist, who can only be disconcerted by such great pride. Yet their dangerous and appalling character bears witness to a supreme ambition that no art, and least of all the art of the novel, can deny itself. Few novelists will ever die from it. There is no reason to fear or, alas, to hope that the world of letters will be depleted from despairing of too perfect a rigour or from a fatal effort of consciousness. In truth there is no good reason why only the poet should have access to that extreme perfection of work exemplified by Mallarmé. Why shouldn't the novelist, simply because he writes in prose, protect what he creates by the scrupulousness, the power to refuse, and the resistance to the facile which in poetry are guarantees of a certain purity. The novelist who reflects upon the work that he is to compose must immediately come to grips with problems so serious and so exhausting that they will necessarily seem impossible. This impossibility must be the secret soul of his work. It faces him with demands before which he may well succumb, but which, as he is defeated, will make him conscious of what it is he desires. Why shouldn't he find within the term creation all the strength that he must draw from it? Why, having rejected the freedom from constraint that would allow him everything but condemn him to do nothing, shouldn't he be concerned with a particular necessity, a necessity outside which his work would be no more than a simulacrum and a figure of untruth? The novelist must impose a law on himself, and his work's solidity will be measured only by the real value of this law and the strength of his will to reject whatever does not conform to it. If he is truly to be an author, the writer's first thought must be to write nothing and do nothing unless it denotes a calculated defeat of chance, denoting thereby its victory.

In addition to these rules, whose usefulness he secretly acknowledges, it is almost inconceivable that the novelist should not accept, as intended for him, those considerations on language that have deeply preoccupied not only Mallarmé but also Hölderlin, Novalis and many others. Yet the novelist's contempt, not only for the language in which he writes, but for all formal problems, is exceeded only by the naïveté of the solutions he arrives at once he pays them any attention. It appears that, in the view of this creator, prose can only transmit some predetermined idea, after which it evaporates, having expired in the reader's mind, where it is entirely replaced by the idea it conveys. But it is obvious that this vocation of prose only applies to everyday language. The novelist has a destiny quite other than that of making himself understood, or rather he must make the reader apprehend what cannot be understood from everyday, inauthentic speech. He undertakes to bring into the absolutely bound-up world of events, images and words the essential dialogue that constitutes him. Thus, by the same path as any other artist, he heads towards those strange tenebrous regions where he seems to awaken in the deepest sleep, towards that pure presence where things appear so bare and so reduced that no image is possible, towards that primordial spectacle where he never tires of contemplating what can be seen only after a complete self-transformation. To ask, then, that every part of his work have a meaning that is definite and certain for someone other than himself is perhaps to ask him to say what he will do. But that is a contingency that he accepts as an external constraint without sacrificing either the overall rigour of his work, or its unity, or the multiplicity of its expressions, or even the absence of meaning, if we can call meaninglessness an obligation upon the mind to display a superior poverty on coming into contact with thought of the richest kind. His book, like Mallarmé's, must tend towards being the absolute that he desires. It exists by itself, and this, the most rigorous, the most necessary existence possible, is the only signification that can be demanded of it. If it persists beyond the thought we have of it, it is perfect. The reader feels driven to despair, ravished by a book that does not depend on him, but upon which he depends in the most sovereign manner, in a relation that threatens his mind and his being.

The novelist's insurmountable difficulty often stems from the breadth and diversity of the solutions suggested by his art and from his incapacity to realize them in their purity. At the mention of formal problems, he thinks only of the language he uses and of the composition's structure. At the suggestion that the essence of the novel is that its form should be its content, that is to say, the fiction upon which it lives, he believes he has to think up a subject, an external plot, a world of characters and events in every way identical to the one in which we live. As to language, if it is impressed upon him that the language of the novel must in some way be as different from everyday language as is poetic language, he is astonished and scandalized by what he understands to be a system of esoteric conventions. These confusions are so numerous as to be inexhaustible. It is as if the writer in prose only pays attention to what he writes by accident. How can he be made to understand that the language of the novel must be singular, in the sense that it depends uniquely on the work of which it appears as a means and an end, but that this language could in no sense be mistaken for literary language in general, a communal language that has been purified, cultivated and loaded with propitious figures? The true language of the novel, if it is always secretly controlled by a rigorously necessary ordering of images and words, can, as far as metaphors are concerned, quite easily offer the reader only the complete absence of metaphor, of recherché expressions, of well-chosen words. It becomes impoverished, arid. It seems to lose its body and its soul. It acts as a warning to the reader, generating, through an unanalysable power, a sense of the tragic fiction it touches upon. A dying language can very well be acknowledged, eventually, by a scrupulous enough novelist, as necessary. To perform that task would require the most thorough knowledge of the means of universal art, near-total dominion over the world of words, the deepest sense of the creation of images and, last, a fatal taste for perfection. Such a novelist, of whom a writer like Joyce bears certain characteristics, would pose the same problems with which Mallarmé exhausted his life and, like Mallarmé, he would gladly live to bring about singular transformations in himself and to draw out of speech the silence in which he must die.

Translated by Roland-François Lack

7

How is Literature Possible? (1942)*

I

We read the book which Jean Paulhan has just devoted to literature and language, *Les Fleurs de Tarbes* [*The Flowers of Tarbes*], with a strange feeling. We enter unwarily into the analyses he formulates, not really sensing the perils towards which the charming, precise sentences, their tight construction a guarantee of safety and order, are precipitated. Everything about it is clear, ingenious, straightforward. Just as the words follow on effortlessly from one another, so a series of sound reasons is elaborated, which seems intended to dispel equivocations and to ensure that any writer is able to proceed with his writing. We calmly witness the disempowering of a certain critical conception, whose defeat, it seems, we can scarcely regret, since it was by nature hostile to conventions and rules. However, an initial feeling of uneasiness begins to emerge. The movement of the thought we would like to follow, all the while remaining marvellously coherent and regular, reveals at the same time a number of discontinuities and allusions, whose meaning is somewhat threatening. Where is this author, who appeared to be quietly carrying out his police duty with exquisite artfulness, taking us? Is he not talking about something other than what he was supposed to be saying? Could there be, hidden within his refutations and arguments, a kind of infernal machine which, invisible today, will one day explode, overwhelming literature and rendering its use impossible? This is the anxiety that Jean Paulhan is able to produce. We read his book unsuspectingly, but when we reach the end, we suddenly see that he has put into question not only a certain critical conception, not only all of literature, but also the mind, its powers and means, and we look back in horror at the abyss we have just crossed – but have we really gone over it? – and which a succession of veils had skilfully hidden from us as we crossed over. Jean Paulhan has given two titles to his work: *The Flowers of Tarbes* or *Terror in Literature*. This ambiguity accurately expresses some of the games he employs in order to manipulate the reader's mind.

---

* Originally published as *Comment la littérature est-elle possible?* (Paris, José Corti, 1942).

To the question: 'what is literature?' the criticism Jean Paulhan calls
terrorist gives the following answer: there is only literature when there are
no commonplaces, when a poem or a novel is not bound by conventions,
artifices, or the traditional figures of style. This terror, whose decrees
have dominated the world of letters for the past 150 years, expresses a
need for purity, a preoccupation with rupture, which goes as far as
forgetting the accepted conditions of language. With Victor Hugo it
rejects 'rhetoric', with Verlaine 'eloquence', with Rimbaud 'poetic old
hat'; but with more recent writers, driven by a distaste for clichés and
tormented by an obsession with revolt, it claims to break with all forms
of discourse and even with all language, seeking in originality the provisional refuge of a rebellion whose success consumes it constantly. The
deprivation of words, the poverty of vocabulary, but also an absolute
mistrust of technique, of well-defined genres and of rules in general,
these are the effects of terror which, from Sainte-Beuve to Taine, from
Romanticism to Surrealism, traps literature in a network of prohibitions,
where it can only fade away. At the entrance to the public gardens in
Tarbes one can see, says Jean Paulhan, this sign: 'It is forbidden to enter
the gardens carrying flowers.' It can also be seen these days at the
entrance to literature. Young writers can only show up empty-handed,
unadorned by the decorations with which art embellished itself naturally
in the past and in all the brilliance and disorder of a freedom which
aspires, in vain, to a primitive state of being.

Why this fear of commonplaces? It is because, according to terrorist
critics, clichés are a sign of laziness and inertia. The writer who takes
refuge in them revels in a kind of indolence which subordinates him to
ready-made forms. He still believes he is thinking for himself; this is his
mistake. He accepts a succession of words which imposes a fixed order
upon him and narrowly confines his thought. The use of commonplace
expressions thus leads to a serious abuse, which is verbalism. The author
who is a victim of conventional sentences is no longer in control of what
he is saying. And his words, triumphing over the exact meaning to which
they ought to correspond, rebel against the mind which attempts to guide
them, weigh upon it with all of their brute force, and make it aware of
how degradingly all-powerful that force is. If we reflect on certain words,
such as *freedom, democracy, order,* and on the disorderliness that can result
if they are used carelessly, it becomes clear to us that writers have good
reason to be vigilant in preventing a facile subservience. Apparently given
over to licence and anarchy, they are in fact engaged in repudiating
chance, darkness, confusion, destroying idols and battling with monsters.

Terror, in brief, as the enemy of commonplaces and rules, is engaged
in a fight against a sickness of language, and in the fear that words, left to

themselves and freed from their meaning, might exert over the minds and hearts of men a formidable power, this terror attempts to restore to inspiration and creative force a boundless empire. Jean Paulhan notes that this conception has found in Bergson's philosophy the privileged doctrine which has led it to self-awareness. Following Bergson's advice, it has invited writers continually to resist practical, ordinary language in order to rediscover the fluid forms of a deeper life. It goes beyond apparent logic, fixed by everyday words, in search of an unexpressed and probably inexpressible reality; it strives to break the network of conventions in order to get through to a world that is still innocent; it lays claim to a virginal contact, to brand-new meanings, finding within this aspiration towards an extreme purity the justification for the imperious decrees which cause it to regard with suspicion the *savoir-faire* and technique proper to all usages of language.

This then is terror, its claims, its hates, its secrets. What are we to think of it? If we look a little more carefully at its grievances, we notice first of all that they don't correspond to the simplest observations and then that they are based on a remarkable kind of illusion. It would be rash to believe that the use of commonplace expressions always presumes laziness or leads to verbalism. There are times when a writer invents his clichés, rediscovers them through a personal effort and uses them as a means of expressing a freshness of sensibility or a naïveté of the imagination. Then there are times when the author knows he is using commonplace expressions, but uses them wilfully precisely because for him they only represent forms of language that are as common as any other word, that are well-suited to their meaning and unable to stand in its way. Clichés are intended to go unnoticed; far from giving the sentences that include them the appearance of verbal excess, they rather have the effect, by dint of their banality, of making them transparent and invisible.

Terror's entire accusation in fact relies upon an optical illusion. Its attention is focused on the author, whom it reproaches for giving in to words, whereas it is the reader, as he comes to grips with commonplaces, who is wholly engaged with words, a prisoner of an uncertain language whose intention escapes him. When the writer uses a cliché, whoever reads it may well ask himself at least a double question: is this, he wonders, a picturesque and empty expression, which translates an important thought with added colour, or is it on the contrary an impressive-looking word which corresponds to nothing? It is this ambiguity which unsettles the use of conventional words and ultimately makes using them a perilous activity. The reader, disturbed and worried, wondering what these words freedom, order and democracy which are put before him mean, ends up accusing the author of verbalism, as if the latter were guilty of having been too preoccupied with words, when in fact he is guilty of having neglected them; far from being too concerned with combinations of language, he pays too little attention to problems of form, whose solution he leaves to his reader, who is thereby condemned to these words and possessed by them.

The drawback, then, of commonplace expressions, of clichés, of a trite sequence of images, is that they subject the reader to equivocation and move him further away from the thought to which he ought to have access. From this perspective, we see how the conception which accuses rhetoric is right to recommend that writers strive for a faithful expression, why it has good reason to denounce the scandal of the commonplace which, instead of acquitting itself honourably of its duty as a scrupulous interpreter, on the contrary fosters obscurity and misunderstanding. But we also see how incomplete this conception is. Terror, so intransigent, so quick to consume figures of speech, is in fact extraordinarily timid. It is content to act after the damage has been done, hunting down clichés when they have already carried out their work of corruption and striking at random without any exact sense of the reasons motivating its exercise of justice. So terror needs to be perfected. And the best way of turning it into a method of preventive action, that is, of dispelling the Janus-faced form that is the commonplace expression, is to take away the latter's power to deceive, to give it a quality of clarity and self-evidence, in short, to make commonplace expressions *common*, since their main flaw, as shown by the preceding remarks, was that they were always oscillating as expressions, never fixed or commonly understood. And the same is true of other conventions, rules, laws and figures of speech. The writer who uses them as advised, who is ready to form them by virtue of a flawless technique and not just to submit to them, is blessed with the grace of an innocent literature and of a language in contact with things. Rhetoric, or perfected terror, as Jean Paulhan says.

It would be a great disappointment to read *The Flowers of Tarbes* without seeing the various levels of meaning of the thought expressed in it, whose enigmatic existence is hinted at in murmurs, in a number of lightning-quick reversals or, conversely, in several slow allusions. Do not think that this book is what it appears to be: the analysis, guided by the subtlest, the rarest and the most felicitous of minds, of a certain critical conception and a proposed ingenious solution to a particular problem. We are in fact dealing with a fundamental question concerning the nature of the mind, its profound division, this struggle between the Same and the Same, which is the means of its power, its torment and its apotheosis. It will become apparent to anyone who tries to read the real book that Jean Paulhan has written, and whose sequel is announced, that behind the ironic reserve which is his art, by means of a seriousness which challenges itself and which puts itself to the test in this challenge, he has posed, in a form that calls to mind the famous Kantian revolution, the following problem: how is literature possible? But since such a question, through the debate into which it draws language and the mind, involves a hypothesis about the nature of the most extreme human darkness, we can catch a glimpse of some of the paths he takes to get to authentic thought and contemplate its native purity, which is also made up of stereotypes, of commonplaces and conventions. These thoughts cannot be summed up in a few words. It is no easy task to try and capture, in a mirror such as this, an image which goes beyond appearances and accounts for them; but once we have made this discovery, when we have learnt to read this book, we realize that we also know how to read almost all others. We will, then, as we retrace our steps and watch the invisible footprints left in the sand, attempt to see how this essay puts into question, through a fundamental doubt, everything that can be written and thought with words.

II

There are two ways of reading *The Flowers of Tarbes*. If we content ourselves with accepting the text, following its signposts and enjoying the first series of reflections it offers, we will be rewarded with a reading that is most pleasing and stimulating to the mind. What could be more ingenious or more immediately satisfying than turns and detours of judgement when confronted with a certain literary conception which it at the same time watches, captivates and demolishes? We leave this spectacle delighted and reassured. Unfortunately, after several allusions hidden by their self-evidence, a number of formal problems and a mysterious conclusion little by little give us pause for thought. Is the book we have just drawn near to the real work we should be reading? Is it not merely its appearance? Might it not only be there to hide ironically another, more difficult and dangerous essay, whose shadows and ambitions we are dimly aware of? At this point we have to take up our reading again, but it would be futile to think that Jean Paulhan ever gives away his secrets. It is only through the uneasiness and anxiety we feel that we are authorized to communicate with the larger questions that he poses, and he is prepared to show us these questions only by their absence.

The first book, the apparent book, is devoted, as we have seen, to the critical conception Paulhan calls terrorist. Let us recall its conclusion:

It is that clichés would no longer be lacking anything if they always appeared to writers as clichés. All we need to do, says Paulhan, is to make commonplaces *common*, and to restore to their proper usage the rules, figures of speech and all the other conventions which suffer a similar fate.

If a writer uses images, unities, rhymes, that is, rhetoric's renewed means, as he is supposed to, he will be able to rediscover the impersonal and innocent language he is searching for, the only one which allows him to be what he is and to enter into contact with the virgin newness of things.

This is, more or less, Jean Paulhan's conclusion. But having reached this ending, the reader has the choice between two possible courses of action. He can stop at this text he has understood, which is important enough to engage his mind. Is not everything perfectly clear now? Is there some remaining doubt, which has not been cleared up? What can we ask of an author who has foreseen everything, even that we will ask nothing more of him? Indeed, this same reader, if he is attentive, will find at the end of the work, just when he is completely satisfied, a few words of retraction, which disturb him and force him to retrace his steps. So he rereads, and little by little, convinced that there is, behind the initial assertions he had contented himself with, a secret he has to find, he tries to go further, looking for the combination by which he will be able to open the true book that is offered to him. First of all he considers raising several objections, in order to attack and if possible to dispel the apparent book from which he has trouble taking his eyes. There is one objection he can try without too great a risk. What is this terror, after all? How has it been able to bring together so many minds, sometimes so different and opposed in almost every way? At first sight we can discern among the terrorists, as Paulhan calls them, two categories of writers who seem very far from having a common understanding about language. For some writers, language's mission is to express thought correctly, to be its faithful interpreter, to be subservient to it as if to a master whom it recognizes. But for other writers, expression is merely the prosaic function of everyday language; language's true role is not to express but to communicate, not to translate but to be; and it would be absurd to see it as nothing but an intermediary, a worthless agent: it has a peculiar quality which it is the writer's duty precisely to discover and restore. Here are, then, what seem to be two types of mind completely foreign to one another. What could they possibly have in common?

A lot more, no doubt, than one would think at first. Let us come back to classical writers. Writing for them is expressing thought by means of a discourse which should not hold our attention, which should even disappear the moment it appears, which should not at any rate cast a shadow over this profound life which it reveals. Art consequently has only one objective: to bring to light this inner world, while keeping it untouched by the crude and general illusions with which an imperfect language would dishonour it. But what else do all the other writers want, who refuse to ask literary language to do the same things as everyday language; and do they want it by some other means? For them too, writing is expressing a secret, profound thought, all the while making sure that they rid language of everything which could make it look like ordinary language, expressing oneself, in other words, through a language which is not an instrument of expression, in which the words could show none of the wear and tear, and the ambiguity, of ordinary life. In both cases, then, the writer's mission is to impart an authentic thought – a secret or a truth – which an excessive attention to words, especially to the well-worn words we use every day, could only imperil.

What confirms the similarity of these two kinds of mind is the identity of their fate. Each of them, carried along by the movement of its own necessity [*exigence*], ends up criticizing language as such, literature as such, and would waste away into silence if it were not saved by a constant illusion. Jean Paulhan has clearly shown what becomes of the first kind. Wanting to make language the ideal site of understanding and self-evidence, they gradually remove from it the commonplace expressions which hamper communication of thoughts, extract from it conventional words, finally rid it of words themselves and, in a futile pursuit of clarity in a language which would say everything without being anything, they die having attained nothing. They end up, in short, cancelling out language as a means of expression, precisely by having demanded that language be nothing other than a means of expression. As for the second kind, they end up feeling the same hostility, because they saw words first of all as having no value in terms of expression, but great value in terms of communication. So they expelled from language those words, figures of speech and turns of phrase most likely to make it resemble a means of exchange or a precise system of substitution. But this necessity [*exigence*] inevitably ended up being all-consuming. If it allowed Mallarmé to restore to certain terms the value of an event, if it gave him the means to explore their inner space to the point of appearing truly to invent or discover them, it forced those who came after him to reject those same terms as already corrupted by usage, to repudiate this discovery as having been vulgarized by tradition and returned to common impurity.

It is quite apparent that in this exhausting search for a power, which a single application will necessarily corrupt, in this endeavour to rid words of their opacity or banality, language is very precisely exposed to its own ruin. And the same can be said for literature in general. Commonplace expressions, the object of ruthless ostracism, have their equivalents in literary conventions, which appear as worn-out rules, these rules themselves, like any form, being the result of previous experiences and, as such, remaining necessarily foreign to the personal secret they should be helping to reveal. The writer has a duty to break with these conventions, which are a kind of ready-made language, even more impure than the

other kind. If he can, he should free himself from all the intermediate
layers which usage has built up and, enrapturing the reader, put him
directly in touch with the veiled world he wants to uncover for him, with
that secret metaphysics and that pure religion, the pursuit of which is his
true vocation.

At this point in the analysis, which Jean Paulhan is guiding us through
with a hardly visible yet sure hand, we will allow ourselves two fairly
serious comments. The first is that this conception which we have
learned to recognize as terror is not just any aesthetic or critical conception; it covers almost the entire realm of letters; it is literature, or at least
its soul, so that when we put terror into question, refuting it or showing
the frightening consequences of its logic, it is literature itself we are
questioning and gradually annihilating. What is more, we are forced to
acknowledge that, apart from a few famous examples, writers of one or
the other type, even those most rigorous and most devoted to their
ambition, have neither given up language nor the form of their art. It is a
fact, literature exists. It continues to be, in spite of the inner absurdity
which inhabits it, divides it and renders it properly inconceivable. The
moment has come, then, to ask the fundamental question: how is literature possible?

III

How is literature possible? It is to this supreme question that we have
been led in studying Jean Paulhan's book. We saw how every writer, out
of a concern that he should not say anything which did not express
perfectly his thought, was condemned to reject not only commonplace
expressions but also language and the conventions and rules of all literary
expression. This is the necessity [*exigence*] motivating the conception
which Paulhan has named terror. This tendency, according to which one
only writes out of a hatred of words, is the soul of literature. There is
deep in every writer a logical demon which urges him to deal a mortal
blow to all literary forms, to become aware of his dignity as a writer by
breaking free from language and literature, in short to put into question,
inexpressibly, what he is and what he does. How can literature exist
under these conditions? How does a writer, who sets himself apart from
other men by the sole fact that he contests the validity of language, and
all of whose energy should be directed at preventing a written work from
taking shape, end up creating a work of literature? How is literature
possible?

In order to answer this question, to see in other words how Paulhan
answers it, we have to follow the movement which can lead to a refuta-

tion of terror. We saw that some writers fought against language because they saw it as an imperfect means of expression and because they wanted it to be completely and perfectly intelligible. Where did this ambition lead them? To the invention of a language without commonplace expressions, that is, a language apparently without any ambiguity, or a language that in fact no longer offers any common measure, entirely removed from understanding. And we also saw that other writers fought against language considered as a means of expression that was too complete or too perfect, and consequently like a non-literary language, and that through their ruthless demands [*exigence*], their concern for an inaccessible purity, they arrived, by hunting down conventions, rules, genres, at a total proscription of literature, satisfied only when they were able to intimate their secret outside all literary form. We must now add, however, that these consequences – a rejection of language, a rejection of literature – are not the only ones which both kinds of writers resign themselves to accepting. It also turns out, necessarily, that their campaign against words, their desire not to take them into account so as to give thought its full weight, their obsession with indifference, all give rise to an extreme preoccupation with language, one of the effects of which is verbalism. This is a significant inevitability, at once regrettable and fortunate. In any case, it is a fact. Anyone who wants, at every moment, to be absent from words, to be present only at the ones he reinvents, is endlessly preoccupied with them, so that of all the authors, those who strive most keenly to avoid the reproach of verbalism are also precisely those who are most exposed to this reproach. *Run away from language, it comes after you*, says Paulhan, *go after language, it runs away from you*. We might think of Victor Hugo, the writer *par excellence* obsessed with words, who indeed did everything he could to triumph over rhetoric, and who said: 'The poet must not write with what has already been written (that is, with words) but with his soul and his heart.'

The same is true of those who, by prodigious asceticism, deluded themselves into thinking that they set themselves apart from all literature. Because they wanted to rid themselves of conventions and forms, in order to be in direct contact with the secret world and the profound metaphysics that they wished to reveal, they were ultimately content to use this world, this secret, this metaphysics as conventions and forms, which they complacently presented, and which constituted both the visible framework and the basis of their works. As Jean Paulhan remarks decisively on this point: 'Castles that come tumbling down,[1] lights in the night, ghosts and dreams (for example) are . . . pure conventions, like rhyme and the three unities, but they are conventions that we happily take for dreams and castles, whereas no one has ever thought they have seen the three unities.' In other words, for these kinds of writers, metaphysics, religion and feelings take the place of technique and language. They are a system of expression, a literary genre, in a word, literature.

So we are now in a position to give an answer to the question: how is literature possible? It is in fact by virtue of a double illusion – the illusion of some writers who fight against commonplace expressions and language by the very same means which engender language and commonplace expressions; and the illusion of other writers who, in renouncing literary conventions or, as they say, literature itself, cause it to be reborn in a form – as metaphysics, religion, etc. – which is not its own. Now it is out of this illusion and the awareness of this illusion that Jean Paulhan, through a revolution we might call Copernican, like Kant's revolution, proposes to establish a more precise and more rigorous reign for literature. Let us note at the outset how bold this revolution is, since what it involves is putting an end to the essential illusion which makes literature possible. It involves revealing to a writer that he only gives birth to art by a vain and blind struggle against it, that the work he thinks he has wrested from common, vulgar language exists thanks to the vulgarization of the virgin language he had imagined, through an excess of impurity and debasement. This discovery is enough to make Rimbaud's silence descend on all of us. But according to Paulhan, just as for a man the fact of his knowing that the world is only a projection of his mind does not destroy this world, but rather guarantees knowledge of it, marks its limits, clarifies its meaning, so a writer, if he knows that the more he fights against commonplace expressions the more subservient he is to them, or if he learns that he writes only with the help of what he detests most, has the chance of seeing more clearly the scope of his power and the means by which he can reign. In either case, instead of being unconsciously controlled by words or indirectly governed by rules (since his rejection of rules makes him dependent upon them), he will seek to master them. Instead of submitting to commonplaces he will be able to make them and, knowing that he cannot fight against literature, that he could only set himself apart from conventions by accepting their constraint, he will receive rules not as an artificial track indicating the path to follow and the world to discover, but as the means of his discovery and the law of his progress through obscurity, where there are neither paths nor tracks.

We now have to try to take one more step, without thinking of going very far. Jean Paulhan has admirably demonstrated that a writer, concentrating single-mindedly on the thought he wants to express or communicate and, for this reason, hostile to clichés and conventions, is condemned to silence or only escapes it through a permanent illusion. So he invites him to give, in his conception of a work of literature, preeminence to the system of verbal expression and to the understanding of a form. One might say that his Copernican revolution consists in no longer making language just turn around thought, but in imagining another, very subtle and very complex mechanism by which thought, in order to rediscover its authenticity, turns around language. Let us stop with this remark and see if we can express it another way. Throughout the various sections of his study, Paulhan accepted – with an obedient submission to common sense which visibly hides a trap – the traditional distinction between signs and things, words and ideas. In actual fact Paulhan, knowing full well how arbitrary the opposition between content and form is and that, in Paul Valéry's words, what we call content is only an impure form, factors this equivocation into his calculations and does not attempt to dispel it. If he were to dispel it, we would see clearly that what he means by thought is not pure thought (all perceived thought is from the outset a language), but a confusion of isolated words, fragments of sentences, a first fortuitous expression – and by language, a regulated expression, the organized system of conventions and commonplace expressions. This observation allows us to say, therefore, that according to Paulhan – at least in the secret book that we assume he has written – thought, in order to return to its source, that is, in order to throw off the loose outer form it is clothed in and which is a travesty of thought, has to yield to clichés, conventions and the rules of language.

In an essay which he has not included in his book, but which is a continuation of its project, *La Demoiselle aux miroirs* [*The Young Lady of the Mirrors*],[2] Paulhan notes that a proper study of the strictest and most faithful kind of translation would provide a method for gaining access to authentic thought. For such a translation would show what transformation, proper to language, expression brings to bear on thought; all one would have to do would be to work out what kind of change the translator necessarily imposes on the text he is translating, and then to imagine within the original text analogous changes in order to work back, ideally, to a thought deprived of language and saved from reflection. Now, as is often pointed out, it seems that the almost inevitable effect on any translation is to make the translated text appear richer in its imagery and more concrete than the language into which it is translated. The translator dissociates the text's stereotypes, interprets them as expressive metaphors and, so as not to replace them with simple, abstract words (which would be a further deformation), he translates them as concrete, picturesque images. This is also how all reflection becomes a travesty of ineffable original thought. Immediate thought, the kind perceived for us by consciousness with a look that decomposed it, is deprived of what we might call its stereotypes, its commonplaces, its abstract rhythm. It is false and arbitrary, impure and conventional. All we recognize in it is our own look. But if, on the other hand, we submit it to the rules of rhetoric, if our attention is surprised by rhythm, rhyme and numerical arrangement, we can hope to see the mind restored to its stereotypes and its commonplaces, reunited with the soul from which it was separated. Thought will become pure, it will become a virginal, innocent contact once again, not when it is set apart from words, but within the intimacy of what is said, through the operation of clichés, which alone are capable of rescuing it from the anamorphoses of reflection.

One might imagine this thought which is revealed in conventions, which both escapes and is kept safe [*se sauve*] within constraints. But that is language's secret, as it is Paulhan's too. All we have to do is imagine that *true* commonplace expressions are words torn apart by lightning and that the rigours of law found the absolute world of expressions, outside which there is nothing but sleep and chance.

Notes

1 The original French *les châteaux branlants* (literally, 'shaky castles') is a cliché used to describe toddlers who have just learned to walk [translator's note].
2 *Mesures*, 15 April 1938 [translator's note: later published in *Oeuvres complètes*, Paris, Editions du Cercle du Livre Précieux, vol. II, pp. 169–83].

Translated by Michael Syrotinski

8

The Novel is a Work of Bad Faith (1947)*

The views on the novel provided by Jean Pouillon's book[1] manage to avoid the vagueness one associates with literary appreciation. They are conscious of their own principles. That is their great merit. When one begins to think about works of literature, it is surprising to realize how long it is possible for such thinking to go on using the most imprecise of notions, unaware of what justifies it and of what it implies. Indeed, such ignorance would seem to be something that is required not only by literature, but also by reflections on literature. To surround works of literature with too many problems, seeking to bring out the sense of those problems, seems to be something the critic has no right to do, as if criticism is possible only if it respects a fundamental ignorance, an ignorance peculiar to art, more precisely if it veils that ignorance by appearing to dispel it with a display of remarks that explain nothing, but provide an alibi for problems which thus remain beyond inquiry, maintained at a cautious remove. In this sense, criticism can be compared to theology. But theology is admirably elaborate and exact, even if its exactness sometimes serves to defend it against questions which it does not consider legitimate. Criticism does not seem even to have a right to precision and rigour; on the contrary, it must make what it talks about comprehensible by introducing into the theoretical domain to which after all it belongs, and into the effort of elucidation it seeks to accomplish, that movement of ignorance, those blind groping steps whose pleasing effects are manifest in literature. It reproduces this ignorance, but must neither study it nor recognize it, let alone turn it into a problem for criticism. It thus raises vagueness to the level of perfection and so inevitably nullifies itself. But such nullity does not disappoint it, since it thereby renders an ultimate homage to its object, which then appears in its true light: as an object capable of rendering contradictory or meaningless any attempt to study it theoretically.

* Originally published as 'Le Roman, oeuvre de mauvaise foi', *Les Temps Modernes*, 19 (April 1947), pp. 1304–17.

This is not to say that such critical modesty does not have its significance. Anyhow, it is not very easy to abandon it and do some rigorous thinking in a domain which, being that of imposture, transforms rigour into yet more bad faith. Mr Pouillon's work on time and the novel opens the way for such an examination because he does not deny himself a concern for clear and precise thinking, and also because he withdraws some of the privileges literature enjoys. On the way he encounters more set-backs than he acknowledges, but if we intend now to set about describing these obstacles, it is not so as to disqualify the principle on which his enquiry is based, because without that enquiry, it would not even have been possible to perceive the difficulties it encounters.

Where can one find ground that is at all firm on which to grasp the novel and not be content with the traditional approximations where it is concerned? Mr Pouillon's method consists in focusing exclusively on those characteristics about which studies emanating from much more elaborate disciplines provide him with distinct views. Hence he demonstrates that the novel brings into play the diverse forms of self-knowledge and knowledge of others; that everything that is known about such forms of knowledge and their conditions must be applied to the novel; that a novel has value only if it respects those conditions; so that we can, theoretically at least, work out a definition of what a good novel is: one which, in the peculiar world of written language, has no other purpose than to reproduce the diverse ways in which beings become conscious of themselves and of others.

Mr Pouillon's concern is to deprive the novel of any position of privilege. The novel as a work is a set of written words, it is a fiction, it is linked to a real and unique being we call the novelist, acting in partnership with another real and more often than not multiple being we call the reader. Mr Pouillon tends to set little store by these features. For him, the problem of expression does not matter. The novel undeniably deploys invented characters with the aid of a fictitious story, but such recourse to the unreal has nothing specific about it: in the real world, every being who lives consciously has recourse to fiction; he is only conscious of himself, only understands himself, is only conscious of others and only understands them in the act of unreality by which he gives himself and others a meaning. Understanding, grasping, seeing: all of that is imagination. To imagine in the way the novel requires is thus not to disregard the real, but rather to put oneself in a position to be able to retain from reality only the act which gives it significance.

Mr Pouillon insists on the fact that the author must not award himself any privileges over the reader. Characters and events must be for him, as he gives them reality by describing them, what they will be for the reader who gives them reality by reading them. This is to say that the knowledge he can have of them is identical to what it would be if they were real. In no way are author, hero and reader in an original situation. They must be, in relation to each other, what real people living among real people are; they can know each other only in the way real people do. More precisely, characters in a novel stand a chance of acquiring novelistic value, if they behave and understand each other in such a way that both author and reader seem to have needed to call upon no special sort of understanding (either writerly or readerly) in order to make them real, but simply find themselves face to face with them the way everyone is with himself and *vis-à-vis* others.

One of Mr Pouillon's errors is not to have brought out the paradoxical nature of his study, yet the paradoxes are there to be seen. It is perhaps right to condemn the privileges the author has compared to the reader, as well as those the novelist has compared to his hero; and right to assert that anyone who writes a story must, in the act of writing it, place himself on a level with the person who will read it – and must also, when calling forth fictional beings with words, stand face to face with them the way he would face real beings who exist independently of him. Yes, that is undoubtedly right. But how is it possible? This question has its importance too.

Mr Pouillon distinguishes between two sorts of novel: the 'novel with' [*le roman-avec*] and the 'novel from behind' [*le roman par derrière*]. In novels of the first type, the writer accompanies his heroes and coincides with them; he is what they are and knows about them only what they know themselves, in all the circumstances in which he portrays them and throughout the developments of the story in which he follows them. With novels of the second type, the writer places himself at a certain distance from the characters and this allows him to judge them, to search out every possible motive for their actions, in a word to analyse them. But he is behind them so as to see them, not behind them in order to drive them and animate them from without: he contemplates them and tries to understand them through reflective knowledge, but what he understands about them always depends upon an existence that does not come from him. In both cases the novelist is ignorant of his heroes up to a point: either because, by becoming one with them, the only knowledge of them he acquires is that of a consciousness which cannot consider itself from without; or because, considering them from without in the way they reflect themselves from within, he must at least respect the retreat that alone allows such knowledge while at the same time rendering it always conjectural and incomplete.

Mr Pouillon seems to find such ignorance normal. At all events it does not appear to him to raise any serious questions. He admits that when a character is described as living in the spontaneity of unreflective consciousness (as is the case, for example, with Benjy in *The Sound and the Fury*), we are faced with a slight difficulty. 'Clearly, I who am writing am not on that level, which means there is a degree of bad faith, as there always is in literature. For if I wish to be an "unreflecting consciousness" then I am not one, since I am obliged to know what one is and thus to reflect.' In the end, he adds, 'this is of no importance, provided that my reflection does not appear in person in the work.' On the contrary, this seems to me to be of considerable importance, and if I referred to Faulkner's Benjy, it is because, in my view, that example provides a very suitable illustration of certain anomalies present in the art of the novel. The first problem is: how can the unreflecting consciousness of an idiot be conveyed as such, be spoken through the medium of a coherent and more or less objective language? The second problem is: how can the act of reflection required to some degree by the effort of novel composition coincide with such an unreflecting existence? And the third problem is: how can the reader gain an impression of this immediate life, that of a dumb idiot, by the roundabout way of the language lent him by a reflecting author? The last problem is the most important one if, according to Mr Pouillon's view of the novel, what counts above all is the point of view of the reader. And it is obvious what the aim must be: the reader, in reading Benjy's monologue, must feel confined within the world of an unreflecting, illogical existence, incapable of speaking and understanding; what he must not feel is, behind that existence, the reflective consciousness of the author who is evoking it. But when is this aim achieved? Is it when the author seeks to become, himself, the stupor he is describing, that is to say, forces language to become as incoherent as possible? Or is it on the contrary when, with the skill and dexerity of a reflective art, he attempts to draw forth, by means of a language artful enough to disappear, the absence of language and reason that he wishes to bring into being? There is nothing to prove that absence of reflection on the part of the author, or recourse to a form in which absence of reflection is constantly present, is the best way to persuade the reader of it or to make him feel it. Where on the novelist's part there is a concerted effort to approach a blind state of consciousness, it is quite possible that the reader will find only affectation, arbitrariness and artistic trickery. In the case of Benjy's monologue, the artifice is obvious: however interior it may be, the language of an idiot in whom language is lacking can only take its place in a written work with the cooperation of the writer who lends it his own. Such language cannot be freed from this anomaly simply through being labelled an interior monologue. Moreover, no one could imagine that what speaks inside a purely stupid consciousness resembles in any way the ordered and basically objective language used by Benjy. We are therefore dealing with an eminently conventional device. But as it turns out the reader forgets these conventions, and little by little, by way of words that are full of artifice, goes out to meet the mute presence which is being presented to him.

The novelist writes, the reader reads. This difference of function is easily forgotten, but it makes it very difficult to apply the rule on illicit privileges formulated by Mr Pouillon. Basically, where does this rule lead? Perhaps it means that the novelist must not so much give up his rights as hide them from the reader, avoid making him aware of them? Very well. Such precautions are essential to all artistic composition. They take account of the difference of perspective between writer and reader, which no theoretical requirement [*exigence*] can cause to disappear. But the result is this: not only are his privileges not abolished, the author adds to them the extra privilege of appearing not to enjoy any, thanks to the camouflaged use he makes of them, while adding to them the double-dealing convention of appearing to renounce all convention while in the process inventing yet another one.

Such trickery does not appear to be what Mr Pouillon wishes, since he writes quite unambiguously: 'We will no doubt be told that it is absurd to reproach the novelist with knowing the end of the story he is telling and organizing his narrative with reference to that end; of course the novelist finishes his novel before we read it, but what we ask of him is that he either writes it as it should be read or makes us read it the way he wrote it.' Nothing could be clearer, certainly, but perhaps nothing could be more contradictory either. For if I wish the reader to see in my book a work in which technique is reduced to a minimum, I may well have to pile on the technique. If I write it with the automatism of spontaneous consciousness, the reader may well discover in this the disguises of a thinking process that reveals itself as it endeavours to conceal itself. In order to be read as I write, I must write differently from the way I shall be read. For Benjy to appear as a mute consciousness carried along by the current, Faulkner must endow him not only with language, but with knowledge of his actions and the ability to find his way in the world of others. One might add that, by requiring the novelist to make us read him the way he writes, Mr Pouillon twists his rule by incorporating within it a desire for intellectual honesty which it does not presuppose. As he tells us, it is to the extent that the novelist's vision corresponds to a real psychological attitude in the reader that a novel has value. The aim is thus to coincide with one of the possibilities for real understanding in the reader. But that can be achieved in numerous ways, and one of them is feigning, trickery or imposture; another is fantasy, unreality or the incredible. Once the reader has become our law, it is his consciousness that provides our guarantee, and it is enough to make him accept an illusion for illusion to acquire all the value of truth.

The novelist gives reality to events and beings that are unreal, using words that he writes. The reader gives reality to them by means of words that are read. As Mr Pouillon quite rightly observes: 'the reader makes what is read real [*en lisant, le lecteur réalise*].' That is why it seems inevitable to him that the novel should express reality. But let us look a little more closely at what happens. Mr Pouillon deals rather cursorily with the role played by expression in the the novel, remaining content to draw the usual distinctions. Hence he recalls that whereas in poetry expression dictates content, in the novel it depends on content, and this allows him to relegate formal concerns to a secondary level. Perhaps that is justified. At the same time, there is a problem which he disregards. Between a sentence read in a novel and the same sentence uttered in real life, the difference is considerable. Why? I can simply recall here one or two remarks developed in other studies.[2] In the world of day-to-day existence, the words that I read do not only disappear into their meaning, no precise image need correspond to that meaning either; it is not a real object that appears behind the word, as a support for its meaning, nor an image of that object either, but an empty set of relations and intentions, an opening on to an indistinct complexity. It is as if, in reality, the superabundance of beings and things which press on us from all sides could only take on meaning in a language that was, first, empty of things, since it is a language of signs, but in addition empty of language, since it is always beyond words themselves. This nullity of language, sustained solely by the void of some possible intention, is what establishes the power of everyday understanding.

But in the novel, even if it is written in the most prosaic prose and with exactly the words that are used every day, a radical transformation occurs, a change that comes from a change in attitude towards words on the part of the person who writes or the person who reads. In narrative [*un récit*], neither writer nor reader sets out from existing reality, given along with their own existence: they both set out from a world that has as yet to be revealed, either because it does not yet exist, since it has yet to enter the world of what is written, or because it exists as a book, but as a book as yet unread. Moreover, both are dealing with a set of imagined elements which in itself will never cease to be unreal, but which both writer and reader will act to realize. How? With the help of words and with words as their starting-point. That is why a narrative sentence cannot confine itself to functioning as a sign, nor to vanishing in the signification produced by terms that instantaneously disappear. Even if, in itself, it counts as little as possible, the language of fiction nevertheless plays a specific role, to the extent that instead of referring us to the reality of existence, it brings us into contact with a fictional world and, for that reason, is indispensable not in order to become the sign of beings and objects already absent, but rather to become the means of making them present for us, of letting us feel them and letting them live for us through words. So, to the extent that it allows writer and reader to give a reality based in words to this world that is otherwise unreal, language acquires importance as a verbal apparatus, with the ambition of establishing itself as a language that is physically and formally viable. This does not mean that, in the novel, the manner of writing matters above all else; it means that the events, the characters and the dialogues of this world of fiction we call the novel are necessarily impregnated with the particular nature of the words on which their reality is based; and that in order to be understood and made real, they need a language capable not so much of signifying them as of presenting them to us, of making them directly visible and comprehensible in its own verbal consistency.

To this Mr Pouillon will object that of course this world of novel fiction cannot be considered unreal; that it is part of reality, not any given physical reality obviously, but part of psychological reality; that this goes without saying; that otherwise it would defy all consciousness and all formulation; finally, that since the imagination it is a product of is exactly the same as that which is active in the processes of cognitive conscious-ness, the involvement of this power proves that there is a continuity between the various psychological attitudes of actual existence and the fictitious situations of existence as it is found in the novel, which there-fore cannot but embody the meaning of those attitudes. But on this point, Mr Pouillon does not seem to be playing fair. Simply on the pretext that imagination is based on the structure of consciousness, and that it is only possible because consciousness is always at a distance from itself, he can hardly claim to consider as equivalent, and identical in meaning, every act of consciousness in which this way of being at a distance from what one is is manifest. Imagining, as the power to make present what is absent, to present it in its absence and as absent, remains an original act. In the same way, in order to dismiss the 'fictitious' it is not enough to recall that the experience procured by imagination is perfectly real, because it is a real experience whose defining characteristic is that it gives us what is unreal and is a relation to something non-existent that appears to us in this non-existence. In the same way, furthermore, when Mr Pouillon examines the classic definition of imagination: 'that which causes something to exist for us that does not exist' and observes that this 'something that does not exist' is the mode of everything that is conscious, that it constitutes the psychological, and hence concludes that imagination is oriented towards psychological existence and not non-existence, he is arguing in an odd manner. For he omits to ask himself whether, among the various ways we are presented with psychological reality (an ambivalent expression it must be said), that which consists in positing a thing as nothing and calling it forth in its very nothingness does not have as its object, more than any other, 'something that does not exist', since in this case it is not simply a matter of something existing according to the consciousness I have of it, but in addition I become conscious of it as something that does not exist, as an unreality.

The novel is a work in which the events and the characters, in so far as they are fictitious, become real through words by means of a twofold act that is perpetually out of alignment: the act of writing and the act of reading. That this fiction should, precisely, need words in order to become real, and that apart from them it has no specific means of becoming manifest, would be enough to prove to what extent fiction forms the essential reality of the novel. On the other hand, it would be quite incorrect to conclude from the fact that the writer makes real through writing, as the reader does through reading, that once this realization has occurred, there is no essential difference between real existence and existence as evoked by the novel. It is rather the opposite. For whatever the intensity with which the novel suggests, and the greater what it suggests is, the more the reader, and doubtless also the writer, entertain with the beings and events of fiction a set of relationships that differ from those that make up real existence; and the more each of them lives in the unreal, sinks deeper into a world where any return to real existence is postponed until later. No doubt the reader's immediate sentiment, like that of the writer (who is often even more naïve), leads him to attribute to an extraordinary degree of reality the spell cast upon him by beings that are so demanding that he cannot be rid of them and must obey them: they are alive, he says, they are real. But this sentiment can quite easily be explained: no, the characters in the truest of novels are not true, nor are they living or real, but as fictitious beings they draw the reader so powerfully into fiction that he lets himself momentarily slip out of the world, loses the world and is lost to it, abandons his points of reference and, giving himself up entirely to a story in which he becomes unreservedly involved, allows it from this point on to take the place of reality for him, considers it as real and, in this readerly existence, makes it his life, all life. That does not prove that fiction has ceased to be imaginary; it proves rather that a real being, be he a writer or a reader, fascinated by a certain form of absence that he finds in words and which words derive from the fundamental power of consciousness, withdraws from all real presence and seeks to live in the absence of life, to derealize himself in the absence of reality, to establish the absence of the world as the only true world.

These remarks make no claim to solve any problems. On the contrary, they pose all manner of problems, and difficult problems at that. I simply wish to argue that, in order to form an idea of the novel, it is necessary first to try and imagine what a fiction is, how it is possible and what attitudes it presupposes in those who become involved in it, whether they create it through writing or produce it through reading. It is perhaps the case that the novel tends in essence to be a fiction that contests itself as fiction, an imagined narrative [*un récit*] that desperately, and by the most diverse paths, seeks to be reunited with the world and with the responsibility and seriousness of the world. If however, as I would argue, this tendency is constitutive of the novel in the sense that the novel could not abandon it and survive, it can only be understood and made meaningful within fiction and on the basis of fiction, against which it is pitted in an unremitting and hopeless struggle.

In the novel, the imaginary demands to be taken as real – and that applies just as much to the writer as it does to the reader (it is in this sense primarily that Mr Pouillon's remark about illicit privileges finds an application). But 'to be taken as real' is something that can occur in two quite different ways. It means that the world of the imaginary takes the place of the real entirely, is substituted for it and effaces it: that, we know, is the ideal of the sort of reading that aims to *take hold* of the reader, cast a spell on him, reduce him entirely to his readerly condition; the sort of reading that seeks, in short, to be so enthralling that it puts whoever embarks on it to sleep; that seeks to be like a sleep from which it is impossible to awaken. But this also means that fiction has value to the extent that it passes for real; that it therefore draws its value from its equivalence with things that exist, and that in return it is also what has value in reality, that it gives reality its meaning, and that it is unfaithful to itself when it is not that towards which we are dimly led by our effort to be in presence with the things and the beings of existence. Which brings us back to Mr Pouillon's standpoint.

Even when it is not symbolic, the aim of the novel is to represent the true relations between beings in the world, because it claims to embody their meaning. This ambition to express the meaning of reality is founded paradoxically on the unreality that constitutes the way of being of things in the novel: being imaginary, it is in the nature of these things to remain always at a distance, set aside from what they are, from what they would be if they truly were, and it is this setting aside of reality which simultaneously gives them their own reality and allows them to make present the process whereby meaning comes to the things of the world, a process which, precisely, is possible only through a retreat from those things and in their setting aside. In addition fictional beings, being always at a distance from themselves, can retain that essential characteristic only by becoming real equivocally, and the role of language is to make them real in a mode of ambiguity and contestation.

A successful novel is destined to attract two contradictory sorts of praise (or blame): for being true to life and for not being so; for being an exact depiction through being fantastical or an unfaithful one through being too faithful. One now begins to suspect where the endless discussion about certain novelists who, for some, are models of realism and, for others, models of creative imagination in fact originates. In a recent study, Mr Albert Beguin reopened the debate as it concerns Balzac by bringing out the surreal nature of the Balzacian world, which is the product of a power of vision that differs sharply from exact and objective observation.[3] These observations raise little or no objection. Mr Pouillon says rather speciously of Balzac that he uses analysis to construct characters that his analysis turns to stone, but who, though deprived of the living force of individual beings, have the power as types to help us to understand real people. Hence in the world itself, they take on the life which they lack, or which is refused them, in the novel. This observation is strange, in that it contradicts the experience of every reader of Balzac, for whom a work such as his is first of all an autonomous world, a closed realm as Mr Beguin puts it, which has its own laws, its perspectives and its proportions, and which, as soon as we cross its threshold, imposes its presence upon us with an authority which takes away from us any right to question it in the name of life 'as it is'. Perhaps Mr Pouillon is right, Balzac's characters are not alive, but if they give the reader the impression that they are, this is not because they explain living beings, but because they render the latter useless and seemingly remote, and because they confine us within the closed world of reading where they reign absolutely. And if Balzac remains the supreme genius of the novel, it is because he dared conceive and give reality to this world of reading with such scope and such inspirational power, that the novel truly appears to be in rivalry with the world and to be capable, through its richness and fecundity, of 'entering into competition' with it and granting the reader who enters therein the illusion of being able to dwell there for almost his whole life.

The world of Balzac can be 'taken for real' because it is set apart from the real. And no doubt it wishes to be considered not as fictitious but as profoundly alive, as the meaning that gives life to the real and which we are so incapable of recognizing in ordinary life that the novelist appears to make it exist in the process of revealing it. But this signifying power to which the novel lays claim does not exist outside the novel, and it cannot even be separated from the universe of the novel considered as a whole: each character does not carry a fragment of this power, nor does such and such an event in the story receive the task of signifying such and such a particular idea. In a novel, the heroes may well be inconsistent or too consistent, too simple or too visible as figures; the novel will not necessarily be less rich for that, or less significant, or less close to the reality that it simplifies. For Mr Pouillon, the novel is made up of characters and the truth of a novel is in direct proportion to how deeply alive its characters are. Why? Because human experience begins only with consciousness, and to ignore this basic fact is to abandon all possibility of coming into contact with human existence. This is a perfectly legitimate and important reminder. But its consequence is not that the fact of subjectivity can be translated only by means of the 'I' of the characters; through the manner in which the writer respects, in existences imagined by him, the real conditions of conscious existence and its relations with other consciousnesses. This is firstly because, were that the case, the novel as a genre would be worthless. Let us recall the definition of the 'novel with', which is the one that approximates most closely to real-life attitudes. 'To be "with" someone,' says Mr Pouillon, 'is not to be reflectively conscious of him, it is not to know him, it is to share "with" him the same unreflecting state of self-consciousness. How indeed could we distinguish between ourselves and him at that moment?' But in fact, how can we not distinguish between ourselves and him? If the 'novel with' proposes a type of relation in which we must live with someone else exactly the way this person lives with himself, we are obliged to discern in this a principle of trickery, for existence offers us nothing of the kind. On the contrary indeed, even if we admit that relations with others are immediate relations, they are such as to allow us to encounter others [*autrui*] only as other, as forever different from us. It is in the novel and only in the novel that we can 'get inside the skin of the characters'; only the reader can let himself slip into an existence that is not his own and, thanks to the fascinating void that reading creates, agree to live outside himself, as if he were no longer anything but others [*autrui*].

This is something we can only describe as trickery, a trickery that is essential to art and to the art of the novel in particular. But this is no cause for alarm, if it is this imposture which provides the truth of art with its point of departure. When Mr Pouillon stresses, in a passage already quoted, that there is always a certain amount of bad faith in literature, he is gently confronting literature with its own lie. Literature cannot be rid of this lie, nor can it conceal it or elude it. It keeps literature in a permanent state of doubt about its own value, to such an extent that this doubt is incorporated into everything it does, is the principle governing its works and the measure of their authenticity.

The novel is a work of bad faith: bad faith on the part of the novelist, who believes in his characters and yet sees himself behind them, who is ignorant of them, who gives them a reality in which they remain unknown and finds in the words of which he is master a means of having them at his disposal without ceasing to believe that they escape him. Bad faith on the part of the reader, who plays with the imaginary, plays at being the hero he is not, plays at taking as real what is fiction, then finally lets himself be caught up in fiction and, in this enchantment that sets existence at a distance, finds a possibility for living the sense of that existence. These relations of bad faith are not unique to the novel, nor to literature in general. But it is in the nature of the novel and of literature to accommodate them as such, to make of them their objective and to succeed, not in overcoming them certainly, but in organizing them into a specific experience, in which the meaning of the human world as a whole can be recovered.

This experience calls for study, in itself and for itself. That is far from being an easy task. One of the first questions it would be useful to ask concerns the fact that the reader (as well as the writer) undergoes an enchantment, and that this is no less active in novels where man is reconciled with himself than in those where he gets lost; in works which claim to be means of discovery as much as in books without an ulterior purpose. True, for the person who writes and for the person who reads, the novel claims to be an instrument of knowledge. But this is a knowledge with its starting-point in the void of fascination, a discovery that presupposes the authority of a far-reaching ignorance, a way of apprehending being whose condition is the reign of absence of being, an absence that seeks to be everything and become real in the dual and paradoxical form of absence and absence of everything. In this universe of enchantment and fascination, what becomes of the contribution of individual beings, their ways of understanding themselves and each other, and of living? To what extent does the notion of character remain predominant henceforth, and in what measure do the spell-binding density of fiction and the existence of a novel *world* succeed in making of the novel more than just a dream? Finally, are not the characters, who need to cast a spell on us in order to become our partners in this game, obliged in their turn to fall prey to this fascination, to be fascinating because they are themselves fascinated, incapable of controlling themselves even when displaying the greatest mastery and lucidity, as in the case of the classical heroes (those of Madame de Lafayette, Benjamin Constant or Stendhal), just as much as with those of Faulkner, about which Mr Pouillon has written some extremely interesting pages? This would explain Malraux's observation:

In literature, the domination of the novel is significant, for the novel is the most unruly of all the arts (not forgetting music), the one in which the domain of the will is most restricted . . . And the point is not that the artist is therefore dominated, but that, for fifty years now, he has chosen more and more what dominates him, and that it is in relation to this that he organizes the artistic means at his disposal. Certain great novels were first and foremost, for their author, the creation of the only thing that was able to submerge him.

The novel could thus be said to be the most striking product of bad faith in language, if this succeeds in constituting a world of untruth in which it is so possible to put one's faith that even its author finds himself reduced to naught by dint of believing in it; and if at the same time it makes of the untruth of this world the element of emptiness in which, finally, there comes into view the meaning of what is most true.

Notes

1 Jean Pouillon, *Temps et roman* [*Time and the Novel*] (Paris, Gallimard, 1946).
2 These are collected in *La Part du feu* (Paris, Gallimard, 1949). A translation of this book is forthcoming from Stanford University Press. [Translator's note.]
3 Albert Béguin, *Balzac visionnaire* (Paris, Albert Skira, 1946).

Translated by Michael Holland

9

Sade's Reason (1947)*

La Nouvelle Justine ou les Malheurs de la Vertu, suivi de l'Histoire de Juliette sa sœur appeared in Holland 150 years ago. It was a monumental work of nearly 4000 pages. The author had rewritten it several times, thereby greatly increasing its size. Overwhelming and almost endless, it immediately threw the world into a panic. If there is a department of forbidden books in every library it is for such a book. We may as well admit that no literature of any epoch has ever produced so outrageous a work and no other volume has ever wounded people's thoughts and feelings more deeply. In our age, which shudders at Henry Miller, who would dare to compete in licence with Sade? Yes, we can safely say that here we have the most scandalous book that has ever been written, and surely this is a reason for taking an interest in it. Here we have a chance of getting to know a work that marks a limit beyond which no writer has ever dared to venture. And so, in some sense, in the world of literature whose values are so relative, we have a true absolute and yet we do not ask it what it has to teach us. It never occurs to us to ask why it is so absolute, what makes it so overwhelming, and eternally more than men can bear. This is a strange example of neglect. And yet it may well be that the very thoroughness of the outrage arises from just this neglect. If we consider the safeguards history has taken to turn Sade into an enormous enigma: if we think of his twenty-seven years of prison, of his confined and ostracized existence, and consider how this segregation affected not only the life of the man but also his posthumous existence so that the ban on his work seems to condemn him, as though still alive, to eternal imprisonment: then we may well wonder whether the censors and the judges who claim to have immured Sade are not really in his service, are not in fact fulfilling the liveliest wish of his libertinism. For Sade always longed for the solitude of the earth's entrails, for the mysteries of a hidden and solitary life. Time after time he formulated the idea that men's greatest excesses demand secrecy, the darkness of the pit and the inviolable solitude of the cell. Now, strange to say, by banning him to

* Originally published as 'A la rencontre de Sade', *Les Temps Modernes*, 25 (October 1947), pp. 577–612. Reprinted in *Lautréamont et Sade* (Paris, Editions de Minuit, 1963 [1949]), pp. 17–49, under the title 'La raison de Sade'.

loneliness the guardians of morality have become the accomplices of his worst immorality. It was his mother-in-law, the prudish Madame de Montreuil, who turned his life into a masterpiece of infamy and debauch when she gave it a prison for its setting. And similarly, if 150 years later *Justine and Juliette* still seems the most outrageous book that can ever be read, this is because it is almost impossible to read it. With the help of author, publisher and Universal Morality, all measures have been taken to ensure that it remains secret, absolutely unreadable as much for its length, style and repetitiveness as for its furious indecency which would, in any case, have hurried it to the librarian's hell.

It is an outrageous book because it is hard to get at and cannot be made public. But it is also a book that proves there is no outrage where there is no respect, and that where the outrage is immense the respect is proportionate. Who is more respected than Sade? Even today many people still believe they would only need to have this accursed work in their hands for a few minutes to make Rousseau's boast – that any virgin who reads a single page of it will be undone – come true. Certainly such respect is a trophy for a literature and a civilization. And so we can hardly resist a longing to whisper to all his present and future critics and editors: when dealing with Sade, at least be respectful to the outrage.

Fortunately Sade holds his own very well. Not only his work, but his thought remains impenetrable – and this although he develops numerous theories, repeats them with disconcerting patience, and reasons with great clarity and very adequate logic. He is a passionate lover of systems. He expounds, he affirms, he proves. A hundred times he goes back to the same problem (a hundred times is putting it mildly) and examines every facet; he weighs all the objections, answers them, finds others and answers these. And as what he says is generally rather simple, and as his language, though prolific, is precise and firm, it seems that nothing should be easier than understanding the ideology which, in his case, is inseparable from his passions. And yet, what *does* lie at the bottom of Sade's thought? What exactly did he say? Where is the method in his system, where does it begin and end? For all his obsession with reason, is there anything more than the mere shadow of a system in the workings of his thought? And why is it that so many well co-ordinated principles fail to form the perfectly solid whole they ought and appear to form? That is not clear either. Here we have the first of Sade's singularities. At every moment his theoretical ideas set free the irrational forces with which they are bound up. These forces both excite and upset the thought by an impetus of a kind that causes the thought first to resist and then to yield, to try again for mastery, to gain an ascendancy, but only by liberating other dark forces by which once again the ideas are carried away, side-tracked and perverted. The result is that all that is said is clear but seems to be at the mercy of something that has not been said. Then, a little further on, what was concealed emerges, is recaptured by logic but, in its turn, obeys the movement of a still further hidden force. In the end everything has been brought to light, everything has been expressed, but equally everything has once more been plunged into the obscurity of undigested ideas and experiences that cannot be given shape.

When he comes up against this way of thinking which is only clarified by the pressure of another thought which, at that moment, cannot itself be clearly grasped, the reader's uneasiness is often extreme. It is not helped by the fact that Sade's declarations of principle, or what might be called his basic philosophy, seem to be simplicity itself. It is a philosophy of self-interest, of pure egoism. Each man must do what he likes, he has no law except his pleasure. The first premise of this morality is absolute solitude. Sade has said and reiterated it in every way: nature has caused us to be born alone and there is no possible relationship between one man and another. My only rule of conduct, then, is my preference for all that affects me agreeably and my indifference to any outcome of my preferences that may result in harm for others. The deepest suffering of others is always less important than my own pleasure. What does it matter if I have to pay for a minor pleasure by a monstrous sequence of crimes, for enjoyment pleases me and is mine, while the effect of crime is exterior to me and cannot touch me.

These principles are clear. We find them developed in twenty volumes and in a thousand ways. Sade is never weary of them. He takes infinite pleasure in relating them to the theories then fashionable, about the equality of individuals before nature and before the law. He proposes arguments such as: since in the eyes of nature all creatures are identical, this identity gives me the right not to sacrifice myself for the preservation of others whose ruin is indispensable to my happiness. Or, again, he draws up a kind of Declaration of the Rights of Eroticism, with for a fundamental principle this idea, applying equally to men and women: give yourself to anyone who desires you, and take anyone you desire. 'What harm do I do, what offence do I commit, if I say to a beautiful creature I meet: "Lend me the part of your body that can give me an instant's satisfaction, and enjoy, if it so pleases you, the part of mine you prefer." ' To Sade such a proposition is irrefutable. For page after page he invokes the equality of individuals and the reciprocity of rights without noticing that his reasoning, far from gaining strength, becomes more crazy. 'An act of possession can never be exercised on a free being,' he says. But what does he conclude from that? Not that it is wrong to do violence against anyone and use them for pleasure against their will, but that no one, so as to refuse him, can plead as excuse an exclusive attachment or 'belonging' to anyone. The equality of all creatures is the right to dispose equally of all creatures, and freedom is the power of subordinating everyone to one's wishes.

When we are up against propositions like these we are apt to imagine that there is something lacking in Sade's mental processes, a sort of lacuna or folly. We get the impression of a deeply disordered thought in bizarre suspense over a void. But then suddenly logic regains the upper hand, objections appear, and little by little the system takes shape. Justine, who, as is well known, stands in this cosmos for stubborn and humble virtue, always oppressed and unfortunate but never convinced of the error of her ways, suddenly declares in the most reasonable way: your principle presupposes power. If my happiness consists in taking no account of the interest of others, in doing them harm as the opportunity arises, the day will surely dawn when the interests of others will consist in doing harm to me. In the name of what will I be able to protest? 'Can the solitary individual struggle against all this?' This, it will be realized, is the classical objection. Sade's hero replies to it explicitly and implicitly in many ways that, little by little, lead us to the core of the universe he inhabits. Yes, he begins by saying, my right is the right of power. And, indeed, humanity for Sade is essentially composed of a few powerful men who have had the energy to raise themselves above the law and above prejudice, who feel they are worthy of nature because she has endowed them with extravagant appetites which they seek to satisfy by every means. These men without parallel generally belong to a privileged class. They are dukes and kings. There is the Pope, himself an offspring of the nobility. They benefit from the advantages of their rank and fortune and by the immunity that their situation assures them. Their birth gave them all the privileges of inequality and they take pleasure in perfecting them with implacable despotism. They are the strongest because they belong to a strong class. 'By the people,' says one of them, 'I mean that vile and despicable class that can only live by dint of sweat and tears: everything that breathes should form an alliance against such contemptible creatures.'

Nevertheless, it must be made clear that if, generally speaking, these princes of debauch represent to their own advantage all that there is of inequality between the classes, this is only a historical accident to which Sade gives no importance in his scale of values. He discerned perfectly clearly that, at the time he wrote, power was a social category, something established in the organization of society such as it was before and after the Revolution. But for all that, he believes that power (and moreover solitude) is not only a state but a choice and a conquest, and only the man who attains power by his own energy is really powerful. In reality his heroes are drawn from two opposite backgrounds: the highest and the lowest, the classes most favoured and least favoured, from among the great of the earth and from the scum of the underworld. From the very beginning both of these classes have the advantage of an extreme situation: the extremity of poverty is as powerful a springboard as the dizziness of fortune. Madame Dubois or Madame Durand revolts against the law because their situation is too wretched for them to be able to conform to it and survive. Saint-Fond or the Duc de Blangis is too far above the law to conform to it without a fall. That is why in the works of Sade there is an appeal to contradictory principles in his apology for crime. For some people inequality is a fact of nature. Certain men of necessity are victims and slaves, without rights, without an existence, and against them everything is permissible. Hence the wild praise of tyranny and of those political constitutions whose aim is to render forever impossible a revolt of the feeble or an enrichment of the poor. 'Let us establish,' says Verneuil, 'that according to the intentions of nature, one class of individuals must of necessity be subject to the other by reason of its weakness and its low birth . . . The law is not made for the people . . . The essential thing in all wise government is that the people should not trespass on the privileges of the great.' And Saint-Fond says: 'The people will be held in a bondage that will render them incapable of ever attempting to gain power or of laying hands on the property of the rich.' Or again: 'What are called sexual crimes will never be punished save among the slave castes.'

Here we seem to be dealing with the wildest theory of extreme and absolute despotism. But the perspective suddenly changes. What does la Dubois say? 'By nature we are all born equal. If fate is pleased to upset this original law, it is up to us to put things right and use our skill to remedy the situation . . . Good faith and patience on our part would only serve to double our chains, whereas our crimes will become virtues, and we would indeed be dupes if we deprived ourselves of them and so fail to lessen a little the yoke we have to bear.' And, she adds, for the poor, only crime can open the gates of life: criminality is the compensation for injustice, just as theft is the revenge of the dispossessed. Thus, as is now clear, equality and inequality, freedom to oppress and revolt against the oppressor are no more than purely provisional arguments by which Sade's hero, according to his social status, affirms his right to power. Soon, moreover, the distinction between those who need crime so as to exist and those who only enjoy existence through crime disappears. La Dubois becomes a baroness. La Durand, a low-class poisoner, is raised above all the princesses whom Juliette unhesitatingly sacrifices to her. The peers become gangsters or brigands (as in *Faxelange*) or else, the better to rob and assassinate fools, they become innkeepers. And the fact that the greater number of the victims of debauchery are chosen from the aristocracy, and must be of noble birth, evens things out. It is to his mother, the Countess, that the Marquis de Bressac declares with superb contempt: 'Your days belong to me, and mine are sacred.'

And now what point have we reached? A few men have become powerful, some through birth, but these have shown that they deserved their power by the way they increased and enjoyed it. Others have risen to power, and the test of their success is that after using crime to gain power they use this power to be free for further crimes. Such is the world. There are those who have risen to the heights, and around them, into infinity, there stretches a dust of nameless and numberless individuals without either power or rights. Now let us see what becomes of the law of absolute egoism. 'I do what I like,' says Sade's hero, 'I only recognize my own pleasure and to assure it I torture and kill. You threaten me with a similar fate for the day I meet someone whose happiness consists in torturing and killing me. But it is precisely to raise myself above this danger that I have acquired power.' When Sade produces answers of this kind we can be sure we are slipping towards an aspect of his thought whose only consistency depends on the obscure forces it conceals. What is this power that fears neither chance nor law, that contemptuously exposes itself to the terrible risks of law conceived as: 'I will do you all the harm I like, do me all the harm you can' and claims that this rule will always be to its advantage? Notice that one single exception is enough to make these principles collapse. If on just one occasion the Man of Power runs into misfortune through seeking nothing but his own pleasure, if in the course of exercising his tyranny he falls a victim, even once, he will be lost. The law of pleasure will be shown to be a cheat, and instead of seeking triumph through abuse, men will return to their mediocre way of life, considered as the lesser of two evils.

Sade knows this. 'And what if luck changes?' asks Justine. And so he will go deeper into his system and show that no evil can ever befall a man who commits himself to evil with sufficient energy. Here lies the essential theme of his work: virtue earns all misfortunes, but vice earns the benefit of a constant prosperity. Sometimes, above all in the early versions of *Justine*, this affirmation appears to be no more than a factitious thesis illustrated, in guise of proof, by the construction of a story of which the author pulls the strings. We tell ourselves that Sade is satisfied with fables, that he is too ready to lay everything at the door of dark Providence whose function is to give the best to those who have chosen the worst. But with *La Nouvelle Justine* and *Juliette* all is changed. There can be no doubt about Sade's deep conviction that misfortune can never befall the man whose egoism is absolute. Better, this egoist is happy in the highest measure, and always will be, and there will be no exception. Is this madness? Possibly. But this notion is bound up in him with forces of such violence that they end by making the ideas they uphold irrefutable to him. It must be admitted that the translation of this conviction into theory is not done without difficulty. Sade has recourse to several solutions, and he tries them out ceaselessly, although no single one can satisfy him. The first is purely verbal. It consists in saying 'no' to the social contract which, for him, is the safeguard of the weak and, in theory, a serious menace for the strong. In practice the Man of Power is well able to make use of the law to strengthen his arbitrary position, but in that event his power depends on the law and so, in theory again, the law is the real source of power. As long as anarchy or the state of war is not in force the sovereign is only the ruler, because, even if the law helps him to crush the weak, it does so by means of an authority created in the name of the weak, and, after all, he is only master by substituting for the strength of the solitary man the false bond of a pact. 'The passions of my neighbour are infinitely less to be feared than the injustice of the law, because my neighbour's passions are restricted by mine, whereas nothing limits or constrains the injustices of the law.' Nothing limits the law because there is nothing above it and therefore it is always above me. That is why it oppresses me even when it serves me. And so, if Sade recognized his own features in the Revolution, it was only in the measure to which the Revolution represented for a time the possibility of a regime without law during the course of the transition from one law to another. He expressed this in these curious observations: 'The reign of the law is inferior to that of anarchy. The biggest proof of my contention is that when a government wants to remake its Constitution it is obliged to plunge itself into anarchy. To abrogate its ancient laws it must needs establish a revolutionary regime in which there is no law. In the end new laws are born of this regime, but the second state is of necessity less pure than the first, because it derives from it.'

Power, in fact, can make any kind of regime serve its ends. It denies authority to them all, and in the core of a world perverted by law it creates an enclosure in which law is silent, and where the sovereignty of the law is ignored rather than resisted. In the statutes of 'The Society of the Friends of Crime' there is an article prohibiting all political activity. 'The Society of the Friends of Crime' respects the government under which it lives and if it places itself above the law it is because, according to its principles, man has no power to make laws which contradict the laws of nature, but the bad behaviour of its members behind closed doors should not cause outrage either to the people or its rulers. And if, in Sade's work, Power should happen to accomplish a political task and be involved in revolution, as in the case of Borchamps who comes to an agreement with the Lodge of the North to overthrow the Swedish monarchy, the motives inspiring it have nothing to do with the will to emancipate the law. 'What motives make you detest Swedish despotism?' one of the conspirators is asked, and the answer is 'Jealousy, ambition, pride, weariness of being dominated, my own desire to tyrannize over others.' 'Does the happiness of the people play any part in your views?' 'I only recognize my own in it.'

If needs be, Power can always maintain that it has nothing to fear from the commonalty of men, who are weak, and nothing to fear from a law whose legitimacy it does not recognize. The real problem is that of the relationship between Power and power. These exceptional men who come from the heights or the depths of society must, of necessity, meet. They are brought together by the similarity of their tastes. The fact that they are exceptional at once sets them apart and draws them together. But what form can the relation between exception and exception take? There is no doubt that this point considerably preoccupied Sade. As always, he proceeds from one solution to another, and finally, at the end of all his logic, he produces out of the puzzle the only solution that matters to him. When he invents a secret society governed by strict rules designed to moderate its excesses, he has the excuse of fashion, for he lived in a time in which the freemasonry of libertinism and Freemasonry in the conventional sense created, within a collapsing society, a quantity of little societies and secret colleges based on complicity of passions and mutual respect for dangerous ideas. 'The Society of the Friends of Crime' is an attempt of this kind. Its statutes, which he analyses and studies at length, forbid the members to give way to their furious desires with each other – these can only be assuaged in two brothels which are constantly replenished by the virtuous classes. Between themselves the members should 'indulge all their whims and do everything', but without cruelty. It is easy to see why. People who only expect pleasure from evil should be prevented from meeting on a plane on which evil might become their undoing. Superior debauchees may make an alliance but they don't clash.

But a compromise of this kind is not enough to satisfy Sade. And so we notice that the heroes of his books are constantly drawn into association by agreements to fix the limits of their power and to impose order on disorder, and yet the possibility of betrayal is always present. Among the accomplices tension never ceases to grow until, at last, they feel less bound by the oath which unites them than by the mutual compulsion to break it. It is this situation that makes the last part of *Juliette* so dramatic, for Juliette has principles. She respects debauchery and, when she meets an accomplished evildoer, sees the perfection of the crime for which he is responsible and the power for destruction he represents, she is not only led into association with him, but is led to spare him if she can, even when this association becomes dangerous for her. And thus she refuses to have the ogre Minski assassinated, even though she is in danger of being killed by him. 'That man is too harmful to mankind for me to deprive the universe of him.' She finally sacrifices another inventor of masterpieces of lechery, but only because she has observed that at the end of his bloody orgies he was in the habit of visiting a chapel to purify his soul. Does this mean that the perfect criminal is immune to the passions in which he indulges? That there remains some final principle by which the libertine can never be either object or victim of his libertinism? Mme de Donis says to Juliette: 'You have told me a hundred times that debauched women don't ruin each other. Are you going to throw over this maxim?' The answer is clear. She does throw it over and Mme de Donis is sacrificed. And so, little by little, perish all the most deeply loved and most distinguished accomplices in debauch; victims either of their loyalty or of their perjury, of weariness or of the strength of their feelings. Nothing can save them, nothing can excuse them. No sooner has Juliette hurled her best friends to their death than she turns to new allies and exchanges vows of eternal trust with them. And they themselves laugh at these oaths, knowing full well that they only assign limits to their debauchery so as to have the pleasure of passing beyond these limits.

The situation is fairly well summarized in the following conversation between several Princes of Crime. One of them, Gernand, says of his cousin Bressac: 'He is my heir. All the same, I swear that my being alive doesn't make him impatient. We have the same tastes and the same way of thinking, and, in me, he is sure to find a friend.' 'To be sure,' says Bressac, 'I will never do you the slightest harm.' Yet this very Bressac remarks that another of his relatives, d'Esterval, who specializes in cutting the throats of passers-by, came very near to assassinating him. 'Yes,' says d'Esterval, 'as a relative, but never as a brother in debauchery.' For all that, Bressac remains sceptical, and they both agree that this last consideration almost failed to restrain Dorothée, d'Esterval's wife. But what does Dorothée answer? 'When I condemn you, I flatter you. My terrible habit of immolating the men who attract me decided your sentence in the very moment I made my declaration of love.' That is clear enough. But given such conditions, what happens to Sade's thesis on the happiness of evil, and his conviction that a man is always happy if he has all the vices and of necessity unhappy if he has a single virtue? In fact, Sade's work is littered with the corpses of debauchees struck down in the height of their glory. Catastrophe befalls not only Justine, who is unique, but also the splendid Clairwill, the strongest and most energetic of Sade's heroines, it befalls Saint-Fond who is assassinated by Noirceuil, and the licentious Borghese who is thrown into a volcano, and a hundred other perfect criminals. These are strange ends and peculiar triumphs for the profligates! How can Sade's mad reasoning be blind to all its own self-contradiction? Because for it these contradictions are really proofs, and we must see why.

From a casual reading of *Justine* we might take it to be simply a coarse tale. We see a young and virtuous girl who is for ever being violated, beaten and tortured, the victim of a destiny bent on destroying her. And when we read *Juliette* we see a perverted girl soar from pleasure to pleasure. A plot of this character is scarcely convincing. But that is because we have failed to pay attention to its most important aspect; noticing only the sadness of one girl and the satisfaction of the other, we fail to see that in reality the stories of the two sisters are identical, that everything that happens to Justine happens to Juliette also, and that both underwent the same ordeals and experienced the same trials. Juliette too is thrown into gaol, thrashed without mercy, threatened with death and endlessly tortured. Her existence is horrible, but – and here we come to it – her sufferings give her pleasure and her tortures delight her. 'Sweet are the chains of the crime one loves.' And I am not even referring to those remarkable torments which are so terrible for Justine and so very pleasing to Juliette. In a scene that takes place in the castle of a corrupt judge the unfortunate Justine is delivered over to really appalling tortures: her sufferings are incredible and it is difficult to know what to think of injustice on such a scale. But what happens? A completely perverted girl, who is present, is so excited by what she sees that she insists that she should immediately undergo the same torments. And she derives infinite ecstasy from them. So it is true that virtue is the cause of man's unhappiness, though not because it exposes him to unfortunate experiences, but because if we eradicate virtue, what was unhappiness turns into an opportunity for pleasure and torment becomes an ecstasy.

For Sade, the sovereign man is inaccessible to evil because no one can do him evil. He is the man of all passions and his passions take pleasure in everything. Some people have received Jean Paulhan's idea of an inherent masochism lying behind the sadism of Sade as the expression of a paradox too witty to be true. But we can see that this idea lies at the heart of the system. The completely egotistical man is the man who can transform all disgust [*dégoûts*] into pleasure [*goûts*], and all revulsion into attraction. Like the Philosopher of the Boudoir, he affirms, 'Nothing disgusts me, everything gives me pleasure, I wish to combine all satisfaction.' And that is why in *Les 120 Journées*, Sade took on the gigantic task of making a complete enumeration of all human eccentricities, aberrations and possibilities. To be at the mercy of nothing he needs to experience everything. 'You will know nothing if you have not known everything, and if you are timid enough to stop at the natural, it will always escape you.'

We can see why the unfortunate Justine's objection: 'And what if luck changes?' cannot impress the criminal. Luck may change and become bad luck, but it will only be a new kind of luck, every bit as desirable and as satisfactory as the other. But you risk the hangman! Perhaps you will end up with an ignominious death! That, replies the debauchee, is my dearest wish. 'Oh Juliette,' says la Borghèse, 'how I would want my follies to lead me, like the lowest of creatures, to the fate to which their wretchedness condemns them. For me the scaffold itself would be the crown of ecstasy. I would be facing death and enjoying the pleasure of expiring as a victim of my crimes.' And someone else says: 'The real debauchee even cherishes the reproaches his appalling behaviour earns him. Have we not seen people who loved even the tortures human vengeance prepared for them, who underwent them with joy, who saw in the scaffold a throne of glory on which they would have been angry indeed not to perish with the same courage that inspired them in the loathsome practices of their crimes? And so we can see men at the last stage of considered corruption.' What can the law do against such Power? It sets out to punish it and succeeds in rewarding it. When it reviles it, it exalts it. And, for the same reason, what can the debauchee do against his equal? The day will come when he betrays and strikes him down, but his very treason gives a sharp pleasure to his victim who sees in it the confirmation of all his suspicions and so dies in the ecstasy of having been the occasion of a further crime (not to mention further pleasures). One of Sade's strangest heroines is called Amelia. She lives in Sweden. One day she sets out to meet Borchamps, the conspirator we have already mentioned. He, in the hope of a mass execution, has just handed over to the King all the participants in his conspiracy, and his treason has excited the young woman. 'I adore your violence,' she tells him. 'Swear to me that one day I too shall be your victim; from the age of fifteen, my mind has been inflamed only with the idea of perishing a victim to the cruel passion of perversion. Obviously I don't want to die tomorrow, my extravagance doesn't go that far, but this is the only way in which I want to die. To make my death the occasion of a crime is an idea that excites me above all others.' A strange wish and well deserving the answer 'I worship your ideas to madness, and I think we shall do great things together.' 'I agree, they are corrupt and perverse.'

So everything becomes clear: for the complete man, who is the whole of man, no evil is possible. If he does harm to others, what ecstasy! If others harm him, what joy! Virtue serves him because it is weak and he can crush it, and vice is agreeable because he derives satisfaction from the chaos it creates, even if at his own expense. If he lives, there is no single event of his existence which he cannot welcome as happy. If he dies, his death is an even greater happiness, and in knowledge of his destruction he sees the crown of a life that is only justified by the need to destroy. Thus he is immune from others. No one can touch him, nothing can deprive him of the power of being himself and of enjoying it. This is the primary meaning of his solitude. Even if, in his turn, he seems to be victim and slave, the violence of the passions that he can slake in no matter what circumstances guarantees him his sovereignty, and makes him feel that in every condition of life and death he remains all powerful. It is for this that, despite the similarity of their descriptions, it seems right to leave the paternity of masochism to Sacher Masoch and of sadism to Sade. With Sade's heroes the pleasures of debasement in no way reduce their mastery, and those of abjection raise them to the heights. All those feelings that we call shame, remorse, love of punishment remain foreign to them. When Saint-Fond says to Juliette, 'My pride is so great that I would like to be served on bended knee and never speak, save through an interpreter, to all that filthy mob that is called the people,' she asks, without any irony, 'But do not the follies of debauchery bring you down from this elevation?' 'For minds that think like ours,' answers Saint-Fond, 'such humiliation is a delicious adjunct to our pride.' And Sade adds by way of comment, 'This is easy to understand: in doing what no one else does, we are unique of our kind.' On the moral plane, there is the same satisfaction of pride in the feeling of being an outcast of humanity. 'The world must shudder when it learns of the crimes we shall have committed. We must force men to blush at being of the same species as we are. I demand that a monument be raised to publish these crimes to the universe, and our names be engraved on it by our own hands.' To be Unique, unique of one's kind, is the true test of sovereignty. And we shall soon see the absolute meaning Sade gives to this word.

Now everything becomes clearer: but at this point we also feel that everything is beginning to be rather obscure. The progression by which the Unique person escapes from the clutches of others is far from obvious. In some ways it is a kind of stoical insensibility which seems to suppose man's perfect autonomy when confronted with the world. But at the same time it is just the opposite because, while he is independent of others who can never harm him, by this very fact the Unique person at once establishes a relationship of absolute domination over them, and this not because the others can do nothing against him, or that daggers, tortures, and acts of humiliation leave him unscathed, but because he has all power over others, and even the pain dealt out by them reinforces the pleasure he derives from power and helps him to exercise his sovereignty. And here the situation becomes rather embarrassing. From the moment at which 'being master of myself' means being 'master of others', from the moment at which my independence ceases to derive from my own will, but comes from the dependence of others on me, it is clear that I remain linked to others and that I have need of them, if only to annihilate them. This difficulty about Sade has often been mentioned. It is not even certain that he was aware of it, and one of the originalities of his exceptional mind possibly comes from this fact: when one is not Sade, a decisive problem arises which reintroduces relations of human solidarity between master and slave; but if one is Sade there is no problem and it is even impossible to envisage one.

There is no space to go over, as one would like, all the numerous texts (and with Sade everything is in infinite profusion) which bear on this situation. The fact is that contradictions abound. Sometimes the violence of debauchery seems almost haunted by this contradiction at the root of its pleasures. The debauchee knows no greater joy than destroying his victims, but this joy is ruined and destroys itself by destroying what causes it. 'The pleasure of killing a woman,' says one of them, 'is soon over: when she is dead she can feel nothing more; the ecstasy of making her suffer ends with her life. . . . Let us brand her, let us flay her; she will suffer from this treatment up to the last moment of her life, and, by its infinite prolongation, our lust will be the more delicious.' Similarly Saint-Fond, bored with simple tortures, would like a kind of infinite death for each person, which is why with remarkable ingenuity he conceives of a raid on Hell, and makes plans to dispose of that inexhaustible source of torture at the expense of people of his choice. Here, in all clarity, we can see how entangled are the relationships that oppression creates between oppressed and oppressor. Sade's hero derives his existence from dealing out death and sometimes, in his longing for an eternity of life, he dreams of a death that he can dispense for ever, so that the executioner and the victim, eternally placed face to face, are endowed with identical power and the same divine attribute of eternity. There is no denying that this contradiction is embedded in Sade's thought. But he commonly manages to transcend it with reasons that give us increased light on the world he inhabits. Clairwill reproaches Saint-Fond with what she calls his unforgivable excesses and, to put him back in the right path, she gives him this advice: 'Replace the idea of pleasure which now fills your head – the idea of prolonging to infinity the tortures of the creature you have destined for death – replace it by a greater abundance of murders: do not try to kill the same individual for ever, which is impossible, but assassinate many more, which is easy.' The large number is, indeed, the elegant solution. To look upon other people from the point of view of quantity kills them more completely than when they are destroyed by physical violence. It may well be that the criminal is indissolubly united to the man he assassinates. But the debauchee who, when he kills his victim, only experiences the need to sacrifice a thousand more, seems strangely free from any complicity with him. In his eyes the victim does not exist in himself, he is not a distinct being but a mere cipher who can be indefinitely substituted in an immense erotic equation. When we read declarations such as: 'Nothing amuses, nothing excites me like large numbers,' we understand better why the idea of equality is used to bolster up so much of Sade's reasoning. All men are equal simply means that no one creature is worth more than another, all are interchangeable and with no more significance than that of a single unit in an infinite enumeration. In comparison with the Unique person, all the others are equally meaningless and the Unique person, by reducing them to nothing, only makes their nothingness more manifest.

This is what makes Sade's world so strange. Scenes of violence succeed one another; the repetitions are infinite and fabulous. In one single session it is common for each debauchee to torture and massacre four or five hundred victims. The next day he begins again, and in the evening follows up with a new holocaust. The order is then slightly changed, excitement is refreshed, and hecatomb is piled on hecatomb. But what of it? Who can fail to see that in these mass executions those who die have lost every shred of reality, and if they can disappear with such derisory ease it is because they have already been annihilated by a total and absolute act of destruction, that they are only present, and that they only die to bear witness to a kind of primordial cataclysm, and to a destruction which is valid not only for them but for all. This is the striking thing. The cosmos through which the Unique person makes his way is a desert; the creatures he meets there are less than things, less than shadows, and when he torments and destroys them he doesn't rob them of their lives but proves their nothingness: it is their non-existence of which he is master and from which he derives his greatest pleasure. As the Duc de Blangis says to the women, gathered together for the delectation of the four debauchees at the outset of *Les 120 Journées*: 'Reflect upon your situation, upon what you are, and what we are, and let your reflections make you tremble. You are here, away from France, in the depths of an uninhabitable forest, behind precipitous mountains whose passes were blocked the moment you crossed them. You are shut up in an impenetrable castle, no one whatsoever knows you are here; you are separated from your friends and from your relations and already you are *dead to the world*.' This must be taken in its strict sense: they are already dead, wiped out, shut up in the absolute emptiness of a Bastille into which existence no longer enters and in which the fact that they are alive only makes us more aware of their 'being already dead', from which their life is indistinguishable.

Naturally we are discounting the tales of necrophilia which, though fairly frequent in Sade, are not generally the 'normal' pursuits of his heroes. Moreover, we should point out that when one of them exclaims 'Ah! what a lovely corpse' and becomes excited by the passivity of death, he had begun by being a murderer, and it is the effects of his aggressive power that he is striving to prolong beyond death. What is characteristic of Sade's cosmos is not the longing to become one with the motionless and petrified existence of the corpse nor the effort to slip into the passivity of a form representing absence of form, a reality that is fully real, immune to the uncertainties of life yet incarnating supreme unreality. On the contrary, in the core of his world lies the demand of sovereignty as affirmed by an immense negation. This negation is achieved through large numbers, and no one particular instance can satisfy it; it is essentially aimed at surpassing the plane of human existence. It is all very well for Sade's hero to master others by his power to destroy them: if he gives the impression that he is never dependent on them, even in view of his need to destroy them, and if he always appears able to do without them, this is because he has placed himself on a plane where no common measure with them is possible, and he has done this, once and for all, by setting as the limits to his project of destruction something infinitely beyond men and their short existence. In other words, to the extent that Sade's hero appears strikingly free in relation to his victims, upon whom he nevertheless depends for his pleasures, it is because violence is aimed, in them, at something other than them, goes way beyond them, doing no more than validate, frantically and to infinity, through each particular case, the general act of destruction by which he has reduced God and the World to naught.

Thus it is certain that in Sade the spirit of crime is bound up with a boundless dream of negation, which is ceaselessly degraded and dishonoured by the weakness of its possibilities of realization. The finest crime which earth has to offer is a mere trifle which could only arouse the debauchee's contempt. Every one of these profligates who, like Jerome the monk, experiences a sense of shame when faced with the mediocrity of his acts, dreams of a crime superior to all that man can do in the world, 'and unfortunately,' Jerome says, 'I can't find it: all that we do is only the shadow of what we would like to do.' 'I want,' says Clairwill, 'to find a crime whose effects would be active for ever, even when I am acting no longer, so that there should be no single instant of my life, even when sleeping, that I was not the cause of some upheaval or other, and that this upheaval would be enough to bring with it a general corruption or chaos of a kind whose effects would be prolonged beyond my lifetime.' And to this Juliette gives a reply calculated to please the author of *La Nouvelle Justine*: 'Try that moral crime which is achieved through writing.' If Sade, who in his system reduces the part of intellectual excitement to the minimum, and who has almost completely suppressed the eroticism of the imagination (because his own erotic dream is to project, on to characters who do not dream but who really act, the unreal processes of his enjoyment: his eroticism is a dream eroticism because it is generally realized through fiction, but the more he dreams of this eroticism the more he demands a fiction from which dreams are expelled and in which debauch is really achieved and lived); if, nevertheless, Sade has in exceptional cases exalted the imagination, it is because he knows perfectly well that the origin of many imperfect crimes lies in an impossible crime only conceivable by the imagination, and this is why he makes Belmor say: 'Oh Juliette, how delightful are the pleasures of imagination. The world is ours in these moments: no single creature can resist us, we devastate the universe and repeople it with new objects only to devastate it again; the means for all crimes are at our disposal, we use them all, and we multiply the horror a hundredfold.'

In his book, which not only contains some powerful thoughts on Sade, but on the problems which Sade's existence illuminates, Pierre Klossowski explains the very complicated character of the relationships between the Sadean consciousness, God and one's neighbour. He shows that these relationships are negative but that, in so far as the negation is real, it reintroduces the notions it suppresses, that is to say that the notion of God and the notion of one's neighbour are indispensable to the consciousness of the debauchee. This is a subject that can be discussed indefinitely because Sade's work is a chaos of clear ideas in which, while everything is said, everything is also disguised. Nevertheless, his claim to originality seems to have a firm stake in the idea that man's sovereignty is based on a transcendental power of negation: a power in no way dependent on the objects it destroys and which, for their destruction, does not even need to suppose their previous existence, because at the moment in which it destroys them it has already, in advance and at all times, considered them as non-existent. Now, this dialectic has at once its best example, and perhaps its justification, in the way in which Sade's All-powerful hero takes up his position before divine Omnipotence.

Maurice Heine has shown the exceptional strength of Sade's atheism. But, as Pierre Klossowski has every reason to remind us, this atheism is not a cold-blooded one. The moment the name of God appears, in even the calmest passage, his language straightaway flares up, his tone is raised and the emotion of hate runs away with his words and throws them into confusion. It is not in the scenes of lust that Sade shows passion, but each time the Unique person sees some trace of God on his path, violence, contempt, pride, the intoxication of power and desire are immediately inflamed. In some way the idea of God is man's unpardonable fault, his original sin, the proof of his nothingness, and an authorization and justification for crime. For no method can be too violent to destroy a creature who has agreed to abase himself before God. Sade writes: 'The concept of God is the only fault for which I cannot forgive man.' This statement is decisive and it is one of the keys of his system. Belief in an all-powerful god, which only allows man the status of a straw in the wind or an atom of nothingness, forces the complete man to seize on this superhuman power by himself exercising, in the name of man and over all men, the sovereign rights which men have given to God. When the criminal makes a kill he is God on earth because he establishes over his victim the domination which the latter associates with the definition of divine sovereignty. The minute a real debauchee observes, even in the mind of the most corrupt profligate, the tiniest trace of religious faith, he immediately passes a decree of death: and this is entirely because the lapsed profligate has destroyed himself and abdicated into the hands of God; he deems himself to be nothing, and so the man who kills him does no more than regularize a situation only slightly disguised by appearances.

Sade's hero denies mankind, and this denial is achieved through the concept of God. For a moment he turns himself into God so that men should be destroyed before him and so realize the nothingness of a creature compared with God. 'You hate mankind, do you not, Prince?' asks Juliette. 'I loathe it. Not a moment passes in which I do not have some project for its violent destruction. No species is more frightful . . . What abjection, how vile it is and how disgusting.' 'But,' interrupts Juliette, 'as for you, can you really believe that you belong to men? Oh, no! for when one dominates them with such force it is impossible to be of their species.' 'She is quite right,' says Saint-Fond, 'yes, indeed we are gods.'

Nevertheless, the dialectic continues on its course: Sade's hero, who has claimed for himself that power over men that men rashly concede to God, never forgets for an instant that this power is entirely negative. There can be only one meaning in being God – to crush men and destroy creation. 'I would like to be Pandora's box,' Saint-Fond goes on to say, 'so that all the evils emerging from my heart should destroy every creature individually.' And Verneuil says: 'If a god really existed, are we not his rivals, for we destroy what he created.' And so, little by little, an ambiguous conception of omnipotence is built up, and about its final meaning there can be no doubt. Pierre Klossowski stresses the theory of Saint-Fond – a man singular among all Sade's heroes in that he believes in a Supreme Being. But the god which he worships is not good but 'most vindictive, barbarous, wicked, unjust and cruel'. He is a being supreme in wickedness, a god of evil. From this idea Sade has developed many brilliant conclusions. He portrays an imaginary Last Judgement which is described with all the resources of his peculiar and ferocious humour. We

hear God scolding the Good in these terms: 'When you saw that everything on earth was vicious and criminal why did you stray along the paths
of virtue? Should not the perpetual misery in which I have deluged the
universe have convinced you that I only like chaos and that to please me
you had to annoy me. Did I not daily give you an example of destruction?
Why did you not destroy? Fools who failed to imitate me.'

But with this in mind, it is clear that such a conception of an infernal
deity is no more than a stage in the dialectic by which Sade's supermen,
after denying man in the name of God, turns to face God and in turn
deny Him in the name of Nature and, finally, to deny Nature by identifying it with the spirit of negation. Negation, which has exterminated the
idea of man, comes to rest, so to speak, for an instant in the evil deity
before taking itself for its object. In becoming God, Saint-Fond has, at
the same time, obliged God to become Saint-Fond; and the Supreme
Being into whose hands the weak man delivers himself so as to break the
power of the strong man, is now no more than a gigantic limitation, a
transcendent bronze idol who crushes each one in proportion to his
weakness. This is hatred of mankind hypostasized and pushed to its
furthest limits. But no sooner has the spirit of negation attained absolute
existence, it can do no more, having thus become conscious of itself as
infinite, than turn against this assertion of absolute existence, as the sole
object now commensurate with negation that has become infinite.
Hatred for men was incarnated by God. Now it is hatred of God that
frees hate itself from God, a hate so violent that at every moment it seems
to give reality to what it denies in order the more to justify itself and
assert itself. 'Were the existence of God true,' says la Dubois, 'I confess
the mere pleasure of perpetually annoying Him would become the most
precious consolation for the necessity in which I would then find myself
of having to believe in Him.' But Klossowski seems to think that such
burning hatred testifies to a faith that has forgotten its name and has
recourse to blasphemy to force God to break His silence. This hardly
seems to be the case. On the contrary, everything seems to show that this
hatred has attached itself to God so particularly only because He provides it with a special justification and a special source of nourishment.
God for Sade is simply a prop for his hatred. His hatred is too great for
any object to be really important to it. Since it is infinite and insatiable it
must eventually feed on itself and be enraptured by this infinity to which
it gives the name of God. 'Your system,' says Clairwill to Saint-Fond,
'has its roots entirely in the deep horror you feel for God.' But it is only
the hatred which is real and, in the end, it will turn against Nature with
the same boldness as it turned against the non-existent God it abhors.

In reality, if matters of religion, the name of God and the people who
make God, namely priests, unleash all Sade's most violent passions, it is

because the words 'god' and 'religion' are just the ones that incarnate all the forms of his hatred. In God, he hates the nothingness of man who gave himself such a master, and the thought of this nothingness infuriates him to such a degree that he can only co-operate with God to punish this nothingness. Next, in God, he hates His divine omnipotence, in which he perceives his own, and so God becomes the image and body of his infinite hatred. Finally, he hates in God His wretchedness, the vacuity of an existence which in so far as it expresses itself as existence and creation is nothing, because what is great and all that matters is the spirit of destruction.

In Sade's system this spirit of destruction is identified with Nature. On this point his thought has hesitated; he needed to get rid of the atheist philosophies then in fashion, for which he could only feel sympathy and in which his reason, always hungry for argument, found inexhaustible resources. But, to the extent that he managed to get beyond the naturalist ideology, and to the extent that he was not taken in by external analogies, he shows us how he accompanied logic to its furthest frontiers and did not retreat before the dark forces that upheld it. Nature is one of the words that – like so many of his contemporaries – he is always ready to use. It is in the name of Nature that he leads the fight against God and all that God represents, especially morality. We have no need to emphasize that Sade's prolificness on this subject is vertiginous. First of all Nature for him is universal life, and for hundreds of pages the whole of his philosophy consists in repeating that the immoral instincts are good because they are natural facts, and that the foremost and final authority is Nature. Put in other words, not morality but facts must rule. But then, embarrassed by seeing that he is being led to give an equal value to the instincts of virtue and of vice, he tries to set up a new scale of values with crime at its summit. His chief argument boils down to saying that crime is more in conformity with the spirit of Nature because it is activity and hence life: Nature, he says, wants to create and needs crime to destroy: all this is established in a very detailed manner, in long boring passages interspersed with occasional striking proofs. Nevertheless, by dint of speaking of Nature and finding himself always up against this sovereign and insurmountable point of reference, little by little Sade's hero becomes irritated and his hatred soon makes Nature so intolerable to him that he covers it with curses and denials. 'Yes, my friend, yes, I loathe Nature.' This revolt has two deep motives. On one hand it seems to him intolerable that the power of unparalleled destruction which he represents has no other end than allowing Nature more room for creation. On the other, in so far as he himself belongs to Nature, he feels that Nature escapes his curses and the more he outrages it the better he serves it, the more he destroys it the more he obeys its law. Hence his mad outbursts of hatred and revolt. 'Oh, you blind and idiotic force, when I have exterminated all the creatures that dwell on earth I will be far from my goal, for I will have done you a service, evil mother, and I only aim at avenging myself for the stupidity and wickedness by which you cause men to suffer by never giving them the means of satisfying the fearful inclinations you inspire in them.' Here we have the expression of a primeval and elementary feeling; man's deepest need is to outrage nature, a need a thousand times stronger than offending God. 'In all our activities we can only inflict suffering on creatures or on shadows, but Nature is not one of these and it is she that I would like to outrage. I would like to upset her plans, reverse her course, arrest the circulation of the stars, overthrow the planets floating in space, destroy what serves her, protect what harms her and, in a word, insult her in her works, and I cannot do it.' Once again in this passage Sade is superficial enough to confuse Nature with her principal laws and this allows him to dream of a cataclysm that could overthrow them: but his logic rejects this compromise and when, elsewhere, he imagines a mechanic who invents a machine capable of disintegrating the universe, he has to admit that no one will ever have deserved better of Nature than such a man. Sade is perfectly aware that to destroy all things is not to destroy the world, for the world is not only universal affirmation but universal destruction, so that the totality of being and the totality of nothingness both represent it equally well. This is why in the history of man the struggle against Nature signifies a dialectical stage very superior to the struggle against God. Without modernizing his thought in any way, we can say that Sade in his century was one of the first to affirm the idea of transcendence in the idea of the world because, as the idea of nothingness is part of the world, one cannot think of the nothingness of the world except within a totality which is always the world.

If crime is Nature's true spirit there can be no crime against Nature and so it follows that there is no possible crime. Sade affirms this, sometimes with the greatest satisfaction, sometimes with the wildest rage, for if he denies the possibility of crime, he is able to deny morality, God and all human values; but if he denies crime he must also reject the spirit of negation and admit that this could destroy itself. And this conclusion he cannot accept and so, gradually, he is led to deny that Nature has any reality. In the last volumes of *La Nouvelle Justine* (particularly in volumes VIII and IX) Juliette denounces all her former ideas and makes up for them in these terms: 'Idiot that I was, before we left one another I was still at the stage of nature and the new systems that I have adopted since then have led me away from her.' Nature, she says, has no more truth, reality or meaning than God. 'You old bitch, Nature, you may be deceiving me as I was formerly deceived by the hideous image of God to which they said you were subordinated. We no more depend on you than on Him. The cause is not necessary for the effect.' So Nature must go, even though the philosopher was so pleased with her and it would have been so agreeable to him to turn universal life into a fearful machine of death. But simple nothingness is not his aim. What he sought is sovereignty achieved through the spirit of negation pushed to its furthest extreme. In turn, he has made use of men, God and Nature to test it. And each of these ideas, when exposed to negation, seemed to gain a certain value. But if one looks at the whole of experience, these moments no longer have the slightest reality because it is of the nature of experience to ruin them and make them cancel each other out. What are men if they are nothingness before God; what is God compared with Nature and what is Nature if she can be compelled to vanish before man who carries in himself the need to outrage her? And here the cycle is complete. We set out with man and we have now come back to man, only he now has a new name; he is called the Unique Person, the only one of his species.

When Sade discovered that in man negation is power, he tried to base man's whole future on negation pushed to its limit. To reach this point he borrowed a term from the vocabulary of his age, imagining a principle whose very ambiguity shows an ingenuity of choice. This is the principle of energy. Now energy is a completely equivocal idea: it is at one and the same time a reserve and an expenditure of force. Affirmation which fulfils itself only by negation, power which is destruction: it is fact and law, datum and value. It is striking that in this forceful and passionate cosmos, far from giving desire the highest position, Sade subordinates it and treats it as suspect. This is because desire militates against solitude and leads to the dangerous recognition of the world of other people. But when Saint-Fond declares, 'My passions concentrated on a single point are like the rays of the sun collected by a magnifying glass – they immediately consume their object,' we can easily see how destruction becomes a synonym for power, though the object destroyed acquires not the slightest value from the operation. There is another advantage of this principle in that it assigns a future to man without imposing on him any recognition of an ideal notion. This is one of Sade's achievements. He claimed to have overthrown the ethic of the Good but, in spite of several provocative assertions, he took great care not to replace it by a gospel of Evil. When he writes, 'Everything is good when it is in excess,' he can be reproached for the uncertainty of his principle, but he cannot be accused of a desire to base the sovereignty of man on the sovereignty of ideas superior to man. No privileged way of behaviour emerges from that statement. We can choose to do anything whatsoever. What matters is that when we do it we are able to effect a coincidence between maximum destruction and maximum assertion. In fact, in Sade's novels, it is precisely in this way that the plot works out. It is not by measure of their greater or less virtue or vice that the characters are unhappy or happy, but according to the energy they show. For, as he puts it, 'happiness is an affair of energy of principle and there can be none of it for the person who is always undecided.' Juliette, when Saint-Fond suggests a plan for destroying two-thirds of France by famine, hesitates and is frightened: immediately she is threatened – why? Because she has shown weakness; her tone of spirit has lowered and Saint-Fond's greater energy is getting ready to make her its prey. That is even clearer in the case of la Durand, a poisoner and incapable of the slightest virtue. Her corruption is complete, but one day the government of Venice asks her to spread the plague. This proposal frightens her, not because it is immoral, but because she fears the dangers that she herself might undergo, and so she is immediately condemned. Her energy had failed, she had met her master and her master was Death. In living dangerously, said Sade, all that matters is never to 'lack the force to go beyond the ultimate limits.' One way of putting it is that this strange world of his is not composed of individuals, but of systems of force, of higher or lower tension. Where the tension is lessened catastrophe becomes inevitable. Moreover, no distinction can be made between Nature's energy and man's: lust is a thunderbolt, just as a thunderbolt is Nature's lust: the weak will be victims of both and the strong will emerge triumphant. Justine and not Juliette is struck by lightning, and yet there is nothing providential in this conclusion. Justine's weakness attracts the thunderbolt that Juliette's energy repels. In the same way, all that befalls Justine makes her unhappy because everything that affects her diminishes her: we are told that her inclinations were *virtuous but low*, and this must be understood literally. All that befalls Juliette, on the other hand, reveals her power to herself and she enjoys it as an increase of herself. That is why, should she die, she would experience the total destruction of death as the total expenditure of her enormous energy and this would raise her to the very pinnacle of power and exaltation.

Sade has understood perfectly that the sovereignty of the man of energy as arrived at by his identification with the spirit of negation is a condition of paradox. The complete man who completely asserts himself is also completely destroyed. He is the man of all passions, incapable of feeling. He began by destroying himself, first as man, then as God and then as Nature, and in this way he has become Unique. Now he can do everything because in him negation has mastered everything. To explain his formation Sade has recourse to a very coherent idea to which he gives the classical name of apathy. Apathy is the spirit of negation as applied to a man who has chosen to be sovereign. It is in some way the cause or principle of energy. Sade appears to argue more or less as follows: the individual today represents a certain amount of force: most of the time he disperses his strength for the benefit of those ghosts called other people, God or the ideal; by this expenditure he wrongly exhausts and wastes his potentialities, but what is worse, he is basing his conduct on weakness, for if he expends himself for others it is because he believes that he needs their support. This is a fatal lapse. He weakens himself by vain expenditure of energy and he expends his energy because he thinks he is weak. The strong man knows that he is alone and accepts that condition: he repudiates the whole inheritance of seventeen centuries of cowardice that would make him turn to others. Pity, gratitude and love are all feelings he destroys, and in destroying them he recuperates all the force he would have expended on those debilitating impulses and, more important, he derives the beginning of a real energy from this work of destruction.

It must be understood, then, that apathy doesn't simply consist in destroying the 'parasitical' feelings, but that it also militates against spontaneity in any passion whatsoever. The perverted man who surrenders himself immediately to his vice is only a failure who will be lost. Even profligates of genius, with all the necessary gifts for becoming monsters, are doomed to catastrophe if they are merely content to follow their inclinations. Sade insists that for passion to become energy it has to be compressed, it must control itself in its course and pass through a necessary moment of insensitiveness: then only will it reach its maximum. In the early period of her career Juliette is repeatedly taken up on this point by Clairwill: she only commits crime in moments of enthusiasm when her passions are inflamed, and she puts lust and the ebullience of pleasure above all else. This is easy and dangerous. Crime means more than mere lust. Cold-blooded crime is greater than crime committed in the heat of passion, but crime committed when sensitivity has hardened is more important than any other, because it is a sombre, secret crime, the act of a soul which has accumulated enormous energy in itself through destroying everything in itself, and this energy will be completely at one with the impulse to total destruction for which it is preparing the way. All great debauchees who live for pleasure alone are great because they have utterly destroyed all capacity for pleasure in themselves. That is why they indulge in frightful anomalies, otherwise the mediocrity of normal pleasures would suffice. But they have made themselves insensitive: they claim to take pleasure in their insensitivity, which is sensitivity denied, and they become ferocious. Cruelty is merely the negation of self, taken to such a degree that it is transformed into a destructive explosion; insensitivity becomes a tremor of one's whole being, says Sade; 'the soul progresses to a sort of apathy which is soon transformed into pleasures a thousand times more divine than those obtainable through weaknesses.'

It is clear that principles play a great part in this cosmos. The debauchee is 'thoughtful, concentrated in himself and incapable of being moved by anything whatsoever'. He is a solitary, unable to endure noise or laughter: nothing should distract him, 'apathy, indifference, stoicism and inner solitude are the pitch to which he must lift his soul.' A transformation of this kind and a work of such self-destruction is not accomplished without extreme difficulty. *Juliette* is a kind of *Bildungsroman*, an apprentices' handbook in which we trace the slow education of an energetic soul. On appearances alone Juliette is entirely depraved from the very beginning. But in reality she has no more than a few inclinations and her mind is untouched: a gigantic effort still needs to be made for, as Balzac says: 'You aren't destroyed by wanting.' Sade points out that in the achievement of this apathy there are dangerous moments. It can happen, for instance, that insensitivity reduces the profligate to such a state of exhaustion that he may easily return to morality. He believes he is hardened, but he is merely weak and a ready prey for remorse: a single impulse to virtue by re-establishing the universe of mankind and of God is enough to destroy all his power; whatever heights he has attained, he collapses, and generally his fall means his death. But if, on the other hand, in this state of prostration, when he experiences no more than a tasteless repulsion for the worst excesses, he can summon up a final increase of energy, to increase his insensitivity by inventing new excesses which revolt him still more, then he will emerge from prostration to all-power, from coldness to extreme will, and 'in revolt on all sides' will enjoy himself in supreme and limitless measure.

One of the surprising things about Sade and his destiny is that, though outrage has no better symbol than he, the outrageous side of his thought should have been for so long unknown. It is not necessary to summarize all the themes he discovered and which the boldest minds of the future needed all their courage to reaffirm. We have merely touched on them and have restricted ourselves to retracing the essential movement of his thought. We could well have dwelt on his conception of dreams, where he sees the mind re-becoming instinct and escaping from the morality of daylight, or on those reflections in which he anticipates Freud, such as: 'It is in our mother's womb that the organs that make us capable of this or that eccentricity were formed: the first object seen and the first words heard are enough to determine the course we take: education is all very well, but it changes nothing.' In Sade there is a moralist of the great tradition and it would be easy to collect a selection of maxims compared with which La Rochefoucauld would seem weak and unsure. He has been reproached for writing badly and it is true that he often writes with a haste and prolixity that try one's patience. But he is also capable of a strange humour: his style achieves an icy conviviality, a cold innocence in its excesses that one might well prefer to all Voltaire's irony – it is a quality found in no other French writer. All these gifts are remarkable, but they were useless, for until Apollinaire, Maurice Heine and André Breton (with his clairvoyant sense of history's hidden resources) opened the way for Sade – and even until the publication of the latest studies by Jean Paulhan, Georges Bataille and Pierre Klossowsky, Sade, the master of the great themes of modern thought and feeling, was no more than a brillant but empty name. Why is that? Because his thought is an achievement of insanity and was moulded by a depravity which the world shunned. Moreover, Sade put forward his work as the theory of this depravity; it is a tracing of it and claims to transpose the most repulsive anomaly into a complete view of the world. For the first time philosophy was publicly conceived as the product of an illness[1] and shamelessly claimed that a system whose only guarantee lies in the preference of a perverted individual can be logical and universal thought.

Here again we come on one of Sade's remarkable originalities. He can be said to have carried out his own self-analysis by writing a text in which he sets down everything that has a bearing on his obsessions and in which he tries to find to what world and to what logic his obsessions are the key. But on the other hand, and here he was a pioneer, he boastfully proved that out of a certain personal and even monstrous conduct a world view could justifiably be drawn, sufficiently important to force great minds, exclusively devoted to the search for the meaning of human existence, to do no more than reaffirm its main perspectives and lend their support to its validity. Sade was bold enough to state that when he fearlessly accepted his strange tastes and took them as the point of departure and principle of all reason, he gave philosophy the most solid foundation possible and was thus able to interpret human destiny as a whole. Such a claim is no longer likely to frighten us, but let us frankly recognize that we are only just beginning to take it seriously and for long it alienated from Sade's thought even those interested in Sade the man. In the first place, what was he? A monstrous exception, absolutely outside humanity. As Nodier said, 'the singularity of Sade was that he committed an offence so appalling that it could not be named without danger.' (In a way this was certainly one of Sade's ambitions: to be innocent by dint of guilt and by his abuses to break for ever the norm or law that could have judged him.) Another contemporary of his, Pitou, writes rather alarmingly: 'Justice had confined him to a corner of some prison, and given every inmate permission to get rid of this burden.' When, later on, he was seen as the example of an anomaly shared by others, there was haste to shut him up in the nameless aberration to which only his name could be applied. Even later, when the anomaly was seen as an achievement of Sade's, when he came to be considered as a man sufficiently free to have discovered a new kind of knowledge and, in any case, a man exceptional as much for his destiny as for his preoccupations; and when at last people saw in sadism a possibility involving the whole of humanity, even then Sade's own thought continued to be neglected, as if it was established that there was more originality and truth in sadism than in the way in which Sade himself interpreted it. Now, when we look closer, we see that his thought is essential, and through the contradictions within which it operates, it brings us, on the problem whose name he illustrates, a more significant viewpoint than any which the most trained and enlightened thinking has hitherto allowed us to conceive. This is not to say that his thought is viable. But it shows us that as between normal man, within whom the sadist is imprisoned as in an impasse, and the sadist who treats this impasse as a way out, it is the latter who in the long run is more aware of the truth and logic of his situation and has the deeper understanding of it, to the point of being able to help normal man to understand himself by helping him to modify the conditions of all understanding.

Note

1   Sade has no compunction about admitting it: 'Man, a creature of peculiar tastes, is sick.'

Translated by Bernard Wall

PART II

The Turning-Point

The 1950s were a decade in which Blanchot established himself once and for all as a an original thinker. As a name he found his niche, becoming a regular contributor to the *Nouvelle Nouvelle Revue Française*, which reappeared in January 1953. Prior to that, while continuing to contribute to Bataille's *Critique* and to *Les Temps Modernes*, he briefly wrote a column in 1950 for *France-Observateur* (which eventually became *Le Nouvel Observateur*). From 1953, however, he gradually confined himself to publishing in the *NNRF*, remaining a regular contributor until May 1968, when his last regular article appeared, significantly entitled 'The Very Last Word'. Despite the fact that it is devoted to Kafka's correspondence, there can be little doubt that it signals a break with the *NNRF* and its team that was politically motivated (see Part III for futher details of Blanchot's involvement in the events of May 1968). However, though his place as a writer is henceforth assured, its location still remains problematical. This is first of all because, having distanced himself from Sartre and the committed literature he defended, Blanchot now found himself being outflanked, both as a writer and as a critic, by a whole range of new and original developments in the 1950s: what was called the 'New Novel' on the one hand (that of Beckett, Robbe-Grillet and Butor); but more substantially, the work of Roland Barthes, whose *Writing Degree Zero* appeared in 1953; the renewal of psychoanalysis with the founding of the Société Française de Psychanalyse in 1953 and the rise of Jacques Lacan; and the development of 'Structuralism' in the wake of Claude Lévi-Strauss's *Structural Anthropology* (1958). As these developments extended and came to occupy the forefront of the intellectual scene in France, Blanchot did not remain impervious to them. Included here are two articles devoted to Barthes, **The Pursuit of the Zero Point** and **The Great Hoax** (on *Mythologies*). His *NNRF* chronicles also contain pioneering studies of Robbe-Grillet and Beckett,[1] as well as responses to Lacan and Lévi-Strauss.[2] These chronicles, however, constitute what amounts to a distraction from the course his own writing was following, both fictionally and theoretically, in these years. The turn from the novel to the *récit*, initiated in *Death Sentence* in 1948, was leading to an increasing exhaustion of the space of narrative, first in *When the Time Comes* (1951) then with *The One Who was Standing Apart From Me* (1953). The concomitant shift from third-person to first-person narrative (initiated in *Thomas the Obscure* and tried out in his last novel, *Le Très-Haut*, rendered superfluous all but the most schematic degree of realism in the 'world' provided by literature, the imaginary substance of which was now constituted by the first-person form itself, in its linguistic presence and its assumptions of presentness. On the critical side, his original preoccupation with the possibility of literature had now become, in rigorous dialogue with Heidegger, an austere and sometimes idiosyncratic exploration of what he will term 'the space of literature',[3] in its onto-logical significance, with reference to authors such as Kafka, Mallarmé and Rilke lying entirely outside the prevailing purview.

But if it can be said that Blanchot was becoming established as an influential but enigmatic outsider at this time, the problematical nature of his marginality goes much deeper. For having become established, Blanchot proceeded to negotiate, in a slow, indirect and sometimes painful digression, the impossible fault-line running through what re-mains his only 'world': namely language. His place as an outsider in relation to the writers and the writing around him thus simply reflects what has been the condition of his own subjectivity since his turn to literature in the 1930s. Now as then, his language – be it that of fiction or that of criticism – is a language of the limits of language. It can thus only encounter the language of others at the point where that language comes up short. All of Blanchot's 'criticism', at the time, amounted to a *stricture* upon the unacknowledged limits of what a given writer had said, a designation and denunciation of those limits for the closure they impose, through language, upon an experience that takes place entirely in language. However, behind what for some came to appear the imperi-ous figure writing in the *NNRF*, lay a mind adrift on its own flood, deprived of the residual definition which its opposition to the Sartrean view had allowed, and turning, from a position outside all other prevail-ing tendencies, to face what increasingly neither literature nor its theory could fully accommodate: the impossible, unthinkable division whereby language, the site of both his mind and his 'world', finds itself endlessly outside itself.

The gradual location of this unlocatable outside, both spatially and epistemologically, is ultimately what Blanchot's thinking offers that is most original. In the 1950s, however, the process was affected by what may be termed an essentializing paralysis. The reasons for this are several. For as long as characters such as Thomas, or the Henri Sorge of *Le Très-Haut*, occupied the fictional space which provides his non-fictional writings with their sole reference, that imaginary world, his only world, posessed its own dynamic, which was similar to that which he had de-nounced in *Nausea*, in that it mediated an essentially impossible situation through a recognizable if absurd fictional world. In taking this imaginary world and its language as its referent, therefore, the language of his critical and theoretical writing retained the subsidiary role of affirming and some-times defining its originality, more often than not so as to point up the shortcomings of other fiction and other thinking about fiction. As the triptych of *récits* beginning with *Death Sentence* developed, however, his fiction began to lose its generic features, until, with *The One Who was Standing Apart From Me* (1953), it is reduced to an almost transparent, near-static confrontation between the 'I' who is narrating it and the nameless 'He' that, in 'his' otherness, it takes as its subject. In short, it becomes more than ever before the equivalent of a *pure novel*, in the sense that the flickering alternation between identity and its absence, whose intermittence, arising out of the silencing of the language of the world, generates the entire vast 'world' of *Thomas the Obscure* and is therefore mediated through it for both writer and reader, has here expanded to occupy almost the entire space of fiction, filling it with the endless, protracted and scarcely mediated present of its own paralysing intermittence. Accordingly, his non-fictional writing began to alter course and develop in two directions. The first leads him initially to an extended meditation in response to the question arising out of the experience of his own *récits*: 'Where is Literature Going?' Of the two articles published successively under this title in 1953, I have included the first, which was reprinted in *Le Livre à venir* [*The Book to Come*] in 1959, under the title **The Disappearance of Literature**. They were followed in 1953 by a piece entitled 'Further than the Degree Zero', a response both to their own question and to Roland Barthes, which appears here with the title it has in *Le Livre à venir*: **In Search of the Zero Point**. A third piece, on Beckett, not included here,[4] continued what was becoming a dialogue between titles (it was called 'Where Now? Who Now?') as did the next one, which seems to reply to it: 'The Outside, the Night'. Already though, a second direction was opening up within this enquiry into the future of literature. The first, while implicitly acknowledging the crisis affecting literature in Blanchot's own writing, in so far as it is the sole referent of what he says, side-steps the crisis in its immediacy both by providing lucid accounts of it (and of its limitations) in the work of contemporaries, and by undertaking a wide-ranging exploration of what might be called the literature of the end of literature, particularly the immense novels of Mann, Broch, Hesse and Musil, which could be said to provide compensation, from within another language, for the vastness that his own fictional language, and hence his 'world', have lost.

The second direction is a more 'nocturnal' one. 'The Outside, the Night' marks the culmination of Blanchot's exploration of the space of literature which, beginning in 1951, eventually took the form of the book bearing that title in 1955. On this path, far from side-stepping the impossible condition lying at the heart of his world in so far as it is literature, he advances, using the language of analysis, into a space which, while never ceasing to be that of language, remains utterly inaccessible to language because, as literature, it is for Blanchot the language of the silence which fell on his world and his identity in the late 1930s. This impossible confrontation between two absolutely estranged forms of language, which is rendered acute by the rarefaction of the language of literature that I have referred to, results in a mode of critical discourse for which Blanchot became renowned, not to say notorious, in which, in an obsessive and dirge-like way, he meditated upon being, nothingness and death. By the time he was putting together *The Space of Literature* in 1955, Blanchot had already begun to negotiate an exit from what was becoming an impasse. The original title of the article, included as an annex in *The Space of Literature* under the title 'Hölderlin's Itinerary', was 'The Turning-Point' ('Le Tournant').[5] At this stage, the turn he refers to was still tentative, whence no doubt the change of title. What it announced, however, was something quite radical: no less than a reversal (what Hölderlin calls 'a categoric reversal') within language, of the priority of analysis over literature, and thus, paradoxical as it may seem, the granting of a new lease of life to a language reduced to silence by literature and given voice hitherto only so as to denounce and refuse. In 1955, that reversal was perceptible only within the work *The Space of Literature* itself, and as such it has so far gone almost unnoticed. Yet the fact remains that this extraordinary work seeks, quite simply, to *be* an instance of the literary space it refers to. Though constituted entirely by the language of analysis, its organization and direction are governed in the way those of *Thomas the Obscure* or *The One Who was Standing Apart From Me* are governed: its discourse is the dis-course of the relationship between discourse and what lies beyond the limits of discourse. Eventually, the effects of this reversal transformed Blanchot's writing entirely, abolishing the existing conventional difference between the language of literature and the language of theoretical analysis to produce a single mode of writing (*écriture*), akin to Derrida's, for which the difference between the two becomes both referent and signifier.

The pieces contained in Part II mark out the phases of this radical transformation from the beginning of the 1950s until the end. **Madness par excellence** (1951) and **Artaud** (1956) extend the preoccupation with the extremes of unreason explored so lucidly in the case of Sade and prepare for the encounter with Foucault's thought later in the decade.[6] But whereas, in focusing on the point of indifference and apathy at the heart of Sade's writing, Blanchot was able not only to confront the dark heart of his own experience but also promote a serious reading of his author, by pursuing this line of investigation beyond reason, however aberrant, into the domain of madness itself, he was straining the capacity of theoretical language to remain within the bounds of rational communication. Not surprisingly, a specialist such as Laplanche could only take issue with the view of Hölderlin contained in the 1951 text.[7] More important, however, is the analysis which Jacques Derrida provides in *Writing and Difference*, which was published fifteen years after **Madness par excellence**, where he accuses Blanchot of essentializing madness and so missing what is unique about it.[8] Flanking the period of writing when Blanchot both took this essentialism to an extreme and discovered the exit from it, **Madness *par excellence*** and **Artaud** also point forward to the period covered by Part IV of the *Reader*, by which time a full dialogue had opened up between Blanchot and contemporaries such as Derrida and Foucault.[9]

On emerging from this phase in his writing, the preoccupation with death that so marked it and rendered it pathetic surfaced briefly again, but in a curiously serene way. The titles of two successive articles in 1955, immediately following 'The Turning-Point', revert to that mode of dialogic exchange which in 1953 accompanied Blanchot's descent into literary space. They are 'On the Verge of Death' ('A toute extrémité') and **The Death of the Last Writer,** included here. Now however, in place of an essentializing dirge there is an intriguing parable, in which analysis and imagination explore the new relationship they have acquired in *The Space of Literature*. Thematically and to some extent formally, this text anticipates Blanchot's next *récit*, *Le Dernier homme* (*The Last Man*) (1957), which marks a break with the increasing rarefaction of the *récits* of the triptych, preparing the way for *L'Attente l'Oubli* (*Waiting, Forgetting*) in 1962 and 'The Infinite Conversation' in 1966.[10] At the same time, with its observations on the dictator, it points in a direction that will prove decisive in Blanchot's negotiation of the turning-point which offers him a way out of what has become an impasse: namely a return to politics.

Dionys Mascolo recalled in the following terms a letter he received from Blanchot in 1958:

> In 1958 de Gaulle seized power. With Jean Schuster – from the Surrealist group – I founded an anti-Gaullist journal with the title *Le 14 juillet*. As soon as the first number appeared, Maurice Blanchot, who since the war had not said a word politically, sent me a letter which I found stunning: 'I want you to know that I am in agreement with you. I refuse all the past and accept nothing of the present.'[11]

This rejection of the past is of course a repudiation of his own Rightist politics in the 1930s. It is also, however, from his own point of view something much more delicate: the breaking of a silence which, as I have tried to show, originally opened up the margin in relation to the world to which Blanchot withdrew through writing, and which he made into his own personal–impersonal 'world'. If this breaking of political silence was possible in 1958, it was because of the emergence of a single, original discourse from the turning-point he reached in 1955. Born of a total loss of world in the pre-war years, this discourse is now seeking to forge a relationship to the real world which has survived, in response to what he calls in 1993 'the responsibility and the exigency of politics'.[12] This is clearly a delicate move. **The Great Hoax,** while generous and responsive to Barthes's *Mythologies,* is interesting above all for the new critical perspective on the social world that it opens up for Blanchot. Revealing the continuing complexity of his marginality, it uses Barthes's critique to expose the fact that, despite appearances, the post- war world is dead though formidably powerful, while implicitly contesting Barthes's *theoretical* response to the fraudulence of myth and the tyranny of ideology, by claiming that 'as Roland Barthes knows . . . literature [is] the affirmation most staunchly opposed to myths' (pp. 165–6). Meanwhile, **Essential Perversion,** which appeared in the second number of *Le 14 juillet,* reveals behind it a formidable, doubtless pent-up critical perspicacity concerning the politics of the post-war years and their culmination in de Gaulle's return, a perspicacity whose energy Blanchot will deploy to full effect over the years that follow. For the time being, the world is once again Blanchot's world. He has gone to the limit of the 'world' constituted by language as literature and, reaching a turning-point, brought about a reversal, whereby literature both displaces the language of theoretical analysis yet allows it to develop. The piece entitled **On a Change of Epoch,** which first appeared in 1960, opens with the words ' "Will you allow as a certainty that we are at a turning-point?" ' followed by the reply ' – "If it is a certainty it is not a turning" ' (p. 174). This is the first of an intermittent series of dialogues or 'conversations' (*entretiens*) in which, by means of a plurality of voices without fixed identity, he will explore the exorbitant relationship between the 'world' of language and the world itself. He now finds himself on the brink of a *step (not) beyond* at which he will remain for another decade, during which time his return to the world will prove less than straightforward.

Notes

1 These are to be found in *The Sirens' Song,* tr. Sacha Rabinovitch (Brighton, Harvester Press, 1982).

2 See 'The Speech of Analysis' in *The Infinite Conversation,* tr. Susan Hanson (Minneapolis and London, University of Minnesota Press, 1993), pp. 230–7. This is a piece which originally appeared in the *NNRF* in 1956, under the title 'Freud'. On Lévi-Strauss, see 'L'Homme au point zéro' ['Man at the Zero Point'] in *L'Amitié* (Paris, Gallimard, 1971), pp. 87–97. This text first appeared in the *NNRF* in 1956. A translation of *L'Amitié* is forthcoming from Stanford University Press.

3 See *The Space of Literature,* tr. Ann Smock (Lincoln, University of Nebraska Press, 1982). Published in French as *L'Espace littéraire* (Paris, Gallimard, 1955).

4 It is much translated (see 'Blanchot in English'), and appears in *The Sirens' Song,* pp. 192–8.

5 'Hölderlin's itinerary' in *The Space of Literature*, pp. 269–76.
6 See 'Forgetting, Unreason', in *The Infinite Conversation*, pp. 194–201. This study was originally published in 1961.
7 Jean Laplanche, *Hölderlin et le nom du père* [*Hölderlin and the Name of the Father*] (Paris, Presses Universitaires de France, 1961), Collection 'Quadrige', pp. 10–12.
8 Jacques Derrida, *Writing and Difference*, trans. Alan Bass (London, Routledge & Kegan Paul, 1978), pp. 172–3.
9 The version of *Madness* par excellence included here comes from the new edition of Karl Jaspers's book *Strindberg et Van Gogh, Swedenborg et Hölderlin* published by Les Editions de Minuit in 1970 (the first French edition dates from 1953, Blanchot's review of the German original from 1951). In a 'Note for a New Edition', Blanchot makes a point of problematizing the word *madness*, describing it as 'a word perpetually at odds with itself and interrogative through and through, such that it would put its own possibility in question and, thereby, the possibility of the language that would include it' (see p. 126).
10 Reprinted in *The Infinite Conversation*, pp. xiii–xxiii.
11 Dionys Mascolo, 'Un itinéraire politique [A Political Itinerary]', *Le Magazin Littéraire*, 278 (numéro Marguerite Duras), June 1990, pp. 36–40 (p. 40).
12 'Pour l'amitié', p. 9.

10

Madness *par excellence* (1951)*

Hölderlin's madness does not disconcert medical science. It can be named. The principal features of his character – uncommunicative, unsociable, over-sensitive; the nervous disturbances which as early as adolescence caused him to fear he'd become completely insensible ('I am numb, I am stone'); the sudden onset of the illness which first manifests itself as a sort of emotional and perceptual weariness, then as a slight behavioural instability; eventually the time when these disturbances turn into a crisis and life in the world becomes impossible, without any interruption, however, in intellectual activity (Hölderlin produces a verse translation of Sophocles which Schiller and Goethe find ridiculous, but which posterity judges to be admirable, and he writes his magnificent hymns); finally, when madness sets him definitively apart, his utterly simple life, most often innocent and seemly, though foreign to the world; the mild affectation of his manners, his refusal to see anyone from outside, the flow of his desultory words and even everything that strikes us as a prodigious survival of his past self (the fact that at certain moments his memory, ordinarily so obscured, appears intact, or that he remains capable of profound observations and true reflections, but especially his constant poetic activity – his hand, so highly favoured, which does not cease writing and sometimes writes the most moving poems, even at the end, during his forty years of walled-in, useless life): all these marvels belong to the normal occurrence of schizophrenia.[1]

But what does this expression mean: the normal occurrence of an anomaly? In asylums, Hölderlin is not an exception. Others resemble him. Like him, they have withdrawn from the world and they live far off in the distance – in themselves, it is said, but 'themselves' is still no one. Unbelievably absent, and yet observant, they listen and are capable of understanding; fallen into a stupor, incoherent, they are the least accessible of men, yet sometimes they awake with their reason undiminished. Like Hölderlin, they are affected, ceremonious and persistent in their insularity. If they speak, their language is an unmitigated chaos, or

*   Originally published as 'La folie par excellence', *Critique*, 45 (February 1951), pp. 99–118. Reprinted as the preface to Karl Jaspers, *Strindberg et Van Gogh, Swedenborg et Hölderlin* (Paris, Editions de Minuit, 1953 [1971]), pp. 9–32.

they may write, or draw. Often, though already gravely ill, they demonstrate brilliant and even excessive intellectual qualities; cold reason is all
in them – all too much: sometimes they are remarkable mathematicians
or, in the language of the doctors, inclined to metaphysics, and they
over-exercise their minds (in this respect Hölderlin, who kept working
more and more and surpassing himself at a time when, in the eyes of the
world, he was already mad, is still no exception).

This sketch shows what a standard analysis, determined to grasp
Hölderlin's own special destiny from a general point of view, would be
like. Next, it would turn to a study of the works. Finally, it would have to
attack the problem of mental illnesses and their relations with creative
activity. This problem attracts the imagination, but 'knowledge' has
never been able to get beyond the stage of the most general assertions.
Ever since the romanticism of Lombroso went out of date, people have
been fond of saying that great artists are great in spite of their aberrations. Van Gogh is mad, but to be Van Gogh it does not suffice to be
mad. It is also said – this is the perspective one meets most often, at least
in France[2] – that illness does not create anything, that it never liberates
any but inferior functions which were already involved in the normal
carrying out of conscious life, but were surpassed or 'integrated' in that
process. Depending on the level at which the dissolution sets in, the
disturbances have a greater or lesser effect on the personality as a whole,
but, whatever their significance, they express only the passage from
superior to inferior, from a complete life to a depleted one, from liberty
to anarchy, in other words, to servitude. That is essentially the idea
Bergson proposed as follows: 'In the domain of the mind, illness and
degeneracy create nothing, and the apparently positive characteristics
which give a novel character to the abnormal condition, are nothing but
a deficiency in the normal condition.' Normality is the abnormal surpassed. And the abnormal is an appearance of riches – in the most
favourable cases – which indicates a real impoverishment (even from this
point of view, it would seem more accurate to say only that madness is a
kind of wealth that depends on an impoverishment, a lack).

Such assertions may have their importance, but as soon as one turns to
a particular case, their usefulness proves surprisingly limited.

Similarly, one might wonder if all general conclusions claiming that
illness has an effect on the work of art, that it favours or impedes the
work's development, may not express a puerile conception of knowledge,
the desire to get behind the enigma once and for all and to defeat it by
keeping well away from it. Wouldn't one do better to approach it, to seek
the point where one can see it without making it disappear, where it can
be grasped in its enigmatic purity, just as it is, not wrapped in a vague
secrecy, but in all the clarity with which it confronts anyone who looks at

it straight on, the clarity it also affords this person who looks right at it, desiring to question it without disturbing it and to let himself be questioned by it?

It is this point of view that Karl Jaspers has adopted in the study devoted to Strindberg, Van Gogh and Hölderlin. This work is no longer new, for it first appeared in 1922 in a collection of writings devoted to applied psychiatry. Recently republished, it now includes a preface which makes its purpose explicit and also confirms the reader in the feeling that Jaspers rightly attaches considerable importance to it. Anyone hoping for a discussion – in terms not apt to delude him – of Van Gogh and Hölderlin and the horizon of illness that surrounds their works, will find this book extremely valuable. The fact that a psychiatrist whose works are considered authoritative has become a superlative philosopher would not in itself suffice to justify this interest. But in the present case the deciding factor is that the authority, the specialist who has studied and questioned patients and learned from them as only this direct contact with them permits, has neither bowed before the incomprehensible nor tried to reduce it by understanding it, but has kept trying to understand it as irreducible. Causal explanation is a requirement which admits no exceptions; but what science explains by designating a cause is not necessarily thereby understood. Understanding seeks what escapes it, and advances vigorously and purposefully towards the moment when it is no longer possible: when the fact, in its absolutely concrete and particular reality, becomes obscure and impenetrable. But that extreme limit is not only the end of comprehension, its moment of closure, but also its opening moment, the point at which it illuminates itself against a background of darkness which it has brought to 'light'. The gaze which has succeeded in grasping something original – and this never happens by chance, but requires great patience and great strength, self-renunciation and at the same time the most personal resolve – does not claim to have seen clearly into the origin; it has simply grasped the perspective from which the event must be confronted in order that its most authentic and extreme aspects be preserved.

It seems that his encounter with Van Gogh was an awesome ordeal for Jaspers. This meeting probably took place in 1912, on the occasion of the Cologne exhibition to which he alludes in his book. Van Gogh fascinated him, he says. On confronting Van Gogh he felt, more clearly although no doubt less physically, what he had felt when coming face to face with certain schizophrenics. It is as if an ultimate source of existence made itself momentarily visible, as if hidden reasons for our being were here immediately and fully in force. This is a shock which we cannot bear for long, from which we must remove ourselves, which we find partly expressed, or soothed, in the great works of Van Gogh, not that we can bear it very long in them, either. It is overwhelming, beyond all measure, but it is not our world: a call arises from it, calling into question, calling to existence, acting upon us productively by pressing us to transform ourselves in the vicinity of what is still the inaccessible.

This vital and profound experience explains why such a study, the first that has sought to shed light upon the sickness and the art of Van Gogh – with few documents and a knowledge of the painting that is more intense than broad – gives us such a lively feeling of the creator's truth and of his destiny. Beyond that feeling, we must understand on our own, measuring ourselves against the exceptional. If a person does not initially see the incomparable in Van Gogh's paintings, then explanations will always lead to misunderstandings and all approaches, however cautious and prudent, will be futile.

Jaspers devotes only a few pages to Hölderlin – important ones, granted, expressing the same inquiry – but perhaps Hölderlin is not so close to him; perhaps the experience of reading Hölderlin was less personal. We would like, with his help, to ask why Hölderlin's madness is so absolutely mysterious, or at least try to see what the angle is from which this mystery must appear to us.

To say of Hölderlin that his case is unique is to draw attention only to exterior circumstances. Nietzsche also went mad, but madness was the death which raised or reduced him to silence, whereas in Hölderlin poetry's necessity persisted, asserting itself and even reaching its highest point beyond death. (This is reminiscent of one of the saints, Saint Bonaventura, who, as Chateaubriand recalls for us, was allowed as a favour by God to leave his tomb in order to finish his memoirs – strange favour! the writer must live on to recount his life and then, no doubt, must survive this survival to recount it in turn, and so on endlessly.) Hölderlin does not just undergo a mild derangement, or even one of those serious but partial forms of alienation which respect the appearance of reason or leave the normal modes of expression untouched. From 1801 to 1805 (in the view of psychiatrists) – starting in 1802 (in the eyes of the world) – he is defenceless against the development of the illness which ravages his mind and makes of him the man whom Schelling, on 11 July 1803, speaks of to Hegel: *am Geist ganz zerrüttet* – the illness which, after 1805, renders him similar in appearance to any one of those insane asylum inmates of whom it is said that they have reached the terminal period; and, in fact, they have arrived at the end, they live their end unendingly. However, from 1801 and even from 1802 to 1805, though his person becomes a foreigner to the world, he writes sovereign works which unwaveringly express his poetic mastery and fidelity. After 1805 poetry does not cease to express itself in him, but it lends him a different voice, wherein it is not foreignness and obscurity that make themselves heard, but rather the simplest feelings, in the most regular form, where rhyme once more has a role to play – and this all during the forty years his death lasted. Schwab, who visited him when he was seventy years old, wrote: 'The magical power which poetic form exerted on Hölderlin was prodigious. I never saw a line by him that was bereft of meaning: obscurities, weak points, yes, but the meaning was always alive, and he still wrote such lines when, during the day, no one could extract anything reasonable from him at all.'

But this is only the outer form of the development in question. As far as medical science is concerned, it is all quite 'in order,' or at least not surprising; it corresponds to what is known about the type of patients to whom nightmares lend a pen. If nevertheless one points out that the poems of Hölderlin's madness – those that were written 'at the end' – far from being more incoherent, more extraordinary, are just more simple, in accord with the most spontaneous feelings which the clearest, though infinitely touching words express, then the psychiatrist can only respond: the final state of the illness was in Hölderlin what it is in other schizophrenics, the only difference being that this end was not the end of just any patient, but of a patient whose name was Hölderlin. But he no longer recognized himself by that name, no longer accepted it. Why, though he was similar in every respect to other madmen, was he foreign to himself, and – except in so far as poetry did not cease to find in him a true voice and a genuine heedfulness – foreign even to the poetic form which had been his?

Jaspers thinks the evolution of the illness begins around 1801. As it continues between 1802 and 1805 without, however, provoking any definitive break, the question that arises is this: are the poems written during this period different, do they reveal in their form, their inner movement, their meaning, a change with respect to the works that were written previously, at the furthest remove from madness? Jaspers thinks so. To this change, which tends toward an always greater freedom of rhythm, outside traditional and regulated forms, there corresponds, in Jaspers's view at least, a change in the feeling of poetic vocation. Granted, Hölderlin is aware of the seriousness of his vocation at every period in his life, but for a long time he is no less aware of the obstacles he encounters within himself, outside himself; he sees his own inadequacy, he feels the weight of an unfavourable time, and it is hesitantly that he struggles with a society which burdens him with unworthy tasks. Even philosophy, which he sadly calls the hospital where the unhappy poet can always find an honourable refuge, bewilders him. But later, in the period that borders on schizophrenia, his uncertainties are effaced; the doubting, suffering consciousness becomes a firm and sovereign strength. His work is concerned less with historical time; the solitary in him no longer worries over his solitude, for he dwells now in the world which he creates, a world closer to myth, where an immediate experience of the sacred reaches fulfilment and is expressed. But the mythic vision which comes into focus in the poems at this period is not a late discovery. Hölderlin sensed early on that nature, the truth manifest in ancient Greek civilization and the divine – these three worlds – were one single world where man was to rejoin and recognize himself. But during the period of schizophrenia this view becomes more present, Jaspers thinks: more immediate, more complete, while at the same time passing into a more general, impersonal, objective sphere. It seems that during this period Hölderlin speaks of the divine according to the experience of it which was visited upon him and in the shock which he received from it.

Of all Jaspers's observations, those that bear upon this experience seem to us the most important. During this period, the works of Hölderlin often allude to the vehemence of divine action, to the danger of the poetic task, to the stormy, excessive ardour which the poet must confront, bareheaded and upright, in order that the light of day, calmed in the song, may be communicated to all and become the tranquil light of the community. What Hölderlin says in these works is not an allegorical manner of speaking, but must be understood as the truth, the meaning – gathered up and entrusted to poetic creation – of an immediate experience.

It seems necessary here to distinguish between two aspects. One can speak of an excessive experience, a plenitude of light, too immediate an affirmation of the sacred. With his reserve, that exemplary discretion which never forsook him, Hölderlin twice makes a veiled allusion to this in his letters: in December 1801, to Bühlendorf (apparently he is not yet ill): 'In the past, I exulted to discover a new truth, a greater conception of what surpasses and surrounds us; now, I just fear resembling the ancient Tantalus who received from the gods more blessings than he could stand'; to Bühlendorf again, in December 1802, after his return from France: 'As it is said of heroes, I can well say that Apollo has struck me.'

Apollo struck him, and that means the power of the elemental, contact with the immediate, the unparalleled moment in the relations between the divine and the poet which Goethe did not know. But here is the other aspect: Hölderlin was struck, yet remained standing; he knew a measureless experience which could not possibly leave him intact, and yet for five years he struggled, with sovereign determination, not to preserve himself and save his mere reason, but to raise to poetic form – to expression in its highest and most masterfully controlled sense – what he had grasped, which is beneath any form and lies short of all expression: it is what Heidegger calls 'the shock of chaos which affords nothing to lean on or brace oneself against, the power of the immediate which checks every direct grasp.'

Jaspers evokes the extraordinary tension which many schizophrenics experience in the first stages of the illness: these patients are dominated by overwhelming experiences which threaten to tear apart the personality, or by instances of rupture that are utterly anguishing because they cause the patient to live without interruption in the imminence of total collapse. These patients do not give up, they struggle energetically, and this tension to maintain continuity, meaning and rigour is often very great. Such patients say: 'I feel that I am going to go mad if I relax even for an instant.' But can one compare such a fate with the destiny of Hölderlin, even if he is grappling with an experience which has an analogous form? The reason he saves is not his, but in a way ours, poetic truth; and this effort carried out at the cost of a struggle which we cannot gauge by the difficulties characteristic of the ill – for we do not know even those difficulties – but which we can only suppose to be infinitely great, the greatest possible: such a costly effort does not aim at perpetuating reason's tranquillity, but seeks rather to give form to the extreme, form which has the vigour, the order, the sovereignty of poetic power at its highest point.

Are we here in the presence of the mystery of Hölderlin? Quite possibly, but perhaps we only see it in its fascinating aspect. We can express this aspect as follows, in line, we believe, with Jaspers's thought: at the same time that the illness begins there appears in the work a change which is not foreign to the initial goal, but which contributes something unique and exceptional, revealing a depth, a significance never before glimpsed. This happened because Hölderlin was able to raise to the supreme meaning – which is that of poetry – the experiences of illness, to link them completely to the whole of his spiritual existence and to master them for and through poetic truth. But it happened also because these experiences, suffered in the tumult of illness, were authentic and profound. Now, such experiences are made possible only by schizophrenia. Jaspers sums up as follows his observations about schizophrenia, or at least certain of its forms: in some patients, it seems that a metaphysical profundity is revealed. Everything transpires as if in the life of these beings something manifested itself briefly which exposed them to shuddering dread and ravishment. They lead their lives more passionately, more unconditionally, in an unbridled way; they are more natural but at the same time more irrational, demonic. It is as if there appeared in the world circumscribed by the narrow human horizon a meteor and, often before any witnesses have taken cognizance of the strangeness of this apparition, the demonic existence ends in psychosis or abandons itself to death.

Demonic existence, this tendency of existence to surpass itself eternally – to assert itself relentlessly with regard to the absolute, in dread and ravishment – must be considered separately from psychosis. But everything happens as if the demonic, which in the healthy man is muted, repressed by the concern for a goal, succeeded at the beginning of these illnesses in coming to light, accomplishing a breakthrough. Not that the demonic, the spirit, is sick; it keeps clear of the opposition sick–healthy. But the evolution of the illness affords an opportunity for the breakthrough, even if only for a brief time. It is as if the soul, stirred in all its reaches, shows its depths in this upheaval, and then, when the shock is over, falls into ruins, becomes chaos, becomes stone.

We must add this: what matters is not only that the ground should shudder, but that it should be rich and worthy of the shock. To understand such a development then, it is necessary to turn towards those who can make it manifest: profound artistic geniuses. There is in them a spiritual existence which schizophrenia appropriates, and what is then created, the experiences and the figures, the forms and the language, have their roots in the spirit, seem linked to the truth of this spirit, and cannot rigorously be conceived except in relation to it, and yet, without schizophrenia, they would not have been possible, would not have been able to manifest themselves in this way.

One senses now why the poems of Hölderlin are unique in literature: nothing can compare with them, whereas Goethe, as supreme representative of humanness, can enter into a comparison with others. Jaspers says this forcefully: Goethe is capable of everything, except the late poems of Hölderlin and the paintings of Van Gogh. In such works the creator perishes; not of exertion, not from excessive creative expenditure; but the subjective experiences and emotions, in relation with the upheaval of the soul – the experiences whose expression the artist creates and which he raises to the truth of an objective form – comprise at the same time the development which leads to collapse. Thus we must repeat: schizophrenia is not in itself creative. In creative personalities only, schizophrenia is the condition (if one adopts provisionally the causal point of view) for the opening of the depths. A poet who in good health was sovereign becomes schizophrenic: such a combination has not occurred again. To see it reappear one must turn to other arts, and then the name of the incomparable is Van Gogh.

But can we leave the question there? Perhaps we can go no further; it is even possible that we have gone too far. For the mystery of Hölderlin is coupled now with the mystery of schizophrenia, and the mysterious essence of this illness has come and installed itself behind the mysterious figure of the poet, making the latter appear as the radiance and the figure of the extremely profound and the invisible. Perhaps this is really the case. There is nothing in this manner of seeing that seems to us to diminish the real meaning of the creative force – and besides, it is truth we seek, not an account that respects or exalts. But precisely, hasn't mystery been over-done in a way which has also strained and altered the exact configuration of the occurrence? Every affirmation is difficult here; and yet:

Jaspers thinks that, starting in 1801, the time at which he situates the beginning of the illness's development, Hölderlin's work shows a profound change; this change appears, according to Jaspers, in the inner and the outer style, and also in the new manner – firmer, more immediate – with which the poet asserts himself and affirms (indifferent, from here on, to the world) the mythic reality of the universe he creates. Jaspers sees here the same conjunction that he sees in Van Gogh: between the curve of the disease's evolution and the changes which profoundly modify the creative style.

Perhaps this is true for Van Gogh, but with Hölderlin it is the opposite that strikes one initially. We are necessarily limited to observations on a general scale, but the essential point remains clear, and Hellingrath, whom Jaspers indeed cites, expresses it: there is no turning-point in the work of Hölderlin, but a continuous development, a supreme fidelity to his goals which he approaches little by little through patient investigation and with a control ever greater and better suited to the truth of what he seeks and what he sees. A change can be discerned in Hölderlin's poetry, a decisive moment which puts him face to face with himself and distances him definitively from the form of his youthful works and even of *Hyperion:* it is the moment when he becomes master of the hymn – of what is termed mythic lyricism. The tragedy *Empedocles* was its first expression. But that moment occurs before 1800, and several of the hymns wherein Hölderlin gives form to poetry in its purest intensity are from that period, which continues up to 1801. The hymn *So, on a Holiday* is from 1800; the elegy *Bread and Wine* belongs to the same interval. The hymns which were written a little later show no change from these models. The last works may seem, by the increased tension and abrupt density of their language, to correspond to a new development; but this departure is not altogether new, it simply indicates that Hölderlin's poetic language does not maintain itself at the point it has already attained, but continues its movement, in fidelity to this movement which it carries ever further, as near as possible to its extreme point, thereby realizing what, at a much earlier period and even right from his youth, he had regarded, in his theoretical conceptions, as the essential poetic form.[3]

It is very difficult to discern the changes Jaspers believes he recognizes in what he considers Hölderlin's new consciousness of himself and in the 'mythic vision' which the poems bring close to us. At the most one can acknowledge differences in attitude between the adolescent and the poet who in 1800 reached the maturity of a thirty-year-old – differences which it would be strange not to encounter. They have to do with youth and maturity, with changes in the times and different experiences; they are linked above all with political history which initially grants the young Hölderlin the perspective of a real revolution, whereas, to Hölderlin at thirty, it brings the deep disappointment of a political world closed to the future. The essential difference, however, lies entirely in this fact: at first, Hölderlin knows that poetry is his vocation; he feels himself called and bound to poetry, but he has not yet tested himself in the plenitude of the poem, the hymn. At first, he does not yet exist; later, his existence has the certainty, but also the infinitely dangerous reality of poetic presence;[4] later, in the end, he will once again cease to exist; having passed into transparency he will no longer be Hölderlin, but just the mystery of his name.

In all this what persistently impresses us is not change but rather fidelity, the continuity of Hölderlin's destiny, the movement which raises him to an always clearer consciousness, not more secure, but more sure of the danger which is his and of the truth of what exposes him to danger. Right from the first he expresses the problem which he feels to be at the centre of his life, and indeed to be the heart, not only of his everyday life but also of poetic life – the problem whose contrary demands he must maintain with firm decisiveness. He expresses it in a form which is entirely abstract yet intimately close to him: how can anything finite and determined bear a true relation with the undetermined? On the one hand, the greatest hostility to formlessness, the strongest confidence in the capacity to give form – *der Bildungstrieb* – on the other, the refusal to let himself be determined, *die Flucht bestimmter Verhältnisse*, the renunciation of self, the call of the impersonal, the demand of the All, the origin. This double movement is translated on the everyday plane by Hölderlin's refusal to accept a pastor's tranquil career, a refusal which he resolutely maintains, but not without feeling it none the less as a shortcoming, for he also belongs to the world which respects limits.[5] On the level of poetic conception the demand is asserted in these terms: *die höchste Form im höchsten Leben*, 'in extreme life, supreme form,' or again: *dem Geistigen sein Leben, dem Lebendigen seine Gestalt*, 'to the spirit its life, to the living its form.' Finally, in the sphere of pure poetic truth, the double requirement will be expressed as the destiny of the poet, who becomes the mediator of the sacred, who is in immediate relation with the sacred and envelops it in the silence of the poem in order to calm it and communicate it to men, a communication requiring that the poet remain upright yet be stricken none the less, a mediation which does not merely result in a torn existence, but is this very division of the poet, the effacement at the heart of the word which, existence having disappeared, continues, affirming itself all alone. And, to be sure, it is easy to provide, for this opposition of the two movements concentrated in destiny's unique moment, a translation into psychiatric language as well, or at least into the language which Jaspers has placed at our disposal: then it becomes a matter of the extreme tension he spoke of, between the overwhelming experience and the sovereign will which undertakes to give it form, to unveil it in the creation.

Yes, this is easy to do, it is even necessary (for the mystery lies also in this simultaneous double reading of an event which can be situated neither in one nor the other of its versions). But here is the extraordinary thing: this opposition and this tension, though they may coincide for an instant with the development of the illness, nevertheless have nothing essentially in common with it, since they do not correspond with the moment of its appearance, but belong to the whole of the life whose firmest and most conscious necessity they form – its constantly deepened and sustained purpose, carried all the way to the goal – so that schizophrenia seems to be just the projection of that life at a certain moment and on a certain plane, the point of the trajectory where the truth of existence in its entirety, having become sheer poetic affirmation, sacrifices the normal conditions of possibility, and continues to reverberate from the deep of the impossible as pure language, the nearest to the undetermined and yet the most elevated – language unfounded, founded on the abyss – which is announced also by this fact: that the world is destroyed.

One might be tempted to say the following: in Hölderlin, poetry reached the depth where illness came to take possession of it. Not that illness, even as the experience of the depths, was necessary to explain this development: poetic power met illness at its extreme point, but did not need illness in order to arrive there. This could be expressed in a different way: Hölderlin is the necessity which doomed the poet to collapse, with the consequence that collapse has in turn taken on poetic meaning. All these formulae, however, seem to us insufficient, too general; they still neglect the essential.

One cannot be content to see in Hölderlin's destiny that of an individuality, admirable or sublime, which, having too intensely wanted something great, had to press on all the way to the point where it broke down. His fate is his alone, but he himself belongs to what he expressed and discovered, not as his, but as the truth and affirmation of the poetic essence. He does not seek to realize (to surpass) himself in a Promethean tension that would doom him to catastrophe. It is not his destiny that he decides, but that of poetry; it is truth's meaning that he takes on as a task to accomplish, and that he does accomplish silently, obediently, with all the strengths of mastery and decisiveness, and this movement is not his own, it is the realization of the true which, at a certain point and in spite of him, demands of his personal reason that it become pure impersonal transparency whence there is no return.

We cannot represent even the principal moments of this evolution. Besides, only the poems have any power here to draw us closer to themselves and to a true understanding of them. What must none the less be said is this: in the elegy *Bread and Wine* Hölderlin evokes night, the derangement that night brings, and the light which continues to keep watch over night:

> Indeed it is fitting to consecrate garlands to Night, and song
> because she is sacred to those astray and to the dead,
> though herself she subsists, everlasting, most free in spirit.[6]

Night is sacred because it touches a sacred region of the world – it touches madness and death – but still more deeply because it is united with the spirit's pure freedom. Beyond night, short of day, this freedom is also the original power in us that no force must stop or repress: day or night, it matters not at all:

> The divine fire also by day and by night impels us
> to set out. Then, come! that we may see open spaces
> [*das Offene schauen*].

Das Offene, the Open, the reason why truth opens up, the original upsurging wherein all that appears is lost, but also founded, in the tear of its apparition, and it is there that we must go:

> That we may seek what is proper to us
> One thing remains sure; whether it be towards noon or late
> towards midnight, always a measure subsists
> common to all . . .

Greece is the mythic country of this common measure. Among the Greeks, no one had to bear life alone and the original cry, lived, exchanged, grasped in common became jubilant acclaim, the power of language. Such a moment is no longer ours. We come too late. The gods live, but overhead, in another world. For man is not always able to sustain plenitude. Our life no longer consists in living divine life, but in dreaming it. Thus the meaning of night becomes apparent, and the truth of derangement: it is a power whereby, in an empty time, we can still communicate with the divine.

Only at times can men bear the plenitude of the divine.
Henceforth our life is a dream about them. But to wander astray
helps, like sleep, and need and night make us strong.

These few signs exist only to indicate in what general direction derangement, at an early stage and in one of its aspects, is situated. Error,
straying, the sorrow of wandering are linked to a time in history, the time
of distress when the gods are absent twice over, because they are no
longer here, because they are not here yet. This empty time is that of
error, when we do nothing but err, because we lack the certainty of
presence, of a 'here'.

>   but so much happens
> nothing takes effect, for we are heartless, mere shadows.

It is this absence of vigour, of deep truth that turns us into shadows and
prevents us from making the events that do, nevertheless, occur (such as
the return of the gods), true. And yet, error, 'to wander astray helps,' *das
Irrsal hilft:* error is a moment of truth, it is the waiting which senses truth,
the deep of sleep which is also vigilance, forgetting, the intimacy of
sacred memory. In all of this, derangement is the silence whereby what is
no longer here, the divine, the true, is however here, here in the mode of
waiting, of premonition, and escapes the disfigurement of the false (the
indefiniteness of error preserves us from falsehood, the inauthentic).

>   In holy night,
> where silent Nature thinks out the days to come
> even in most crooked Orcus
> does not a straightness, a rightness prevail?

This I discovered.[7]

That is why the poet must consent to stray: it is necessary that at a
certain moment he become blind. He descends into the night, the night
that provokes the frightful stupor, but his heart remains awake, and this
wakefulness of the heart which precedes the first light and makes it
possible, is the courageous premonition of dawn (*Chiron*).

The poet is the intimacy of distress; he lives the empty time of absence
profoundly, and in him error becomes the deep of derangement, where
he recaptures steadfast strength, the spirit at its freest point. That is the
original power for which he bears witness and to whose possibility he
attests, by founding it. Night in him becomes the intimacy of night,
immune to weariness and tranquil somnolence; and the sterility of the

empty moment becomes the plenitude of waiting, the reality of the future, the premonition which divines and presents.

> But now day breaks. I waited and saw it come
> and what I saw, it is holy, now be my word.[8]

Waiting has ripened time. In the poet waiting is not that of a life plunged in particularity, but that of all nature, of nature as all, the All itself. In the poet, therefore, waiting becomes vision, just as true language makes what it calls come. And what it calls is the day, not the prudent day (*der besonnene Tag*), but the day that rises, that is its own beginning, the origin, the point where the Sacred communicates and founds itself in the firm resolve of language.

The poet is now the relation with the immediate, with the undetermined, the Open, wherein possibility finds its origin, but which is the impossible and the forbidden, to men and to gods: the Sacred. Of course he does not have the power to communicate the incommunicable, but in him – through the relation which he sustains with the gods, with the portion of divinity which resides in time, the deep of pure becoming – the incommunicable becomes what makes communication possible, and the impossible becomes pure power, and the immediate, the freedom of a pure law. The poet is the one in whom transparency becomes daybreak, and his word is what restrains the limitless, what gathers in and contains the infinitely expansive strength of the spirit, on the condition that this word be authentic: the poet's must be language which mediates because in it the mediator disappears, puts an end to his particularity, returns to the element whence he comes: divine sobriety.

The poet – to the extent this can be said – is the locus of a dialectic of derangement, which reproduces and makes possible the very movement of the true, the movement causing error to blossom into truth. When, in the elegy *Bread and Wine*, Hölderlin speaks of poets who, in the time of distress, go from country to country like the priests of Bacchus, this movement, this perpetual passage is the misfortune of wandering, the disquietude of a time without repose, but it is also the fecund migration, the movement that mediates. This wandering makes of rivers a language and of language the dwelling *par excellence*, the power whereby day abides and is our abode.

Hölderlin lives doubly in distress. His time is the empty time when what he has to live is the double absence of the gods, who are no longer *and* who are not yet. Hölderlin is this *and* which indicates the double absence, separation at its most tragic instant, but thereby he is also the *and* which unites and joins, the pure word wherein the emptiness of the past, the emptiness of the future become real presence, the 'now' of breaking day, the irruption of the Sacred. At that instant, distress changes into superabundance, and misfortune is no longer solitude's poverty, but the fact that the poet is all unto himself excessive richness, the wealth of the All which he must bear all alone, since he belongs to the empty present of distress. His solitude is the understanding into which he enters with the future; it is the prophetic isolation which announces time, which makes time,

> too bright, too dazzling this good fortune comes
> and men avoid it

And that is why the days which are 'plenitude of happiness' are also 'plenitude of suffering'.

In the last hymns, those at least which we can regard as the latest in Hölderlin's *oeuvre*, he alludes more and more frequently to the weight he has to bear, the 'heavy burden of logs' which is daylight, the burden of day breaking. And it is always against a background of extraordinary pain that the certainty of dawn is expressed – such is the rigorous regard for poetry which makes it his duty to lose himself in the daylight in order to present the day.

Why this destiny? Why does he have to lose himself? We must say this once again: it is not excess that the gods punish in the man who becomes the mediator; it is not punishment for an offence that sanctions his ruin, but the poet must be ruined in order that in and through him the measureless excess of the divine might become measure, common measure; this destruction, moreover, this effacement at the heart of language is what makes language speak, and causes it to be the sign *par excellence*. 'That which is without language, in him becomes language; that which is general and remains in the form of the unconscious, in him takes the form of the conscious and concrete, but that which is translated into words is for him what cannot possibly be said' (*Empedocles*).

Hölderlin knows this: he himself must become a mute sign, the silence which the truth of language demands in order to attest that what speaks nevertheless does not speak but remains the truth of silence. From the heart of madness, such is 'the last word' which he makes us hear still:

> A sign, that is what we are, deprived of meaning,
> deprived of pain, and we have almost
> lost the power of speech in a foreign land.

Such is the last word, to which we may relate no other utterance save this one, voiced in a hymn composed a little earlier:

And suddenly, she comes, she swoops upon us,
the Stranger,
the Awakener
the voice that forms men.

During his madness, some writers remembered he was still alive and came to see him.[9] Bettina speaks of a madness 'so great, so gentle'; she says to Sinclair, Hölderlin's most faithful friend: 'It is a revelation and my thought is inundated with light. One would think that language, dragging everything with it in a rapid fall, had inundated the senses and, when the cascade drained off, the senses were weakened and the faculties devastated.' – 'That is it, exactly,' said Sinclair. 'To listen to him makes one think of the wind's vehemence, he seems possessed of deep knowledge, then everything disappears for him into darkness, he sinks down.' These accounts are fine and significant, but perhaps one should prefer the simplest words, those of the carpenter Zimmer, at whose home Hölderlin lived from the time of these reports until the end. 'To tell the truth, he is no longer mad at all, not what you'd call mad' (conversation between Zimmer and G. Kühne, 1836). 'He sleeps well, except during the hottest seasons: then, all night he goes up and down the stairs. He doesn't hurt anyone. He serves himself, dresses and goes to bed without any help. He can also think, speak, play music and do everything he used to do. If he has gone crazy, it is from being so learned. All his thoughts have stopped at a point which he keeps turning around and around. It makes you think of a flight of pigeons wheeling round a weather vane on the roof. He can't stand being in the house, he goes into the garden. He bumps into the wall, gathers flowers and herbs, he makes bouquets then throws them away. All day he talks out loud, asking himself questions and answering them, and his answers are hardly ever positive. There is a strong spirit of negation in him. Tired from walking, he retires in his room and declaims at the open window, out into the void. He doesn't know how to unburden himself of his great knowledge. Or else, for hours at his piano' (the Princess von Hombourg had given him a piano from which he had cut certain of the strings), 'ceaselessly, as if he wanted to drag out every last shred of his knowledge, always the same monotonous melody. Then I have to go work with all my might with my plane so I don't go off my head. Often, on the other hand, he plays very well. But what bothers us is the clicking of his fingernails which are too long. The honorifics?' (Hölderlin assigned ceremonial titles to himself and to others.) 'That's his way of keeping people at a distance, for no one should misunderstand, he is after all a free man, and no one should step on his toes.'
Hölderlin died on 7 June 1843. Lotte Zimmer recounts his death as follows: he was suffering from a 'catarrh.' In the evening, he played the

piano some more and came to have supper with his hosts. He went to bed but got up again almost immediately and came to tell the young woman he couldn't stay in bed, he was so frightened. He took some more of the medicine the doctor had given him, but the fear only got greater. 'And then if he didn't die, very gently, almost without a struggle.'

(1953)

Note for a New Edition

These pages – reread after more than two decades more or less without recollection by the one who cannot, however, completely forget having written them and who even recognizes them – strangely resist him even as he reads, resisting his desire to modify them. Why? It's not that they are true, or even untrue, and even if they were, that would of course not be the reason for the resistance, nor could it be caused by their constituting a closed discourse upon which judgements of truth or of value would no longer bear. What is the reason, then? I leave the question as it is. I will pose another one. It is based on this word: madness. In general, we ask ourselves, through the intermediary of experienced practitioners, whether a particular individual falls under the sentence which such a word contains. If we must employ it, we restrict it to an interrogative position. Hölderlin was mad, but was he? Or else we hesitate to give it any specialized meaning, not just because of scientific uncertainty, but because we do not wish, by specifying it, to immobilize it in a determined system of knowledge: even schizophrenia, though evoking the extreme forms of madness, the separation which from the start already distances us from ourselves by separating us from all power of identity, still says too much about all this or pretends to say too much. Madness would thus be a word perpetually at odds with itself and interrogative through and through, such that it would put its own possibility into question and thereby the possibility of the language that would include it, and therefore the interrogation as well, inasmuch as it belongs to the play of language. To say: Hölderlin is mad, is to say: is he mad? But, right from there, it is to make madness so utterly foreign to all affirmation that it could never find any language in which to affirm itself without putting this language under the threat of madness: language gone mad simply inasmuch as it is language. Language gone mad would be, in every utterance, not only the possibility causing it to speak at the risk of making it speechless (a risk without which it would not speak), but the limit which every language holds. Never fixed in advance or theoretically determinable, still less such that one could write: 'there is a limit,' and thus outside all 'there is,' this limit can only be drawn by its violation – the transgression of the untransgressible. Drawn by its violation, it is barred by its inscription. This accounts (perhaps) for the surprise and the fright which seize us when we learn – after Hölderlin and after

Nietzsche – that the Greeks recognized in Dionysos the 'mad god': this is an expression which we render more familiar by interpreting it as: the god who would drive you mad, or the madness that makes one divine. But the 'mad god'? How is it possible to receive what comes upon us with the force of such an anomaly? A god, not distant and responsible for some general insanity, but present, presence itself in its revelatory suddenness – the presence of the mad god?

The 'mad god', come from the Greeks, signals to us, even if we cannot help calming him down into a metaphor, however fearsome a conceptual metaphor it may be, for example, this one: presence is presence only as madness, which leads us to think that presence, the excess which exceeds every present – the withdrawal of the mark which marks the opening – would be the limit that never presents itself, any more than death does. Of course the word 'mad' and the word 'god' do not speak to us in the same way they spoke to the Greeks. But in the difference the same exceptional strangeness is none the less indicated, for the Greeks had no other god able to bear, as if it belonged to his essence, the description 'raving' (mainomenos), without on that account being the god of madness. Such is the enigma Dionysos presents to us: an enigma which, again, we translate in vain by speaking of the god of ecstasy, of terror and of savagery. A mad god, as Hölderlin and as Nietzsche always knew and knew unto no longer knowing, still awakens in men of today an unmasterable thought, whether they understand it as the premonition that even divine order is under the threat of a disturbance which is 'outside' it while none the less belonging to it, or whether this thought causes the presence of the god who is only presence, and the radical exteriority which excludes all presence including that of the god, to surge up, through Dionysos, in an incompatible alliance. The mad god: the presence of the outside which has always already suspended, forbidden presence. Let us say: the enigma of the Eternal Return which, born by Nietzsche, was born no less, perhaps, by Hölderlin.

M.B. (1970)

Notes

1 In another terminology, it would be called prococious dementia with schizophrenic syndrome. This is not the place to recall the debates about these names and what they represent.

2 This point of view is represented, for example, by J. Delay and by H. Ey (under the influence of Jackson). Pierre Janet's attitude is very similar. Psychoanalysis includes other views, however. Jacques Lacan, in his book on paranoia, by no means sees psychosis as deficiency.

3 In the dissertation he composed at the end of his studies, the one which gave him the right to the title *Magister*, writing of Pindar, he defines the supreme form of art in this

manner: *die gedrängte Kurze, der kurze gedrungene Styl,* condensed brevity, brief and dense style.

4 To his friend Neuffer, who is not only a poet, he writes (July 1797): 'You have another, happy activity on which your feeling of being someone rests, so you are not annihilated as soon as you are not a poet.'

5 The danger of passion, he says to his brother (March 1798), lies in its being 'that uncertainty into which the incapacity to adopt a determined behaviour *vis-à-vis* an undetermined object throws us' (the object is unique and yet wants to remain undetermined).

6 Translator's note: English prose translations of Hölderlin's verse are by Michael Hamburger, in *Hölderlin, Selected Verse* (London, Anvil Press Poetry, 1986).

7 *Dies erfuhr ich,* I have experienced this. (*Lebenslauf* (*The Course of Life*), second version.)

8 *So, on a Holiday.*

9 The documents on Hölderlin's life during the years of his madness are almost all gathered together in the book by E. Trummler, *Der Kranke Hölderlin.* Several of these documents have been reproduced in the fine book wherein Pierre Jean Jouve and Pierre Klossowski have translated some of the *Poems of his Madness.*

Translated by Ann Smock

11

Artaud (1956)*

At the age of twenty-seven, Artaud sends some poems to a journal. The editor of the journal politely turns them down. Artaud then tries to explain his attachment to these flawed poems: he is suffering from such a dereliction of thought that he cannot simply disregard the forms, however inadequate, which he has wrought from this central non-existence. What is the worth of the resulting poems? An exchange of letters follows, and Jacques Rivière, the journal's editor, suddenly suggests publishing the letters written about these unpublishable poems, some of which will now, however, appear in an illustrative, documentary capacity. Artaud accepts, on condition that the truth should not be disguised. This is the famous correspondence with Jacques Rivière, an event of great significance.

Was Jacques Rivière aware of the anomaly here? Poems which he considered inadequate and unworthy of publication cease to be so when supplemented by the account of the experience of their inadequacy. As if what they lacked, their failing, became plenitude and consummation by virtue of the overt expression of that lack and the exploration of its necessity. Rather than the work itself, what interests Jacques Rivière is clearly the experience of the work, the movement which leads up to it, and the obscure, anonymous trace which, clumsily, it represents. More than that, this failure, which does not in fact attract him as much as it will subsequently attract those who write and who read, becomes the tangible sign of a central event of the mind, on which Artaud's explanations shed a surprising light. We are coming close, therefore, to a phenomenon to which literature and indeed art seem linked: namely, that there is no poem which does not have its own accomplishment as a poem as its implicit or explicit 'subject', and that the work is at times realized, at times sacrificed, for the sake of the very movement from which it comes.

We may recall here Rilke's letter, written some fifteen years earlier:

* Originally published as 'Artaud' in the *Nouvelle Revue Française*, 47 (November, 1956), pp. 873–81. Reprinted in *Le Livre à venir* (Paris, Gallimard, 1959), pp. 53–62.

The further one goes, the more personal and unique life becomes. The work of art is the necessary, irrefutable, and forever definitive expression of that unique reality . . . It is in this respect that the work affords extraordinary help to whoever is compelled to produce it . . . This gives us a sure explanation of the need to submit ourselves to the most extreme ordeals, but also, it seems, to say nothing of them until we immerse ourselves in our work, not to diminish them by talking about them: what is unique – what no one else could understand or would have the right to understand, that particular derangement which is our own – can only acquire any worth by taking its place in our work [*travail*], there to reveal its law, an original figure which the transparency of art alone makes visible.

Rilke intends, therefore, never to communicate directly the experience from which the work comes, the extreme ordeal whose value and truth only arise from its immersion in the work in which it appears – visible, invisible – in the distant light of art. But did Rilke himself always maintain this discretion? And did he not articulate this discretion precisely to break it even as he safeguarded it, knowing moreover that he did not have the power to break it, no more than anyone has, but could only keep in contact with it? That particular derangement which is our own . . .

The Impossibility of Thinking which is Thought

Jacques Rivière is impeccably understanding, attentive and sensitive. But, in their dialogue, there is a clear degree of misunderstanding which none the less remains difficult to define. Still very patient at this time, Artaud keeps a constant watch over this misunderstanding. He sees that his correspondent is seeking to reassure him by promising that the future will bring the coherence which he lacks, or else by showing him that the mind's frailty is necessary to it. But Artaud does not want to be reassured. He is in contact with something so serious that he cannot bear it to be assuaged. This is because he is also aware of the extraordinary, and for him almost unbelievable, relationship between the ruination of his thought and the poems which he is able to write despite this 'veritable decay'. On the one hand, Jacques Rivière fails to perceive the exceptional nature of the event, and on the other, he fails to see what is extreme about these works of the mind which are produced on the basis of a mental absence.

When he writes to Rivière with a calm penetration which impresses his correspondent, it is no surprise to Artaud to be in command of what he wants to say. It is only his poems which lay him open to the central loss of thought from which he is suffering, an anxiety which he later evokes in trenchant terms and, for instance, in the following form: 'What I am speaking of is the absence of any mental lapse, a sort of imageless, feelingless, cold suffering, which is like an indescribable collision of abject failures.' Why then does he write poems? Why does he not content himself with being a man using language for everyday ends? Everything suggests that poetry, linked for him 'to this sort of erosion, at once essential and ephemeral, of thought', thus essentially involved in this central loss, at the same time gives him the certainty that it alone can be the expression of this loss, and promises, to a certain extent, to save this loss itself, to save his thought in so far as it is lost. So it is that he comes to say, in a fit of impatience and arrogance: 'I am he who has most keenly felt the bewildering disarray of his language in its relation to thought . . . I become lost in my thought exactly as one dreams, as one suddenly drifts off in thought. I am he who knows the innermost recesses of loss.'

He is not concerned with 'thinking clearly, seeing clearly', with having coherent, appropriate, well-expressed thoughts, all of which aptitudes he knows he possesses. And he is annoyed when friends say to him, you think very well, it's a common experience to be lost for words. ('I am sometimes thought to be too brilliant in the expression of my inadequacies, my fundamental failings, and my professed helplessness for this expression to be anything but a fiction, a complete fabrication.') He knows, with the profundity afforded by the experience of suffering, that thinking is not simply having thoughts, and that the thoughts he has only make him feel that he has not 'yet *begun* to think'. This is the dire torment with which he is struggling. It is as if, despite himself and through a woeful error at which he cries out, he has reached the point where thinking is always already not being able to think yet – an 'im-power', as he puts it, which is, as it were, essential to thought, but which makes thought a most painful lack, a debility which immediately radiates out from this centre and, consuming the physical substance of whatever it thinks, at every level divides into so many individual impossibilities.

That poetry is linked to the impossibility of thinking which is thought, this is the truth which cannot disclose itself, because it always turns away, requiring that he experience it beneath the point at which he would really experience it. This is not only a metaphysical difficulty, it is the ravishment of suffering, and poetry is this perpetual suffering, it is 'darkness' and 'the night of the soul', 'the absence of a voice to cry out'.

In a letter written some twenty years later, when he has undergone ordeals which have made him a difficult, fiery being, he says with the utmost simplicity: 'I started out in literature by writing books in order to say that I could not write anything at all. My thought, when I had something to write, was what was most denied me.' And again: 'I have only ever written to say that I have never done anything, never could do anything, and that, when doing something, in reality I was doing nothing. All my work has been and can only ever be built on nothingness.' Common sense immediately poses the question why, if he has nothing to say, does he not in fact say nothing? We may reply that one can content oneself with saying nothing when nothing is merely almost nothing; here, however, we are apparently confronted with such a radical nullity that, in the exorbitance it represents, the danger of which it is the approach, the tension it provokes, it demands, as if it were the price to be freed from it, the formulation of an initial word which would banish all the words which say something. How could someone who has nothing to say not endeavour to begin to speak, to express himself? 'Well, my particular weakness and my *absurdity* consist in wishing at all costs to write and to express myself. I am a man who has endured great mental suffering and, as such, I have the *right* to speak.'

Descriptions of a Struggle

In a movement which bears his own particular authority, Artaud approaches this void which his work – of course, it is not in fact a work[1] – will exalt and denounce, span and safeguard, fill as it is filled by it. At the outset, before this void, he still seeks to recapture some plenitude of which he thinks he is sure, and which would put him in touch with his rich instinctive capacities, the integrity of his feeling and an adherence to the continuity of things which is so consummate that, within him, it is already crystallizing into poetry. He has, he believes he has, this 'deep-seated aptitude', as well as a wealth of forms and words with which to express it. But 'at the point where the soul is preparing to organize its treasures, its discoveries, this revelation, at that unconscious moment when the thing is about to emerge, a superior, malevolent will attacks the soul like an acid, attacks the mass of word and image, attacks the mass of feeling, and, as for me, it leaves me gasping for breath, as if at the very gates of life.'

It is easy to say that Artaud is the victim here of the illusion of the immediate, but everything begins with the way in which he is banished from the immediate which he calls 'life'; this comes about, not through some nostalgic swoon nor through the sensory oblivion of a dream, but rather through a rupture so conspicuous as to introduce into his very core the affirmation of a perpetual deviation which becomes what is most distinctively his own and, so to speak, the shocking revelation of his true nature.

Through an unerring and painful exploration, then, he comes to reverse the terms of this movement, according first place to dispossession instead of the 'immediate totality', whose simple lack this dispossession had at first seemed to be. What comes first is not the plenitude of being, but the breach and the fissure, erosion and laceration, intermittence and gnawing deprivation: being is not being, it is this lack of being, a living lack which makes life faltering, elusive and inexpressible, except through the howl of savage abstinence.

When he thought he had the plenitude of 'indivisible reality', perhaps Artaud was only sensing the shadowy depths projected behind him by this void, since the only evidence within himself of this complete plenitude is the awesome power which denies it, an immense negation which is always at work and capable of an infinite proliferation of emptiness. This is so dreadful a pressure that it ex-presses him, even as it demands that he devote himself entirely to producing and to sustaining its own expression.

However, at the time of the correspondence with Jacques Rivière, when he is still writing poems, he clearly nourishes the hope of becoming a match for himself, an ambition which the poems are destined at once to accomplish and to thwart. At this time, he says that he is 'thinking at a lower level'; 'I am beneath myself, I know – it grieves me.' Later, he remarks: 'It is the contradiction between my deep-seated aptitude and my external difficulties which causes the torment which is killing me.' At this point, his anxiety and guilt stem from thinking beneath his thought, which he therefore keeps behind him, assured of its ideal integrity, so that, in expressing it, if only in a single word, he would reveal himself in his true stature, his own incontrovertible witness. His torment comes from being unable to acquit himself of his thought and, within him, poetry remains the hope, so to speak, of annulling this debt which, however, it can only extend far beyond the limits of his existence. One sometimes has the impression that the correspondence with Jacques Rivière, the latter's disregard for his poetry and his interest in the central turmoil which Artaud is only too inclined to describe, that these displace the centre of his writing. Artaud had been writing against the void, endeavouring to evade it. Now he is writing so as to expose himself to it, to try to express it and draw expression from it.

This displacement of the centre of gravity – which *The Umbilicus of Limbo* and *The Nervometer* represent – is the painful constraint [*exigence*] which compels him, forsaking any illusion, to pay heed henceforth to one point alone: the 'point of absence and futility' around which he wanders with a sort of sarcastic lucidity, a sly good sense, to then be driven by movements of suffering in which one can hear wretchedness cry out, as only Sade before him could cry out, and yet, like Sade again, without any compliance, and with a power to fight which is at all times the equal of the void he is embracing. 'I want to get beyond this point of absence and futility – this stagnation which is debilitating me, making me inferior to everything and everyone. I have no life, I have no life! My inner spark is dead . . . I cannot manage to *think*. Can you understand this emptiness, this intense, lasting nothingness . . . I can go neither forwards nor backwards. I am fixated, confined around a single point which is always the same and which all my books convey.'

We must not make the mistake of reading as analyses of a psychological state the precise, unflinching and detailed descriptions of this which Artaud offers us. Descriptions they are, but of a struggle. This struggle is in part imposed on him. The 'void' is an 'active void'. The 'I cannot think, I cannot manage to think' is an appeal to a deeper thought, a constant pressure, a forgetting which, unable to bear being forgotten, none the less demands a more complete forgetting. Thinking now becomes this step back which is always to be taken. The struggle in which he is always defeated is always engaged again at a lower level. The powerlessness is never powerless enough, the impossible not the impossible. But at the same time, this struggle is also what Artaud wants to pursue, for in this fight he always clings to what he calls 'life' – this explosion, this blazing vitality – which he cannot bear to lose, which he wants to unite with his thought, and which, with a magnificent and dreadful obstinacy, he categorically refuses to distinguish from thought, whereas the latter is nothing other than the 'erosion' of this life, its 'emaciation', the depths of rupture and decay where there is neither life nor thought, but only the torture of a fundamental lack in which the demand issuing from a more decisive negation already asserts itself. And it begins all over again. For Artaud will never accept the scandal of a thought separated from life, even when he is subjected to the most direct, savage experience ever known of the essence of thought understood as separation, of this impossibility which thought asserts against itself as the limit of its infinite power.

Suffering, Thinking

It would be tempting to draw a parallel between what Artaud says and what Hölderlin or Mallarmé tell us, namely that inspiration is first of all that pure point where inspiration is lacking. But we must resist the temptation of these too general affirmations. Each poet says the same, and yet it is not the same, it is, we feel, unique. Artaud's contribution is distinctively his own. What he says is of an intensity which we should be unable to bear. There speaks here a suffering which refuses any depth, any illusions and any hope, but which, by that refusal, offers thought 'the ether of a new space'. When we read these pages, we learn what we never succeed in knowing: that the fact of thinking cannot be anything other than devastating; that what is to be thought is that which, in thought, turns away from thought and inexhaustibly exhausts itself in it; that suffering and thinking are secretly bound together for, if suffering, when it becomes extreme, is such that it destroys the power to suffer, thus, in time, always destroying, ahead of itself, the time in which it might be grasped and accomplished as suffering, then the same is perhaps true of thought. Strange relations. Could it be that extreme thought and extreme suffering open the same horizons? Could suffering, in the end, be thinking?

Note

1 'As I said, no works, no language, no words, no intellect, nothing. Nothing but a splendid Nervometer [*Pèse-Nerfs*].'

Translated by Ian Maclachlan

12

The Disappearance of Literature (1953)*

One sometimes finds oneself asking strange questions such as 'What are the tendencies of contemporary literature? or 'Where is literature going?' Yes indeed, a surprising question, but what is more surprising is that, if there is an answer, it is an easy one: literature is going towards itself, towards its essence which is disappearance.

Those who feel the need of such general assertions can turn to what is called history. It will teach them the meaning of Hegel's famous remark, 'Art is for us a thing of the past,' a remark made audaciously in the face of Goethe, at the time of the blossoming of Romanticism, when music, the plastic arts and poetry were to produce major works. Hegel, opening his lectures on æsthetics with this solemn remark, knows this. He knows that art will not want for works, he admires those of his contemporaries and sometimes prefers them – he can also misjudge them – and yet 'art is for us a thing of the past.' Art is no longer capable of bearing the demand for the absolute. What now counts absolutely is the consummation of the world, the seriousness of action, and the task of real freedom. It is only in the past that art is close to the absolute, and it is only in the Museum that it retains value and power. Or else, and this is a worse disgrace, with us art has fallen to the point of becoming a mere aesthetic pleasure or cultural accessory.

All this is well known. It is a future which is already present. In the world of technology we may continue to praise writers and make painters wealthy, to hold books in esteem and expand our libraries; we may keep a place for art because it is useful or because it is useless, shackle it, diminish it, or leave it free. In this last, favourable case, the fate of art is perhaps least favourable. Apparently, if it is not sovereign, art is nothing. Hence the artist's discomfiture at still being something in a *world which none the less offers no* justification for the artist.

* Originally published as 'Où va la littérature (I)', *Nouvelle Revue Française*, 7 (July 1953), pp. 98–107. Reprinted in *Le Livre à venir* (Paris, Gallimard, 1959), pp. 285–95, under the title 'La disparition de la littérature'.

An Obscure, Tormented Pursuit

This is, crudely, what history says. But if we turn to literature or the arts themselves, what they seem to say is quite different. It is as if, by taking a deeper, more exacting perspective, artistic creation were drawing closer to itself, just as the times, following movements foreign to that creation, are rejecting its importance. The perspective in question is not, however, more overweening: it is *Sturm und Drang* which thinks to exalt poetry through the myths of Prometheus and of Muhammad; what is thereby glorified is not art but the creative artist, the powerful individual, and whenever the artist is preferred to the work, this preference, this glorification of genius signifies a degradation of art, a retreat from its own power, the pursuit of compensatory dreams. These muddled, yet admirable ambitions, such as Novalis expresses mysteriously – 'Klingsohr, the eternal poet, does not die, but remains in the world' – or as Eichendorff evokes – 'The poet is the world's heart' – are in no way similar to those announced after 1850, to choose the date from which the modern world moves more decisively towards its destiny, by the names of Mallarmé and Cézanne, ambitions which are upheld by the movement of all modern art.

Neither Mallarmé nor Cézanne evokes the artist as an individual who is more important and more prominent than anyone else. They do not seek glory, that blazing, radiant void with which artists since the Renaissance have always sought to crown themselves. They are both of them modest, turned not towards themselves, but towards an obscure pursuit, towards an essential concern, the importance of which is not connected with the assertion of their own individuality, nor with the ascent of modern man; it is incomprehensible to almost everyone, and yet they adhere to it with a determination and a methodical force, of which their modesty is but the concealed expression.

Cézanne does not glorify the painter, nor even, except through his work, painting, and Van Gogh remarks, 'I am not an artist – how crude it is even to think it of oneself,' adding, 'I say this to demonstrate how foolish it seems to me to speak of gifted and ungifted artists.' In the poem, Mallarmé has the presentiment of a work which does not refer back to anyone who made it, the presentiment of a decision which does not rely on the initiative of any particular, privileged individual. And, contrary to the ancient notion according to which the poet says, 'it is not I who speak, it is the god speaking in me,' this independence of the poem does not indicate a proud transcendence which would make literary creation the equivalent of the creation of a world by some demiurge; it does not even signify the eternity or immutability of the poetic sphere, but quite to the contrary it reverses the values we customarily accord to the words 'making' or 'doing' [*faire*] and 'being'.

This surprising transformation in modern art, occurring at the very time when history is suggesting quite different tasks and goals for humanity, could appear to be a reaction against these tasks and goals, an empty effort to affirm and to justify. This is untrue, or is at best only superficially true. It does happen that writers and artists respond to the call of the community with a frivolous retrenchment, and to their century's compelling tasks with the naïve glorification of their idle secrets, or with a despair which causes them to recognize themselves, as did Flaubert, in the condition they reject. Or else they think they can save art by enclosing it within themselves, art then simply being a mood and 'poetic' meaning 'subjective'.

But precisely with Mallarmé and with Cézanne, to use these two names symbolically, art does not seek such meagre havens. What counts for Cézanne is 'achievement', not Cézanne's moods. Art is powerfully directed towards the work, and the work of art, the work which has its origin in art, shows itself to be an affirmation quite different from those works which may be gauged in terms of labour, value and exchange – different, but not their opposite: art does not deny the modern world, nor the world of technology, nor the effort to liberate and transform which relies on that technology, but it expresses and perhaps establishes relations which *precede* any objective, technological achievement.

This is an obscure, difficult, anguished pursuit, an essentially perilous experience in which art, the work, and the truth and essence of language are questioned and placed at risk. This is why, during the same period, literature depreciates, is stretched on Ixion's wheel, and the poet becomes the bitter enemy of the figure of the poet. At first sight, this crisis and this criticism simply remind the artist of his condition in the powerful civilization in which he plays so small a part. Both crisis and criticism seem to come from the world, from social and political reality, and seem to submit literature to a judgement which abases it in the name of history: it is history which criticizes literature and pushes the poet aside in favour of the publicist whose task serves the interests of the time. This is true, but, in a remarkable coincidence, this extraneous criticism echoes the experience peculiar to literature and art, which they effect on their own account, and which lays them open to radical questioning. The sceptical genius of Valéry and the steadfastness of his *partis pris* contribute to this questioning just as much as do the violent assertions of surrealism. Similarly, it would seem that there is almost nothing in common between Valéry, Hofmannsthal and Rilke, and yet Valéry writes, 'My poetry has had no other interest for me than to suggest thoughts on the poet' and Hofmannsthal, 'The innermost core of a poet's

essence is nothing other than the fact of knowing himself to be a poet.'
As for Rilke, it would not be a misrepresentation of him to say of his
poetry that it is the lyrical theory of the poetic act. In all three cases, the
poem is the depth which opens onto the experience which makes it
possible, the strange movement which goes from the work towards the
origin of the work, the work itself become the restless, infinite pursuit of
its own source.

It must be added that, while historical circumstances exert their pressure on such movements to the extent of appearing to govern them – so it
is said that the writer, who takes as the object of his activity the uncertain
essence of that activity, is merely reflecting what is becoming his own
precarious social position – they are not on their own capable of explaining the significance of this pursuit. We have just cited three names which
are roughly contemporary with each other and with major social transformations. We chose the date of 1850 because the 1848 Revolution marks
the moment at which Europe began to open up to the full development
of the forces shaping it. But everything we have said about Valéry,
Hofmannsthal and Rilke could have been said, and at a much deeper
level, about Hölderlin, who nevertheless precedes them by a century, and
for whom the poem is essentially the poem of the poem (more or less as
Heidegger remarks). The poet of the poet, the poet with whom the
possibility, the impossibility of singing itself becomes the song, such is
Hölderlin and such, to cite a new name, a century and a half younger, is
René Char, who echoes Hölderlin and, in this echo, evokes for us a very
different notion of duration from that grasped by a simple historical
analysis. This does not mean that art, works of art, much less artists,
oblivious of time, attain a reality which eludes time. Even the 'absence of
time' towards which we are led by the literary experience is in no sense a
region of timelessness, and if, through the work of art, we are brought
back to the upheaval of a true initiative – to a new, unstable manifestation
of the fact of being – this beginning speaks to us in the very heart of
history, in a way which perhaps opens the path to inaugural historical
possibilities. All of these problems are obscure. To present them as clear,
or even as susceptible to clear formulation, could only lead us into
acrobatics of writing and deprive us of the help which these problems can
offer, namely to resist us forcefully.

What we can sense is that the surprising question, 'Where is literature
going?' doubtless expects its response from history, a response which to
some extent it has already been given; but at the same time, by a ruse in
which the resources of our ignorance are in play, it turns out that in this
question literature, taking advantage of history which it anticipates,
questions itself and indicates, not a response by any means, but the
deeper, more essential sense of the particular question it harbours.

Literature, the Work, Experience

We are speaking of literature, the work, and experience; what do these words express? It would seem wrong to see in the art of today a simple occasion for subjective experiences or a dependence on the aesthetic, and yet, in respect of art, we constantly speak of experience. It would seem right to see in the concern which drives artists and writers, not the pursuit of their own interests, but a concern which demands to express itself in works. The works ought, then, to play the most important part. But is this the case? Not at all. What attracts the writer, what stirs the artist, is not directly the work, but its pursuit, the movement which leads to it, the approach of what makes the work possible: art, literature and what these two words conceal. So it is that the painter prefers the various states of a painting to the painting itself, and the writer often wishes to accomplish almost nothing, leaving in fragmentary state a hundred tales whose interest had been to lead him to a certain point and which he has to abandon in order to try to go beyond that point. And so it is that, in a further surprising coincidence, Valéry and Kafka, separated by almost everything, close to each other in their sole concern to write rigorously, come together in asserting that, 'All my work is nothing but an exercise.'

Similarly, we may feel annoyed to see, taking the place of so-called literary works, an ever greater mass of texts which, in the guise of documents, chronicles, remarks in almost rough form, seem to be oblivious of any literary intention. We may say that this has nothing to do with the creation of artistic objects, or that these are manifestations of a false realism. But what do we know of this? What do we know of this approach, even if unsuccessful, to a region which eludes the grasp of ordinary culture? Why should not this anonymous, author-less speech [*parole*], which does not take the form of books, which passes and wishes to pass, alert us to something important, about which what we call literature also wishes to speak to us? And is it not remarkable, but enigmatic, remarkable in the manner of an enigma, that this very word 'literature', a belated word, a word without honour, which is mainly of use for manuals, which accompanies the ever more encroaching advance of the prose writers, and refers, not to literature, but to its shortcomings and excesses – as if these were essential to it – is it not remarkable that this word should become, at a time when contention is growing more intense, when genres are becoming more diffuse and forms dissipated, at a time when, on the one hand, the world no longer needs literature, and on the other, each book appears alien to all the others and indifferent to the reality of genres, at a time when, moreover, what seems to be expressed in works is not the eternal verities, not types and characters, but a demand which stands against the order of essences, that at such a time literature, thus contested as a worthwhile activity, as the unity of genres, as a world which might offer refuge to the ideal and the essential, should become the increasingly present, albeit hidden, preoccupation of those who write and, in this preoccupation, should offer itself to them as that which has to reveal itself in its 'essence'.

A preoccupation in which, it is true, what is at issue is perhaps literature, but not as an assured, definite reality, an ensemble of forms, nor even a tangible mode of activity, but rather as that which never directly reveals, confirms, or justifies itself, which one only approaches by turning away from it, which one only grasps when one goes beyond it, in a pursuit which must in no way be concerned with literature, with what it 'essentially' is, but which, on the contrary, is concerned with diminishing it, neutralizing it, or, more accurately, with descending, in a movement which ultimately eludes and disregards it, to a point where all that seems to speak is impersonal neutrality.

Non-literature

These are necessary contradictions. All that matters is the work, the affirmation which is in the work, the poem in its compact singularity, the painting in its own space. All that matters is the work, but ultimately the work is only there to lead to the pursuit of the work; the work is the movement which takes us towards the pure point of inspiration from which it comes and which it seems it can only reach by disappearing.

All that matters is the book, such as it is, far away from genres, outside the categories – prose, poetry, novel, chronicle – with which it refuses to align itself, and whose power to impose its place and determine its form it denies. A book no longer belongs to a genre, every book pertains to literature alone, as if literature held in advance, in their generality, the secrets and formulae which alone allow what is written to be accorded the reality of a book. It would seem, therefore, as if, the genres having dissolved, literature alone were asserting itself, shining alone in the mysterious light which it propagates and which each literary creation multiplies and reflects back on it – as if, then, there were an 'essence' of literature.

But the essence of literature is precisely to evade any essential characterization, any affirmation which would stabilize or even realize it: it is never already there, it is always to be rediscovered or reinvented. It is never even certain that the words 'literature' or 'art' correspond to anything real, anything possible, or anything important. It has been said that being an artist is never knowing that there is already art, nor indeed that there is already a world. The painter does, no doubt, go to the museum and so has a certain awareness of the reality of painting: he knows painting, but his canvas does not, knowing rather that painting is impossible, unreal, unrealizable. Whoever affirms literature in itself affirms nothing. Whoever seeks it only seeks that which slips away; whoever finds it only finds what falls short of or, worse still, lies beyond literature. This is why, in the end, it is non-literature which each book pursues as the essence of what it loves and passionately wishes to discover.

We must not, therefore, say that every book pertains to literature alone, but rather that each book determines it absolutely. We must not say that every work draws its reality and value from its power to conform to the essence of literature, nor even from its right to reveal or affirm this essence. For a work can never take as its object the question which sustains it. A painting could never so much as begin if it set out to make painting visible. It may be that every writer feels as if he is called upon alone, through his own ignorance, to answer for literature, for its future which is not only a historical question, but, across history, is the movement through which, while necessarily 'going' outside itself, literature none the less means to 'come round' to itself, to what essentially it is. It may be that being a writer is a vocation to reply to that question which anyone who writes has the duty to maintain with passion, truth and mastery, and which none the less he can never discover, least of all in setting out to reply to it – the question to which he can at most give an indirect response through the work, the work of which one is never master, never sure, the work which will not answer to anything but itself and which makes art present only where art conceals itself and disappears. Why is this?

Translated by Ian Maclachlan

13

The Pursuit of the Zero Point (1953)*

That books, writings, language are destined for transformations to which, unknown to us, our customs are already opening up, but which our traditions still refuse; that libraries strike us by their otherworldly appearance, as if, after a cosmic journey, we suddenly discovered there, with curiosity, surprise and respect, the vestiges of another, more ancient planet, frozen in an eternity of silence – one would have to be most unfamiliar with oneself not to notice these things. Reading, writing – we have no doubt that these words are called upon to play a very different role in our minds from the one they still played at the beginning of this century: this is obvious, we learn it from any radio set, any television screen, and still more from that murmur around us, that anonymous, continuous humming within us, that marvellous, unheard, agile, tireless speech which provides us at every moment with an instant, universal knowledge, and makes us the pure point of passage of a movement by which each of us has, in advance, always already taken the place of everyone.

These prognoses are within our grasp. But what is more surprising is that, well before the inventions of technology, the use of radio waves and the appeal of images, one would only have had to attend to the pronouncements of Hölderlin or Mallarmé to discover the direction and extent of these changes which nowadays we calmly take on board. In order to arrive at themselves, poetry and art, in a movement which has to do with the times, but also through demands of their own which have shaped this movement, have proposed and affirmed much greater upheavals than those whose striking manifestations we now see, on another level, in our everyday amenities. Reading, writing, speaking, these words, understood in terms of the experience in which they are accomplished, give us an inkling, according to Mallarmé, that, in the world, we neither speak, nor write, nor read. This is not a critical judgement. That speaking, writing, that the demands contained in these words are no longer adapted to the modes of comprehension necessary for work and specialized know-

* Originally published as 'Plus loin que le degré zéro', *Nouvelle Revue Française*, 9 (September 1953), pp. 485–94. Reprinted in *Le Livre à venir* (Paris, Gallimard, 1959), pp. 296–307, under the title 'Recherche du point zéro'.

ledge to be effective, that speech may no longer be indispensable to our understanding one another, this indicates, not the destitution of this world without language, but rather the choice that it has made and the vigour of this choice.

Dispersion

Mallarmé separates the regions in question with remarkable brutality. On one hand, there is useful speech, an instrument or a means, the language of action, of work, of logic and knowledge, a language which transmits immediately and which, like any good tool, disappears with regularity of use. On the other hand, there is the speech of the poem and of literature, where speaking is no longer a transitory, subordinate and habitual means, but instead seeks realization in an experience peculiar to it. This brutal separation, this division of realms which endeavours rigorously to determine the respective spheres, should at least have helped literature to gather around itself, to make it more visible by giving it a distinctive, unifying language. But we have witnessed the opposite phenomenon. Until the nineteenth century, the art of writing forms a stable horizon which its practitioners do not contemplate ruining or exceeding. Writing in verse is the bedrock of literary activity, and nothing is more conspicuous than verse, even if poetry remains elusive within this rigid frame. It is tempting to say that in France at least, and probably in any classical period of writing, poetry is given the task of gathering within itself the risks of art, thereby saving language from the dangers to which literature subjects it: common understanding is protected from poetry as the latter is made very visible, very distinctive, a domain enclosed by high walls – and at the same time poetry is protected from itself by being firmly delineated and accorded such precise rules that poetic indeterminacy is disarmed as a result. Voltaire still writes in verse perhaps in order that, in his prose, he should only be the purest, most effective prose-writer. Chateaubriand, who can only be a poet in prose, begins to transform prose into art. His language becomes speech from beyond the grave.

Literature is only a domain of coherence and a common region as long as it does not exist, as long as it does not exist for itself and conceals itself. As soon as it appears in the distant presentiment of what it seems to be, it flies into pieces, it sets out on the path to dispersion in which it refuses to be recognized by precise, identifiable signs. As, at the same time, traditions remain powerful, humanism continues to seek the assistance of art, prose still wants to fight for the world, there results a confusion in which, at first sight, one cannot reasonably try to decide what is at issue. In general, limited causes and secondary explanations are found for this disintegration. The blame is laid on individualism: each writer is said to write in accordance with a self whose purpose is to be distinct from all others.[1] Blame is also laid on the loss of common values, the profound divisions in the world, the break-up of ideals and of reason.[2] Or else, to re-establish a little clarity, the distinctions of prose and poetry are restored: poetry is consigned to the disorder of the unpredictable, but it is noted that the novel nowadays dominates literature, and that the latter, in the novel form, remains faithful to the everyday, social designs of language, remains within the limits of a circumscribed genre, capable of channelling and specifying it. The novel is often said to be monstrous but, with a few exceptions, it is a well-bred, highly domesticated monster. The novel is identifiable by clear signs which do not lend themselves to misunderstanding. The predominance of the novel, with its apparent freedom, its audacities which do not imperil the genre, the unobtrusive reliability of its conventions, the richness of its humanist content, is, as formerly the predominance of formally regular poetry, the expression of the need we feel to protect ourselves from what makes literature dangerous: as if, at the same time as its poison, literature urgently sought to dispense for our benefit the antidote which alone allows its untroubled, lasting consumption. But perhaps what makes literature innocuous also spells its doom.

In answer to this quest for subordinate causes, we must reply that the break-up of literature is essential and that the dispersion to which it is succumbing also marks the moment at which it approaches itself. It is not the individuality of writers which explains why writing is taking a position outside any stable horizon, in a fundamentally disunified region. Deeper than the diversity of temperaments, moods, or even existences is the tension of a pursuit which places everything back into question. More decisive than the rending apart of worlds is the demand which rejects even the horizon of a world. Neither should the word 'experience' lead us to believe that, if literature today appears to us to be in a state of dispersion unknown in previous eras, it does so because of that licence which makes it the site of constantly renewed experiments. No doubt, the feeling of limitless freedom seems to drive the hand which seeks nowadays to write: we think we can say everything and say it in every way, and so nothing holds us back, everything is at our disposal. Everything is a great deal, is it not? But ultimately everything is very little, and anyone who begins to write, in the insouciance which bestows mastery of the infinite, finally notices that, at best, he has devoted all his efforts simply to pursuing a single point.

Literature is no more varied than it used to be; it is perhaps more monotonous, as one might say of the night that it is more monotonous than the day. It is not disunified because it has been left to a greater degree at the mercy of the arbitrariness of those who write, or because, being outside the genres, rules and traditions, it allows free reign to a multiplicity of chaotic ventures. It is not the diversity, extravagance and anarchy of its experiments which make literature a dispersed world. We must put it differently and say that the experience of literature is the very ordeal of dispersion, it is the approach of that which escapes unity, an experience of that which is without understanding, without harmony, without legitimacy – error and the outside, the ungraspable and the irregular.

Language, Style, Writing

In a recent essay – one of the few books in which the future of letters is inscribed – Roland Barthes distinguishes between language, style and writing.[3] Language is the state of common speech as it is given to each of us together, at a certain moment in time, and according to our particular part of the world; it is shared by writers and non-writers alike. No matter whether one endures it with difficulty, unerringly welcomes it, or deliberately refuses it, language is there, a testimony to the historical state into which we are thrown, surrounding and exceeding us – it is for all of us the immediate, although fashioned profoundly by history and very remote from any beginning. As for style, it is the dark side, linked with the mysteries of blood and instinct, a violent depth, a density of images, the language of solitude in which there blindly speak the predilections of our bodies, of our desires, and of our secret time which is inscrutable to us. The writer, unable to choose his language, can no more choose his style, this necessity of his mood, this rage within him, this tumult or this tension, slowness or speed, which come to him from a deep intimacy with himself, about which he knows almost nothing, and which give his language as distinctive an accent as his own recognizable demeanour gives his face. All of this is still not what we must call literature.

Literature begins with writing. Writing is the collection of rituals, the conspicuous or discreet ceremonial which, independent of what one wants to express and the way one expresses it, heralds the event that what is written belongs to literature and that whoever reads it is reading literature. This is not rhetoric, or it is rhetoric of a particular sort, destined to convey to us that we have entered that enclosed space, separate and sacred, which is the space of literature. For instance, as Barthes shows in a chapter which is rich in reflections on the novel, the past historic tense, which is alien to the spoken language, serves to signal the art of narrative; it indicates in advance that the author has accepted the linear, logical time that is narration – narration which, clarifying the sphere of chance, establishes the security of a firmly circumscribed story which, having had a beginning, will assuredly lead to the happiness of an ending, even if the latter should be unhappy. The past historic or indeed the preference accorded to the third person says to us, this is a novel, just as the canvas, paints and, formerly, perspective used to say, that is painting.

Roland Barthes is heading towards this observation: there was a time when writing, being the same for everyone, met with innocent assent. At that time, all writers had but one concern: to write well, that is, to take the common language to a higher level of perfection or of harmony with what they were trying to say; there was for one and all a unity of intention, an identical doctrine. The same is no longer true today. Writers, who are distinct from one another in their instinctive language, are even more opposed in their attitude towards literary ceremonial: if to write is to enter a *templum* which imposes on us, independent of the language which is ours by birthright and by organic inevitability, a certain number of habits, an implicit religion, a murmur which alters in advance what we are able to say, loading the latter with intentions which are all the more effective for being tacit, then to write is, first of all, to wish to destroy the temple before erecting it; it is at least, before crossing its threshold, to ponder the constraints of such a place, the original misdeed which the decision to confine oneself there will constitute. To write is ultimately to refuse to cross the threshold, to refuse to 'write'.

We can thus grasp, can more clearly discern the loss of unity from which current literature is suffering, or on which it prides itself. Each writer makes writing his problem, and makes this problem the object of a decision which he can change. It is not only in their vision of the world, the features of their language, the fortuities of talent, or their particular experiences, that writers part company: as soon as literature manifests itself as a milieu in which everything is transformed (and embellished), as soon as one realizes that this ambience is not a void, that this brightness does not simply illuminate, but distorts by shedding the light of convention on objects, as soon as one senses that literary writing – genres, signs, the use of the past historic and of the third person – is not merely a transparent form, but a world apart where idols reign, where preconceptions lie dormant, and where, invisibly, the powers which falsify everything reside, then it becomes imperative for everyone to try to free themselves from this world, and it becomes tempting for everyone to ruin it in order to reconstruct it free of all previous use, or better still to leave the space empty. To write without 'writing', to bring literature to that point of absence where it disappears, where we no longer have to fear its secrets which are lies, that is 'writing degree zero', the neutrality

which every writer deliberately or unwittingly seeks, and which leads
some to silence.

A Total Experience

This way of seeing things[4] should help us to gain a better grasp of the
extent and gravity of the problem which confronts us. It appears at first,
if one rigorously follows the analysis, that, free from writing, from this
ritual language with its habits, its images, its emblems, its well-tried
formulae, of which other civilizations – Chinese, for instance – seem to
offer far more accomplished models, the writer returns to an immediate
language or to that solitary language which instinctively speaks within
him. But what would this 'return' mean? This immediate language is not
immediate, it is laden with history and even with literature, and above all,
this being the essential point, as soon as anyone who writes tries to grasp
it, it changes in nature beneath his hand. Here we may recognize the
'leap' which literature is. The common language is at our disposal and
places the real at our disposal, it names things, gives us them by setting
them aside, and itself disappears in so doing, always blank and unappar-
ent. But once it has become the language of 'fiction' it falls out of use,
becomes uncommon, and as for what it designates, we still think, no
doubt, that we apprehend it as in everyday life, much more easily even,
since now it is enough to write the word 'bread' or the word 'angel'
immediately to have at our disposal, to do with as we will, the beauty of
the angel and the flavour of the bread – indeed, but on what conditions?
On the condition that the world in which alone it is given to us to use
things should first of all have collapsed, that things should have grown
infinitely distant from themselves, should once again have become the
unavailable remoteness of the image, and also that I should no longer be
myself and should no longer be able to say 'me'. A fearsome transformation. What I have through fiction, I have, but on the condition of being
it, and the being by which I approach it is what parts me from myself and
from any being, just as it makes language, no longer that which speaks,
but that which is – language become the workless depth of being, the
milieu in which the name becomes being, but neither signifies nor
reveals.

A fearsome transformation, elusive moreover, and first of all imperceptible, constantly slipping away. The 'leap' is immediate, but the immediate eludes any verification. We only know we are writing when the leap
has already been accomplished, but to accomplish it, one must first write,
write endlessly, write from infinity. To seek to recover the innocence or
naturalness of the spoken language (as Raymond Queneau invites us to

do, not without irony), is to maintain that this transformation could be calculated in the manner of an index of refraction, as if we were dealing with a phenomenon fixed in the world of things, whereas it is in fact the very void of this world, a call one only hears if one is oneself changed, a decision which consigns anyone who takes it on to the realm of the undecided. And what Roland Barthes calls style, visceral, instinctive language, a language inseparable from our secret depths, that which, therefore, should be closest to us, is also what is least accessible to us, if it is true that, to regain hold of it, we would not only have to put aside literary language, but also to encounter and then to silence the empty depths of ceaseless speech, what Eluard perhaps had in mind when he spoke of 'uninterrupted poetry'.

Proust first of all speaks the language of La Bruyère, of Flaubert: this is the alienation of writing, from which he gradually frees himself by writing constantly, letters above all. It is, it seems, by writing 'so many letters' to 'so many people' that he edges towards the movement of writing which will become his own, revealing the form which nowadays we admire as marvellously Proustian and which naïve scholars relate to its organic structure. But who is it that speaks here? Is it Proust, the worldly Proust, the one who has the vainest social ambitions and a hankering for the Académie Française, the one who admires Anatole France, the one who writes the *Figaro*'s society column? Is it the Proust who has vices, who leads an abnormal life, who takes pleasure in torturing rats in a cage? Is it the Proust who is already dead, motionless, buried, the one whom his friends no longer recognize, a stranger to himself, nothing other than a hand which writes, which 'writes every day, at every hour, all the time' and as if outside time, a hand which no longer belongs to anyone? We say Proust, but we sense strongly that it is the wholly other which writes, not simply someone other, but the very demand to write, a demand which employs the name of Proust, but does not express Proust, which only expresses him by disappropriating him, by making him Other.

The experience which literature is is a total experience, a question which admits no limits, which refuses to be stabilized or reduced, for example, to a question of language (unless within that perspective alone everything begins to tremble). It is the very passion of its own question and forces whoever it attracts to enter completely into this question. It is therefore not enough for it to make suspect literary ceremonial, hallowed forms, ritual images, fine language, and conventions of rhyme, measure and narrative. When one encounters a novel written according to the conventions of the past historic and the third person, one has, of course, in no way encountered 'literature', but no more has one encountered what would keep literature at bay or thwart it, nothing, in truth, which prevents or ensures its approach. Hundreds of novels, such as are written today, written masterfully or carelessly, in a fine style, enthralling, boring, are all of them equally foreign to literature, and this in turn is no more attributable to mastery than to carelessness, to casual language than to elevated language.

In directing us, through an examination of great importance, towards what he calls the zero of writing, Roland Barthes has also perhaps indicated the moment at which literature could grasp itself. But this is because, at this point, it would no longer simply be a blank, absent, neutral writing, it would be the very experience of 'neutrality', which one never hears, for, when neutrality speaks, only he who imposes silence on it prepares the conditions of hearing, and yet what there is to hear is that neutral speech, that which has always been said, cannot stop saying itself, and cannot be heard, a torment which the pages of Samuel Beckett bring us closer to sensing.

Notes

1 There are none the less complaints about the monotony of talent and the uniformity or impersonality of works.
2 But there is virtually nothing which, in literary terms, distinguishes the Catholic novelist from the Communist novelist, and the Nobel prize and the Stalin prize reward the same practices, the same literary signs.
3 Roland Barthes, *Writing Degree Zero*
4 The important point is that the same effort has to be carried out with respect to literature as Marx carried out with respect to society. Literature is alienated, and is so in part because the society to which it is related is founded on the alienation of humanity; it is so also as a result of demands which it betrays, but nowadays it betrays them in both senses of the term: it acknowledges them and falls short of them in purportedly denouncing itself.

Translated by Ian Maclachlan

14

The Death of the Last Writer (1955)*

Let us imagine the last remaining writer, upon whose death, without anyone realizing it, the minor mystery of writing would also be lost. To add something fantastical to the situation, let us suppose that this Rimbaud-like character, who is even more mythical than the real one, hears the speaking that dies with him fall silent too. And let us finally suppose that this irrevocable end is somehow noticed within the world and orbit of human civilizations. What would be the outcome? Apparently there would be a massive silence. This is usually what people say, out of politeness, whenever a writer dies: a voice has fallen silent, a way of thinking has faded away. What silence there would be, then, if nobody were to speak any longer in that lofty manner which is the speaking of works of art and the distant echo of their fame.

Let us pursue this dream. Epochs such as this have existed, will exist, and fictions of this kind turn into reality at certain moments in the life of each one of us. Contrary to all common sense, on the day when the light is extinguished, the age without speech will announce its coming, not in silence, but by the retreat of silence, by a break in the density of silence and the arrival of a new sound through that break. There will be nothing grave or tumultuous to be heard, barely a murmur, adding nothing to the vast urban tumult from which we think we suffer. Its only trait will be its ceaselessness. For once heard, it cannot cease being heard, and as it is never truly heard and escapes our understanding, it also cannot be ignored, and is all the more present the more one tries to disregard it: for it is the reverberation, in advance, of what has not been said and never will be said.

The Secret Speech without Secrecy

What is heard here is not a noise, although, as it grows nearer, all around us becomes noise (and we must remember that we do not know today

* Originally published as 'Mort du dernier écrivain', *Nouvelle Revue Française*, 27 (March 1955), pp. 485–91. Reprinted in *Le Livre à venir* (Paris, Gallimard, 1959), pp. 318–25.

what noise might be like). It is rather a kind of speaking: it speaks, it does not cease speaking, it is like the void itself speaking, an insubstantial, insistent, indifferent murmur, which is doubtless the same for everybody; and though it is without secrecy, it isolates each individual, cuts him off from others, from the world and from himself, and leads him on through taunting labyrinths, drawing him ever forwards while yet standing still, simultaneously repulsive and fascinating, beneath the common world of everyday words.

The strangeness of this speaking is that, while it may seem to be saying something, it may in fact be saying nothing. One could even say that depth itself is what speaks within it and what can be heard is itself unheard of. To each individual, though with surprising aloofness, with neither intimacy nor felicity, it seems to say what might be most personal to him, if only for a moment he could hold it in his grip. It is speaking that is not deceitful, since it promises nothing, says nothing and speaks always for each person alone; it is impersonal and speaks entirely from within, even though it is the outside itself, and is present in the only place in which, hearing it, one might hear everything, which is nowhere and everywhere; lastly, it is silent, since it is silence speaking, silence become the false speaking that is never heard, the secret speech that is without secrecy.

How might one silence this speaking? How to hear it, how not to hear it? It transforms days into night, turns sleepless nights into an empty, piercing dream. It is beneath all that is said, behind each familiar thought, submerging, overwhelming imperceptibly all decent human words, like the third partner in every dialogue, the echo that resounds in all monologue; its monotonous quality might lead one to believe it rules by patience, crushes by lightness, dissipates and dissolves all things like the fog, diverting men from the power of loving one another, by the fascination without object that it substitutes for all passion. What is it? Human speech? Or the speech of the gods? Speech that has not been uttered and demands to be spoken? Is it the speaking of the dead, a kind of phantom, a gentle, innocent tormentor, like a ghost? Is it the very absence of speech that is speaking? Nobody dares to discuss this, nor even mention it. And each one of us, in his dissembled solitude, seeks a way of his own to make it vain, the speaking that wants for nothing better than that, to be vain and yet vainer still: for this is the form of its dominion.

A writer is someone who imposes silence on this speaking, and a work of literature is, for whoever finds their way into it, a rich dwelling-place of silence, a firm defence and lofty wall erected against this speaking immensity that is addressed to us, but only with the effect of making us turn aside from ourselves. If, in this imaginary Tibet, where nobody could be found bearing the holy signs any more, all literature were to cease speaking, what would be lacking would be silence, and it would be that very lack of silence which would perhaps reveal the disappearance of literary speaking.

Faced with any great work of painting or sculpture, the self-evidence of a particular silence touches us like a surprise that is not always restful: rather, the silence is palpable, at times harshly imperious, at times supremely indifferent, and at others agitated, lively and joyful. And any true book is always in part a statue. It rises forth and organizes itself like a silent power that, through silence, gives shape and form to silence.

One could object that, in this world in which the silence of art will suddenly be lacking, and in which the dark nakedness of an empty, foreign speaking, capable of destroying all others, will assert itself, there will still be, in the absence of any new artists or writers, the treasure-house of earlier works, the sanctuary of museums and libraries where each of us will be able to come in secret to find peace and tranquillity. But we must suppose that, on the day when errant speaking takes over, we will see a very peculiar disruption affect all books: it will win back those works that, for a moment, had held it in check but which, to a greater or lesser extent, are still its accomplices, for it constitutes their very secret. In any good library there is a department of forbidden books, an underworld housing the books one must not read. But in each great book there is another kind of underworld, a centre of unreadability in which there watches and waits the entrenched energy of this speaking that is not a speaking, this gentle breath of endless recapitulation [*du ressassement éternel*].

The end is easy to imagine, and the masters of the age will not think of sheltering in Alexandria, but only of condemning its library to the flames. No doubt, each and every one will experience an overwhelming disgust for books: people will rage against them and voice their vehemence and distress, expressing all the paltry violence to be found at times of weakness when dictatorship beckons.

The Dictator

There is much to be said about the word dictator. The dictator is the man of *dictare*, of imperious repetition, the one who, each time the danger of foreign speaking is at hand, claims to struggle against it by imposing orders that are both beyond question and without content. Indeed, he seems to be its avowed enemy. To that which is limitless murmur, he opposes the authority and distinctness of the slogan; to the insinuation of that which cannot be heard, the peremptory cry; for the wandering complaint of the ghost of Hamlet's father who, beneath the earth, like the old mole, here, there, roams without power or destiny, he substitutes the fixed speech of royal reason, which commands and never doubts. But instead of being summoned into existence to cover over with his steely cries and decisions the fog of ambiguity of ghostly speaking, isn't this perfect adversary, this man of the moment, in reality not rather the product of the very thing he opposes? Is he not rather its parody, its false replica, its mask, emptier still than what it veils, when, in response to the prayers of weary, disconsolate men, in order to escape the awful yet not deceitful rumble of absence, people turn towards the presence of the categorical idol that asks only obedience and promises the endless quiet of inner deafness?

Dictators, then, come naturally to take the place of writers, artists, thinkers. But whereas the empty speech of dictatorship is the frightened, deceitful extension of what one prefers to have screamed in the streets rather than have to accept and placate in oneself by great personal concentration, the writer has a quite different task and also a quite different responsibility: that of entering, more than anyone else, into a relation of intimacy with the initial murmur. Only at this price can he impose silence upon it, hear it within this silence, then express it, after transforming it.

Without an approach such as this, and without undergoing this ordeal with a steady heart, the writer does not exist. It is true that this non-speaking speech is very much like inspiration, but it is not the same; for it leads only to the place that is unique for each one, the underworld to which Orpheus descended, which is a place of dispersion and discordance, in which all of a sudden he has to confront speech and find within it, and within himself and the experience of the whole of art, that which transforms powerlessness into power, loss of direction into direction, and non-speaking speech into a silence on the basis of which it can really speak and voice the origin within it, without destroying humankind.

Modern Literature

These are not simple matters. The temptation of literature today to move ever closer to the solitary murmur is linked to many things belonging to our time, to history, to the very movement of art itself. The result is to make us almost hear, in all great modern works, that which we would be forced to hear if all of a sudden art or literature ceased to exist. That is what makes these works unique and why they strike us as dangerous, since they are born immediately from danger and are barely able to bring it under their spell.

Undoubtedly there are many different ways (as many as there are works of art and styles of art) in which the speech of the wilderness can be mastered. Rhetoric is one of these means of defence, efficiently conceived and even diabolically arranged to ward off the peril, but also to make it necessary and urgent at the right points where relations with it can become graceful and rewarding. But rhetoric is such a perfect protection that it forgets the reasons it was marshalled in the first place: not only to repel the speaking immensity, but also to attract it, while diverting it, and to be an outcrop amid the flurry of the sands, and not a picturesque local fortification visited only by walkers on their Sunday outings.

It may be noted how often in certain 'great' writers there is something vaguely peremptory about their voices, something which borders on trembling and nervous anxiety, and which is reminiscent, in the area of art, of the domination of *dictare*. It is as though they remain confined within themselves, or some belief, or their own firm, but soon closed and blinkered consciences, waiting to take the place of the enemy that is within them, which they can shut out only with the magnificence of their language, the splendour of their voices, and a commitment to their faith or even lack of it.

Others take on a neutral tone, a self-effacing, barely ruffled transparency, by which they seem to offer solitary speaking a controlled image of itself, a frozen mirror, so to speak, so as to tempt it to gaze at its own reflection – though, often, the mirror remains empty.

Admirable Michaux,[1] for he is the writer who, at his most faithful to himself, has joined forces with the foreign voice, somehow suspecting he has been caught in a trap, and senses that what is being expressed here, with all its humorous inflections, is no longer his own voice, but a voice imitating his own. In order to sneak up on the voice and capture it back, his only weapons are redoubled humour, calculated innocence, cunning deviations, retreats, abandonments, and at the moment he succumbs, the sudden sharp twist of an image piercing the veil of the murmuring voice. The struggle is pushed to the limit and the victory is marvellous, but goes unnoticed.

There is also chatter and what goes under the name of interior monologue, which is no way reproduces, as one well knows, what a man says to himself, since man does not speak to himself and the intimacy of man is not silent, but mostly dumb, reduced to a few sparse signs. Interior monologue is a crude and superficial imitation of the uninterrupted and ceaseless flow of non-speaking speech, whose strength, let us remember, lies in its weakness; it cannot be heard, which is why one never ceases hearing it, and it is as close to silence as possible, which is why it destroys silence entirely. Lastly, interior monologue has a centre, the personal pronoun ('I') that reduces everything to itself, whereas the speaking that is other has no centre, is essentially errant, and is always on the outside.

Silence must be imposed upon this non-speaking speech. It must be returned to the silence that lies within it. It must, for a moment, forget what it is so that, by a threefold metamorphosis, it may be born to true speaking: the speaking of the Book, as Mallarmé will say.

Notes

1 Translator's note: the poet and artist Henri Michaux (1899–1984) is the author of a series of often fantastical poetical texts, including accounts of bizarre imaginary journeys and explorations of strange drug-induced hallucinations. Blanchot writes about Michaux's work at greater length in an essay entitled 'L'Infini et l'infini', *Nouvelle Revue Française*, 61, (January 1958), pp. 98–110.

Translated by Leslie Hill

15

The Great Hoax (1958)*

That we live in a fraudulent world where our gestures, our words and thoughts – our writings too, of course – come to us supplied with a deceptive meaning which we do not detect, which not only gets accepted by us as our own, as if it came naturally from ourselves, but which within us and by means of us dodges and divides and changes form, with the result that we ourselves employ this duplicity, sometimes for our own, barely conscious purposes, sometimes in the service of greater powers whose accomplices or victims we are: none of this, presumably, should surprise us, since Montaigne, Pascal and Montesquieu, then Hegel, Marx and Freud, in short, an impressive number of thinkers and learned men have pointed it out and demonstrated it to us, sometimes with a precision well able to dispel all doubts.

Yet we are not really aware of it. The extremely general form of this denunciation, as I have just expressed it, in itself gives rise to misperceptions. It mixes together ideas and arguments very different from each other, as if the better to render the type of trickery it warns against anodyne and innocuous. If we are informed that all men are completely deceived, by Descartes's evil genius, for example, Sade's God or the cosmic malice or benevolence in science fiction, or again by some impersonal mechanism said to be put in motion inevitably even by the most flawless usage of language and thought, we can be quite certain that this disclosure is part and parcel of the hoax, a more dangerous form of which it is simply designed to cover up.

The great advance achieved by Marx and by Freud consisted in adapting the forms of this altogether abstract fraud to the particular circumstances of history – collective and personal history. Right away we feel accountable and individually targeted by the gaze of these great denouncers. As long as it is a question of all men, of all times and of everything we say and do, everything is all right; the matter concerns only everyone, that is to say, no one. But when we must learn to distrust ourselves, because we have such and such an income, activity or even dream; when, moreover, we come to suspect that certain of our ways of being and of

* Originally published as 'La grande tromperie', *Nouvelle Revue Française*, 54 (June 1957), pp. 1061–73.

speaking take advantage of us in a broader conflict which, at every instant and every step pits us against other men with whom we believed ourselves to be united, then wariness, dated and localized, becomes graver, and we begin to take seriously this deception which is specific to us though conforming to general laws, which is hidden yet manifest and possessed of its own exact and scientifically discernible bases, which is proven and nevertheless inadmissible.

Men have always sensed a huge deception. The entire culture of the East tells us so. But what is more intriguing is that we seem to have been prepared to draw from this disturbing situation an almost happy feeling; yes, a vast, calm sort of happiness. For to be duped is first off to be innocent. To participate in this great celestial fraud through one's consciousness of it is to do nothing, even at one's most active, except yield to the pleasure and vanity of a prodigious entertainment, and if one must accomplish painful acts, it is to lighten the pain of this useless operation till it is but a game. We are mere playthings; thereby we are granted the right to every form of play.[1]

Children, whose suspicion that they are constantly being deceived is ever vigilant, show us the connection between games and an uncertain, indefinite deception which renders all acts thrilling, solemn and wondrous. Childhood is the metaphysical age of deception. But, when children perceive that certain grown-ups, generally their parents, are the instigators of this duplicity directed against them, then everything is apt to become more serious; distrust solidifies. The dividing line which until then, at least in bourgeois milieux, split the world in two – on one side family members and close friends, the luminous world of the good, and on the other side the street, ill-dressed people, night prowlers, evil – distressingly passes right through the territory children had felt to be secure: their parents may still embody the good, but it is a good which can't be trusted, and craftiness is required to protect oneself against it. Indefinite, marvellous beguilement takes the deliberate form of the lie: mystification is humanized.

It is in the eighteenth century that the idea of a plot secretly fomented by some men against others brings trickery down from heaven and ignites within each individual a specific distrust, ready to flare up in violent action. To us this seems very puerile. Priests as conscious agents of a universal conspiracy, the world divided up into a small group of men who know, who choose and decide, a great number of others who know less and do not decide but act in conformity with the secret knowledge, and the ignorant masses, compelled to act and live in total incomprehension of the meaning of their movements – this view worthy of a novel, which in fact does fuel novels up through Radcliffe, Jean-Paul, Goethe and *The*

Visionary by Schiller, seems to us painfully crude by comparison to the labyrinthine ideas of the Orient. And so it is. But this crudeness has considerable educational importance. It restores concrete reality to mystification, gives it a social form, lends it a human face and, dividing the world strictly between tricksters and the tricked, makes the former responsible and inclines the latter to violence. The idea of a plot presupposes the intention to deceive. 'I have nothing to do with it' loses currency as an excuse. The Revolution and the Terror are propelled by the idea of a responsibility which is always entire and won't stand for any qualification. It's always all or nothing. To be suspect in the slightest is to be completely guilty, and that means death. To be suspect is to have within oneself something obscure and indecipherable, which must be read, inversely, as the proof of a clearly and intentionally evil undertaking – of membership in a shady intrigue from which death will separate one right away, in the most decisive and, as it were, trenchant manner. The plainly displayed death by the guillotine's blade is meant precisely to cut clean through the snarl of the plot which no one would ever manage to untangle. This clarity is the clean decisiveness of reason, and reason also has the sharpness of that cut which isolates the head and, in certain cases, ironically prepares its apotheosis.

The nineteenth and twentieth centuries have unfortunately complicated things and established the category of guilty innocents. The work required to explain the kind of mystification to which men are apparently given, and to show how, without directly wanting to or even being aware of doing so, they deceive each other and themselves, motivates every aspect of these two centuries. This is the great task of modern thought. The notion of an unconscious, in the form made current by a simplistic interpretation of Freud, is one of these types of explanation, but we ought to bear in mind that it is to Hegel that we owe the most convincing perspective – also the most insidious – on this process of deception, its necessity and possible resolution. On this point Marx owes everything to Hegel. The idea of alienation comes expressly from Hegel, and Marx simply limited its application[2] – perhaps mistakenly – while at the same time enriching it by showing it operating originally in economic and social phenomena. I will not go back over the meaning of this process: how it happens that man must separate himself from himself and from nature in order to assert himself; how he has to plunge part of himself into the objects and works which separation – that is, negation – enables him to complete; how he ceases to recognize himself in what he makes; how, from this difference between the work where his negation is already realized and what he thinks of it (the knowledge he has of it), there results a delay, a clouding over, a disfigurement, but also a disquietude: man is always late with respect to himself and to the part of himself which he has brought to fruition; his thought lags behind his action and his language also relies, in order to say what is, on forms and categories which no longer correspond to that reality. This tardiness is disturbing, but not only disturbing, for the perpetual unevenness between what we do, say and think, obliges us to become conscious of the difference, to deepen our awareness of it in our efforts to abolish it, whence an ever more vigorous development which wards off falsifying stabilization.

The important point, from our perspective, is how thin the idea of alienation has become. What in Hegel and even in Marx still had great formative value[3] is practically nothing more today than an insult. Alienation is considered to be the conscious doing of the ruling classes: they impose ways of speaking and thinking which serve to perpetuate their former supremacy. Again we lapse into the idea of an intentional falsification. How does this happen? Consciousness is mystified and mystifying, in the sense that what it thinks and says can only be thought and said in a form which alters its content, or else superimposes on the truth of the content a falsifying signification which covers it up, changes it or even uses this parcel of truth the better to put over the intended deception. (A classic example, which I formulate by over-simplifying: I reflect upon man in general and I say: either human nature is depraved or else man is by nature good. These lofty thoughts signify in reality nothing other than this: we must renounce the idea of modifying the current conditions of man – bourgeois society – for there is an immutable, eternal human nature; let us then not disturb private property.) Naturally, I am not always aware when I speak, or especially when I listen, of this other speech which necessarily accompanies my own. Thus I am a sort of clown of language who thinks he is master of what he says, all the while speaking exactly the way a greater master causes him to. Should I happen to sense this, I come upon a strange, fantastic scene which gives me the impression of a glinting void: I suspect another who is, however, me, of fooling me incessantly; I am ready to extend this duplicity, simulation and dissimulation to everything and make of it the basis of thought until, in this excessively general view of consciousness ever foreign to itself, I unexpectedly encounter the very ideology most apt to mask reality and stabilize mystification. Whence a certain anger, the idea that only action and violence will put an end to this trickery and that, if there is mystification, it is because there are mystifiers and one must deal with them first.

The influence of militant Marxism has accelerated the simplification. A more and more direct and meagre vocabulary is considered sufficient. The ruling class is no longer content to benefit from illusion, it gives birth to lies and undertakes to organize deception. Fascism was a spectacular version of this active lie. Imperialism is another. The opium of the people is no longer just religion; all manifestations of culture and pleasure bear the poison within themselves and spread it. Thus the accusation is general, but it is also merely general. It remains surprising that a doctrine which ceaselessly calls ideologies into question has never undertaken to analyse them precisely, has produced nothing that could pass even for a sketch of a science of ideologies,[4] has not even described their role in our everyday life. This is a surprising lacuna (as if Marxism were no less frightening to Marxists than to others; as if they feared they'd find in it who knows what dangerous novelty). But that is why any book which would fill the gap is so important, and why we owe our attention to *Mythologies* by Roland Barthes,[5] if we are really concerned about the silent and perpetual hoax which is inside and outside us, which is the air we breathe and the breath of our words. How could we be indifferent to this effort to rectify images, this exposure of our ulterior motives?

I doubt, however, that this more accurate reading of ideology will please everyone. Yet the resistance mounted against it and the character of this resistance will also surely teach us something. Every month for two years, most often in *Les Lettres Nouvelles*, Roland Barthes has published a relatively short text in which he comments on an incident he chooses at will from our banal reality: sometimes a very small event, an advertising slogan, something said by an actress; or some object of collective curiosity, Minou Drouet, for example, or the speeches of Monsieur Poujade; or again, one of our more lasting institutions, the Tour de France, the strip-tease, the wrestling match. All such incidents contribute, through the intermediary of the press, the radio and cinema, to the intimacy of our life, and they compose its substance even when we think we remain untouched by them. This is what we all live on, let there be no doubt about it. Roland Barthes offers a commentary, then, on our everyday life, but a commentary which is actually a reading. The manner of approaching the smallest events – the empty ones with which we fill our empty moments – as if it were a matter of a text to be read, and of bringing to light, in this apparently insignificant, perfectly obvious text, a more hidden and thus more crafty meaning, is in itself very characteristic. It comes in part from phenomenology and from psychoanalysis. These two great methods, different as they are one from the other, share certain traits: first, they are interested in everything – there are no more areas of special interest – and second, they approach things with the supposition that they hold more meaning than meets the eye, and perceive in them a series of latent meanings nested and folded into one another, which are to be exposed without violence, by a slow and patient approach whose movement should somehow reproduce its meaning – the direction and the aim which its meaning comprises. That is why phenomenology seems, in some of its undertakings, to be only a description, a description which would be a 'decryption', a way of deciphering the hidden centre of meanings by going towards them according to a movement which mimes that of their constitution and also by a sort of sovereign negligence, capable of leaving aside the presuppositions of all naïve knowledge. Thus one sees why Husserl, no less than Freud and no less than Marx, figures among the great denouncers.

Roland Barthes's book will have its place in this same enterprise. In it one finds collected those brief essays, severe and sprightly, entertaining and threatening, wherein we are obliged to discover with alarm all the active collaboration in politically and philosophically serious designs which our passive participation in the superficiality of our day-to-day existence implies: when we look at photographs of actors from a famous studio, when we use soaps and detergents, curious about the whiteness which is so highly recommended to us, and about the deep foam which is lavished on us, or when we eat our extremely rare steak and become interested in Einstein's brain, don't we feel, with a lazy complicity, that we are playing our part in a game which is by no means innocent, thinking something a little different and speaking otherwise than it seems? And we have the impression that we would do well to look closer. In bygone days we were warned about the candid air of the devil, who liked to wear the mask of the good; then Freud came along and revealed to us all our disguises; but it was still only a question of us and our responsibility with regard to our dreams or our souls: that was a great deal, it wasn't much. Now, it's the whole wide world that is at issue, and triviality weighs more heavily upon us.

Little myths add up to major mystification; Roland Barthes's book teaches us this. But it teaches us something else as well: in a long final essay, where he is no longer interested in the content of the myth but in its form, he manages to isolate, purely and simply, the meaning of this form, and to determine the conditions for its use, discovering the way myth imposes itself without either concealing or giving itself away. Thus Barthes's book is a formalist study of ideologies. The conjunction of these terms alone indicates the boldness of the book. The entire study is remarkable. Roland Barthes shows that myth today is essentially a language. Next he shows that this language resides underneath another which it empties and impoverishes, so as to introduce, as if surreptitiously, behind the factual meaning it displays, its intent: a value which it seeks to impose. If one uses Saussurian formulae, it is a matter of two interlocking semiological systems, the second manoeuvring the first. It's a case of borrowing a language. One language steals another and uses it as an alibi, presenting itself in the other right along with the (factual) meaning of the other, so as to pass off the political, moral or religious value – the teaching which it seeks to make us accept – in the innocent guise of a statement of fact. What was a sign becomes a signal, what had designated proclaims but the proclamation – and this is the essence of the fraud – keeps the form of a neutral language which aims only to make statements. The proclamation installs within a language that shows and names another one that commands and enjoins: it signifies in two senses of the term: by notifying – as when the authorities notify someone of his dismissal or eviction (by transmitting an order, then, or a value judgement) – all the while simply making something known, and seeming thus to denote and to communicate only a judgement of fact.

Roland Barthes uses the following example: an illustrated magazine shows a young Black dressed in a French uniform, who, facing the French flag, gives the military salute. The image, taken by itself, says only this: here is a Black soldier saluting the French flag. It's a piece of information, the transmission of a fact which really and indubitably occurred. But let us look more closely and listen inside ourselves: what does this image say to us? This, for example: 'France is a great empire; all her sons, regardless of colour, serve under her flag; how proud this Black is to be French; what a fine answer to the anti-colonialists, etc.' (This second language, having a clear gist but no specific content, can easily go on forever.) Now let us observe this legerdemain carefully: in the second language there is a political doctrine, a whole moral and political system, a complex set of values, which may be very good or very bad; that is not the issue. What makes this a mythic expression is that it presents itself under the auspices of a tiny factual truth within which it presumes to lodge and to sum itself up as a reality, the reality of 'this fine Black saluting the flag just like one of our own boys'. One could say: the image and the statement it signifies – 'somewhere a uniformed Black salutes the flag' – do actually prove the existence of something like the French Empire. Granted. However, the image is not being employed to assure us of the existence of this Empire but rather of its civilizing excellence, its value and, since the fact which is represented is real, the reality of this value: its proof. We have clandestinely and illegitimately moved from one mode of thinking and one system of expression to another which, however, is irreducible to the first.

The implication is that everything serves myth and that there is no limit other than a formal one upon the exercise of its power and its scope. Perhaps, though, one might remark as follows: of course we always speak on top of another language. In everything we say there is a thickness of language, a sediment of words always supplied in advance, in which ours establish themselves comfortably and almost silently. We hardly ever say anything; we just move like fugitives into a prearranged communications system, speaking a language that is already spoken, not even speaking it, but letting ourselves be spoken in it or simply letting it speak in our stead. This substitution is the primary feature of all language, not only of mythic language. In fact, although mythic language makes use of the void in language which is also plenitude, it does not institute that emptiness. But what characterizes mythic language is not only that it is a language on top of another one (in this case, one should say underneath another), but, most important, that it is a didactic language, swollen up with pretentious aims and arbitrary values, inside another language which disguises it in the candour of a bit of factual truth, or in other words, dresses a convention up as *nature*.

The myth of today lodges in insignificant affirmations of the harmless and picturesque variety which none but a pedant could possibly suspect of seriousness, and which it secretly loads up with a supply of distorting significance – a real stowaway travelling in the hold of our words. Roland Barthes quotes this information from a newspaper, after the armistice in Indochina: 'For his first meal General de Castries ordered French fried potatoes.' Later, the President of the Veterans of Indochina observed: 'General Castries's gesture of ordering French fried potatoes for his first meal has sometimes been misunderstood.' And here is Roland Barthes's commentary: 'What we were asked to understand is that the request of the General was by no means a vulgar, materialistic reflex, but a ritual episode whereby the General came home to his French ethnicity and appropriated it anew. The general knew our national symbolism well; he knew that the potato prepared in this manner is the nutritional sign of "Frenchness".' In reality it is possible that he had an innocent yen for the dish which for some time he had not been able to enjoy, but mythology doesn't let anything go unused: everything must have significance and value; everything must say a little more than it actually says and take on an obscure sacramental meaningfulness. Everything is enrolled in one or another of the primary concepts which night and day inhabit our thoughts.

There we have, I believe, one of the conclusions that should be drawn from these abuses. We are devoured by signs, we smother under the weight of values, we consume them and thirst for them. Everything transpires as if we were happy only when surrounded by these signals, behind which are hidden enormous systems we have no desire to control. That is why a tricolour or a red flag pleases us more than a patriotic or a revolutionary speech. And each day new images function as myths, or old formulas return which, to our surprise, have not lost their magic appeal for us. The expression 'army morale' periodically furnishes a good example of this. It is composed of noble words which are not necessarily political: 'morale' (which simultaneously reads as 'moral') and 'army' – young men whose fate concerns us – are powerful realities and principles. But what indefinable hybrid and fantastic idol is formed by these words put together? And if to them is added this third, rather vague but also rather alarming term, 'dangerous' (which is understood as 'disastrous') we arrive at this unique and forceful expression, 'dangerous for army morale,' which functions like the word *mana* or *taboo* in other cultures and whose religious influence we all undergo. In the enemy camp, the words 'counter-revolution', 'defence of the proletariat', 'class struggle' exert exactly the same power. All these expressions have lost their meaning and no longer function at all except as signals, ethical forces, allusions to formidable transcendent principles which it is forbidden to approach, especially for the purposes of a precise analysis.

Here we touch upon explicit politics and, consequently, the phraseology is a little less hidden (though still very effective). But in all areas we are exposed to this hyper-language, these empty utterances overloaded with intentions, whose object is not to communicate with us according to their rigorous meaning, but to serve as ostentatious figures, as gestures, as signals which set off in us reprobation or approbation, depending on the type of systems involved and the orchestration of the relevant ceremonies. Stendhal's little factual truths have become ritual tokens, 'significant' because of this hyper-sense which manipulates words and commands our adherence by candidly taking shape right in them. Speaking of the Abbé Pierre, Roland Barthes remarks upon our amazing taste for icons and observes how confident we feel in a vocation when it is spectacularly guaranteed by a face and a picturesque costume in which all the signs of the apostolic legend can easily be discerned.

What accounts for this? Whence this 'consumption of signs' characteristic of us, this frightful pressure which values exert upon us?[6] Nietzsche thought he could change everything by calling for a transmutation of values. But that is not even a first step. It is against the very notion of value that thought must be defended, for thought is as if infested with value which, offering it the alibi of hyper-sense and the prestige of what must be, removes from thought the responsibility of thinking according to what is, and poorly, always somewhat short of thought.

Poverty of thought and poverty of language. Modern literature, as Roland Barthes knows, through the disavowal of this hidden hyper-sense which is afforded it by literary form, and by the use of a given genre or of particular literary conventions and indeed of everything which indicates literature as literature – through its perpetual opposition, its violent contrariness, its refusal of itself and of all natural legitimacy – is one of the paths opened yet always closed back up, towards that essential poverty, that rigorous privation and practically mortal retrenchment which make literature as poetry the affirmation most staunchly opposed to myths. I imagine it will inevitably be said that this frail literature, scarcely existing, is not much to count on in the struggle against the great hoax. True, it is not much. But here weakness, and the language that models itself on what lies short of all force, impede the trickster more than strength, his inevitable accomplice.

Notes

1 Our good fortune to be just a moment in the divine game has been movingly expressed by Plato.

2 For Hegel, objectification is in itself an alienation of the logos. For Marx, objectification is not an alienation, it is natural: man objectifies himself by nature and 'alienation is simply an essential secondary process,' introduced by history and to which history will put an end. One grasps here the dangerous primacy accorded by Marx to nature. Here begins the ill-considered realism of his epigones. (See *Logique et Existence* (Paris, PUF, 1953, where Jean Hyppolite clarifies this point.)

3 Heidegger also noted the importance of alienation and of the Marxist conception, which clarified, confirmed, but also covered up the more original forgetting of being. 'Homelessness is coming to be the destiny of the world. Hence it is necessary to think that destiny in terms of the history of Being. What Marx recognized in an essential and significant sense, though derived from Hegel, as the alienation of man has its roots in the homelessness of modern man . . . Because Marx by experiencing alienation attains an essential dimension of history, the Marxist view of history is superior to that of other historical accounts.' See *Letter on Humanism*, (*Basic Writings*, ed. David Farrell Krell (New York, Harper and Row, 1977); translation by Krell, slightly modified). Heidegger adds, perhaps a bit hastily, that as far as he can tell, Sartre hasn't been able to recognize what is essentially historical in being; this is why existentialism can't possibly reach the only dimension where there can be fertile dialogue with Marxism. He addresses the same criticism to Husserl and phenomenology (*Letter on Humanism*, written in autumn, 1946).

4 There is no thoughtful Marxist who does not recognize the positive meaning of 'ideologies'. Tran-Duc-Thao, who is, granted, an exceptional Marxist, writes: 'The autonomy of superstructures is as essential to the understanding of history as is the evolution of productive forces.'

5 Roland Barthes, *Mythologies* (Paris, Editions du Seuil, 1957). For a (selective) English translation see *Mythologies*, trans. Annette Lavers (London, Jonathan Cape, 1972).

6 The relation between the order of values and the proliferation of 'signs' is a close one. Values are not stated but signalled.

Translated by Ann Smock

16

Essential Perversion (1958)*

When one reflects calmly, as one should, on the events of May 1958, something soon becomes clear: if all that one sees is their political aspect and thinks that this aspect is sufficient to define them, the verdict one will pass on them, even if it is an unfavourable one, will still implicitly be favourable towards them. That is why the refusal of what has happened by the men of politics has often appeared feeble, and more obstinate than firm. What happens in the case of political analysis? The point is, precisely, that it analyses, it dissociates: it sees in what has happened a plurality of facts, distinct in their origin and with conflicting meanings, correcting and neutralizing each other – de Gaulle counterbalancing the men of the 13th May; what was murky about them serving merely to bring out the clear light of his unique apparition. What is more, though the revolt by the army may have appeared regrettable, de Gaulle, being not just a soldier but a special sort of soldier, was ideally designated to defuse the political ambitions of the army. Lastly, there was the mediocre regime that came before, its inability to change its ways or solve serious problems; in that case too a solution has been provided, under conditions of sufficient legality, and it is an advantageous one, even if it is open to criticism: who could possibly oppose this constitution in favour of the other one, or indeed of any other one? Whence the unavoidable conclusion: all in all, we are better off with de Gaulle, and when you think what we could have in his place, what a blessing he is.

This common-sense view comes so naturally that it must be there in all of us. It amounts to politics considered as opportune behaviour. Opportunism, in this case, becomes equivalent to political truth. Considered as an opportune decision, the solution bearing the name de Gaulle may appear either dubious or satisfactory (things can always be found in his favour, just as others can be found in his disfavour): such discussions are endless and virtually useless.

However, even among those who use the arguments of opportunism to justify their approval or their disapproval, as among the vast majority of people, struck dumb in the face of an awkward tangle of good and bad

* Originally published as 'La perversion essentielle', *Le 14 juillet*, 3 (June 1958), p. 6.

which they are unable to unravel, there is the feeling that something quite different has happened, a grave alteration that in part eludes political judgement, since it involves decisions made at a deeper level of agreement or disagreement. That being the case, we may continue to approve or disapprove weakly; we may also maintain a neutral stance; yet we feel, through our unease and our discomfort, the wrong (in almost a physical sense) that is done to thought by this way of eluding events that concern it. A deeper understanding or misunderstanding is concealed by our choice. And our refusal to see clearly is already part of the 'yes' that secretly bows and compels us.

The regime [*le pouvoir*] that emerged from the events of May is singular in appearance. This singularity contributes to the unease affecting our judgement, as well as to the reassurance it is content with. It is a regime with a name, that of de Gaulle; this name qualifies it and guarantees it, but is not enough to define it. Is it a dictatorship? No. Dictatorship is power placed in the hands of an individual, who has struggled for power and concentrates it about his strongly individual presence. There is certainly nothing good about it, but there is nothing alarming about it for thought either. Dictatorship is a human power, the dictator is manifestly a man, his regime is the exercise of unbridled force. Naturally, dictatorship rapidly degenerates. Dictators exploit their personal charisma; they turn themselves into emperors, they dominate. But their rise is always that of an individual. They are men. They can be combated simply and without words. None of these features applies to de Gaulle, nor directly to the regime he represents. De Gaulle did not seize power; he is not a man of action. In the past he did briefly turn to politics, but with embarrassment, clumsily, drawn into the role by the bizarre passivity that is characteristic of him, but soon convinced of his mistake. That is why it is meaningless to attack him by reminding him that he once represented a political party. He is not a man of action. To act is no concern of his. The extreme care he exercised so as not to take power, but to let power come to him, offer itself to him, with the help of the men of impure action with whom, at the same time, he did not wish to appear to be associated, is quite remarkable. Was it a wish to preserve an appearance of legality? No, since at first he refused to carry out even the minor formalities necessary for his enthronement. Was it because he had too proud and even vain an idea of himself? I don't think so. It was not out of respect for his own person, but out of respect for the impersonal power he represents, that feeling of sovereignty which it is incumbent on him to affirm, and which is compatible only with a minimum of action.

The sovereignty he incarnates is apparently the exaltation of one man. On one level it glorifies a name while also exploiting its glorious memory;

it says that this person is irreplaceable, is unique (unique signifying that, from the standpoint of political expediency, de Gaulle is without rival, but also, from another angle, that he is without equal, so that he is unique because he represents the sacred and mysterious value of the unique; that is why emphasis is placed, psychologically, upon his solitude: he is a man apart, he is separate, he is the anointed one); finally, this person is providential. This title, which became attached to him straight away, is self-explanatory. Providential means: designated by some Providence and declaring itself to be providence. The power [*pouvoir*] vested in a man of providence is no longer a political power, it is a power [*puissance*] of salvation. His presence as such is salutary, efficacious in itself and not through what it will do.

But at this point the perspective changes. The omnipotence vested from the outset in this one man was most extraordinary; everyone asked themselves: are there any limits to what he will do with it? But they were obliged to observe, to their surprise (but also with shamefaced relief), that he did nothing with it. This was because he could do nothing with it. Because the significance of the authority that belongs to him is that it is too high and too great to be exercised. Hence the situation which gradually became apparent: de Gaulle can do anything, but in particular, nothing. Being all-powerful, the respect he has for this omnipotence (the sentiment he has of being the whole of France, not just of representing it, but of rendering it visible and remotely present in its intemporal reality) debars him from using it to make any specific political decision. So that, even if he had any political ideas, he could not apply them. He is not the man with a specific political programme, he is comprehensive sovereignty ('I have understood you' [*'je vous ai compris'*]), which comprehends everything and, in this comprehension, satisfies all requirements. His is a remote, undivided sovereignty, constantly at a remove from the manifestations expected of it. It is a far cry from simple, profane dictatorship. A dictator is constantly on show; he does not speak, he shouts; his word always has the violence of the shout, of the *dictare*, of repetition. De Gaulle manifests himself, but out of duty. Even when he appears, he seems to be a stranger to his own appearance; he is withdrawn into himself; he speaks, but secretly or under cover of majestic commonplaces, and his faithful people live by the exegesis of his ambiguous words. Truly he is providential man, if Providence, according to Malebranche, is incapable of any particular action, and can only become manifest in the most general of ways.

I admit that this is a rather simplified view, but it does not distort the main feature of what I am talking about, namely the transformation of political power into a power of salvation. Destiny is currently in power:

not a man whom history has made remarkable, but some power that is above person, a force emanating from the highest values, the sovereignty not of a sovereign person but of sovereignty itself, in so far as it has become identified with the sum total of all the possibilities offered by a destiny. Which destiny? The answer to that is simple: it is the august affirmation, above and beyond all the accidents of its history, of a nation as destiny. De Gaulle's own past sheds light on this answer, which is not necessarily related to the idea he may have of himself. In the past, he was called the Symbol. In grave times, his task was to represent national permanence and certainty, above a disastrous abyss. He was the visible presence of a great but absent nation. He personified it. It is always dangerous to identify the reality of a country with a person, and even more so to raise his history ideally above history itself. But in those days, de Gaulle was nothing, a man without a past, without a future, and the value of his action came from the firmness of a refusal to which no power corresponded. This was an extraordinary experience for a man. He never ceased, in a way, to be passive; he did nothing, he could do nothing, at most he preserved and safeguarded by his presence, haughtily maintaining a set of invalid rights, an authority without content, while immense active forces, in which he played only a nominal role, worked gradually to translate into reality the affirmations of an Idea.

Out of this experience there gradually emerged in him the awareness of a sovereignty of emergency, coinciding, in those dramatic hours when all seemed plunged into emptiness, with the essential presence of the nation's destiny. What was characteristic of those times was the manner in which this emptiness manifested itself. In 1940, nothing was more pathetic or more self-evident: where once there had been France, there was now nothing but a void and, suspended above this void that had opened up in history, the almost visible, almost tangible affirmation, in a man who was himself unknown and faceless, of France in the persistence of its destiny and the very prophecy of its own salvation. De Gaulle has remained obsessed by the emptiness of that void, but he also remains intimately familiar with it, and retains a sense of its necessity. He has written it into the constitution. He has made it, in a way, legal. For France to raise itself to the level of destiny, and for the power that represents it to become a sovereignty of salvation, she must become aware of this void which, as a result of her institutions and her divisions, is a constant threat to her. In 1946 de Gaulle suddenly withdraws, so that the country, discovering the void in the form of a power vacuum, may arrive at the decisions that will ensure its unity. But the country sees nothing, the operation is a failure. In 1958 the operation succeeds magnificently. In the face of the problems created by a senseless war, and plunged into a despair that has turned into social disturbance as a result of the problems of this war, feelings begin to organize themselves (and be organized) into doubt. A vacuum seems about to open up, when in the same moment, in the guise of a man of destiny, there approaches the very essence of national sovereignty, which alone can fill that vacuum. But what is so striking is the fact that, no sooner is de Gaulle in power, than there is indeed (apparently) no longer anything but him and a vacuum. The political forces collapse. The social forces withdraw. Everything falls silent. It is like a mysterious conditioned reflex. Even men capable, for powerful inner reasons, of showing opposition, remain silent and seemingly absent. The vacuum must not be disturbed. The yes vote in the referendum is no more than the exorbitant expression of this vacuum. And the vacuum does its job, which is to *consecrate* as a power for salvation the authority of a single man. What would happen if we did not have such a man? The answer is now clear: a vacuum or void is all that would remain.

But that is a misleading answer. History does not repeat itself. From 1940 to 1944 the great active forces, namely those of the Allies, kept de Gaulle away from the action, but also left him the freedom of his ideal authority. The allies of today, those whose action has brought him as it were passively to power, have by no means vanished, especially since, owing to the inactive sovereignty of sacred power, they are totally free to act, and thereby give political content to a power and a regime that are majestically without content. The identity of these forces is known, but insufficiently as yet, and from an anecdotal angle, which serves more to hide them than to define them. In particular, anecdote and analysis have been used to present them as isolated forces, bearing no significant relationship to the regime they have brought into being. Or else attempts have been made to prove, on the contrary, that there were anecdotal relations between de Gaulle and the conspirators. This is to turn everything into pure spectacle. The important thing is that what happened on 13th May, and what happened afterwards, go together to form a whole, and that they have reality and meaning only when taken together. The important thing is that the movements which can crudely be labelled an expression of colonial sentiment, a nationalist upsurge, the effects of technocratic pressures, the transformation of the army into a political force, the transformation of political power into a force for salvation, all constitute, in their entangled relations with each other, differing as they do in origin, form and character, an identical phenomenon of shifting significance, yet one that is unique, and as such extremely grave.

One of the consequences of this is that the regime is not what it appears, since it is constantly occupied by different forces, striving to realize themselves through it, and from which it cannot distance itself without appearing to be less than itself. In the foreground we have the Sovereign Presence, the affirmation of a power that is not political but essentially religious, wielding the crudely perverted values of the sacred (the privileged destiny of one man, his predestined epiphany: he saved us once, he will save us every time, he is the saviour; he is the eternal fatherland; each time the fatherland is in danger, it is incarnated in this man, to whom Providence has entrusted its decisions).

In so far as the colonialist reflex is an expression of despair (just as the nationalist upsurge is a form of distress), a collective despair, focused in collective unrest resulting in displays of ferment that can be called either racist or fascist, it is easy to see how the salvation through destiny symbolized by de Gaulle appeared to constitute an appropriate response. However, ferment needs slogans and fetish words (only utter the word integration and peace will be achieved, the happy past restored); it requires violent satisfactions, spectacular deeds, executions, and warlike operations; or, failing that, clandestine conspiracies (secrecy and spectacle are equally necessary to such ferment). And this type of disorderly outburst is not congenial to the lofty sovereignty, which is far removed from such vulgarity, has no intention of being identified with it, yet cannot be critical of it either, since it is there to understand it, to recognize it and protect the essence of its aims, without however fulfilling them directly, which would anyway be impossible.

Through a whole series of imperceptibly downgraded emanations, the supreme authority of the One must therefore be communicated, without suffering deterioration, to power zones lying deeper and deeper within the real, and which are authoritarian in their form, dictatorial in their aims, and destined to achieve the ends in whose name the 13th May took place (Algeria as part of France; the war waged to the death and imposing its logic upon everything; the army continuing, in the name of that logic, to exert its authority, which inevitably can only be political in nature). Hence, behind a sovereignty of a religious (and anachronistic) nature lies the promise or the presence of much more modern manifestations of political activism, from the permanent intriguing of the various factions, to the threats of the praetorians (if de Gaulle goes, you'll have the paratroops), by way of what was already the tight control exercised by the police forces, down to political gangsterism pure and simple. Similarly, we see the forces of neocapitalism using the mystique of sovereign oneness, distorting its ideal meaning to make it correspond to the requirements of economic supremacy, which requires a centralized power, both in the service of planning and so as to ensure technocratic efficiency. In this case, the sovereign is no longer the saviour, called upon by the despair of crowds driven by instinct; he is not the war leader required by the army, capable of seizing power in the name of war and in the name of the army; he is the director, a being of an impersonal nature, who directs, supervises and makes decisions in accordance with the requirements of modern capitalist organization.

I grant that these forces are divided, that they are secretly in conflict with each other, and that these violent contradictions, far from having died down behind the noble façade of unity, have moved in to power, or to the edges of power, as they seek, through the intermediary of a simple, narrow, Debré-style nationalism, to translate into their own terms the hymn to sovereignty. This struggle has only just begun. We are at the beginning of a process in which the war, a senseless war, as devoid of sense as it is of outcome, remains the determining factor. What will come of it all? It is not for me to prophesy. I simply observe that there has rarely been a regime more false, not through the falsehood of men, but because of an essential corruption of political power: the regime is authoritarian but without authority; behind the mask of unity it could not be more divided; beneath a guise of power and efficacy, it is incapable of either decision or choice; claiming to acknowledge the responsibility of a person, designated in person, it shelters beneath the name of that person a welter of irresponsible actions, as well as the supremacy of faceless economic forces. This is a strange regime, and these are grave occurrences: not just grave but unbearable. Everything is becoming perverted into wretched confusion: we see de Gaulle's adversaries placing all their hope in him while his zealots profane him (blasphemy being a part of religion); while his closest friends, those whom he placed in government himself, seem bent on ruining what he seeks to represent. All of which occasionally makes it tempting to see the entire situation as both uncanny and unreal, with that unreality whose light, unfortunately, is often seen when history is about to end.

As for those who say (either openly or silently): yes, we are for de Gaulle, we are in his hands and we are content with this sovereign vocation that raises him religiously above every dispute, because if he went we could fear the worst, we would have a dictatorship, to them it must be replied: you have saved nothing by betraying what is essential, for behind the sovereignty that is everything but can do nothing, you already have potentially, and tomorrow you will have in its full force, that dictatorship that necessarily ensues whenever political power is corrupted to become a force for salvation.

Translated by Michael Holland

17

On a Change of Epoch (1960)*

'Will you allow as a certainty that we are at a turning-point?

– If it is a certainty it is not a turning. The fact of our belonging to this moment at which a change of epoch, if there is one, is being accomplished also takes hold of the certain knowledge that would want to determine it, making both certainty and uncertainty inappropriate. Never are we less able to get around ourselves than at such a moment, and the discrete force of the turning-point lies first in this.

– Can we be so sure? I mean, were this the case, that would not be certain either. You have in mind Nietzsche's words: "The greatest events and thoughts are comprehended last; the generations that are contemporaneous with them do not experience such events – they live right past them." Nietzsche also says, in a phrase frequent citation has come to exhaust: "Thoughts that come on doves' feet guide the world; it is the stillest words that bring on the storm." But note that Nietzsche does not say the storm will be silent.

– For Nietzsche the storm is speech, the speech of thought.

– When the French Revolution occurs, everyone knows it except Louis XVI. Today when it is manifestly a matter of a change much more important – one by which all the previous overturnings that have occurred in the time of history come together to provoke a break in history – everyone has a presentiment of it, even if each of us cannot affirm that we know it. This is a knowledge that is not within the scope of any particular individual.

– Yet you yourself affirm it.

– Because I am no more than an episodic voice, a speech without contour. And of course I affirm more than I know. But what I mean to say is not without signs: it goes about in the streets and this steady, anonymous current runs strong; we must try to hear it.

– And it says we have arrived at the time of a break that separates times?

– It says this, perhaps, in the manner of the ancient oracle, when Pythia spoke in a language of violence and of the elements that the poet-inter-

* Originally published as 'Entretien sur un changement d'époque', *Nouvelle Revue Française*, 88 (April 1960), pp. 724–34. Reprinted in *L'Entretien infini* (Paris, Gallimard, 1964), pp. 394–418, under the title 'Sur un changement d'époque'.

preter – transcribing, describing – was to elevate to the calmer and clearer language of men.

– An obscure language.

– Not obscure, but open to that which is not yet truly divulged, though none the less known to all. A language into which passes precisely the indecision that is the fate of the turning – an individual turning point and a turning of the world.

– An uncertain, indecisive fate that therefore remains always unaccomplished.

– Uncertain today for a very different reason: because this accomplishment is of a kind such that it escapes our historical measures. Recall Herodotus, who is known as 'the father of history.' One enters his books as into a country upon which day is about to dawn. *Before this there was something else, it was mythical night. This night was not obscurity. It was dream and knowledge; between men and event relations other than those of historical knowledge and its separating force. Herodotus stands on the crest that separates night from day: not two times, but two kinds of clarity. After him there falls upon men and things the clear light of historical knowledge.*

– You speak like a book.

– Because I am citing one.[1] And I will cite again the question it formulates: would this light that begins with Herodotus and becomes steady with Thucydides not also have its time? And if in reading Herodotus we have the sense of a turning, have we not, in reading our years, the certainty of a change even more considerable, a change such that the events that offer themselves to us would no longer be bound together in the manner we are accustomed to calling history, but in another with which we are not yet familiar?

– Is it the end of history that you claim to announce – at this moment when history becomes universal and speaks imperiously in the consciousness of everyone?

– I am not proclaiming it, nor does it proclaim itself directly. What is proclaimed, in fact, is apparently the contrary: the all-powerfulness of historical science that penetrates down to the most profound layers, those that have never before been historical. This discovery is itself a sign. We discover that there was a time without history, a time for which the terminology proper to historical times is unsuited – terms and notions with which we are familiar: freedom, choice, person, consciousness, truth, originality and, in a general sense, the state as the affirmation of a political structure. Just as the originary eras were characterized by the importance of elementary or telluric forces, so today the event we are encountering bears an elementary character: that of the impersonal powers [*puissances*] represented by the intervention of mass phenomena, by the supremacy of a machine-like play of these forces, and by the seizure of the constitutive forces of matter. These three factors are named by a single term: modern technology. For the latter includes collective organization on a planetary scale for the purpose of establishing calculated planning, mechanization and automation, and, finally, atomic energy – a key term. What up to now only the stars could do, man does. Man has become a sun. The astral era that is beginning no longer belongs to the bounds of history. Are you in agreement with this presumption?

– There's a fitting word. And how can one not agree with something necessarily so vague that to oppose it would be the sign of a thought just as confused? I recognize that to hear talk of the end of history is always pleasurable. I can see that the domination of values and of the historical sciences could go hand in hand with the exhaustion of the forces making history (if these words have a meaning). I grant that when walking in the street, one breathes in thoughts such as these. But one breathes them in, one does not think them; as soon as they are formulated they lose their storybook charm. I have heard it said that we are in the process of crossing the time barrier. This kind of metaphor abounds in the work of Teilhard de Chardin, who does not fail to add, with the naïveté proper to him: it is as a scholar that I speak; I have not left the terrain of scientific observation.

– Is it a metaphor? It suggests to us something important and troubling: that we are at the end of one discourse and, passing to another, we continue out of convenience to express ourselves in an old, unsuitable language. That is the greatest danger. It is even the only one. The street is therefore much wiser than the painstaking thinkers who wait until they have new categories with which to think what is happening. I would remind you that theologians have sometimes spoken of "the smell of the end of time", a sort of *sui generis* experience that, amid real historical phenomena, would allow one to discern the breakthrough: being heading for its end.

– No doubt the smell of atomic explosion. Nietzsche, another theologian, already asked us: "Do we smell nothing as yet of divine decomposition?" And Heraclitus said before anyone else: "If all things turned to smoke then we would discern things with our nostrils." But he did not make the nose into a theological organ. Note that I have nothing against the smell of the end of time. It is even possible that the kind of mixture of vague science, confused vision and dubious theology one finds in the writings of Teilhard may also have value as a symptom, and perhaps a prognostic: one sees this kind of literature develop in periods of transition. What is distressing is that this sincere and courageous man is unaware of the horrible mix with which he must content himself; while speaking in the name of science, he speaks as an author of science fiction.

– Now here is a title with which, in his place, I would not be displeased.

Something in these authors speaks that I do not always find in the greatest books. And don't forget that Kant himself wrote a treatise on "the end of all things".

– It is precisely in strong, forcefully systematized thinking that undertakes to think everything, and history as a whole, that a possibility such as the end of history can have meaning. So it is with Hegel and Marx: in the case of Hegel, it is the development of absolute knowledge, the final achievement of a coherent discourse; in the case of Marx, the advent of the classless society in whose final state there will no longer be any power [*puissance*] of a properly political form. Here, at least, we have a dividing line, a criterion by which to judge things. We more or less know of what we speak.

– I have nothing as coherent to offer you, it is true, and this lack of a rigorous system is not necessarily an advantage. But must we take advantage of this to diminish Teilhard by designating him as a poor man's Hegel or a vestry Marx, as do, I think, certain pious men? Criticism has little hold on me. What is weak does not need us to grow weaker, but we ought to preserve and reinforce what is strong. What counts in the case of Teilhard is that he was a competent prehistorian, and it is as a prehistorian intimate with the ancient earth (one who has weighed ancient crania and delved into the profound layers) that he learned to form an idea of man's future. One might say that this beginning prior to the beginning, this language prior to speech that the images of an originary time speak, everything we now see and have never been able to see, give a certain clairvoyance with which to discern the invisible future, suggesting relations with the spirit of the earth and an understanding that is not disconcerted or frightened by the great metamorphoses that are being accomplished today.

– Your very language is becoming obscure – a sign, in fact, of clairvoyance. But what relation is there between the ancient knowledge of the earth that romanticism so generously ascribed to early times and modern technology, which is thought to direct against nature an inordinately destructive power of attack and negation? Can one say anything serious in taking such a tack?

– Nothing. Moreover, I am simply speaking in the name of Jünger's book, which meets up with Teilhard in a striking way. It is perhaps the same romanticism, the same magical presentiment, to wit, that the earth, finally unified and open to its depths, will become animate and, merging with humanity gathered up into itself, become a living star capable of a new brilliance. Teilhard speaks of a noosphere. Jünger says that our planet has acquired a new skin, an aura woven of images, of thoughts, melodies, signals and messages. This, he says, is a higher degree of spiritualization of the earth. It passes above nations and their languages,

above word and sign, war and peace. The stone axe extended the
arm; technology is the projection of mind. To be sure, technology first of
all glorifies matter; but the materialism affirmed here by Jünger is
neither empty nor superficial (as his mediocre adversaries contend), it is
depth itself. And in undertaking the most profound penetration of
matter, in no longer simply using matter but arriving at a manipulation
of the processes that command the genesis of matter, intelligence has
embarked upon an extreme adventure of unforeseeable consequences –
consequences of which it has an intimation each time Mother Earth
begins to tremble and each time man is able to take this shaking in hand
and capture it. This shaking and this grasp put the entire traditional
structure into question, along with the ancient rights, ancient customs,
and freedom; they precipitate the decline of the paternal gods and
develop every anonymous force – a movement to which correspond
an insatiable hunger for energy, a Promethean ardour of means and
methods, vulcanism (fire and radiance), the emergence of unwonted
forces, and a stirring of the serpent of the earth, but also the withdrawal
of the heroic forces in favour of the titanic ones, as is natural when
the technician takes precedence over the useless warrior. You have no
objections?

– No, none.

– That's not a good sign. Does this alliance of romanticism and
technology, or this romantic interpretation of technocracy, seem to you
to play on the weak parts of the imagination? But even taken this way, it
is not without meaning. The philosophy of nature, whose significance
Hegel did not fail to recognize, tapped here 150 years ago one of its
sources. That it should emerge anew today, spanning history, shows that
it represents an enduring presentiment and knowledge. Reduced to their
simplest terms, what do these views signify? That, hidden in what is
called modern technology, there is a force that will dominate and determine all of man's relations with what is. We dispose of this force at the
same time as it disposes of us, but we are ignorant of its meaning; we do
not fully understand it. Jünger draws out and makes this mysterious
dimension of technology shine with the help of the old images of magic
romanticism, as Teilhard also does with his manner of speaking of a
science that is but a foreknowledge [*une prescience*]. Far from being
frightened by this mystery, both of them rejoice in it and put their trust
in it. Both have faith in the future, and they love the future: a future not
only of years but of superior states. That is good.

– I wonder whether, on the contrary, your authors don't have a kind of
horror of the future since they refuse to entertain the incompletion that
it necessarily holds in it. One could say they do everything to turn away
from the simple truth of our death: the fact that it is always premature

and before term. Hence their haste to affirm that an epoch has ended, a time is over. There is surely something barbaric in this end of history that you, that your authors, announce.

– Yes, barbaric, I would agree. It is a foreign truth: it flatters curiosity, but runs against it as well. Let's consider this for a moment. Naturally, if historical values pass and come to an end, this signifies their dominion in this end that only begins. We do not think absolutely the idea of the end, we think it only in relation to the idea of beginning. The end revokes the beginning. But what was the beginning of history? The end of mythico-heroic times, the end of Homer and Heracles; none the less an end that has never ended but prolonged itself in history. This trait is easily brought forth. Historical man is bound up with the myths of heroic times in so far as he sometimes affirms himself by combating them, at other times by identifying with them. In originary time (the time of prehistory) there are no heroes; man is without a name, without a visage. He belongs to living nature and lives in the pleasure and pain of the earth. The mythical hero already has a name and a genealogy; he no longer takes pleasure in nature, he wants to conquer it: he struggles, he annihilates. With him are born the virile gods, and he himself seeks to complete himself in becoming a half-god. Historical man preserves myth and preserves himself from it. Certainly, his principal task is to conserve his dignity – his humanity – against the mythical powers. But within history the moral of heroic myths does not cease to act as a model: that of the great personality, appearing in wartime, in the sacrifice of the hero for the fatherland, and in state governance where the great man as father, as guide, and as providential man belongs, even during history itself, to the world of heroes and gods. The decline of the heroic myth that characterizes our time is therefore another sign of this end of history whose dawning clarity you do not wish to accept, seeing in it only twilight. The hero disappears from universal consciousness; just as the name disappears, so the personality. What new cult did the Great War engender? Only one: that of the unknown soldier. And the unknown soldier is the glorification of the anti-hero; he is the unperceived, the obscure, ghostly stranger who abides in the memory of a people by virtue of being forgotten. This memorial of non-remembrance, this apotheosis of namelessness is an invitation to recognize that the time of the hero – and of heroic literature – is past. I don't miss it.

– You prefer the myth of the end of time, the fear of worldwide catastrophe that shakes men's imaginings day and night.

– It is not a preference that I wish to indicate. But the possibility to which you allude is naturally a sign of the greatest magnitude. When, for the first time in the history of the world, one has at hand the material power to put an end to this history and this world, one has already departed historical space. The change of epoch has occurred. This can be simply expressed: henceforth the world is a barracks that can burn.

– You seem to rejoice in this. But are you sure it's the first time? Perhaps you've forgotten the Bible. Biblical man constantly lives from the perspective you describe as new, warned by Jahweh that if men persevere in their practices they will be annihilated and creation abolished. History is born under this threat, the very threat of historical time.

– Then the fire came from above. Today it comes from here below.

– I could easily respond that when God promises to destroy humanity, should it continue to behave badly, he turns the decision over to humanity. Everything always finally depends upon man, whether there be God or whether there be the atom.

– Be there God or the atom, the point is precisely that everything does not depend on man. In God's time this was very nearly clear – also offensive, I grant it. Today the danger comes from the illusion in which we live of being the masters of what is carrying itself out under the englobing name of modern technology. I do not rejoice in this power to end that is conferred on us in a still scarcely intelligible manner. I have no liking for the bomb. I simply note that it is but a sign, a crude sign, of the extreme peril that necessarily marks the passage from one time to another, and perhaps from history to a trans-historical epoch. I allude here to a thinker with whom you are familiar: he often says that each time, denouncing the danger of the bomb, we hasten to invite knowledgeable men to put nuclear energy to peaceful use we do no more than procure for ourselves an alibi and bury our heads in the sand. The bomb gives visible notice of the invisible threat that all modern technology directs against the ways of man. The American chemist Stanley, a Nobel Prize winner (as you can well imagine), made this statement: "The moment draws near when life will be no longer in God's hands but in those of the chemist who will modify, form, or destroy every living substance at will." We read such statements every day, statements made by responsible men, and we read them along with other news items in the papers with negligence or with amusement, and without seeing that through the force of modern technology the way is being paved for an attack that makes the explosion of the bombs signify little in comparison.

– In fact, the end of everything isn't much. And what do you conclude from this? That we must preach a crusade against the world of technology, condemn it as an *opus diabolicum* and prepare huge fires upon which to burn learned men? Must we begin by destroying the contemporary world out of fear that it may not take this task upon itself?

– Were we able, I would not wish to. Fortunately, we belong to this world; we will not escape it. And in its lack of measure, which frightens us, we are frightened because not only the threats but also the hopes it holds in store for us are beyond measure. We must simply be clear-sighted, or try to be. The danger does not really lie in the bomb. It is not in the unwonted development of energy and technology's domination; it is first of all in our refusal to see the change of epoch and to consider the sense of this turning. The threat will grow as long as we have not determined it as a risk. I would even say that the danger is perhaps solely provoked by our old language, a language that obliges us to speak in the style of history and the discourse of representation where the word war continues to be in use, and along with it the old mythical images, the pretensions of prestige, frontier customs and the habits of a politics of heroics, whereas we all sense that the very idea of war, as well as the traditional idea of peace, have fallen into ruin. Hence there results a new state of affairs without war or peace, an unsettled strangeness, an errant and in some sense secret, vast space that has little by little overgrown our countries and where men act mysteriously, in ignorance of the change they themselves are in the midst of accomplishing.

– When I listen to your ambitious nocturnal evocations, I wonder if the real danger does not also lie in suggesting in a vague sort of way that we no longer run the risk of war, on the pretext that such a word belongs to an anachronistic vocabulary. It may well be anachronistic. We will die necessarily, and in any case in an anachronistic manner, whether we belong to history or to this beyond of history whose existence you have argued for. But, in reality, you do not believe in the risk of absolute catastrophe. Father Teilhard de Chardin, with the logic of his lyrical optimism, already stated that the danger of a nuclear explosion capable of blowing up the world seemed to him negligible. Negligible! It is true, he took comfort in invoking, in his terminology, "a planetary instinct of conservation" – he, too, probably ashamed of the old ecclesiastical language that would have obliged him to speak of Providence. Perhaps you yourself, along with Jünger and the romantics, have faith in some technocratic providence or some unknown harmony into whose sphere you think that man, crossing history, cannot fail to fall?

– I shall answer simply: I love the future that you do not love.

– I love the future more than you: *I love being ignorant of it.*'

Note

1 This book, first published in German, is by Ernst Jünger, *An der Zeitmauer: Zum Weltgeist des Atomzeitalters* (Stuttgart, Ernst Klett Verlag, 1959); *Le Mur du temps, Essai sur l'âge atomique*, trans. Henri Thomas (Paris, Gallimard, 1963).

Translated by Susan Hanson

PART III

Our Responsibility

The title of Part III echoes that of Blanchot's contribution to *Texts for Nelson Mandela*, a collective volume originally published in 1986.[1] If I have chosen it to define the developments which the section covers, this is because, from 1958 onwards, his life was transformed in each of the directions in which the title points: on the one hand, abandoning the language of a failing 'I' for that of a resolute 'We', he emerged from the remote solitude of literature[2] into a new experience of friendship;[3] on the other, he once again became responsive to the reality of the world, with a response that is now the discovery of a responsibility. In fact, this return was long overdue. Before 1940, in advance of what appeared to be the end, Blanchot placed a margin of indifference between what remained of himself and what the world was about to become. The end came, but (to use the terms of *The Madness of the Day*) 'the world hesitated, then regained its equilibrium.'[4] With time therefore, what he sought to occupy as a margin increasingly took on the reality of a hiatus. Meanwhile, as the 'world' provided by literature became more and more rarefied, the incongruity of his position, topographically speaking, became acute. Rather like Mallarmé, experiencing an age of historic change as no more than 'an interregnum for the poet',[5] Blanchot lived his marginality increasingly anachronistically. Whereas in the 1930s it constituted a mode of relation to the world, and to the end that seemed about to come, by the 1950s it had become an obstacle to all relation, a stance, even a pose: history was passing him by, the world lived on.[6] Then, at a stroke, he abandoned this stance and once again entered his time.

This move back into history did not simply take him back into the course of things, however: he remained at a margin of the world. This is because, as the notion of 'our responsibility' indicates, neither the self nor the world was the same for Blanchot in 1958 as they formerly were. Had they been, the political situation which had emerged by then could only have appealed to him: the integrity of the nation preserved from the twin threat posed by the loss of its colonial status and a military coup, by a powerful, historic father-figure standing above party politics, and so guaranteeing the stability of the State while neutralizing its democratic excesses. The refusal of what Pétain and Vichy offered, because it originated in a foreign power, could now be vindicated in the espousal of a truly national version of that order.

But this option was no longer available to Blanchot. Not, as some have hinted, because of political opportunism, nor simply because he is an inveterate extremist. Rather, by dismantling the subjectivity that politics had hitherto determined, the practice of literature into which Blanchot withdrew disabled it, politically, once and for all, making it in the first instance totally intractable to the politics of Vichy; but also, subsequently, just as impervious to the pattern of political action being repeated around the name of de Gaulle. This is because literature, in providing a 'world' for Blanchot in advance of the end, brought forward the end: the dismantled, 'literary' subjectivity he acquired came into existence in a 'world' whose reality as a world presupposed the real extinction of the world itself. Consequently, although 'the world hesitated, then regained its equilibrium,' its survival, though historically real, was for Blanchot the survival of a world that had, historically, come to an end. If the world lived on, therefore, it lived on as something dead: not through a process of palingenesis but, like Poe's Mr Valdemar or Kafka's Gracchus or Lazarus,[7] as something dead but somehow persistently alive. Hence any form of existence, either personal or political, that did not take account of this could itself appear now only an anachronism to him.

The break with the past expressed in the letter to Mascolo was thus a complex move: not so much a refusal of his existing political position – that is to say, a refusal of a refusal – as an acknowledgement that, in the present, that refusal could now cease merely to be something negative and take on new and original political significance. Prior to the Occupation, the silence into which Blanchot withdrew amounted to political death. The silent writing subject of literature found a political voice only when politics sought to determine the course and nature of art, whereupon it opposed an active resistance to politics, in the name of those essential values which art alone henceforth preserved. Now that refusal, without changing in nature, could be exerted politically not from without (from within a margin of indifference to what the world was becoming), but from within. What had changed? Quite simply, the post-war world had become indistinguishable from the 'world' in which Blanchot had existed since the late 1930s. Dead yet living on, it displayed precisely that interminable relation to its own end, that refusal 'to have done with it', that characterized the 'world' provided by literature. The values that could only be defended against politics from within art are now no longer solely the values of art (considered as the only world in which a failing, undone subject can live on), but essential human values that lie at 'a deeper level of agreement and disagreement' than politics, as Blanchot says in **Essential Perversion** (p. 168), but at a level whose reality is now to be found located in the post-war world.

In short, what happened in the years leading up to 1958[8] is that the failing subject who retreated, in the late 1930s, into what Blanchot subsequently termed the 'essential solitude' of art,[9] discovered, with time, that the openness and lack of unity that characterized its condition was no longer a state of radical alienation from the world, but rather an openness to others which, in the world where existence has its place, offered radically new political possibilities for the defence of essential human values, both on the part of the defenders and at the level of what is to be defended. The conflict between existence and essence, which lies at the heart not only of Blanchot's pre-war politics, but of Western politics as a whole, is here resolved, at least in principle: in a reversal more radical than any Sartre would ever achieve, the subject ceases absolutely to defend essential values individually, because the individual has ceased historically (with the end of history) to be commensurate with those essential values. In returning to the world, therefore, the no-longer-individual subject can exist, politically, only through participating in a collective refusal of the perversion of those values by a political system which is structured around the sovereignty of the individual (de Gaulle). In short, collective existence, expressed as refusal, becomes the sole guarantee of what is essential, but in the process defines the essential in a new and original way.

This new relationship between existence and essence determined the course of Blanchot's life and writing for a decade, following his re-emergence as a political voice in 1958. Arising out of the intellectual resistance to the return of de Gaulle came the 'Manifesto of the 121', a declaration of support for those who refused to bear arms against the Algerian people, which was framed by Blanchot.[10] Simultaneous with this, but extending beyond it, was the attempt to found an international review, bringing together writers from France, Germany, Italy and Great Britain, in search of a new mode of writing, appropriate in its form and subject-matter to the change of epoch occurring in Europe.[11] Finally, with May 1968 came the founding of the Comité d'Action Etudiants-Ecrivains (the Students' and Writers' Action Committee) or C.A.E.R., at the most extreme wing of intellectual participation in the movement that delivered the *coup de grâce* to de Gaulle's power.[12] At every stage, 'the responsibility and the exigency of politics' which brought Blanchot back to the world determine a mode of action that seeks to be both collective and impersonal.

Throughout this decade of renewed political response, however, the issue of *responsibility* undergoes profound transformation. Initially, it may be said, Blanchot worked to eliminate it, as an issue, from the political activity to which he had returned. The refusal which motivated him at this time, as he says in the first of his contributions to *Le 14 juillet*, 'Le refus' ('The Refusal'), remains a solitary one for all those who experience it: 'men who refuse and are linked by the force of refusal know that they are not yet together. It is precisely the time of a common affirmation that has been taken away from them.'[13] This solitude is not a solipsism, however: in it the subject (who is, significantly, anonymous) is responding to others: 'When we refuse, our gesture of refusal is . . . as far as possible, anonymous, for the power to refuse is not accomplished from within ourselves, nor in our name only, but from a beginning in what is poorest which belongs first of all to those who cannot speak.'[14] The turning-point which Blanchot had reached is clearly visible here: this solidarity in refusal with those without language (what he calls 'the amity of this resolute No')[15] is undoubtedly the beginning of a sense of responsibility for the oppressed, not to say for the proletariat. The world in which the subject who has lost his political voice now moves and speaks is a world in which others too are reduced to silence. Yet at the same time, in principle and in practice, refusal is an appeal for a brotherhood in solitude to those who, like him, are without language politically because they have lost it, rather than because they have never possessed it; to a yet to be established community of defective individuals (who as such will probably never constitute a community except in this mode of 'yet to be'), rather than to those who have not yet acquired the status of individuals.

This, it seems to me, is the profound significance of the way Blanchot framed the 'Manifesto of the 121', which he justifies in **The Right to Insubordination.** Those who would have preferred to support a *duty* of insubordination were wrong, he says, because 'an obligation depends on a prior morality . . . ; when there is duty, all you have to do is close your eyes and carry it out blindly.' A right, on the contrary, 'is a free power for which each person . . . is responsible and which binds him completely and freely' (see p. 197). This paradoxical formulation reveals that, in returning to politics in 1958, Blanchot brings with him the vestiges of the position into which he withdrew twenty years earlier, and which he explores indirectly in **Sade's Reason** as well as in 'Literature and the Right to Death':[16] in the vacuum left behind by the collapse of all value and all law, the strong are those *individuals* who, from within a margin or interval of indifference and apathy, both to their own security and to that of others, refuse all the chimeras that rush to fill that vacuum in the name of the sovereignty of their own imagination. Now, nothing remains of that imaginary world, for Blanchot the writer, but the endlessly deferred encounter with the Other in his absolute vulnerability, which first *The One Who was Standing Apart From Me* then *The Last Man* explore. At the same time, the world from which he retreated is increasingly becoming filled with the silent call of countless such others. His 'world' and the world are beginning to coincide. The language of relation, to and in the one, is now being called forth by the Other.

At the turning-point marked by 1958, however, it is clear that he continues to seek to speak with the same *sovereign* voice, in the world of others, as he did in the 'world' provided by literature. This does mean that the sovereign refusal that he continues to oppose to all recognizable forms of political organization is now exercized in the name of others, not of art. It is in other words a form of responsibility, and as such it was not without its effect.[17] It remains, however, a *sovereign* refusal; its language remains that of essential solitude; consequently the subject giving voice to refusal, who has hitherto existed exclusively in the autonomous world of literature, turns out to be fundamentally unsure of himself once he enters the world of men. The encounter with alterity in literature, with its attendant experience of anonymity, becomes a source of radical uncertainty initially, when it is replicated in the real world. Hence the ambivalence over the 'we' that forms the subject of this 'resolute No'. In short, though he finds himself at a turning-point, Blanchot is clearly uncertain at first which way to turn in response to the call from others he now encounters in the world. This is, however, not simply a shortcoming: though it is impossible to analyse here, the particular form of dissident radicalism practised at the time by Blanchot, Mascolo, Antelme and others, prolonging as it does an attitude to Marxism first developed by the Surrealists between the wars, constitutes an important and original phase in the emergence of a libertarian, post-Marxist form of 'communism' in France and elsewhere. At the same time, as a position it was untenable politically, or at least it proved to be so in Blanchot's case. Throughout the decade separating de Gaulle's return and May 1968, he continued to write and act politically; and if Levinas is to be believed, when May came he was overjoyed.[18]

Yet, as **Disorderly Words** reveals, however much he felt in tune with the events of May, and however alert he was to their revolutionary potential, politically they could only lead to an impasse. There is a powerful continuity between his attitude in 1958 and what he writes in 1968. Now as then, the forms of political organization provided by the Constitution of 1958 (whether in support of it or in opposition) are absolute anachronisms: the world to which they could apply is dead. There has been, he says, a stop (*un arrêt*) (p. 205); between the liberal-capitalist world and the present there is an absolute hiatus (p. 204). But now, unlike 1958, the refusal of the old world is not focused by a single issue and the responsibility to which it appeals: it is total, active and revolutionary. The present is the present of 'the exigency of Communism' (p. 204); the break it constitutes legitimizes sweeping away the old order entirely; responsibility and friendship fuse in an act of affirmative refusal.

At the height of this movement of enthusiasm, however, the texts published anonymously in *Comité* point towards an impasse which caused Blanchot to retreat from politics once and for all after May 1968. However original the position that evolved between 1958 and 1968, it remained limited by the conditions under which the refusal that informed it originally came into being. On the surface, this is apparent from what could be seen as an alarming return to the revolutionary rhetoric of the pre-war period. Now as then, violence and destruction are what Blanchot is calling for. On a deeper level, moreover, this position displays the same essential contradictoriness that overtook Blanchot as the 1930s progressed, even though this is accepted now rather than endured. But the fact remains that a revolution that takes place to the extent that it is merely possible, putting a stop [*arrêt*] to everything and causing society to fall apart is, politically speaking, a mirage. However powerful the refusal it exerts against a world that refuses to see that it is dead, the living world it speaks for – that of the 'exigency of Communism' and the responsibility with and for others that this establishes – simply cannot exist: it is a utopia.[19]

It is this limitation that puts an end to Blanchot's political involvement after 1968. But though it is a limitation, it is not a defect in his thinking. At two levels, Blanchot can be seen to be working something out, during this decade, which is of decisive significance both for him and for thought in general. On one level, this leads to the discovery that 'the exigency of Communism', in whose name all existing forms of social organization are being refused, is primarily a *theoretical* one. Between it and the liberal-capitalist world, Blanchot says, 'the *theoretical* hiatus is absolute' (p. 204); and to bring to light the refusal it motivates in its simultaneously negative and affirmative singularity, is 'one of the *theoretical* tasks of the new political thinking' (pp. 200–1). At the 'revolutionary' brink to which he had returned in 1968, thirty years on, the acknowledgement that the 'exigency of politics' dictates a praxis that is confined to thought (and writing), with all that this implies for the concept of revolution in the twentieth century, inaugurates the final phase of Blanchot's development as a writer, which is examined in Part IV: **The Step Beyond**.

On the other related level, as well as the exigency of politics, it is the responsibility this entails that is finally clarified. The uncertainty apparent in 1958 over where to turn, in response and out of responsibility to the Other, is at last resolved. In a move that is as decisive, both for Blanchot and for Western thought, as the shift of politics into theory and writing, the Other in whose name refusal must be offered ceases to be the vague *political* Other of 1958, who is no more than a pale, post-Marxist after-image of the victim of capitalism, the proletarian, and becomes the absolute victim of Western culture and society, immolated historically along with a world that has died yet persistently lives on: the Jew.

Almost twenty years later, in the long text included in this section, **Intellectuals under Scrutiny** Blanchot embraces the whole period of his political activity in a meditation on the role and responsibility of the intellectual since the Dreyfus Affair. In passing, the collective action of 1958 and 1968 is evoked, for its significance but also for its limitations: for 'abuse of authority' (p. 225) in the case of the Manifesto of the 121; as 'an exception [which] provides no solution' (p. 224) in the case of the events of May. The detachment which these judgements display, and which permits Blanchot in addition to reflect, indirectly at least, upon the implications of his own political position in the 1930s,[20] is provided by a relation to Judaism and the Jew which, by 1984, is long established as the exigency governing his writing. The turn towards Judaism and its Other is long in preparation, however, and is not without its difficulties. Indeed, the issue of friendship, which is the focus of the ambivalence regarding the Other evident in 1958, continues in the 1980s to prove problematical. In *Michel Foucault As I Imagine Him* (1986), Blanchot defends the memory of May 1968 in the following terms:

> whatever the detractors of May might say, it was a splendid moment, when anyone could speak to anyone else, anonymously, impersonally, a man among men, welcomed with no other justification than that of being another person.[21]

And he returns to this defence of the camaraderie of May at the end of his homage to Foucault, when, evoking the Greek notion of *philia*, he observes:

> he would be tempted to call on the ancients for a revalorization of the practices of friendship, which, although never lost, have not again recaptured, except for a few of us, their exalted virtue.[22]

Yet in 1993, at the end of 'Pour l'amitié', this celebration of the bond between equals that so intruded upon Blanchot's response to the call of the oppressed in 1958 is sharply countered. Having returned once again to May, in order this time to distinguish between the camaraderie in *tutoiement* imposed by the movement and the friendship uniting him, Mascolo and others ('friendship has no room for camaraderie'),[23] he interrupts an elegiac concluding meditation on the difference between the two with the words:

> Greek *philia* is reciprocity, exchange between Same and Same, but never openness to the *Other*, discovery of *Autrui* in so far as one is responsible for him, recognition of his pre-excellence, an awakening and a sobering up by this *Autrui* who will never leave me alone.[24]

And he concludes: 'That is my salute to Emmanuel Levinas, the only friend – oh distant friend – to whom I say *tu* and who says *tu* to me.'

By now, the uncertainty still apparent in these texts has long since been gathered up and worked through in Blanchot's writing, remaining at most a problem at the personal level from which he is speaking here. Previously, however, it formed the focus of a long, slow negotiation with the Other, lasting for the entire decade between 1958 and 1968, and central to which is a debate with that friend among friends, Emmanuel

Levinas. When *Totality and Infinity* appeared in 1961,[25] Blanchot published no less than three successive articles, in the dialogue form inaugurated in **On a Change of Epoch**, in response to Levinas's book. He clearly had difficulties with the latter's argument, both in so far as it is essentially a religious one,[26] and for the status it gives the Other (*Autrui*). And in what can only appear an extraordinary move, Blanchot devotes the third of his articles, not to Levinas at all, but to Robert Antelme's account of his prison-camp experiences, *L'Espèce humaine* ('Humankind'), which first appeared in 1947, and about which he says:

> Each time the question: who is '*Autrui*' emerges in our words I think of the book by Robert Antelme, for it not only testifies to the society of the German camps of World War II, it also leads us to an essential reflection. (p. 235)

It is difficult not see at work here a powerful resistance to the specificity of Jewish experience in the broadest sense (Antelme was not a Jew, his camp was not an extermination camp). Indeed Blanchot is so wary of Levinas's philosophy of the Other that, as a preliminary to his examination of Antelme's book, he proposes that the word quite simply be withdrawn.[27] The issue at stake is of the deepest significance for the development of Blanchot's thought and cannot properly be examined here. In 1962, let it simply be said, that 'deeper level of understanding and misunderstanding' which lies beyond politics for him in 1958, may well be an openness to others and a discovery of responsibility; the otherness of *Autrui* remains determined primarily by his friendship for Antelme, Mascolo and others (a *philia*), rather than by his friendship for Levinas; while the responsibility that the name *Autrui* evokes is one that the name also obscures in Blanchot's view, if it leads to memory of the camps rather than to 'an essential reflection', since:

> *autrui* is a name that is essentially neutral and . . . far from relieving us of all responsibility of attending to the neutral, it reminds us that we must, in the presence of the other who comes to us as *Autrui*, respond to the depth of strangeness, of inertia, or irregularity and idleness [*désœuvrement*] to which we open when we seek to receive the speech of the Outside.[28]

Yet it is clear too that Blanchot's thinking is being powerfully challenged at this time, by Levinas and more generally by the question of the Other borne by Judaism and the fate of the Jews in the twentieth century. Shortly after the series of studies inspired by *Totality and Infinity*, he published a piece entitled **Being Jewish**. The peremptoriness of tone perceptible in the earlier pieces is still there: the dismissal of God in 'Knowledge of the Unknown'[29] is echoed in **Being Jewish** by the words:

> Here we should bring in the great gift of Israel, its teaching of the one God. But I would rather say, brutally, that what we owe to Jewish monotheism is not the revelation of the one God, but the revelation of speech as the place where men hold themselves in relation with what excludes all relation: the infinitely Distant, the absolutely Foreign. (p. 233)

Now, however, the refusal of 'theology' no longer deflects the question posed by Judaism, which, having received a tentative response from Blanchot in 1959 (though this was through the intermediary of a 'literary' form, the Hasidic stories presented by Martin Buber in *Gog and Magog*),[30] is now explored in terms of Jewish experience. The next year (1963), in a review of Edmond Jabès's *Book of Questions*, Blanchot writes: 'In history, the central break is called Judaism,' and goes on to extend his exploration of 'being a Jew'.[31] And in 1968, an article in homage to the Heidegger expert Jean Beaufret is headed with the words:

> For Emmanuel Levinas, with whom, for forty years, I have been linked by a friendship that is closer to me than myself: in a relationship of invisibility to Judaism.[32]

These words were omitted when the article was included in *The Infinite Conversation* in 1969. But by then, the developments that had been slowly taking place over the decade had found more substantial expression. The third of the pieces devoted to Levinas, on Antelme, is separated from the other two; a number of paragraphs from it (including the call for the term *Autrui* to be withdrawn) are used as the basis for a third piece in *The Infinite Conversation*, 'The Relation of the Third Kind', written specially for the volume and in which Blanchot brings to the fore the *philosophical* nature of the question posed by Judaism. More significantly, perhaps, the article on Antelme is placed in a later section of the book, which is given the title originally given to the article (**The Indestructible**), but where the article comes second to the one written after it in 1962, **Being Jewish**.

With this adjustment, it would seem clear that Blanchot wished in 1969 to turn once and for all in the direction of the Other of Judaism in preference to the Other of camaraderie and of friendship considered as *philia*. The next year, he makes his first direct reference to the Holocaust.[33] The step taken here will lead him, once and for all, beyond yet not beyond the entire frame in which his life and work have so far developed, to a relation of witness to Judaism in writing whose endurance is attested by the piece with which this Part ends, **'Do Not Forget'**.

Notes

1 *Texts for Nelson Mandela*, ed. Jacques Derrida and Mustapha Tilli (New York, Seaver, 1987). Originally published as *Pour Nelson Mandela*, avant-propos de Dominique Lecoq (Paris, Gallimard, 1986).

2 This remoteness was also geographical. Between 1947 and 1957, Blanchot revealed in 1989, he lived in Eze-Villages, near Cannes. In 'Pour l'amitié' he refers again to that period: 'I was living far away. The "I" is already incongruous and improper. . . . I was silently absent' (pp. 8–9).

3 There may be said to be four phases to what Blanchot refers to as *l'amitié* in his life: the comradeship of the pre-war activism; the almost clandestine friendship with Bataille between 1940 and the latter's death in 1962; the friendship with Dionys Mascolo, Robert Antelme and Marguerite Duras which took shape during the 1950s; encompassing all of these – and lying above and beyond friendship as we shall see – what he has called the 'invisible' relation to Judaism which binds him to Emmanuel Levinas, 'my oldest friend, the only one I feel entitled to address in the *tu* form' (see p. 244).

4 *The Madness of the Day*, tr. Lydia Davis (Barrytown, New York, Station Hill, 1978), p. 6. This *récit* first appeared in 1949.

5 Stéphane Mallarmé, 'Autobiographie', a letter to Paul Verlaine dated 19 November 1885.

6 At the Liberation, Sartre was at pains to relegate writers such as Bataille and Blanchot to the status of pre-war figures. During the 1940s and 1950s, it was by comparison with his conception of the writer's commitment that Blanchot's position acquired its definition.

7 See *La Part du feu* (Paris, Gallimard, 1949), p. 316.

8 The break with the past expressed in his letter to Mascolo is not a bolt from the blue: two years earlier, Blanchot was involved with Mascolo, André Breton and others in a 'Committee of Revolutionary Intellectuals', which sought to respond to events in Hungary and Poland, as well as to counter the anti-democratic developments at home. See Gerard Legrand, *André Breton et son temps* (Paris, Le Soleil Noir, 1976), p. 85 for a brief account of the first meeting of this Committee in 1956.

9 See *The Space of Literature*, tr. Ann Smock (Lincoln, University of Nebraska Press, 1982), chapter 1: 'Essential Solitude'. This piece was first published in January 1953.

10 The text of the Manifesto was published in English as 'A Declaration Concerning the Right of Insubordination in the Algerian War', *Evergreen Review*, 4, 15 (Nov.–Dec. 1960) [unpaginated].

11 A dossier of documents relating to this project is published in *Lignes*, 11 (September 1990), pp. 161–301.

12 The ephemeral organ of this movement was entitled *Comité*. Everything published in it was anonymous.

13 'Le Refus', in *L'Amitié* (Paris, Gallimard, 1971), pp. 130–1 (p. 130).

14 Ibid., p. 131.

15 Ibid., p. 130.

16 See *The Gaze of Orpheus*, tr. Lydia Davis (Barrytown, New York, Station Hill, 1981), pp. 21–62. This was originally published as 'La littérature et le droit à la mort' in *La Part du feu* in 1949.

17 The 'Manifesto of the 121' remains the most significant undertaking on the part of French artists, writers and intellectuals in the post-war period. It was, moreover, fraught with consequences for those who signed, if their careers depended directly or indirectly

upon the State. Blanchot and others were questioned and charged, as he recalls in 1993 in 'Pour l'amitié' (pp. 10–11). Several years previously, Alain Robbe-Grillet evoked the same episode with some glee: 'the examining magistrate who interrogated Maurice Blanchot about the "Manifesto of the 121" . . . eventually had to request sick-leave on the grounds of moral exhaustion' (in *Angélique ou l'enchantement* (Paris, Editions de Minuit, 1987), p. 204). The enduring significance of the Manifesto is reflected in the decision by *Le Nouvel Observateur* in 1988 to bring together as many of the original signatories as possible, in protest against repression in Algeria. Blanchot refused to sign because the text of the declaration did not explicitly condemn Islamic fundamentalism. (I am grateful to M. Serge Lafaurie for providing me with this information.)

18 See 'Levinas: au nom d'autrui' 'Levinas: in the Name of the Other', an interview with Luc Ferry, Raphaël Hadas-Lebel and Sylvaine Pasquier, in *L'Express*, no 2035 (13 July 1990), pp. 60–6: 'did you know that the barricades of May filled him with joy?' (p. 64).

19 During this decade, Blanchot is aware of the risk that what he and others are seeking to achieve may be utopian. As he says of their attempt at a collective undertaking, in one of the preparatory documents published in the 'Dossier of the International Review': 'we must test it through experience, and if it is a utopia, then be willing to fail utopianly' (*Lignes*, p. 180).

20 Though ostensibly concerning Paul Valéry's attitude during the Affair, it is difficult not to hear a more personal reflection in the words: 'There would thus seem to be a moment, in every life, when the unjustifiable prevails and the incomprehensible is given its due' (p. 213).

21 *Michel Foucault As I Imagine Him*, trans. Jeffrey Mehlman, in *Foucault, Blanchot* (New York, Zone Books, 1987), pp. 61–109 (p. 63; translation modified).

22 Ibid., pp. 108–9.

23 'Pour l'amitié', p. 14.

24 Ibid., p. 16.

25 Emmanuel Levinas, *Totalité et infini* (The Hague, Martinus Nijhoff, 1961); translated by Alphonso Lingis as *Totality and Infinity: An Essay on Exteriority* (Pittsburgh, Duquesne University Press, 1969).

26 In 'Violence and Metaphysics' (*Writing and Difference*, tr. Alan Bass (London, Routledge & Kegan Paul, 1978), pp. 79–153), Jacques Derrida takes Blanchot to task over his use of the terms 'theological context' to define the limitations of Levinas's argument (p. 103). Clearly sensitive to the criticism, Blanchot adds the following footnote to the piece when it is included in *The Infinite Conversation*: ' "Context" here, as Jacques Derrida very aptly observes, is a word that Levinas could only deem inappropriate – just as he would the reference to theology' (note to p. 56).

27 'The Relation of the Third Kind (man without horizon)', in *The Infinite Conversation*, pp. 66–74: 'Perhaps . . . it is time to withdraw this term *autrui*' (p. 72).

28 Ibid.

29 'Let us leave aside God – the name is too imposing' (*The Infinite Conversation*, p. 50.) The French could equally well be rendered as 'Let's leave God out of this'.

30 'Gog et Magog', in *L'Amitié* (Paris, Gallimard, 1971), pp. 259–71.

31 In 'Traces', *L'Amitié*, pp. 246–58 (p. 252).

32 'Parole de fragment' (The Fragment Word), in *L'Endurance de la pensée. Pour saluer Jean Beaufret* (Paris, Plon, 1968), pp. 103–9. In *The Infinite Conversation*, pp. 307–13. A last-minute crisis, the facts surrounding which have still to be fully established, prompted Blanchot to add the homage to Levinas to his contribution to the volume.

33 In 'Fragmentaires', *L'Ephémère*, 16 (Winter 1970), pp. 376–99. In *Le pas au-delà* (Paris, Gallimard, 1972), *passim*. The fragment in question is to be found on p. 156.

18

The Right to Insubordination (1960)*

MADELEINE CHAPSAL – Why did you sign this Declaration?

MAURICE BLANCHOT – I should like to say to begin with that this
Declaration is a solemn act and that it is quite self-sufficient; any
individual commentary on it runs the risk of weakening it, mitigating
its effects, or else depriving it of the collective character that is one of
its important distinguishing features. Having made these reservations,
I shall answer that it is as a writer that I signed this text: not as a
political writer, nor even as a citizen involved in the political struggle,
but as an apolitical writer who felt moved to express an opinion about
problems that concern him essentially. What form do these problems
take? We know that there are young Frenchmen currently being pro-
secuted for refusing to bear arms against the Algerian people; and
others for having given assistance to Algerian fighters. These are the
simple facts. They were not invented by us, they are known to
everyone, everyone talks about them and everyone has an opinion
about them: the newspapers, the political parties, the courts. It
seemed to us that, faced by facts of such gravity, and given the debate
unfolding before public opinion in France and abroad, it was our duty
not to remain silent, but to express a firm opinion of our own. This
decision to speak is contained in the closing declarations of the text.
One of the main purposes of the Declaration is to bring out the
particular responsibility of intellectuals: when the democratic order is
corrupted or decays, it falls to them, independent of any purely
political allegiance, to say in simple terms what seems to them just.

M.C. – And you say that insubordination has become a right?

MAURICE BLANCHOT – Yes indeed. I believe that all the force of the
Declaration, all of its power to unsettle, comes from the authority with
which it utters one word, the word insubordination, a solemn word
of utmost refusal: the right to insubordination. I say right and not
duty, a term that some people, in an ill-considered way, wished the
Declaration to use, no doubt because they believe that the formulation

---

* Originally published in *Le Droit à l'insoumission* (Paris, Maspero, 1961), pp. 90–3.

of a duty goes further than that of a right. But that is not the case: an obligation depends upon a prior morality, that vouches for it, guarantees it and justifies it; when there is duty, all you have to do is close your eyes and carry it out blindly. In that case, everything is simple. A right, on the contrary, depends only on itself, on the exercise of the freedom of which it is the expression. Right is a free power for which each person, for his part and in relation to himself, is responsible, and which binds him completely and freely: nothing is stronger, nothing is more solemn. That is why one must say: the right to insubordination; it is a matter of each person's sovereign decision. But something must also be added: the right to insubordination in the Algerian war. Because – and it is important to stress this – the Declaration is not a call to anarchy, denying and contesting the authority of the State in all circumstances. Here too, those who would have wished the Declaration to be more assertive, to assert as a general rule the right to refuse all military obligations, were in fact merely looking for an alibi: that refuge always provided, for good conscience, by the theoretical expression of an absolute right bearing no relation to reality. What is important, what is decisive, is to state that, in the situation precisely defined by both the Algerian war and the transformation of military power into political power, traditional civic duties have ceased to count as obligations. That is what the Declaration states essentially.

M.C. – Are you not afraid that talk of insubordination will lead the nation into anarchy?

MAURICE BLANCHOT – But the anarchy is to be found in the fact that the army has been allowed to become a political force, and also in the fact that the present regime came to power thanks to a military *coup d'état*, which consequently condemns as illegal from the outset the imperious order which it claims, in its august way, to represent and to impose on us. Since May 1958 we have been in a state of anarchy, that is the truth of which everyone is dimly aware. For since May 1958, everyone knows that the army has become a political force, claiming the right to decide the fate of the nation as a whole. We know that the army, thanks to the immense material force it represents, as well as the importance it has acquired precisely because of the Algerian war, has the power to overturn governments, change regimes and impose decisions of its choosing. This transformation of the power of the military is a crucial fact, of unprecedented gravity. Well, what we are saying is that, given that state of affairs, the refusal to assume one's military duty takes on a completely different meaning. By claiming for

itself the right to have a political attitude, the army must recognize in
return that every young Frenchman has the right to judge whether or
not he is willing to be enrolled in the sort of political party that many
of its highest-ranking members are seeking to make of it. Some of
them accept, and that is their business. Others refuse: this refusal is
henceforth a fundamental right.

M.C. – Insubordination is a very serious act. Are you not afraid you will
persuade young men to take such serious action and that their entire
lives will be affected as a consequence?

MAURICE BLANCHOT – As soon as we are willing to say that the
Algerian war is unjust and criminal, we have said all that is necessary
in order to justify the refusal to take part in it. When, on three
occasions, after Melun, General de Gaulle solemnly declared that the
war and the fighting in Algeria were absurd, he himself alerted young
Frenchmen (or else the words he utters have no meaning) that henceforth, to take part in the fighting was to take part in something utterly
meaningless. We have said and are saying nothing different. I would
however like to add one thing: deep down, and though they are only
vaguely aware of it, the great majority of the French people are
convinced that this war is unjust and, precisely, absurd. One might
therefore expect them to be ready to revolt against the fact that their
sons are taking part in it. But the idea must be turned round: because
their sons are taking part in it – even if only as automata, through the
automatic nature of military service – they can no longer recognize
that this war is unjust, and they become its accomplices. That way, the
army has a hold over everyone: the sons, physically, and because it
changes them little by little; and the parents, who feel solidarity and
complicity with their sons. That is the trap. The army is the trap. This
can never be pointed out enough, nor denounced enough.

M.C. – Do you think that signing such a Declaration can have a political
effect?

MAURICE BLANCHOT – You mean: won't it be politically ineffectual?
I think the answer must be: it does not seek to have any immediate
political effect, or more precisely: it will be effective precisely in so far
as it has taken no account of any considerations of practical and
political efficacy, for example by attempting, through a compromise
over the terms in which it is expressed, to rally as many people as
possible. It is an act of judgement, that is its significance and that is its
strength. It is not merely a manifesto of protest. It is a Declaration,
and a declaration which decides, in the absence of any legitimate
authority, what it is right to refuse and to demand. It is therefore

nothing but words? That is true, but words with all the authority of a solemn utterance for which all those who pronounce it feel henceforth responsible, and ready to uphold it calmly, firmly, as long as necessary, whatever the consequences.

Translated by Michael Holland

19

Disorderly Words (1968)*

Affirm the Break

(1) The ultimate goal, which is to say, also, the immediate, obvious goal, which is to say the goal that is hidden, direct and indirect: *affirm the break*. *Affirm it*: organize it so as to make it more and more real, more and more radical.

What break? The break with the powers that be, hence with the notion of power, hence everywhere that power predominates. This obviously applies to the University, to the idea of knowledge, to the language relations to be found in teaching, in leading, perhaps to all language, etc., but it applies even more to our own conception of opposition to the powers that be, each time such opposition constitutes itself to become a party in power.

(2) Radically affirm the break: that is the same as saying (this is its first meaning) that we are *in a state of war* with things as they are, everywhere and always; that we are exclusively in a relation with a law that we do not recognize, a society whose values and truths, whose ideals and whose privileges are alien to us; that the enemy we face is thus all the more dangerous for seeming more indulgent, but is one with whom it is understood that we will never collaborate, in any way, and not even on tactical grounds.

(3) To be the bearers of this break is not merely to dislodge, or attempt to dislodge, from their integration within the social order those forces that promise a break, it is to make sure that really, and each time it occurs, refusal, without ceasing to be active refusal, does not remain a *purely negative moment*. That, politically and philosophically, is one of the most powerful characteristics of the movement. In this sense, radical refusal such as that borne by the movement, and such as that which we have to bear, goes way beyond simple negativity, in so far as it is the negation even of what has not yet been advanced and affirmed. To bring

* Originally published as 'Affirmer la rupture', 'La mort politique', 'Le communisme sans héritage', 'Tracts, affiches, bulletins', 'Rupture du temps, révolution', in *Comité*, 1 (October 1968), pp. 4–5, 8, 13–14, 16, 18. A selection of these pieces, some translated, was published in *Libération*, 28–29 January 1984, p. 23, under the title 'Mots de désordre'.

to light the singular character of this refusal is one of the theoretical tasks of the new political thinking. This theoretical undertaking obviously does not entail drawing up a programme or a platform, but rather, independent of any programmatic project, indeed of any project, maintaining *a refusal that is an affirmation*, bringing out or maintaining an affirmation that does not come to any arrangements [*s'arranger*], but rather undoes arrangements [*dérange*], including its own, since it is in relation with dis-arrangement [*le désarrangement*] or disarray [*le désarroi*] or else the non-structurable.

This decision about a refusal that is not a power, neither a power to negate, nor a negation depending upon an affirmation that has always already been either advanced or projected, is what is referred to when we bring in to the 'revolutionary' process the term *spontaneity*, provided we recognize that this notion of spontaneity must, in several respects, be handled with caution, implying as it does a number of dubious ideas – for example, a sort of vitalism or natural self-creating power, etc.

Political Death

When from time to time, speaking of so and so as it were obliviously, we say: 'he is politically dead,' we know that this opinion does not affect another, it affects us all, more or less. We have to accept it, and even bid it welcome and lay claim to it. Political death keeps watch in all of us, like 'a light inside the tomb', so as to guard us against all distraction, all day-to-day musing, all easy recrimination – more precisely, all possibility of survival. Political death, that which allows one to accept the unacceptable, is not an individual phenomenon. We all take part in it, whether we wish to or not. And in French society, the higher you rise the greater this death becomes, reaching, at the top, a state of derisory excess: a presence which is that of humanity petrified. If in this country today there is a man who is politically dead, it is the man who bears – but does he bear it? – the title of President of the Republic, a republic from which he is as cut off as he is from any living future. He is an actor, playing a role borrowed from ancient history, just as his language belongs to a role, is imitated speech, which is sometimes so anachronistic that it appears always to have been posthumous. Naturally, he does not know this. He believes in his role, believing he is magnifying the present when he is parodying the past. And this dead man, unaware that he is dead, is awe-inspiring with his great dead man's stature, and that dead obstinacy that passes for authority, and from time to time the awful, distinguished vulgarity which signifies the dissolution which comes of being dead. His is a strange, insistent presence, in which we see the perseverance of a world of old,

and in which, let us not forget it, we too feel ourselves dying, sumptuous-
ly, laughably.

For he himself is nothing, he is merely the delegate of our political
death, a victim himself, a mask behind which nothingness lies.

The first task is therefore to get rid of this superior alibi, then, at every
level, the alibi of alibis. Let us not believe that we are politically alive
because we involve ourselves with moderation in orthodox opposition.
And let us not believe we are intellectually alive, because we are involved
in a highly developed culture where dissidence is the rule, and where
criticism and even negation are signs that we belong. Some time ago, a
Minister declared – with the lack of intelligence of those who are vain –
that the fate of the world would not be decided in Bolivia. It is just as
likely to be decided there as in France, where the only principle of
government is stability, and where the only change one can look forward
to is the death of a ghost-like old man, who seems constantly unsure
whether he is in the Pantheon or not, or whether his memory, which
forgets nothing, has not simply forgotten the imperceptible event of his
end: which is to say the end of a sham.

If he survives, let us take advantage of his survival in order to become
fully aware of our own state of living death, which we share with him,
while reserving the additional right to denounce our destruction, even if
this is by means of words that are themselves already destroyed. From
this, here and there, today, tomorrow, others will perhaps derive a new
and vigorous power to destroy.

Tomorrow, it was May: the infinite power of destruction – construction.

Communism without a Heritage

We must repeat to ourselves those simple things that we constantly
forget: patriotism, chauvinism, nationalism have nothing that distinguishes them from each other, except that nationalism is the coherent
ideology to which patriotism gives sentimental expression (as illustrated
still by such lamentable declarations as 'I am wedded to France'). Everything that allows men to become rooted, through values or sentiments, in
one time, in *one* history, in *one* language, is the principle of alienation
which constitutes man as privileged in so far as he is what he is (French,
of precious French blood), imprisoning him in contentment with his own
reality and encouraging him to offer it as an example or impose it as a
conquering assertion. Marx said with calm forcefulness: *the end of alienation can only begin if man agrees to go out from himself* (from everything that
constitutes him as interiority): *out from religion, the family and the State.*
The call to go out, into an outside that is neither another world nor what

lies behind the world, is the gesture that must be opposed to all forms of patriotism, whatever they may be.

■ Patriotism has the most extraordinary power to integrate, since it is that which, in our intimate thoughts, in our everyday deeds and in political developments, works to reconcile everything, be they deeds, men or classes, and to prevent all class struggle, to establish unity in the name of particularizing values (national particularism raised to the level of a universal) and to ward off necessary division, which is that of infinite destruction. The day international Communism, in a tactical ruse, agreed to serve the national community and was ashamed to be seen as the foreign party [*le parti de l'étranger*], it lost what Lenin called its soul. Even to speak of the fatherland of revolution, or the fatherland of socialism, is to use a most unfortunate metaphor, one most likely to kindle the need to be at home somewhere, to submit to the Father, to the law of the Father, to the blessing of the Father. It just takes one word, and the man who wished to free himself becomes reconciled. The party in turn becomes patrial. The socialists (no more ridiculous for that than other intransigent progressives) say with touching emotion admittedly: for us, our party is our family, and naturally you would sacrifice everything for the survival of the family, starting with socialism. I say that the glorious call 'my country or death', were it not that it promotes the word death and thus the word life, could well simply lead to a frightful mystification, for the country, precisely, is death, the false life that is sustained by dead values, or else the tiresomely tragic death of heroes, those hateful heroes.

■ Communism: that which excludes (and is itself excluded from) any already constituted community. The proletarian class: a community with no other common denominator than penury, lack of satisfaction, lack in every sense.

■ Communism that is accommodating: whereas Lenin, not afraid to use the word, said that the *soul* of Communism is what makes it *intolerable, intractable*. To reflect on the error of humanism is to reflect on the error of easy-going Communism [*le communisme commode*], that is to say Communism which, in wanting to lose nothing, ends up being reconciled with everything, including those human, all too human values: national values.

■ Communism cannot be the heir to anything. We must get that into our heads: not even the heir to itself. It is rather called upon constantly to allow the legacy of the centuries, however venerable, to be lost, at least momentarily, but at the same time radically. The theoretical hiatus is absolute; the break that has occurred is decisive. Between the liberal-capitalist world, our world, and the present of the exigency of Communism (a present without presence), there is merely the hyphenation of a disaster, of a change that is astral [*un changement d'astre*].

Tracts, Posters, Bulletins

To write *about* is, in every respect, inappropriate. But to write about the event that is destined, precisely, (along with others) to prevent us from ever again writing *about* – be it in epitaphs, commentaries, analyses, eulogies or condemnations – is to falsify it in advance and to have always already missed it. We shall therefore never write about what took place or did not take place in May: not out of respect, nor even a concern not to place restrictions on the event by circumscribing it. We admit that this refusal is one of the points where writing and the decision to break coincide: each of them always imminent and always unpredictable.

■ Already, by the dozen, books are being published on the subject of what took place or did not take place in May. In general they are intelligent, partially correct, useful perhaps. Written by sociologists, teachers, journalists and even militants. Naturally, no one expected to see disappear, through the strength of the movement (even though it does in a way forbid it), the reality and the possibility of the *book*: that is to say completion, finishing off.

■ The book has not disappeared, it must be recognized. However, let us observe that everything in the history of our culture and in history itself that has constantly destined writing not for the book, but for the absence of the book, has constantly anticipated, and at the same time prepared for, this upheaval. There will still be books, and worse still, fine books. But the writing on the walls, a mode that is neither inscriptional or elocutionary, the tracts hastily distributed in the street that are a manifestation of the haste of the street, the posters that do not need to be read but are there as a challenge to all law, the disorderly words, the words, free of discourse, that accompany the rhythm of our steps, the political shouts – and bulletins by the dozen like this bulletin, everything that unsettles, appeals, threatens and finally questions without waiting for a reply, without coming to rest in certainty, will never be confined by us in a book, for a book, even when open, tends towards closure, which is a refined form of repression.

■ In May there is no book about May: not for lack of time or the need to 'act', but because of a more decisive impediment: it is all being written elsewhere, in a world without publication; it is being distributed in the face of the police and in a way with their help, violence pitted against violence. This stop [*arrêt*] put to the book, which is also a stop put to history, and which, far from taking us back to a point preceding culture indicates a point lying way beyond culture, is what is most provocative to authority, to power, to the law. May this bulletin prolong that stop, while preventing it from ever stopping. No more books, never again, for as long as we remain in contact with the upheaval of the break.

■ Tracts, posters, bulletins; street words, infinite words; it is not some concern for effectiveness that makes them necessary. Whether effective or not, they belong to the decision of the moment. They appear, they disappear. They do not say everything, on the contrary they ruin everything, they are outside everything. They act and reflect fragmentarily. They leave no trace: they are a trait without trace. Like the words on the walls, they are written in insecurity, received under threat, are themselves the bearers of danger, then pass with the passer-by who passes them on, loses them or forgets them.

A Break in Time: Revolution

As soon as, through the movement of those forces tending towards a break, revolution appears as something *possible*, with a possibility that is not abstract, but historically and concretely determined, then in those moments revolution *has taken place*. The only mode in which revolution is present is that of its real possibility. At that moment, there is a stop, a suspension. In this stop, society falls apart completely. The law collapses: for an instant there is innocence; history is interrupted. Walter Benjamin:

> The conscious desire to break the continuity of history belongs to the revolutionary classes in the moment of action. It is just such a consciousness that expresses itself in the July revolution. During the evening of the first day of the struggle, simultaneously but as a result of separate initiatives, in several places people fired on the clocks in the towers of Paris.

Translated by Michael Holland

20

Intellectuals under Scrutiny: An Outline for Thought (1984)*

Jean-François Lyotard recently published some useful pages, with the title 'The Tomb of the Intellectual'.[1] But the artist and the writer, constantly in search of their own tombs, are not so deluded as to believe that they will ever lie in them. A tomb? Were they to find one, they would resemble the crusaders who, according to Hegel, set off to free Christ in his age-old sepulchre, knowing full well that, as their faith told them, it was empty, so that were they to succeed, all they would set free would be the sanctity of emptiness. Which is to say that, were they to find it, their task would not be over: it would just have begun, with the realization that it is only in the endless pursuit of works that worklessness [le désœuvrement] is to be found.

That being so, I wonder whether artists and writers do not bring aid and succour, through the necessity of their lack of success and their distress, to those we call intellectuals and whose burial is perhaps premature. Intellectual is such a name of ill repute, easily caricatured and a convenient insult. Whoever recalls the Algerian war also recalls having been despised for being an intellectual, and for that reason not at all disposed to deny being one.

Today it is in himself that the intellectual is seeking the reasons for his decline and perhaps for his self-denial. It would seem that the universal idea is no longer what he has in view, as was once thought to be the case during the Enlightenment. Just as Spengler, following the Great War, jubilantly announced the decline of the West, there are those who believe they are announcing the end or ruin of reason, considered as having the same value for everyone and as binding upon everyone, and announcing this as a new idea, when the whole of the twentieth century has sought to replace reason with an Unreason, in subtle or cunning guise, which would not overturn it but be the affirmation of its ground (or its abyss). To seek out how, from a starting-point in the irrational and its realm, the unconscious, by way of erotic violence and the death drive, it was possible to allow an affirmation of hope in a reasonable society where the

* Originally published as 'Les Intellectuels en question', *Le Débat*, 29 (March 1984), pp. 3–28.

ambiguous possibilities of sublimation would continue to bear fruit – such was Freud's task, yet one always under threat from Freud himself. Similarly, Nietzsche incessantly struggles against Nietzsche, demystifying the True but without exalting mystery, casting doubt not only on the universal but on legitimate thinking about the Universe, debasing oneness, but unable to free himself from the eternal return of the Same, and hence failing to disrupt the equivalence of Dionysos and Apollo.

I shall not venture to decide whether it still makes sense to distinguish between the part played by the rational and the part played by the irrational in the work of Heidegger, so reductive do these words appear in relation to a way of thinking which holds them to be inadequate, or the legacy of an impoverished Cartesianism; nor even to decide whether Heidegger's fatal mistake in adhering (however briefly) to National Socialism finds its explanation in some area of his philosophy (the hegemony of the philosophical over the political, and the certainty that it is the destiny of the German people to incarnate that hegemony by repeating the demands of Greek thought),[2] or whether we should invoke his naïveté or his astonishing blindness, that 'naïveté' which makes him write, to justify himself for having accepted the post of Rector of the University of Freiburg in 1933: 'At that time I saw in the movement that had come to power a possibility for unifying and renovating the people from within, a way towards finding its historical, Western determination.'[3] (How could he see such a thing in a movement that had no other ambition than to identify 'people' with 'race', and no other programme than that of ensuring the domination of a so-called Aryo-Germanic race – by eliminating all those who appeared not to belong to it, starting with the Jews? The fact is that, at that time, Heidegger would occasionally have done better to be a mere intellectual.)

As this last remark implies, I am not one of those who are content to seal up the tomb of the intellectual – first and foremost because I don't know what is meant by the term. What is there to be said about intellectuals? Who are they? Who deserves to be one? Who feels discredited if he is told he is one? Who fits the bill? Not the poet or the writer, not the philosopher or the historian, not the painter or the sculptor, not the scientist, even if he is a teacher. It would seem that you aren't one all the time any more than you can be one entirely. The intellectual is a portion of ourselves, which not only distracts us momentarily from our task, but returns us to what is going on in the world, in order to judge or appreciate what is going on there. In other words, the intellectual is all the closer to action in general, and to power, for not getting involved in action and not exercising any political power. But he is not indifferent to them. In standing back from politics he does not withdraw from it, he has not retired from it, but rather attempts to sustain this space of retreat and this effort of withdrawal [*retirement*] so as to take advantage of this proximity at a distance and install himself there (in a precarious installation), like a look-out who is there solely to keep watch, to remain watchful, to wait with an active attention, expressive less of a concern for himself than of a concern for others.

Does that mean that the intellectual is no more than a simple citizen? That would already be quite something. A citizen who is not content merely to vote according to his needs and his ideas, but who, having voted, takes an interest in the results of this unique act, and while keeping his distance with regard to any action that is necessary, reflects upon the sense of that action and, by turns, either speaks out or is silent. It would seem the case then that the intellectual is not a specialist in intelligence (i.e. a specialist in non-specialism). Intelligence – the skill of a mind that is adept at giving the impression that it knows more than it does – does not make an intellectual. The intellectual knows his limits. He accepts that he belongs to the animal kingdom of the mind, but he is not credulous: he doubts, he approves when necessary, he does not applaud. That is why he is not the man of commitment [*l'engagement*], to use an unfortunate term which often rightly made André Breton lose his temper. Which is not to say that he does not take sides; on the contrary, having made up his mind in accordance with the thinking which appears to him to be the most important – thinking about the perils and thinking against the perils – he is the obstinate one, the man of endurance, for there is no greater courage than the courage of thinking.

And yet, what is there to be said about the intellectual? He is said to be outdated, because he continues to be concerned about the universal at a time when totality as a system has demonstrated its misdeeds no less than its crimes, so rendering highly suspect anyone who, even though not claiming to think in place of others, claims the right not to turn in upon himself, for what is far off is as important to him as what is close, and what is close is more important to him than himself. Certainly, the word intellectual and the use of the word are by no means fixed. Etymology provides no protection. *Intelligere* alerts us to its dependency with regard to *legere* and the prefix *in*, and *legere* in turn opens onto the *logos* which, before it signifies language (speech, mark), expresses the gathering in to itself of what is dispersed inasmuch as it must remain dispersed. Dispersion and gathering in, such could be said to be the respiration of the mind, the dual movement which does not become unified, but which intelligence tends to stabilize so as to avoid the dizzying prospect of an ever-deepening investigation. These words of Paul Valéry's are frequently cited: 'The intellectuals' business is to stir up all things underneath their signs, their names or their symbols without counterbalancing that by real actions.' What is most noteworthy about that is the facile opposition set up between signs and actions. The intellectual is thus a sort of mathematician who works on symbols, combining them with a certain coherence yet without any relation to the real. He says the True (what seems to him true), he says the Just, he says the Right, which is to say the Law or even the ideal. But things have at once to be rectified and made more specific. He is not a pure theoretician, he is between theory and practice. He makes himself known, gets worked up and bestirs himself whenever, in precise cases, justice appears to him to be under attack or under threat by higher authorities.

But what is the origin of the power he gives himself, in order to pass judgement tumultuously on things about which, in principle, he makes up his mind without any more knowledge than the humblest citizen? It lies in a notoriety owing to success which apparently has nothing to do with what he makes so bold as to judge. A Nobel prizewinner in chemistry (to take a random example) will grandly lay down the law to politicians and judges on matters which are foreign to him. This appears unreasonable, but it is not entirely so. To succeed in any field of specialism is to invoke by virtue of one's success a power to understand and to succeed that derives from the universal. However, protest by intellectuals is often, too often, unconcerned with knowing what motivates their protest; they fail entirely to display, in protesting, those patient qualities required by their work, they hastily read newspapers which are themselves either ill-informed or partisan, and sign petitions written in an approximate language which negates the value of their moral judgements. As if morality, when applied to politics, could free itself from all rules, all method, and from those precautions without which there is no knowledge, only opinion. So sure are they of being right in heaven that they dismiss not only reason in the world, but the world of reason also.

Needless to say, the power, the justification and the definition of intellectuals change with the times (and the centuries). The *Aufklärung* shines with a brilliance which, though illusory, nostalgically illuminates the period. Paul Valéry regretted that he was not born in the eighteenth century, perhaps because he was rather drawn to the contented decline of a gentle society, lit by dying gleams, while beginning to sense that, already issuing from it, there was a barbaric society whose barbarism was necessary (apparently) so as to make applicable the finest of principles, which would revolutionize humanity. The nineteenth century also remains the century in which writers played a political role, both through their reputations and through their writings. Even Bonaparte had difficulty choosing between words and battles, and one might even say that he only won victories for the sake of the fine proclamations by which he concluded them. But let us leave aside Lamartine, Hugo and all those who in the nineteenth century are preparing the vocation thanks to which intellectuals will receive their derisory name at the time of the Affair (a curious word to designate the set of values involved in the humiliation of Dreyfus). It is well known (and Bredin's fine book has recently reminded us)[4] that intellectuals recognized themselves as such in those years when the defence of an innocent Jew, whose torment anticipated that of the racial camps in the twentieth century, was not just of interest because it was a just cause, but was their Cause: what justified them in writing, knowing and thinking. The strange thing about their intervention is that it was collective, whereas what they themselves answered to was an exaltation of singularity, so that there thus came into being an individualistic universalism which, under other names, still retains its power of attraction. Let us simply note the objections which certain people levelled at them. 'Intellectual skills,' said Brunetière, 'are only of relative value. I thus have no hesitation in placing such and such a farmer, or such and such a merchant of my acquaintance, well above certain scholars, certain biologists or certain mathematicians I shall not name.' Elsewhere he says, with his proverbial heavy-handedness: 'The intervention by a novelist, even a famous one (Zola), in matters of military justice appeared to me as out of place as would be the intervention of a colonel in the gendarmerie in a discussion about the origins of Romanticism.' Note the expression 'military justice'. There is, according to the nonintellectual Brunetière takes himself to be, no universal idea of what is just and what is unjust. Justice in itself does not exist. Justice must take account of other values than itself. It cannot ignore those supreme values: the greatness of the Army, its utility in the service of the Fatherland and the certainty that the nation to which one belongs by an accident of birth incarnates civilization itself, which brings him back to earthly justice.

In this respect, the Dreyfus Affair remains an inexhaustible subject for meditation. For the first time, an appeal against the verdict in a rigged trial gives rise to an 'Intellectuals' Manifesto'. The pejorative name is laid claim to as a glorious title or a guarantee of Truth. Those involved are, in general, writers who would later on be called avant-garde, defending in the same impulse the demands of right and of justice and the demands of writing, considered as that which must submit to nothing but itself. Brunetière (to remain with him) suspects them of believing they are supermen, and Barrès, more artfully and with greater logic, denounces their contradictoriness in believing themselves to be 'aristocrats of thinking', a 'line-up of the elite', while claiming to be the representatives of justice for all, a democratic justice. And he makes this clever remark: 'A semi-culture destroys instinct without replacing it with a conscience.' Instinct is the knowledge of roots (the earth, the dead, blood); conscience is progress towards absolute knowledge, by way of an identification of Right with the State. Is Barrès aware that he is stammering out the language of Hegel, that 'abhorrent Hun'? At least Durkheim's retort is a calm one (I paraphrase): we accord ourselves no superior privilege, but we demand to exercise our human right and speak in the name of reason alone, a reason which our professional habits have trained us to serve.

To which Barrès once again will reply that there are no grounds for appealing to reason, to thought, in order to judge the facts that incriminate or exonerate Dreyfus. First of all 'there is no such thing as freedom of thought . . . we are not the masters of our thoughts. They do not come from our intelligence. They are ways of reacting which express very ancient physiological predispositions.' That is why Dreyfus's treason has no need of proof, no need to be established, and cannot be disputed. Were he innocent, he would still be a traitor precisely because he is not a true traitor, but merely a 'rootless person, ill at ease . . . in our old French garden'. And even if innocent, he is guilty of stirring up in his defence these intellectuals who 'judge everything in the abstract' and, by deciding in the name of the universal, are contributing to the ruin of 'French morality', 'French justice'. 'I am not an intellectual,' Barrès says, 'and above all I wish people to speak in French.'

It would take only minor changes to these texts for us to rediscover in them everything that appeared surprising about the Moscow trials. They contain the same logic, that of a party or a fatherland that is always right. The 'patriotic forgery', extolled by Maurras along with a section of *la France profonde*, ushers in the right to rewrite history, to manipulate it so that it corresponds to a higher Good which none may dispute. All that is lacking there is the Confession. And strangest of all, Dreyfus seems to have all the qualities that, in other times, could have led him to make the supreme sacrifice, that of admitting to a crime he did not commit, in the event that this admission might have served the Army, the Fatherland and the public Good. But there was in this man, whom so many of those who defended him misjudged, a superior inability to default on what he called Honour, that is to say his very humanity – something he expressed in these words: 'My life belongs to my country, my honour does not.' In other words, perhaps he was 'lacking' that dialectical sense for which falsification is necessary for truth, error is an integral moment in the revelation of knowledge, and justice always remains relative with regard to its future as an absolute. And he, who never said that he was persecuted as a Jew, was saved because he had received from a Judaism of which he was ignorant the power to be a 'stiff- necked' man, incapable of breaking or even of bending.

That appalling affair, during which were uttered, against the Jews and those who stood by them, words as violent as the most violent of those with which the Nazis worked themselves up in order to justify the final solution ('we must roast the Jews'), had the merit – the sombre merit – of obliging intellectuals to reveal themselves to themselves, and of entrusting them with a simple demand [*exigence*] (the demand for truth and justice, the call for freedom of the mind against fanatical vehemence) from which they drew a new authority and sometimes a moral gain. The fact remains that one of the most illustrious among them (not at the time, though he had already written on Leonardo da Vinci) signed the notorious subscription to the glory of the forger Henry ('it was,' said Alain, 'a pretty fine example of the follies that the fanatical mind was capable of'). That is a stupefying example. In the *Notebooks*, where he confided only in himself, Paul Valéry did try once at least (but thirty years later) to explain his attitude. Let us read this text which, it must be said, is disappointing and hardly enlightening: 'Not "vicious", that is to say suffering at the sight of suffering – however I suddenly feel no pity in my heart for anyone who gambles on my compassion – or wishes to achieve his aims by resorting to invocations to Justice, Humanity etc. So much so that, even when such entreaties to Idols are justified – I take up a position in injustice and reassure myself by my disgust at this charade, of which I have seen many an example. This provides me with an explanation for my attitude during the celebrated affair.' And he adds these words: 'For to invoke Humanity is not to be a man. I knew those men to be in no way free of the weaknesses of men, or of men of letters – and I saw them, in this particular case, become inflamed, or act inflamed, for a cause.'

Paul Valéry often wrote that he had a poor 'historical' memory: 'I *know* I have lived such and such a period – But nothing of it comes back to me. I am incapable of reconstituting.' In that case, we have to admit that, in this paltry explanation, he has not only forgotten his commitment on the side of those who persecuted Dreyfus, he has rather forgotten himself also. What grievances does he invoke against those who defend the innocent man? He says they appealed to his pity by employing big words like Justice and Humanity. And he does not want to be moved to pity through recourse to what seem to him to be idols. He prefers to be unjust (he does not dispute therefore that justice speaks in favour of the ailing man on Devil's Island), he 'takes up a position in injustice' rather than take part in a charade where men who have weaknesses, even the weaknesses of men of letters, claim to represent Humanity and seek to turn it, with mediocre passions, into a sublime cause. He responds with retrenchment; which means he will remain above and outside the fray. But if we accept that, why then does he become inflamed in his turn by the cause of Major Henry? Why does he allow himself to be moved to pity by the sorry plight of the widow and the orphan, whom the miserable death of the forger leave destitute? Why, passion for passion, does he prefer the basest sort to the passions which make the mistake of calling themselves 'passion for truth, passion for justice, intolerance of lying, impatience at falsification'? Is it a liking for paradox? But he will maintain that paradox for its own sake does not appeal to him, and he is certainly right. Did he let himself be led on by the company and the opinions that his job at the War Ministry obliged him to frequent? Or else did he come under the influence of personalities such as Léon Daudet (thanks to whom, he will later say, he wrote the 'Introduction to the method of Leonardo da Vinci'), or friends such as Pierre Louÿs, or writers such as Léautaud – the latter a subscriber to the monument to Henry, 'in the name of order, against Justice and against Truth' as he put it? Perhaps, and since we have left the high ground of thought for the regions of what is uncertain, it must be recalled that in his youth, as he himself admits, he went through a 'military' phase. 'My "military" period – 1895. Mind of a Bonaparte . . . that type of politico-strategic reasoning. I wrote the *Methodical Conquest.* I believe I could have succeeded at a certain type of politics.' And it is also the period when, among the six people living whom he admires (Stéphane Mallarmé, Henri Poincaré), he nominates the bold colonizer Cecil Rhodes. He thus keeps company, in thought at least, with men who, when they act, do not take account of moral questions or appeals to finer feelings. Which is why he objects equally to the notions of Barrès, which he will describe (later it is true) as charlatanism: the Soil where lie the dead, the cult of the Self ('nothing from Barrès'), all themes that are foreign to him, because they appeal unjustifiably to his finer feelings which, because they are very strong in him, are always in horror of themselves: 'I found it ignoble, indecency or hypocrisy, to . . . preach virtue, fatherland, humanity.' Which is not to say that, as moralism and immoralism irritate him in equal measure, he is without morality. His own morality is often stated by him, reduced to these two principles: 'A. Do not increase (if you can help it) the quantity of suffering. B. Let us try and make something of man.'

From this cursory examination, which could be refined and of course gone into in greater depth, it is clear to me once more how that great upsurge of reason and sensibility in favour of an innocent man may well have appeared to him too violent and too political for him to let himself be moved by it, but I can find nothing that can justify his allowing his name to be associated with the names of those who called, in the worst terms, for the death of the Jews and the elimination of their defenders. There would thus seem to be a moment, in every life, when the unjustifiable prevails and the incomprehensible is given its due. And it is all the more absurd in that, from the very outset, Mallarmé his peerless master took the side, discreetly at least, of what was most just – not to mention Gide who made the same decision and whose resolution, precisely,

Valéry tried to shake (this was therefore close to his heart). A painful memory and a painful enigma.

If the Dreyfus Affair seems to distinguish intellectuals by defining them, and occasionally by glorifying them, it shows also how onerous that glory is, and that it forces onto them a vocation which transforms them and is perhaps too much for them. When you are struggling for innocence to be restored to a man like Dreyfus, it is not just a matter of pleading a case and examining the evidence in a trial. It is more than just a system that is being called into question, it is society, it is religion, from which anti-Semitism derives as from a contaminated source. Hence the intellectual is tempted to forget the Just Man, and raise him to the reality of a symbol in which the latter does not recognize himself. He becomes a moralist, a political being, even a mystic, as is the case with Péguy, who will heap injury on the one he defended in terms as unjust as those which were used to condemn him. Let us recall that eloquence, which was perhaps sublime, but unquestionably odious: 'Consecrated a hero in spite of himself, consecrated a victim in spite of himself, consecrated a martyr in spite of himself, he was unworthy of that triple investiture. Historically, truly unworthy. Inadequate, below standard, incapable, unworthy of that triple consecration, of that triple investiture.' Words which, read carefully, are absurd, and which show what *debasement* the intellectual exposes himself to in becoming the messenger of the absolute, the substitute for the priest, the superior being bearing the mark of the sacred.

But do we even have the right to talk of debasement? That would suppose that we could assign rigorous boundaries to the situation of the intellectual, which he would not have the right to exceed. Yet as soon as he defends the innocent man, he cannot confine himself to simple testimony, he has to go beyond that, to make a Cause of the man he is defending and, implicitly, to require him to be worthy of that Cause. Soon he substitutes himself for that man. The moral case with which he identifies will cease to be his sole combat, the end of ends, and will become a means, even if it is undeniably a noble means, since it is a matter of changing the social structures which permitted the iniquity, and forming the project for a new society (democracy) where justice, equality and fraternity will no longer be under threat. 'We were fully determined to transform the revisionist coalition into a permanent army in the service of human right and of justice' (Léon Blum). Whence eventually a political transformation which will ensure the existence of the Republic, and without which it is doubtful whether the rehabilitation could have been obtained. For Dreyfus, an officer and proud to be one, who moreover has the misfortune to be rich and does not consider himself different from ordinary Frenchmen, has nothing about him that could authorize him to incarnate the 'universal victim-subject', whose actual existence, according to Lyotard, is the only thing that could excuse the writer for momentarily becoming an *intellectual* in order to defend him, and in defending him, proclaim values having value for everyone. It is well known that Guesde opposed Jaurès because for him, the essence of socialism lay in defending the proletariat, where injustice is at its peak, and dissociating oneself from disputes between the rich which do not call into question capitalist society as a whole. Dreyfus is rich. The fact that he is being wrongly accused by his peers is merely an effect, a further illustration of the generalized iniquity constituted by his membership of the ruling class. This analysis does not just divide Guesde and Jaurès. For a long time it will divide Jaurès himself. What does he write at the much later date of 1898? 'The trial is the occasion for two fractions of the privileged class to clash with each other: on one side the opportunist groups, Protestant and Jewish, on the other the clerical and military groups, grapple with each other.' And it is at the same period that the celebrated words of the socialist Viviani ring out: 'They would not do as much for someone who was poor.' Something which will also be said, but at the very beginning of the Affair, by 'the first Jew to stand up for a Jew', Bernard Lazare, replying to P.V. Stock who had asked him to intervene: 'if he were a poor soul, I would be concerned for him. But Dreyfus and his family are very rich.' A Jew and rich, a Jew and an officer, he is thus doubly suspect and doubly ineligible for the consideration that would be shown to a man without means. Let us not forget that, no sooner was Dreyfus found guilty than there was no one, except his 'admirable brother', to defend him, while Jaurès, Clemenceau and the Dreyfusards of tomorrow were regretting that such a traitor, 'unclean of soul', 'abject of heart', had not been condemned to death, whereas 'ordinary soldiers, guilty of some momentary misconduct, are shot without pardon or pity.' Class justice as always. From which one may conclude that it perhaps takes intellectuals to get back to the simple idea of justice, a justice as abstract and as formal as the idea of man in general can be.

It is difficult to be an intellectual, the more so given that it is impossible to be one alone, whereas the personal demand such a person seems destined to be the bearer of (at least in so far as he is a writer) confines him within a solitude from which he cannot emerge without some cost. Remaining with Bredin's book, I shall cite two facts which show that the intellectual is not necessarily to be found where he should be, or more exactly that he remains impossible to find until after the event. In 1897 the Dreyfus Affair starts again with the 'attempt to rehabilitate the traitor'. Who does Léon Blum count upon in this task, to support him in this obligation? Naturally enough, it is on the writer he admires the most, 'who was for me not only a master and a guide', around whom 'we formed . . . a school, almost a court.' Léon Blum therefore goes to see him: 'I can recall the proud and charming graciousness of his welcome . . . I am sure that he felt true friendship for me, almost the concern of an elder brother.' And who is this refined writer who, because he writes 'well', could not possibly, so it would seem, withhold his support for an equitable Cause? None other than Barrès, a man whose ideology, which is none the less evident even then, will make of him a master of injustice. As for Barrès, in order to resist the Dreyfusards he will rely on Anatole France, a writer whose caution, whose classicism and whose great renown do not place him in the ranks of those audacious people who are ready to risk their reputations in a uncertain combat. But Anatole France, along with Sully Prudhomme, will take part in it with unexpected fervour. Blum is mistaken, Barrès is mistaken. Romain Rolland writes unashamedly to Lucien Herr (as if it were merely a matter of good taste): 'As you know very well, I make no secret of my anti-Semitic feelings. I would however put aside these feelings and think only of justice, if it were not that justice clearly occupies a secondary place in the preoccupations of those who defend Dreyfus.' Meanwhile, Dreyfus is dying. What does anyone care? Even the anti-Semitic feelings that are given vent in that period, with a vehemence one can scarcely conceive, are insufficient to explain the division of opinion and of judgement.[5] The celebrated Colonel Picquart, who dislikes Jews and who, according to certain witnesses, expressed himself with vulgarity on the day Dreyfus was stripped of his rank, started with indignation when, on discovering the plot of which the latter was the victim, he heard the deputy chief of staff say to him: 'What do you care if that Jew stays on Devil's Island?' (the implication being: that Jew, a Jew, that is to say a subhuman). His reply: 'But since he is innocent.' To which the high-ranking soldier retorted: 'If you say nothing, no one will know.' It is at this moment that Picquart strips himself of his rank, of his office and even of his duty to the State, becoming the stubborn intellectual whose obstinacy about being just will lead, as with Socrates, to prison if not to death. 'What you are saying is abominable. I do not know what I shall do; but whatever happens, I shall not take this secret with me to my grave.'

The words by which this decision is made must be firmly borne in mind. For the man who is in power, or who has institutional responsibilities, justice can be lost sight of behind duties that are not necessarily negligible. Furthermore, in a society based on right there are specialists in justice, whose profession is to be able competently to read books in which individual judicial rulings are recorded, and to draw on these in support of their attempts at redressing or preventing either serious or minor injustice. That being the case, what can the intellectual contribute – he who, despite his name, often does not know very much, but who at least sticks by a simple idea, which says there is a requirement [*exigence*] that must be sustained, come what may? It is this simplicity that gives him his strength, but which is exasperating as well, because it is so lofty that it seems oblivious of circumstances. It culminates in the extreme presumption that one can judge the judges, and invest with a higher authority the very people who claim that they have no right to any. There is Luther, who stands where he is and cannot do otherwise. There is Socrates, who says yes to death, and calmly refuses the way out that would allow him to escape his sentence. There is the stiff-necked Jew. There is the obligation to come to the assistance of others which, according to Hermann Broch, takes precedence over everything to do with one's own work. There is, finally, for the person whose vocation is to remain in retreat, far from the world (in that place where speech is the guardian of silence), the pressing necessity to expose himself to the 'risks of public life' by discovering a responsibility for someone who, apparently, means nothing to him, and by joining in the shouting and the clamour, when, on behalf of that which is closest, he has to give up the sole exigency that is properly his own: that of the unknown, of strangeness and of distance.

When the intellectual – the writer – makes up his mind and declares himself, he suffers perhaps irreparable damage. He absents himself from the only task that matters to him. It may well be that he loses once and for all the right to utter the unexpected. Between two imperatives, which at the same time have nothing imperative about them, he yields to the one for which he is not suited. It would be so easy for him to remain on the sideline. What then is this command from without, to which he must respond and which obliges him to take his place in the world again and assume an additional responsibility which may lead him astray?

Today the sense of the Dreyfus Affair is clear. But when you realize how many 'prejudices' a man like Jaurès had to overcome in order to reach the decision he then upheld with passion, you understand why it took so many years to give back his innocence to an innocent man. Whatever Léon Blum may have said about it, the Affair was a turning-point. It revealed that anti-Semitism, that age-old poverty of intellect, was, without anyone realizing it, going to divide modern times and prepare the ground for social change on an unsuspected and terrible scale. Such a claim may appear excessive. The 14–18 War appears as just an ordinary war. But I recall the conversation with Léon Brunschvicg that Emmanuel Levinas relates, in which the two events are compared for the way their outcomes, though satisfactory, were at the same time unsatisfactory: 'The men of my generation,' said Brunschvicg, 'experienced two victories: the Dreyfus Affair and 1918.' And after a hesitant silence, he added laconically: 'And now the two battles which were won are about to be lost again.' That was in 1932. What is so striking about

this assertion, murmured one morning as if it were a confidence destined
to be forgotten, such was the burden of misfortune it bore? First, the fact
that those who participated in the Dreyfus Affair took away from it, less
a memory of the injustice that had been done, than of the victory over
injustice which was eventually won. Democracy had proved the stronger.
A just truth, opposed to the vehemence of passions, imposed itself thanks
to the persistence of the evidence. It was a victory for conscience and for
reason, which, in Dreyfus as much as in Brunschvicg, claimed to represent only humanity, not so as to deny Judaism, but to recognize it in the
demands of reason, considered as inseparable from moral consciousness.
But then, lo and behold, what seemed to have been won, though with
difficulty, and at times in desperation, is again put in jeopardy. Not only
does Dreyfus in a way become guilty again: innumerable Dreyfuses are
condemned, without trial, to a death worse than death. Brunschvicg,
with his faith in a society of minds, may seem a naïve thinker compared
to someone like Heidegger, and yet it is Heidegger who blunders and
trips himself up, while it is Brunschvicg who goes straight to the heart of
the matter, by recognizing in Nazism an upsurge of myths, which will
give rise to frenzy and crimes unprecedented even in a history not short
of bloodshed.

However the 14–18 War, which does not appear to be an ideological
war, even if it begins with the defeat of internationalism, provides the
latter with its most devastating opportunity. Let us recall, if only in a few
words, something that we rather tend to forget: namely that there is no
firm socialist concept of war, or else that the socialist tradition is highly
inconsistent. Even Marx, in 1870, calls on the workers of every country
to take part resolutely in the national war, which should not, however, be
a war of conquest. The misinterpretations surrounding the memory of
the French Revolutionary Wars, owing to their legendary magnificence,
impose the vague idea that war and social emancipation go together. It is
Guesde who, as far back as 1885, foreseeing a war between Russia and
England, speaks of 'fruitful war' or cries '*Vive la guerre.*' 'The war which
is about to break out, whichever way it ends, will serve a revolutionary
purpose.' Guesde may well appear more of a polemicist than a theoretician. But Kautsky and Plekhanov and Lenin hardly think differently:
'The international proletariat, true to its revolutionary point of
view, must agree to all war – be it defensive war or a war of conquest
[an offensive war equally well therefore] – that looks likely to remove
an important obstacle on the road to revolution' (Lenin). Though it
failed, the revolution of 1905, which resulted from a military defeat,
confirmed the need for a war and for a lost war – and not a partial war,
but a war which will shortly be called total: in any case, a significant
catastrophe.[6]

As a result, the socialism born of the war will thereafter constantly be a 'war socialism'.[7] First of all because war is waged against it, from without and from within, so that the party is obliged to become militarized (prepared as it already is to be an instrument of war), and this in turn requires obedience to a single leader who, thinking and acting for everyone, demands absolute loyalty, without criticism, without doubt and without thought. Let us not forget that it was Trotsky who, in 1919 (vainly at the time as it happened), called for the 'militarization of the entire Soviet economy, that is, the permanent militarization of the entire working population – workers and peasants – under the authority of the man who is to direct the Tcheka, and with a rigorous system of both productivity bonuses and also severe penalties, in cases where stipulated tasks are not carried out'.[8]

These thoughts are excessively schematic and would therefore need qualifying. They do, however, throw into relief an orientation and a tendency. The importance of the military and industrial complex, which today lies at the heart of the Soviet system, is no more than a refined form of that initial war-like logic. And the Polish regime provides another sign of this, which ought not to have come as a surprise. A general, whether mediocre or not, is always the best bet to carry out the functions of the failing party. It was out of war that so-called proletarian socialism was born; it is through war that it spread; it is in war and under threat of war that it survives and remains in force. The famous words of Guesde unwittingly remain the decisive verdict: 'As for the socialists, knowing as they do on what necessary cataclysms the new order and the society of the future depend, their ardent desire can only be that this end to the most unbearable of regimes should begin.'

Such a conception, such a conviction, which is as simplistic as it is desperate (wars must precede revolutions), goes back a long way, much further back than the foolhardy forms of a scarcely scientific socialism might lead us to believe. For the decisive characteristic of justice (justice for others [*autrui*]) is that it brooks no delay, so that as a consequence it can let slip no opportunity – be it dangerous or doubtful – to fulfil itself. (Levinas pertinently cites this line from Bialik: 'And if justice exists, let it immediately appear.') Impatience is the exigency that torments and imperils the poetic spirit just as much as the spirit of justice. Let us recall certain episodes from Jewish mysticism, as Buber evokes them in *Gog and Magog*. The Seer of Lublin, a great Hasidic master, observing from a distance the formidable events of the Western world: the French Revolution, the Napoleonic Wars and Bonaparte's monumental glory as the century's master, was ready to see nothing but insignificance in it all, were it not that he sensed in Napoleon a demonic force capable of raising up the abyss and, through the excess of the evil he represented, of cooperating in the hope for salvation, and even hastening the coming of the Messiah. From there stem the debates between him and his pupil, the 'Holy Jew', concerning that riskiest of questions: ought one to promote Evil, bring it to a paroxysm, and hence precipitate catastrophe, so that at the same time deliverance may draw nearer? Couched in religious terms, this is the controversy which will, in the twentieth century, prove the great intellectual dispute, and which goes on today, in a form which only appears to be new.

The war lost in a great country had sparked off a liberating revolution, which certain of those who held liberation most dear quickly realized could re-engender despotism on an even wider scale. The same war, lost in another great country, where on the other hand social democracy was strong, subjected the latter to such trials that it was incapable of preventing the advent of a tyranny which would once again mobilize the entire people, reign using every form of violence, concentrate within a single individual all the powers of sovereignty and give to the new society, as its guiding principle, indeed its sole purpose, the recognition of race as the foundation of all values. It was some time, strange to say, before this last aspect was taken cognizance of. Perhaps it was the fact that Italian Fascism (also the fruit of a war without decisive victory) masked the truth of National Socialism, making it seem a dangerous imitation, though of little significance and unlikely to last. Fascism, which caused surprise with its name, no less than with what was seen as the new alliance between a certain form of socialism and national fervour,[9] was greeted with few misgivings. To be at one and the same time a socialist (in the service of the people) and a patriot (in the service of the nation), under the aegis of a weak and reassuring monarchy, appeared as a good way of countering the ambitions of Bolshevik Communism. The surprising thing was that Communism, with its internationalist vocation, officially renounced all its ecumenical ambitions, while Fascism, which originally claimed to be relevant to one country only, developed a tendency to spread like an epidemic and presented itself as a universal model. Why this reversal? What is it about Fascism that is so attractive? There is a short answer: the irrational, the power of spectacle and a hybrid resurgence of certain forms of the sacred: in other words, precisely what is needed by a society wishing once more to open itself to myths; something that seems cruelly lacking then in the democratic regimes, even those that helped give the war a victorious outcome. But the point is that, because of the means it was obliged to resort to, the war, even though victorious, contributed dangerously to weakening democracy and to making people oblivious of its significance, by associating it with the enormous and absurd misfortunes of combat rather than with its triumphs. That is no doubt why there was almost glad acceptance that democracy should momentarily disappear in the USSR, if this obliteration was necessary for the advent of a definitive freedom, and of a State which would suppress itself so as to establish the reign of full justice. Democracy was worn out, so to speak; it had lost its radiance, it was identified with day-to-day mediocrity; and its disastrous weaknesses were highlighted by the economic difficulties created by the war. It was to require considerable merit on the part of intellectuals, or the majority of them, to gather round and defend a regime for which they felt no respect, and in order not to yield to the fascination of the irrational, the fecundity of which was often demonstrated by their works and their art (Surrealism). They were anti-Fascists out of a love of freedom and an innate sense of justice. But how many of them saw that Hitler's despotism was not a tyranny of a sort that had already existed, but that, if he was so relentless in his pursuit of Judaism and of the Jews, it was because the latter incarnated, in the highest degree, not only a refusal of all forms of servitude – they, the slaves who came out of Egypt – but a rejection of myths, a forswearing of idols, the recognition of an ethical order manifesting itself in respect for the Law. In the Jew, in the 'myth of the Jew', what Hitler wanted to annihilate was, precisely, man freed of myths. Whether or not he was fully aware of it, he chose the right target and accurately defined his struggle. But who at the time read *Mein Kampf*? People were content to see in his furious anti-Semitism merely an obsession, an extravagant folly, or the legacy of the fashionable anti-Semitism which reigned in Vienna.

When intellectuals began to unite against Fascism in every country, but primarily against National Socialism, the question soon arose as to how it was to be resisted. Demonstrating was all very well. By saying 'Fascism will not get through' opinion was of course alerted to it; but it was not really stopped from getting through. So more was needed, and again the need for war became a subject for discussion. Was National Socialism not equivalent to war? Hitler said not; no sooner had he come to power than he made a declaration of peace which amazed the nations. And in any case, he had other tasks. And so many lies had been spread about concerning Germany during the 14–18 war, that people were unwilling to believe the frightening stories coming from over there. However, the Rhineland was invaded. We know today that that was the decisive moment. Should force be used to oppose it? The majority of the French government thought so; military preparations were even ordered; one or two journalists supported the decision. But how many intellectuals stood up then to help an already wavering government? Who had the strength to protest at the threats of the English? After all, the Rhineland belonged to Germany, there was no question of a return to the nationalist excesses of Poincaré when he occupied the Ruhr. In this way, anti-Fascism laid down its arms, pacifism imposed the duty on it not to imitate Hitler. Munich happened on that day. The other Munich, the one that is still remembered and which revealed the moral abjection of the democracies, was inevitable from then on, as was the probable immensity of a defeat which could at the time be sensed but not imagined.

I recall these familiar episodes because they show how the ideological relations between socialism and war had changed by this time. The sincere pacifism of Simone Weil is proof of this. The pacifism of Alain, her teacher, was no less exemplary. War no longer appeared as a good way of imposing revolution, but on the contrary as a perversion of it. The prime enemy was the police and military system, wherever it was to be found. Hence anti-Fascism, though definitely not ready to capitulate, was unwilling to combat Fascism using the methods it extols, and which in part define it. 'Fascism,' said Alain (I cite him often because his influence was great at the time), 'is the military order extended into peace-time.' Which meant at least that there was not, and would never again be, peace.

The Spanish Civil War was cruel proof of this, and it changed once again the outlook of the intellectuals. Here was a war with which they could identify and which they would be allowed to take part in, in return for a minimum of military obedience. It was perhaps, under another guise, Jemmapes and Valmy. Above all, the intellectual was able to put to the test his conviction that no decision should be without risk. That lesson was sometimes forgotten; it remains resolutely true. An intellectual should not just judge or take sides: he is someone who puts himself at risk, and answers for his decisions, if necessary, with his freedom and his existence. He constantly incurs a twofold danger: that of giving up his 'creative' powers by giving up his solitude; that of involving himself in support of a public declaration which he is not even sure can justify his 'sacrifice'.

The Resistance in which so many intellectuals took part, one way or another, followed on from the Spanish Civil War. It was a terrible war, without guarantees and perhaps without hope, but it was also a war without uniforms in which, most of the time, you killed no one, where obedience was not blind, but where being underground changed your life more thoroughly than any regular sort of discipline, and where the need to do nothing that might provoke reprisals against civilians or imperil innocent hostages imposed difficult choices. That rule was not always respected, but it constantly applied. In this way, the intellectuals – some of them – experienced the dark struggles which make war and revolution resemble each other; they learned also how hard it was to sustain a just moral correlation between means and ends. And finally they encountered fraternity and friendship, while remaining individuals in a struggle they had chosen.

I should like quite arbitrarily to stop here, and put forward or repeat one or two observations. For as long as they have borne the name, intellectuals have never done anything other than cease momentarily to be what they were (be it a writer, a scientist, or an artist), so as to respond to moral dictates which are both obscure and imperious, since they concern justice and liberty. Vague words, and powerful, unclear assertions. From the Dreyfus Affair to Hitler and Auschwitz, the proof is there that it was anti-Semitism (along with racism and xenophobia) which revealed the intellectual most powerfully to himself: in other words, it is in that form that concern for others obliged him (or not) to abandon his creative solitude. The categoric imperative, losing the ideal generality given to it by Kant, became the one which Adorno formulated more or less thus: *Think and act in such a way that Auschwitz may never be repeated*; which implies that Auschwitz must not become a concept, and that an absolute was reached there, against which other rights and other duties must be judged.

But there is another lesson, which is harder to perceive. It is that intellectuals, attached as they generally were to the principle of freedom, did not heed the fact that the good (the liberation of a people) would be gravely compromised, the day it required or even tolerated that evil (war) should hasten or ensure its advent. This is not unique to our times, nor even to the recent past. It is striking that Robespierre should have sensed almost immediately that war, even if victorious, would destroy the Revolution, and that, just as you must not 'offer freedom at bayonet-point', so military tyranny could never be to the good, whatever its goals: 'War is good for officers, for the ambitious, for speculators, for the executive . . . this option does away with all other concerns, you have washed your hands of the people when you have given them war.'[10] The Terror (and all terror) comes in part from there. The problem of war and its relation to the liberation of society is one that intellectuals have perhaps never succeeded in clarifying. (For it will always be tempting to reply that if revolution needs war in order to impose itself, it is because it is itself a war, or else because the methods of war – the law on suspects, the suppression of the rules of democracy, concentration camps – are necessary for it to endure.)

The third difficulty which the intellectual cannot elude has not changed since the Dreyfus Affair, even if at that time the justice of the cause made it possible not to linger over it: it is that the writer, the artist and the scientist divert and misappropriate the influence they have acquired, and the authority they owe to their own particular activity, in order to employ them in the service of political choices or moral options. That was the case with Zola. That was the case with Sartre. It was, more recently, the case with an actor of renown [Yves Montand] who, because he excels at his art, was expected to make political or moral statements on every subject. Such statements derived from his fame as an actor both a value and an audience which cannot be described as excessive, but which demonstrate that one citizen is not the equal of another. This was constantly a dilemma for Sartre. Prematurely famous, and however modest by nature, he felt there was vested in him a responsibility which obliged him to take sides far beyond anything he had the right to pronounce upon, speaking and writing according to his dreams or his hopes, until the moment when he was forced to recant in the face of what was self-evident. So he turned against his status as a writer, which had given him such importance and brought him a fame he had wished to place at the service of others: he would no longer be a writer, would no longer be an intellectual of the classic sort, but a 'new intellectual' (with generous but muddled obligations), yet one whom he could not debar from writing altogether, until finally the ordeal of blindness condemned him to a silence that he endured courageously.

There is probably no remedy for this difficulty. But it can be alleviated if the intellectual manages to make it clear that he is one only momentarily and for a fixed cause, and that, as a supporter of that cause, he is merely one among others, with the hope (be it vain) of losing himself in the obscurity of everyone, and becoming one with an anonymity which is, in fact, his profound yet constantly thwarted goal as a writer or an artist.

To conclude once again, I will cite something Michel Foucault wrote some time ago: 'For a long time, the so-called "left-wing" intellectual spoke, and was accorded the right to speak, as the master of truth and justice. He was listened to, or claimed the right to be listened to, as the representative of the universal. To be an intellectual was to some extent to be the conscience of all.' There is little that can be said in response to this warning. When a number of us took part in the May 1968 movement, they hoped to be preserved from any ambition in the singular, and in a way they succeeded, through not being singled out for attention, but treated in the same way as everyone else, the strength of the anti-authoritarian movement making it almost easy to forget all particularity, and impossible to distinguish between young and old, the unknown and the too well-known, as if, despite the differences and the incessant disputes, each person recognized himself in the anonymous words inscribed on the walls and which, in the end, even when on occasion they were the result of a collective effort, never declared themselves the words of an author, being of all and for all, in their contradictory formulation. But of course, that was an exception. It provides no solution, even if it gives an idea of a revolution that does not need to succeed or achieve a fixed goal, since, whether it endures or does not endure, it is sufficient unto itself, and since the failure that eventually rewards it is none of its concern.

Thinking back to the anti-colonial struggle, the role the intellectuals played in it and, as a case in point, the initiative represented by the 'the Declaration of the 121 on the right to insubordination in the Algerian war', I observe that there too, those who declared themselves made no claim to be announcing a universal truth (insubordination for its own sake and in all cases), but were doing no more than support decisions that they had not taken, acknowledging responsibility for them and, in so doing, *identifying themselves* with those who had been forced to take them. No doubt they were giving their endorsement in this way, saying to the authorities: if you strike at people who are unknown, you will have to strike at people who are less so: thus, once again, using their modest or great fame in order to say, in their turn, what is just and what is unjust – but in a way that was not without risks, although the risks entailed were not great enough to conceal from them the abuse of authority with which their initiative remained if not tainted, at least marked.

In this there is a moral constraint which some cannot elude, which others refuse. It is beyond all judgement. For my part – and this shall be my personal confession – there is scarcely a day when, in the most vulnerable part of my memory, I do not recall these terrible words, inscribed in a fragment of René Char's:

> *I want never to forget that I have been forced to become – for how long?*
> *– a monster of justice and intolerance, a cooped-up simplifier, an arctic*
> *individual with no interest in the fate of anyone who is not in league with*
> *him to kill the hounds of hell. The round-ups of Jews, scalpings in police-*
> *stations, terrorist raids by Hitler's police on stunned villages, lift me off*
> *the ground, strike my chapped face with a red-hot slap of molten iron.*

That was written in 1943 ('Notes to Francis Curel'). That improbable date hangs suspended above our heads. Its return is always possible. And it is that date, in my view, which denies intellectuals any hope of disappearing and so shying away from being questioned, from the torment of being questioned.

Notes

1 *Le Monde*, 8 October 1983. [Subsequently included in *Tombeau de l'intellectuel et autres essais* (Paris, Galilée, 1984).]

2 In thus expressing myself so inadequately, I am referring to a study by Philippe Lacoue-Labarthe entitled 'La Transcendance finit dans la politique', published in a collective volume *Rejouer le politique* (Paris, Galilée, 1981). To my surprise, this text, which is largely devoted to the 'Rectorate Speech' and which is in no way polemical, but rather examines Heidegger's thought without bias, keeping its distance from fanatics on both sides, is to my knowledge cited nowhere, not even in the recent *Cahier de l'Herne* on Heidegger

[1983], which however offers an exhaustive bibliography. This silence is in itself significant.

3 The more important Heidegger's thought is taken to be, the more it is necessary to try and clarify the sense of his political adhesion in 1933–4. At a push, it is possible to argue that it was in order to serve the University that Heidegger agreed to become its Rector. One can even go further and play down the importance of his adhesion to Hitler's party, seeing it as a pure formality intended to ease the administrative duties of his new post. But there remains the inexplicable and indefensible fact of Heidegger's political declarations, in which he expresses his agreement with Hitler, either in order to extol National Socialism and its myths by hailing the 'hero' Schlageter; or by recommending a vote for the Führer and his referendum (on withdrawal from the League of Nations); or by encouraging his students to respond positively to the Labour Service – and all of that in the language of his own philosophy, which he placed without a qualm in the service of the worst of causes, and hence discredited it by the use to which it was put. That, for me, is the gravest responsibility: what took place was a falsification of writing, an abuse, a travesty and a misappropriation of language. Over the latter, from then on, there will hang a suspicion.

4 Jean-Denis Bredin, *The Affair. The Case of Alfred Dreyfus*, trans. Jeffrey Mehlman (London, Sidgwick & Jackson, 1986).

5 Ghéon, who complacently uses anti-Jewish language such as 'filthy Yids', is a supporter of Dreyfus. He often annoys Michel Arnauld (Gide's brother-in-law), who thought he saw in 'Dreyfusism' the 'enthusiasm of offended reason'. When he was still only Drouin, the same man wrote letter after letter to Valéry in an attempt to change his mind.

6 Needless to point out, a vague reminiscence of Hegel plays its part in this thinking.

7 I am giving this expression a different meaning from the one it usually has.

8 I should like at this point to pay homage to Boris Souvarine and to *La Critique Sociale*, from which I borrow without always acknowledging it (Editions de la Différence). Boris Souvarine wrote some highly illuminating articles about socialism and war. So did Simone Weil, who published some 'Reflexions on War' in 1933. However, in paying homage to Souvarine, I cannot but protest at the violent, unjust and false criticism which, in a preface to the new edition of his journal, he directs at Georges Bataille, about whom he says that, fascinated by Hitler, he would certainly have joined the camp of the Occupant after the defeat, had he had the courage of his convictions. Boris Souvarine, who spent those dark years in America, admits that all he can cite in support of his accusations are rumours and not proofs. Since I had the privilege, from 1940 onwards (more precisely, from the end of that sinister year), of seeing Georges Bataille almost on a daily basis and discussing a whole range of subjects with him, I can vouch for his horror of Nazism, as well as of the Pétain regime and its ideology (family, labour, fatherland). He came to regret the pages he wrote on 'The psychological structure of Fascism' (published of course in *La Critique Sociale*), and which could have lent themselves to misunderstanding. Finally, he occasionally spoke to me of Boris Souvarine, and always with great esteem and consideration. As, with the passing years, witnesses to the period are becoming fewer, I cannot remain silent while there is still time, and allow credence to be attached to claims which I know to be incontrovertibly untrue.

9 This was already Bismarck's ambition, and one wonders whether Heidegger did not see in Hitler another Bismarck. He did after all write, with considerable simplicity: 'I believed that, having taken over responsibility in 1933 for the people as a whole, Hitler would be bold enough to disengage himself from the Party and its doctrine, and that everything would come together in the area of renovation and unification with the aim of

making the Western World assume its responsibilities. This conviction was a mistake, and I recognized as much with the events of 30 June 1934. If I intervened in 1933 it was to say yes to the national and to the social (and not to nationalism), and not to the intellectual and metaphysical foundations upon which the biologistic doctrines of the Party were based, because the social and the national, as I saw them, were not in essence related to a biologist and racist ideology'. (Letter to the President of the Political Purges Committee, 1945, *Cahiers de l'Herne.*)

10 Quoted from Simone Weil's article on war.

Translated by Michael Holland

21

The Indestructible

(i) Being Jewish (1962)*

Attention, waiting. Waiting, affliction. To reflect historically upon these words that are so difficult to pronounce, all the while maintaining their abstract simplicity, is to expose oneself to the even greater difficulty of undergoing the ordeal of a history to which Simone Weil was obliged (by what necessity of thought, what pain in thinking of it?) to close her eyes. Why must she, too faithful to Greek clarity, forget that every reflection upon a fundamental injustice passes by way of the condition that has for thousands of years been allotted to the Jews? Why, in turn, are we so uneasy as we reflect upon it? Why, in reflecting upon it, do we stop our reflection at a certain moment; accepting, if we must, what is negative in the Jewish condition – once again enlightened (assuming that it is a question of light) about a negative extremity – but thereby missing the positive significance of Judaism? Is it, perhaps, through fear of playing into the hands of nihilism and its most vulgar substitute, anti-Semitism? But perhaps this fear is the very way in which such forces still impose themselves upon us, and even by our refusal. We will not cease to see this equivocation at work.

The Jew is uneasiness and affliction [*malheur*]. This must be clearly said even if this assertion, in its indiscreet sobriety, is itself unfortunate [*malheureuse*]. The Jew has throughout time been the oppressed and the accused. He is, he has been, the oppressed of every society. Every society, and in particular Christian society, has had its Jew in order to affirm itself against him through relations of general oppression. One could say – borrowing this expression from Franz Rosenzweig – that there is a movement of history that makes every Jew the Jew of all men, which means that every man, whoever he may be, has a particular relation of responsibility (a relation not yet elucidated) with this 'Other' ['*Autrui*'] that is the Jew. 'To be Jewish,' says Clara Malraux, 'means that nothing is given to us.' Heine said: 'Judaism? Do not speak to me about it, doctor,

* Originally published as 'Etre juif', *Nouvelle Revue Française*, 116 and 117 (August and September 1962), pp. 279–85 and 471–6. Reprinted in *L'Entretien infini* (Paris, Gallimard, 1969), pp. 180–90, as section 1 of the chapter entitled 'L'Indestructible'.

I would not wish it even upon my worst enemy. Injury and shame is all it brings: it is not a religion, it is an affliction.' Being Jewish would be, then – we are coming to it – essentially a negative condition; to be Jewish would be to be from the outset deprived of the principal possibilities of living, and in a manner not abstract, but real.

Still, is Jewish existence only this? Is it simply a lack? Is it simply the difficulty of living that is imposed upon a certain category of men by the hateful passion of other men? Is there not in Judaism a truth that is not only present in a rich cultural heritage, but also living and important for the thought of today – even if this thought challenges every religious principle? There is an astonishing sign of barbarity in the fact of having to ask such a question, and also in the audacity felt in asking it. Albert Memmi wonders why the Jew should always have to disavow himself, why he is refused the right to be different.[1] Is anti-Semitism so embedded in our ways of being that, in order to defend those it assails, we can find no other means than to take from them the entirety of their existence and truth, making them disappear in an unreal human abstraction, which, moreover, is later held against them? 'A Jew is nothing but a man like any other! Why speak of the Jews?' And if one calls him by name one seems to be lacking reserve, to be pronouncing a dangerous, even injurious word, as though being Jewish could have only a pejorative meaning rather than designating a grave truth and an exceptionally important relation.

Sartre described anti-Semitism rigorously. He showed that the portrait accusation drawn up against the Jew reveals nothing about the Jew but everything about the anti-Semite, inasmuch as the anti-Semite projects the force of his injustice, his stupidity, his base meanness, and his fear onto his enemy. But in affirming that the Jew is no more than a product of the others' gaze, and is only Jewish by the fact of being seen as such by the other (which thereby obliges him either to deny or to claim his identity), Sartre tends to recognize Jewish difference, but merely as the negative of anti-Semitism. It is certainly true that anti-Semitism has modified Jewish existence (if only by threatening it, making it more scarce, and at times exterminating it); and perhaps it has affected the idea that particular Jews have of themselves – but this on the ground of a prior 'historical' reality and authenticity one has to call Judaism, and which defines in an implicit manner the relation of every man to himself. Being Jewish, therefore, cannot be the simple reverse of anti-Jewish provocation; nor is it a break with the incognito into which the Jew must vanish, not only to be secure but in some sense to be himself – absence thus being at the same time his refuge and his definition. Being Jewish signifies more, and doubtless something it is essential to bring to light.

This can only be the fruit of long work and a meditation more personal than erudite. There is a Jewish thought and a Jewish truth; that is, for each of us, there is an obligation to try to find whether in and through this thought and this truth there is at stake a certain relation of man with man that we can sidestep only by refusing a necessary inquiry. Certainly, this inquiry will not be entertained here as proceeding from a religious exigency. Let us acknowledge this beforehand. Let us also declare that it is not a question of the interest we bring to facts of culture. Finally, let us acknowledge that what the Jewish experience can tell us at this level cannot pretend to exhaust the meaning that gives it its richness. Each one understands what he can. Moreover, the principal thing is perhaps not to be found in a lengthy development, but already and almost entirely in the words themselves: being Jewish.

When in his turn Pasternak asks 'What does being Jewish signify? Why does it exist?' I believe that among all the responses there is one in three parts that we cannot avoid choosing, and it is this: it exists so the idea of exodus and the idea of exile can exist as a legitimate movement; it exists, through exile and through the initiative that is exodus, so that the experience of strangeness may affirm itself close at hand as an irreducible relation; it exists so that, by the authority of this experience, we might learn to speak.

Reflection and history enlighten us on the first point with painful evidence. If Judaism is destined to take on meaning for us, it is indeed by showing that, at whatever time, one must be ready to set out, because to go out (to step outside) is the exigency from which one cannot escape if one wants to maintain the possibility of a just relation. The exigency of uprooting; the affirmation of nomadic truth. In this Judaism stands in contrast to paganism (all paganism). To be pagan is to be fixed, to plant oneself in the earth, as it were, to establish oneself through a pact with the permanence that authorizes sojourn and is certified by certainty in the land. Nomadism answers to a relation that possession cannot satisfy. Each time Jewish man makes a sign to us across history it is by the summons of a movement. Happily established in Sumerian civilization, Abraham at a certain point breaks with that civilization and renounces dwelling there. Later, the Jewish people become a people through the exodus. And where does this night of exodus, renewed from year to year, each time lead them? To a place that is not a place and where it is not possible to reside. The desert makes of the slaves of Egypt a people, but a people without a land and bound by a word. Later, the exodus becomes the exile that is accompanied by all the trials of a hunted existence, establishing in each heart anxiety, insecurity, affliction and hope. But this exile, heavy as it is, is not only recognized as being an incomprehensible malediction. There is a truth of exile and there is a vocation of exile; and if being Jewish is being destined to dispersion – just as it is a call to a sojourn without place, just as it ruins every fixed relation of force with *one* individual, *one* group, or *one* state – it is because dispersion, faced with the exigency of the whole, also clears the way for a different exigency and finally forbids the temptation of Unity–Identity.

André Neher recalls these stages of Jewish presence (the presence of a non-presence) in one of his books. First of all, of course, the Jew has the right to the name Jew (I know none more worthy of being claimed); but one must not forget that before being Jewish the Jew was an Israelite, that before being an Israelite he was a Hebrew (today becoming an Israeli), and that to be Jewish is thus to bear without bending the weight and the fullness of all these names. Here I will rapidly take up again André Neher's remarks.[2] The Jewish man is the Hebrew when he is the man of origins. The origin is a decision; this is the decision of Abraham, separating himself from what is, and affirming himself as a foreigner in order to answer to a foreign truth. The Hebrew passes from one world (the established Sumerian world) to something that is 'not yet a world' and is none the less this world here below; a ferryman, the Hebrew Abraham invites us not only to pass from one shore to the other, but also to carry ourselves to wherever there is a passage to be made, maintaining this between two shores that is the truth of passage. It must be added that if this memorial of the origin that comes to us from so venerable a past is certainly enveloped in mystery, it has nothing of the mythical about it. Abraham is fully a man; a man who sets off and who, by this first departure, founds the human right to beginning, the only true creation. A beginning that is entrusted and passed on to each of us but that, in extending itself, loses its simplicity. The Hebrew himself will not remain Hebrew. The relation, through migration and march, with the Unknown that one can know only by way of distance, becomes, with the filing out of Jabbok and in the night of Penuel, enigmatic contact: the struggle about which one knows nothing since what is at stake is the truth of the night, that which is not to be retained when day breaks. Jacob runs headlong into the inaccessible outside whose partner he becomes, struggling not to overcome it, but to receive it in the very night of the word that he firmly stands up to until the moment when it comes to him as benediction. Thus marked, the Hebrew, becoming Israel, becomes the one who is not like the others; election is an alteration. The one who is subject to the brusque interpolation of the Foreign, the one who is responsible for the ambiguous choice that sets him apart, is at the mercy of this strangeness that he risks making into a power, a privilege, a kingdom and a State. Israel's solitude – a sacerdotal, a ritual and also a social solitude – comes not only from the passions of the men who live adjacent to it, but also from this particular relation with itself that placed this extreme, infinite distance, the presence that is other, in its proximity. Thus is born the Jew. The Jew is the man of origins; he who relates to the origin not by dwelling but by distancing himself from it, thus saying that the truth of the beginning is in separation. Israelite, he is in the Kingdom. Jew, he is in Exile, and is as though destined to make of exile a kingdom. André Neher says: 'How can one be in Exile and in the Kingdom, at the same time vagabond and established? It is precisely this contradiction that makes the Jewish man a Jew.' (A contradiction that Neher is perhaps too inclined to translate into dialectical terms, whereas it signifies a contrariety for which dialectics is unable to account.)

Let us insist now upon a single point. The words *exodus, exile* – as well as those heard by Abraham, 'Leave your country, your kinsmen, your father's house' – bear a meaning that is not negative. If one must set out on the road and wander, is it because, being excluded from the truth, we are condemned to the exclusion that prohibits all dwelling? Or would not this errancy rather signify a new relation with 'truth'? Doesn't this nomadic movement (wherein is inscribed the idea of division and separation) affirm itself not as the eternal privation of a sojourn, but rather as an authentic manner of residing, of a residence that does not bind us to the determination of place or to settling close to a reality forever and already founded, sure and permanent? As though the sedentary state were necessarily the aim of every action! As though truth itself were necessarily sedentary!

But why this refusal to found the 'concept' of the true on the need to dwell? Why does errancy substitute for the dominion of the Same an affirmation that the word Being – in its identity – cannot satisfy? It is not simply a question of privileging becoming; nor is it a question of introducing a purely idealist claim in rejecting all that is terrestrial. It is with the Greeks that we find the primacy of the world of ideas – a primacy that is none the less simply a way for the visible to reign invisibly. It is with the Christians that we find the disavowal of the here below, an abasement of life, a scorn for presence. To leave the dwelling place, yes; to come and go in such a way as to affirm the world as a passage, but not because one should flee this world or live as a fugitive in eternal misfortune. The words exodus and exile indicate a positive relation with exteriority, whose exigency invites us not to be content with what is proper to us (that is, with our power to assimilate everything, to identify everything, to bring everything back to our I). Exodus and exile express simply the same reference to the Outside that the word existence bears. Thus, on one hand, nomadism maintains above what is established the right to put the distribution of space into question by appealing to the initiatives of human movement and human time. And, on the other hand, if to become rooted in a culture and in a regard for things does not suffice, it is because the order of the realities in which we become rooted does not hold the key to all the relations to which we must respond. Facing the visible–invisible horizon Greek truth proposes to us (truth as light, light as measure), there is another dimension revealed to man where, beyond every horizon, he must relate to what is beyond his reach.

Here we should bring in the great gift of Israel, its teaching of the one God. But I would rather say, brutally, that what we owe to Jewish monotheism is not the revelation of the one God, but the revelation of speech as the place where men hold themselves in relation with what excludes all relation: the infinitely Distant, the absolutely Foreign. God speaks, and man speaks to him. This is the great feat of Israel. When Hegel, interpreting Judaism, declares, 'The God of the Jews is the highest separation, he excludes all union' or 'In the Jewish spirit there is an insurmountable abyss,' he is merely neglecting the essential, which, for thousands of years, has been given expression in books, in teaching and in a living tradition: this is the notion that if, in fact, there is infinite separation, it falls to speech to make it the place of understanding; and if there is an insurmountable abyss, speech crosses this abyss. Distance is not abolished, it is not even diminished; on the contrary, it is maintained, preserved in its purity by the rigour of the speech that upholds the absoluteness of difference. Let us acknowledge that Jewish thought does not know, or refuses, mediation and speech as mediating. But its importance is precisely in teaching us that speaking inaugurates an original relation in which the terms involved do not have to atone for this relation or disavow themselves in favour of a measure supposed to be common; they rather ask and are accorded reception precisely by reason of that which they do not have in common. To speak to someone is to accept not introducing him into the system of things or of beings to be known; it is to recognize him as unknown and to receive him as foreign without obliging him to break with his difference. Speech, in this sense, is the promised land where exile fulfils itself in sojourn since it is not a matter of being at home there but of being always Outside, engaged in a movement wherein the Foreign offers itself, yet without disavowing itself. To speak, in a word, is to seek the source of meaning in the prefix that the words *exile, exodus, existence, exteriority* and *estrangement* are committed to unfolding in various modes of experience; a prefix that for us designates distance and separation as the origin of all 'positive value'.

Assuredly, it would be rash to claim to represent Judaism by allowing God's name to vanish into thin air – although the discretion with regard to this name and the silence that measures it, in so many important texts, authorize the interpreter not to pronounce it if he can do without it. With regard to Greek humanism, Jewish humanism astonishes by a concern with human relations so constant and so preponderant that, even when God is nominally present, it is still a question of man; of what there is between man and man when nothing brings them together or separates them but themselves. The first word that comes to Adam from on high after he has lapsed is: 'Where are you?' It falls to God to express the pre-eminent human question: 'Where is man?' – as though, in some sense, there had to be God in order that the questioning of man might reach its height and its breadth; but a God speaking a human language, so that the depth of the question concerning us is handed over to language. Inquiring about the nature of the commandments, Franz Rosenzweig makes this remark: 'I could not venture to present any of the commandments as human. . . . But neither can I present the divine nature of the Torah in its entirety in a manner other than does Rabbi Nobel: "And *God* appeared to Abraham; Abraham raised his eyes and he saw three *men*."'[3] Let us recall Jacob. He has just struggled with his opponent of the Night, who said to him in an already significant manner: 'You wrestled with Elohim as with men'; and Jacob, giving this place the name Penuel, says: 'I have seen God [*Elohim*] face to face and my life is preserved.' Then, a little later, he meets his brother Esau, whom he has much reason to fear, and says to him: 'If I have won favour in your sight, then accept this gift from me; for I have seen your face as one sees the face of God, and you were pleased with me.' An extraordinary expression. Jacob does not say to Esau 'I just saw God as I see you' but 'I see you as one sees God,' which confirms the suggestion that the marvel (the privileged surprise) is indeed human presence, this Other Presence that is *Autrui* – no less inaccessible, separate and distant than the Invisible himself. It also confirms the terrible character of such an encounter, whose outcome could only be approbation or death. Whoever sees God risks his life. Whoever encounters the Other [*Autrui*] can relate to him only through mortal violence or through the gift of speech by receiving him.

As arbitrary as it may be to limit ourselves to these remarks, I do not think the direction they take alters the truth. And this truth is that whoever wishes to read the meaning of the history of the Jews through Judaism ought to reflect upon the distance that separates man from man when he is in the presence of *Autrui*. Jews are not different from other men in the way racism would have us believe; they rather bear witness, as Levinas says, to this relation with difference that the human face (what in the visage is irreducible to visibility) reveals to us and entrusts to our responsibility; not strangers, but recalling us to the exigency of strangeness; not separated by an incomprehensible retribution, but designating as pure separation and as pure relation what, from man to man, exceeds human power – which is none the less capable of anything. Anti-Semitism, in this sense, is in no way accidental; it gives a figure to the repulsion inspired by the Other [*Autrui*], the uneasiness before what comes from afar and elsewhere: the need to kill the Other, that is, to submit to the all-powerfulness of death what cannot be measured in terms of power. One could perhaps say that anti-Semitism has three characteristics: (1) it turns all the 'positive' values of Judaism into negatives and, first of all, the primary affirmation of the distance that is 'infinite,' irreducible, impassable (even when it is passed over), with which Judaism confronts us; (2) it transforms into fault (into an ethically and socially condemnable reality) this being negative to which it reduces the Jew; (3) it does not restrict itself to a theoretical judgement, but calls for the actual suppression of the Jews in order better to exercise against them the principle of denial with which it has invested their image. A denial so absolute, it is true, that it does not cease to *reaffirm* the relation with the infinite that being Jewish implies, and that no form of force can have done with because no force is able to meet up with it (just as one can kill a man who is present, and yet not strike down presence as an empty never-present presence, but rather simply cause it to disappear). The anti-Semite, at grips with the infinite, thus commits himself to a limitless movement of refusal. No, truly, excluding the Jews is not enough, exterminating them is not enough; they must also be struck from history, removed from the books through which they speak to us, just as the presence that inscribed speech is what must finally be obliterated: the speech before and after every book and through which, from the farthest distance where all horizon is lacking, man has already turned towards man – in a word, destroy '*autrui*'.[4]

(ii) Humankind (1962)*

'Each time the question: Who is "*Autrui*"? emerges in our words I think of the book by Robert Antelme, for it not only testifies to the society of the German camps of World War II, it also leads us to an essential reflection.[5] I don't mean to imply that his book spells out a full response to the question. But even without taking into account the years or the circumstances it portrays (while none the less taking them into account), what impels this work towards us is what remains of the question's interrogative force. Through reading such a book we begin to understand that man is indestructible and that he can none the less be destroyed. This happens in affliction. In affliction we approach the limit where, deprived of the power to say "I", deprived also of the world, we would be nothing other than this Other that we are not.

* Originally published as 'L'Indestructible', *Nouvelle Revue Française*, 112 (April 1962), pp. 191–200. Reprinted in *L'Entretien infini* (Paris, Gallimard, 1969), pp. 191–200, under the title, 'L'espèce humaine', as section 2 of the chapter entitled 'L'Indestructible'.

– Man is the indestructible that can be destroyed. This has the ring of truth, and yet we are are unable to know it through a knowledge that would already be true. Is this not merely an alluring formulation?

– I believe Robert Antelme's book helps us advance in this knowledge. But we must understand how heavily such a knowledge weighs. That man can be destroyed is certainly not reassuring; but that because of and despite this, and in this very movement, man should remain indestructible – this fact is what is truly overwhelming: for we no longer have the least chance of seeing ourselves relieved of ourselves or of our responsibility.

– As though the inexorable affirmation in man that always keeps him standing were more terrible than universal disaster. But why the indestructible? Why can he be destroyed? What relation is there between these two words?

– I read in Antelme's book: "*But there is no ambiguity; we remain men and will end only as men. . . . It is because we are men as they are that the SS will finally be powerless before us . . . [the executioner] can kill a man, but he cannot change him into something else.*" Here is a first response: human power is capable of anything. This means that man has power over what has to do with the whole and with the power that resides in me: power, in other words, over the Self-Subject itself. In this sense, alienation goes much further than is said by those who, through a need for logical security, hold on to the *ego cogito* (understood as the inalienable foundation of every possibility of being alienated). Man can do anything; and first of all, he can deprive me of myself, take from me the power to say "I". In affliction – and in our society affliction is always first the loss of social status – the one who suffers at the hands of men is radically altered. Having fallen not only below the individual, but also below every class and every real collective relation, the person no longer exists in his or her personal identity. In this sense the one afflicted is already outside the world, a being without horizon. And he is not a thing; even useless, a thing is precious. The deported person is not a thing belonging to the SS: when still working as a labourer, his work gives him, however little, the value of a man exploited; but for the essentially deported person, the one who no longer has either a face or speech, the work he is forced to do is designed only to exhaust his power to live and to deliver him over to the boundless insecurity of the elements. Nowhere any recourse: outside the cold, inside hunger; everywhere an indeterminate violence. "*The cold, SS,*" Antelme says profoundly. In precisely this way he blocks the enemy's endeavour. What force would want is to leave the limits of force: elevate itself to the dimension of the faceless gods, speak as fate and still dominate as men. With an unfaltering instinct, Antelme holds himself at a distance from all natural things, keeping himself from seeking consolation in the serene night, the beautiful light, the splendour of a tree: "*By looking at the sky, everywhere black, the SS barracks, the mass of the church and the farm, the temptation could come upon one to confound everything on the basis of the night. . . . History mocks the night that would do away instantly with contradictions. History closes in more relentlessly than God; its exigencies are far more terrifying. On no account does history serve to give peace to one's conscience.*" And in another passage: "*Francis wanted to talk about the sea, I resisted. . . . The sea, the* water, *the sun, made you choke when bodies were decomposing. It was with these very words . . . that one risked no longer wanting to take a step or get up.*" This is what bears meditation: when through oppression and terror man falls as though outside himself, there where he loses every perspective, every point of reference and every difference and is thus handed over to a time without respite that he endures as the perpetuity of an indifferent present, he has one last possibility. At this moment when he becomes the unknown and the foreign, when, that is, he becomes a fate for himself, his last recourse is to know that he has been struck not by the elements, but by men, and to give the name *man* to everything that assails him.

So when everything ceases to be true, 'anthropomorphism' would be truth's ultimate echo. We should, therefore, complete Pascal's thought and say that man, crushed by the universe, must know that in the last instance it is not the universe but man alone who kills him. But it is precisely in affliction that man has always already disappeared: the nature of affliction is such that there is no longer anyone either to cause it or to suffer it; at the limit, there are never any afflicted – no one who is afflicted ever really appears. The one afflicted no longer has any identity other than the situation with which he merges and that never allows him to be himself; for as a situation of affliction, it tends incessantly to de-situate itself, to dissolve in the void of a nowhere without foundation.

– This is the trap of affliction. But here Antelme's book teaches us a great deal. The man of the camps is as close as he can be to powerlessness. All human power is outside him, as are existence in the first person, individual sovereignty and the speech that says "I". It is truly as though there were no Self other than the self of those who dominate and to whom he is delivered over without appeal; as though his own self, therefore, having deserted and betrayed him, reigned among those who predominate, leaving him to an anonymous presence without speech and without dignity. And yet this force that is capable of everything has a limit; and he who literally can no longer do anything still affirms himself at the limit where possibility ceases: in the poverty, the simplicity of a presence that is the infinite of human presence. The Powerful One is the master of the possible, but he is not master of this relation that does not derive from mastery and that power cannot measure: the relation without relation wherein the "other" is revealed as "*autrui*". Or, if you will, the relation of the torturer to his victim, about which so much has been said, is not simply a dialectical relation. What limits his domination first of all is not his need of the one he is torturing, be it only to torture him; it is rather that this relation without power always gives rise, face to face and yet always infinitely, to the presence of the Other [*l'Autre*] as that of the Other being who is *Autrui*. Hence the furious movement of the inquisitor who wants by force to obtain a scrap of language in order to bring all speech down to the level of force. To make speak, and through torture, is to attempt to master infinite distance by reducing expression to this language of power through which the one who speaks would once again lay himself open to force's hold; and the one who is being tortured refuses to speak in order not to enter through the extorted words into this game of opposing violence, but also, at the same time, in order to preserve the true speech that he very well knows is at this instant merged with his silent presence – which is the very presence of *autrui* in himself. A presence no power, even the most formidable, will be able to reach, except by doing away with it. It is this presence that bears in itself and as the last affirmation what Robert Antelme calls *the ultimate feeling of belonging to mankind*.

– So that, fallen away from my self, foreign to myself, what is affirmed in my place is the foreignness of the other who is *autrui*: man as absolutely other, foreign and unknown, the dispossessed and the wandering or, as René Char puts it, the unimaginable man by whose presence passes the affirmation of an infinite exigency.

– "*Our horror, our stupor,*" Antelme states, "*was our lucidity.*"

– But what happens none the less to the one who is no longer a presence – a terrifying transformation – in the first person? Destroyed as a Subject, that is, in this sense, essentially destroyed, how can he respond to this exigency that is the exigency of the presence in him?

– Here again Antelme's book gives us the right response, and it is the book's most forceful truth. When man is reduced to the extreme destitution of need, when he becomes "someone who eats scraps," we see that he is reduced to himself, and reveals himself as one who has need of nothing other than need in order to maintain the human relation in its primacy, negating what negates him. It must be added that need now changes; radicalized in the proper sense of this term, it is now no more than a need that is barren, without pleasure and without content: a naked relation to naked life where the bread that one eats answers immediately to the exigency of need, just as need is immediately the need to live. Levinas, in various analyses, has shown that need is always at the same time pleasure, which is to say that in eating I not only nourish myself in order to live, but already have taken pleasure in life, affirming myself and

identifying with myself in this first satisfaction. But now what we encounter in Antelme's experience, the experience of man reduced to the
irreducible, is the radical need that relates me no longer either to myself
or to my self-satisfaction, but to human existence pure and simple, lived
as lack at the level of need. And it is still no doubt a question of a kind of
egoism, and even of the most terrible kind, but of an *egoism without ego*
where man, bent on survival, and attached in a way that must be called
abject to living and always living on, bears this attachment to life as an
attachment that is impersonal, as he bears this need as a need that is no
longer his own need proper but as a need that is in some sense empty and
neutral, thus virtually the need of everyone. "To live," as he more or less
says, "is then all that is sacred."

– One can therefore say that when, through oppression and affliction,
my relation with myself is altered and lost – making of me this foreigner,
this unknown from whom I am separated by an infinite distance, and
making of me this infinite separation itself – at this moment need
becomes radical: a need without satisfaction, without value, that is, a
naked relation to naked existence; but this need also becomes the impersonal exigency that alone bears the future and the meaning of every value
or, more precisely, of every human relation. The infinite that is the
movement of desire passes by way of need. Need is desire and desire
becomes confounded with need. It is as though in nourishing myself at
the level of subsistence it is not I whom I nourished; it is as though I
received the Other [*l'Autre*], host not to myself but to the unknown and
the foreign.

– Yet we must not believe that with need everything is already saved: it
is with need that everything is at stake. In the first place, man can fall
below need; he can be deprived of this lack, dispossessed of dispossession. But more must be said. Even at the level of this need that is
sustained without satisfaction, at a level where, rather than a self-
possessed will, there is in me a quasi-impersonal affirmation that alone
sustains the fact of being dispossessed; when, therefore, my relation with
myself makes me the absolutely Other [*l'Autre*] whose presence puts the
power of the Powerful radically into question, this movement still signifies only the failure of power – not "my" victory, still less "my"
salvation. For such a movement to begin truly to be affirmed, there must
be restored – beyond this self that I have ceased to be, and within the
anonymous community – the instance of a Self-Subject: no longer as a
dominating and oppressing power drawn up against the "other" that is
autrui, but as what can receive the unknown and the foreign, receive
them in the justice of a true *speech*. Moreover, on the basis of this
attention to affliction without which all relation falls back into the night,
another possibility must intervene: the possibility that a Self outside me

become not only conscious of the affliction as though this Self were in my place, but become responsible for it by recognizing in it an injustice committed against everyone – that is, it must find in this injustice the point of departure for a *common demand*.

– In other words, through the intermediary of an exterior Subject who affirms itself as being the representative of a collective structure[6] (this would be, for example, class consciousness), the one who is dispossessed must be received not only as *"autrui"* in the justice of speech, but also placed back into a situation of dialectical struggle so he may once again consider himself as a force,[7] the force that resides in the man of need, and, finally, in the "proletarian". We always come back, then, to the exigency of this double relation.

– Yes, and this is what Antelme's book expresses explicitly on several pages that should be cited, were it not fitting to preserve their entire meaning by leaving them within the general movement that belongs to reading. I would like to add that the significance of this book ought now to appear more clearly. It is not, as I have said, simply a witness's testimony to the reality of a camp or a historical reporting, nor is it an autobiographical narrative. It is clear that for Robert Antelme, and very surely for many others, it is a question not of telling one's story, of testifying, but essentially of *speaking*. But which speech is being given expression? Precisely that just speech in which *"Autrui"*, prevented from all disclosure throughout his or her entire stay in the camp, could, and only at the end, be received and come into human hearing.

Let us once again recall that during their stay, all of them found themselves (in a movement that was necessarily painful, partial, unfinished and impossible to realize) deprived as it were of a self and constrained to be the other [*autrui*] for themselves. Among those who were deported there were doubtless relations that allowed them to re-establish an appearance of society, that therefore allowed each one the occasion to feel himself or herself momentarily a self *vis-à-vis* someone in particular, or even to maintain a semblance of force in confronting those who were the Powerful (if only because the political struggle continued in the rest of the world and was preparing a new day). Had it been otherwise, everything would have immediately given way to a dying without end. But what in this situation remains essential, its truth, is the following: the camp confined no more than a bondless entanglement of Others [*hommes Autres*], a magma of the other [*autrui*] face to face with the force of a Self that kills and that represents nothing but the untiring power to kill. Between these deported persons who are Other and this Self of Force no language is possible; but neither is there any possibility of expression between these Others. What is then said is essential, but in *truth* heard by no one; there is no one to receive as speech (save through the momentary exchanges in which, through camaraderie, a self comes back to life) the infinite and infinitely silent presence of *autrui*. Now each one has no relation with words other than the reserve of speech, which he must live in solitude, and must also preserve by refusing any relation of false language with the Powerful, for such a relation could only definitively compromise the future of communication.

To speak in refusing, but in reserving speech.

So now we understand this reserved speech of *autrui*; a speech un-heard, inexpressible, nevertheless unceasing, silently affirming that where all relation is lacking there yet subsists, there already begins, the human relation in its primacy. It is this truly infinite speech that each of those who had been handed over to the impossible experience of being for himself or herself the "other" [*autrui*] felt called upon, now back in the world, to represent to us in speaking endlessly, without stopping, for the first time. Antelme says this, saying immediately the essential from the first words of his book: "*During the first days that followed our return, we were all, I think, seized by a veritable delirium. We wished to speak, to be heard at last.*"

– Yes, one had to speak: to entitle speech in responding to the silent presence of the other that is *autrui*. The unique authority of this speech coming directly from this very exigency.

– It was, in fact, the most immediate exigency that can be. I have to speak. An infinite demand that imposes itself with an irrepressible force. And it was as well an overwhelming discovery, a painful surprise: I speak, am I speaking? Could I now truly speak? Nothing more grave than this being able to speak from the basis of the impossible, the infinite distance to be "filled" by language itself. "*And yet*," says Robert Antelme, "*it was impossible. We had hardly begun to speak and we were choking.*"

– Why this wrenching? Why this pain always present, and not only here in this extreme movement but already, as I believe it is, in the most simple act of speaking?

– Perhaps because, as soon as two individuals approach one another, there is between them some painful formulation of the kind we expressed in beginning. They speak, perhaps, in order to forget it, to deny it, or to represent it.

– That man is the indestructible that can be destroyed? I continue to be wary of this formulation.

– How could it be otherwise? But even if we are to delete it, let us agree to keep what it has most plainly taught us. Yes, I believe we must say this, hold onto it for an instant: man is the indestructible. And this means there is no limit to the destruction of man.

– Is this not to formulate a radical nihilism?

– If so I should be quite willing, for to formulate it would also perhaps already be to overturn it. But I doubt that nihilism will allow itself to be taken so easily.'[8]

Notes

1 Albert Memmi. *Portrait d'un Juif* (Paris, Gallimard, 1962).

2 André Neher. *L'existence juive* (Paris, Seuil, 1962).

3 See the work of Isaac Heinemann, adapted by Charles Touati, *La Loi dans la pensée juive* (Paris, Albin Michel, Collection Présences du Judaïsme, 1962).

4 Without any further conclusions, let me anticipate an objection. I can indeed understand why many who are horrified by anti-Semitism wish to silence those who accuse the Jews by attenuating the importance of the question that comes to us from them. They protest against what they call the metaphysics of the Jewish question; they say it feeds hate for the Jews because this hate is nourished by a myth that has nothing to do with the real conditions of existence. One must therefore deny this question any meaning that would not be simply historical and seek the means to respond to it only in the history that brought it to us. No doubt. But here distinctions must be made. I observe, on the one hand, that anti-Semites too seek fundamentally only to avoid the metaphysical exigency that Judaism poses to each of us by way of Jewish existence, and that it is in order better to suppress this question that they want to suppress all Jews (that is to say, radically denounce being Jewish). To neglect this aspect of anti-Semitism is to renounce coming to grips with its gravity, to renounce finding in it one of its roots, and therefore to refuse to see what is at stake when, in the world, in whatever form it may take, anti-Semitism affirms and strengthens itself. But on the other hand, certainly, the relations that link being Jewish to a people or to a specific nation are also historical relations that must not be considered as being outside history; and these are relations that the work of men in history is called upon to change. At the end of his book, Albert Memmi asks: 'Is this all in the past? I think it is, in part. It is possible that we have entered into an entirely new period of history that will see the progressive liquidation of the oppression undergone by the Jew. But in addition to the fact that regression is always possible, this process has only begun. And it has already begun several times.' The rebirth of the State of Israel, as well as our greater consciousness of what conditions of oppression are may cause us to advance along this path. It ought to remain clear, however, that the question expressed by the words 'being Jewish' and by the question of the State of Israel cannot be identical questions, although each modifies the other. I recall Hermann Cohen's remark regarding the Zionists, as cited by Rosenzweig, who neither criticizes it nor assents to it: 'These hearty souls want to be happy.' After the advent of Hitler he would not have been able to entertain this reflection so simply. For then it became manifest that it was not a question of being happy, but of being. But the hunger for life implies, precisely as Rosenzweig says it does, the metaphysical obligation to live (and perhaps also to be happy), so that to ensure the possibility of a free existence to a people – be it by the reconstruction of a 'place of sojourn', and by the perhaps dangerous means of a national claim – is still the most urgent task. Yet if this task itself, which passes by way of the edification of a dwelling place and, finally, of a state, partially responds to the question of safeguarding the Jews, it cannot constitute a response to the question that being Jewish poses, which is a universal question. We can be assured that this task only produces the question in a new light. Here I will cite a remark of André Neher. He notes that Theodor Herzl, and in a general way Zionist ideology, have proposed a purely Western solution for a situation that is specifi-

cally Oriental (perhaps it would be better to say: a situation exceeding all determined historical signification); this solution entails a State, as though the entire movement carried by Judaism ought to tend towards nothing other than the foundation of a State conceived on the nineteenth-century model, claiming for itself the reality of the Law, and affirming the whole, transcendence. I cite again André Neher: 'The question of whether the State of Israel shall be religious or laic – whether it will be capable of realizing itself in a sharing or in a synthesis of these two dimensions (or even in being neither laic nor religious) – does not fall within the province of political parties but of philosophers: the entire Jewish vocation is in question.' I would be tempted to conclude by saying that in the society that is being tried in Palestine – a society caught up in struggle, under threat and also threatened by nothing less grave than the necessity of this struggle for 'safeguarding' (as is also the case in the societies that have issued from Marxism or been liberated from colonial bondage) – it is philosophy itself that is being dangerously measured against power inasmuch as this society, like the others, will have to determine the meaning and the future of 'nomadic truth' in the face of the state.

5 Robert Antelme, *L'Espèce humaine* (Paris, Gallimard, 1978, c. 1957).

6 Why collective? Because it is a question of coming back to truth as the affirmation and the question of the whole; totality cannot be posited, either in knowledge or in action, unless the subject does so in and as a movement toward that 'totality', and is, himself, already a form of the whole.

7 But this (should it be necessary to state it explicitly) is the most difficult: first because there is a kind of irreducible opposition between the man that is Other [*l'homme Autre*], the absolutely deprived, and any kind of force, even if this force is protective. Robert Antelme says this with a decisive simplicity: 'A suspicion always hangs here over the man who is still strong. . . . He does not defend us by the means that are ours, but with the force of muscle that no one here possesses. And this man, doubtless useful, effective, does not seem to be one of us.'

8 With the experience that he draws from himself and from his learning, Gerschom Scholem has said, speaking of the relations between the Germans and the Jews: 'The abyss opened between us by these events cannot be measured. . . . For, in truth, it is impossible to realize completely what happened. Its incomprehensible nature has to do with the very essence of the phenomenon: it is impossible fully to understand it, that is to say, integrate it into our consciousness.' Impossible, therefore, to forget it, impossible to remember it. Also impossible, in speaking about it, to speak of it – and finally, as there is nothing but this incomprehensible event to say, it is speech alone that must bear it without saying it.

Translated by Susan Hanson

22

'Do Not Forget' (1988)*

Permit me to write to you by letter, something without pretension, rather than attempt to reach you in an interview of which I am incapable.

In a way, Judaism is so close to me that I do not feel worthy to speak of it, except to convey that closeness and the reasons for that closeness (even that though, can I express it?). Is it not presumptious to hope to be able to express it one day? Will there ever be a day on which to express it? The answer is: not in any time to come [*l'avenir*], but perhaps in the future [*le futur*] (cf. Levinas in the journal *Spuren*, no. 20).[1]

The great debt I owe to Emmanuel Levinas is, I believe, well known. He is today my oldest friend, the only one I feel entitled to address in the *tu* form. It is also known that we met at the University of Strasbourg in 1926, where so many great teachers made philosophy anything but mediocre for us. Was this encounter the result of chance? It could be said. But our friendship was neither hazardous nor fortuitous. Something profound drew us together. I won't say that this was already Judaism, but rather, in addition to his cheerfulness, a sort of solemn, noble way of envisaging life by investigating it without a trace of pedantry. At the same time, it is to him I owe my first encounter with Husserl, and even with Heidegger, whose lectures he had attended in a Germany already stirred up by perverse political impulses. We left Strasbourg for Paris at almost the same time, but although we never lost touch entirely, it took the misfortunes of a disastrous war for the ties of our friendship, which could be said to have slackened somewhat, to become firmer again, particularly since, while a prisoner of war (in France initially), he entrusted me, through what amounted to a secret request, with the task of watching over those dear to him, who were, alas, vulnerable to the perils of a heinous political system.

I shall venture no further down the winding path of biography, whose memories are nevertheless very vivid for me. It was obviously the Nazi persecutions (they were perpetrated from the outset, contrary to what certain professors of philosophy would have us believe, so as to persuade us that in 1933, when Heidegger joined the party, National Socialism

* Originally published as ' "N'oubliez pas" ', a letter to Salomon Malka, *L'Arche*, May 1988, pp. 68–71.

was still a respectable doctrine, undeserving of condemnation) that made us feel that the Jews were our brothers, and that Judaism was more than just a culture, more than just a religion even, because it was the foundation of our relationship to others [*autrui*]. I shall refrain from any lengthy commentary on Emmanuel Levinas's work, about which you yourself have spoken so excellently, except to repeat that it must be studied and meditated with the utmost vigilance. That is what it teaches us before all else: reading is not enough, understanding and absorbing are not enough; what matters is to be watchful and to be wakeful. We think we respect others by grudgingly leaving room for them, but others demand (without demanding) all the room. Just as others are always higher than I am, closer than I am to God (that unpronounceable name), so the dissymmetrical relation from them to me is the foundation of ethics and puts me under obligation, with an extraordinary obligation that weighs down on me (ethics, in Levinas, still belongs to the philosophical, as it does in Kant, for whom practical Reason takes priority over pure Reason).

The Relation of the I to the Other

You also ask me about Martin Buber, who reawakened Judaism at a time when assimilation was threatening to eclipse it. We are grateful to Martin Buber for everything he has given us, in an enchanting style which sometimes recalls that of Chagall. Rightly or wrongly, there is in him that radiancy of Hasidism, with all its marvellous stories whose humour is so richly instructive. But it must not be forgotten that Hasidism, which bears little relation to that of the Middle Ages, marks the rebirth of Judaism, following the catastrophe constituted by the apostasy (the conversion to Islam) of the false Messiah, Shabtai Tsvi (as our friend David Banon transcribes it).

I would like here to make the point that, especially in the nineteenth century, the Christians and the non-Christians who took an interest in Judaism were looking for a secret doctrine, the mysticism incarnated in the name Kabbala. In that way, without intending to, they turned the Jews into the bearers of an interesting but perhaps malevolent mystery. Hence the feeling that Jews are a race apart, and that they can only live among themselves. This is the justification for all ghettos, and they in turn anticipate the sinister concentration camps, where there was nothing save waiting for death.

Martin Buber taught us the excellence of the relation of the I to the Other, revealing to us, through stirring us emotionally (but also by appealing to our reason) the richness and the beauty of the *tu* form. The relation from I to You as *tu* is a privileged one; it differs essentially from the relation from I to That [*Cela*]. It is the encounter that precedes all possibility of relation, an encounter in which the unhoped for, unexpected reciprocity is fulfilled, in that blinding instant about which we remain in doubt, even when we are sure of it. But does this reciprocity not make us forget that the I can never be on an equal footing with the Other, when that other is Others [*Autrui*]? That is precisely the lesson of Levinas. It is knowledge that is not merely knowledge. It leads us down a more difficult path, because we shall only find ourselves on it if we have gone through an upheaval in philosophy that places ethics at the beginning and even before any beginning. In this way, we discover Others not in the happy or laborious equality of friendship, but in a state of extreme responsibility that puts us under obligation, takes us hostage even, revealing to us the strangeness of the dissymmetry between You [*Toi*] and me. A Me without me, deprived of the self-sufficiency of subjectivity, trying to divest itself of what it is and even of being, not in search of a purely personal asceticism, but in an attempt to come up to the ethical obligation that I recognize in the countenance [*le visage*], and in the invisibility of the countenance that is not the face [*la figure*], but the weakness of Others in their exposure to death; or that I recognize in the 'Saying' [*le Dire*] with which, when I speak to Others, I appeal to them, in an interpellation or invocation where the addressee is out of reach, being always beyond me, surpassing me and towering above me.

These are very inadequate propositions, which I shall try to compensate for by seeking leave of Jean Halperin to repeat again with him: 'What is proposed, or rather promised, with Levinas is a surplus, something beyond the universal, a singularity which we may call Jewish and which still *awaits* thinking. Which means it is prophetic. Judaism as what for ever surpasses thinking, in that it has always already been thought; but as what, at the same time, carries responsibility for the thinking that is to come: that is what we are *given* by this other philosophy which is that of Levinas, and which is both burden and hope, the burden of hope.'

Heidegger's Unforgivable Silence

All of which makes it difficult for me to go back over the dismal Heidegger 'dispute' which you ask me about. There is nothing that can be said about it that does not inspire a degree of horror. Clearly, the book attacking Heidegger is an unsatisfactory book, and fully deserves the media uproar by which we have been deafened, but perhaps also woken up. The fact remains that the central matter of Heidegger's responsibility in adhering to National Socialism permanently raises the most serious problems as far as his thought itself is concerned. Was it a decision forced on him by events, one to which the man who had written *Sein und Zeit* did not subscribe and which therefore left his thought intact? On this essential point, Heidegger responded clearly to Karl Löwith in 1936, that is to say two years after he had resigned from the Rectorship. And what was that response (there is no mention of it in Farias's book)? 'It was my conception of historiality (*Geschichtlichkeit*) – (or put more simply, of historicity) that provided the basis (*die Grundlage*) for involvement (*Einsatz*).' I would add: for political involvement, but equally well for philosophical involvement. In that conversation, Karl Löwith questions the man who had been his teacher no further. We may assume that, given his own particular way of employing the German language, historically is not simple temporal succession, but a response to a call from destiny, and depending upon whether or not one heeds the call, one contributes or does not contribute to a radical change of epoch. Heidegger himself, in the posthumous testament in *Der Spiegel*, admits that in the advent of Hitler he had hailed the grandeur and the splendour of a new beginning. What begins is always what is most important for him: it is the upsurge of absolute renewal, the interruption that suspends our relation to established laws and values, perhaps even to the 'gods'. And in a sense, this was true. But that interruption, which was for Heidegger the promise of a Germany heir to the excellence of Greece, and as such, and at whatever price, called on to enlighten the world by dominating it, was also for us, and first of all for the Jews, the interregnum where all rights and all redress ceased, where friendship became unsure, where the silence on the part of the highest spiritual authorities left us without assurance, not only under threat, but uneasy at being unable to respond in the way we should have to the silent appeal of others.

The disaster which followed affected Heidegger, since, on resuming his lectures, he urged his listeners to go away and reflect, on the occasion of the opening of an exhibition about German prisoners of war and their maltreatment by the Russians. This was a reflection on certain victims, for whom Hitler was in part responsible to the extent that the war against Russia was his doing. But there was utter silence as far as other victims were concerned, the six million Jews whose only fault was to have been born Jews, and who represented Judaism as a whole which the aim was to wipe out. A silence we are advised today by a certain doctor of philosophy not to break. In other words we should not invoke Auschwitz, so as not to turn it into an argument, an automatic and unthinking term, and in that way show a respect which would in turn, however, give respectability to Heidegger's unforgivable silence.[2]

Must it be repeated (yes, it must) that Auschwitz, an event which makes a ceaseless appeal to us, imposes, through testimony, the indefeasible duty not to forget: remember, beware of forgetfulness and yet, in that faithful memory, *never will you know*. I stress that, because what it says refers us to that which there can be no memory of, to the unrepresent-able, to unspeakable horror, which however, one way or another and always in anguish, is what is immemorial.

Hence this quotation which I beg to cite, because it lets the unknown name that Auschwitz remains be heard (holocaust, extermination, *shoa*, words beyond naming): *The holocaust, an absolute historical event, historic-ally dated, that total burning where all history caught fire, where the movement of Meaning collapsed, where giving, without pardon, without consent, was ruined without giving rise to anything that could be affirmed, or denied, the gift of passivity itself, the giving of what cannot be given. How can it be kept safe, even if only in thought, how can thought be made into what might keep safe the holocaust where all was lost, including the safekeeping of thought.*[3]

I do not feel empowered to add anything to that, but simply to salute you, in this language and in another, and to thank you for bidding me welcome, in these my declining years.

Maurice Blanchot

NB It is not for me here to examine further the work of Heidegger, which has exerted such fascination – a term that already calls into question a way of thinking subject to a language which the play of etymology perhaps leads outside the field of philosophy, and which only ever affirms subject to the artful reservations of a necessarily disguised denegation. Hence it is that a major sociologist, while very much a stranger to Heidegger's 'discourse', can make the following suggestion: 'It is perhaps because he never really knew what he was saying that Heidegger could say, without having really to say it to himself, what he did say. And it is perhaps for the same reason that he refused to explain his involvement with the Nazis [we saw however that, talking to Karl Löwith during the period when Nazism was triumphant, he recognized and accepted re-sponsibility for the concordance between his thought and his radical involvement.] Really to do so would have entailed admitting to himself that essential thought had never thought the essential, that is to say the social unthought [*l'impensé social*] which is expressed through it.' That is Pierre Bourdieu's conclusion. He would not accept that he is implicitly exonerating Heidegger (he claims he is not putting him on trial) by implicating all philosophical activity, whose possibilities (primarily the expressive possibilities) Heidegger can be said merely to have pushed to their extreme.

But a very recent book by Lyotard, entitled *Heidegger and 'the Jews'*,[4] must also be read (he explains why he uses inverted commas, without being totally convincing). He shows that Heidegger is very close to the terrible anti-Semitism of the young Hegel. Heidegger's silence 'shows up the mistaken way in which all "knowledge" confronts the Other under the name of the truth of being'. Finally, he says of Granel, who has attempted to extract from Heidegger's National Socialism a 'truth', a 'grandeur' truer and greater than Heidegger himself conceived of them (disciples are like that), that in so doing he is defaulting gravely on the debt which is our only lot, (that is to say) which consists in not forgetting that something has become Forgotten, nor what horror the mind is capable of in its frenzy to make sure it is forgotten. 'Our' lot, but whose lot? That of the non-people of survivors, Jews and non-Jews, termed 'the Jews' for the occasion, whose existence as a group is based on the authenticity of no primeval root, but solely on a debt of interminable anamnesis. The reminiscence, the memory of the Law which only gets forgotten if the time is not available in which to study it, and act in such a way that I never feel acquitted of my responsibility towards others, in whom there is revealed the trace of him who is never there, who is always already past and gone: God perhaps, but not the God of power, promise and salvation, of whose retreat Auschwitz is the mark.

Notes

1 Do you recall what Levinas said to you one day, during an interview: 'Judaism is an essential modality of all that is human'? An essential modality, but one that usually goes unrecognized, or is buried out of sight, or worse, perverted and eventually impugned.

2 Your readers will recall Levinas's Talmudic reading (on forgiveness, 1967), in which he argues that many Germans could be forgiven, but not Heidegger, because of his mastery (he is the Master), his 'perspicacity' and his 'knowledge'. But what if it was his 'knowledge' that closed his eyes and made him incapable of any confession? What an increase of responsibility then, and one that perhaps weighs down on us too.

3 See *L'Ecriture du désastre* (Paris, Gallimard, 1980), p. 80. [Translator's note.]

4 Jean-François Lyotard, *Heidegger and 'the Jews'*, trans. Andreas Michel and Mark S. Roberts (Minneapolis, University of Minnesota Press, 1990). [Translator's note.]

Translated by Michael Holland

PART IV

The Step Beyond

The question remains, however: what made the turn to Judaism in the 1960s possible? What was it that, without simply opening up fresh territory, led Blanchot to a beyond offering the possibility of a responsiveness and a responsibility towards the Other as personified by the Jew in Western history and culture? Furthermore, in the absence of any turn (back) to God on Blanchot's part, what significance did this new exigency in his writing have?

The answer to all three questions is the same: Blanchot finally overcame the last remaining form of the dead world he had spent thirty years refusing, first from within literature, then politically; a form hitherto unassailable in its essence because it provided the means and the resource for all the other refusals he had offered: namely language, the form or forms offered to subjectivity by language. For as long as his subjectivity remained confined within literature and the 'world' it provided, language and its forms ensured the endless deferral of the last word (what he calls in **The Ease of Dying** 'the word capable . . . of ending all words' (p. 304), so making it impossible for Blanchot, despite the silence that had fallen upon him politically, to 'have done with it' once and for all. Language was, in short, the essential condition of subjectivity for him, even though its product was a divided Subject. However, with the exhaustion of this 'world', the reversal of the priority of analysis over literature and the corresponding discovery, in the world he had given up for literature (and for dead), of the mute call of an Other as vulnerable as that encountered in the 'world' of literature, the persistence of language ceased to be a guarantee of survival for subjectivity and, with his return to the world of others, proved a persistent obstacle in the way of that return becoming real.

For though the increasingly anachronistic nature of the stance he maintained during the post-war years was eventually broken in 1958, his return to the world left one dimension of that stance intact. The retreat into literature in the late thirties imposed a silence upon the subject of politics. But though literature became the language of that subject's loss of language, and the only 'world' in which, though lost, subjectivity could survive, it (he) had not disappeared from language: though reduced to silence, the *position* of that subject, while empty, nevertheless remained intact. Within literature, its language and its 'world', Blanchot's fictional practice consists, over twenty years, of subjecting the language of that mute subject, in the form of first-person narrative (*le récit*), to slow and gradual exhaustion, until with *The Last Man*, it is becoming interchangeable with a language whose subject, *il* (he or it), is becoming indeterminate and impersonal.[1] But however great the divorce eventually effected in the language of his fiction, between the existing forms of subjectivity in language and the

subjectivity that Blanchot had been elaborating for twenty years in the
'world' of literature, in 1958, on his return to the political world,
those forms, which inevitably remain the forms in which that world
continued (and continues) to articulate its subjectivity and respond to
its Other, equally inevitably accompanied that return, finding a new
lease of life in response to 'the exigency of politics'. In other words, not
yet having forged a language commensurate with his own subjectivity that does not depend, indirectly, upon the language of subjectivity
still current in the world, with his return to the world, that dependency exerts a major limitation on his ability to be a subject in that
world, either politically (together with others) or responsibly (for others
(*autrui*)).

The difficulties traced in the previous part all stem from here. Lucidly
denouncing in de Gaulle the personification of a world unaware that it is
dead, he is unable to see that he too is burdened by the dead weight of
his own lifeless subjectivity. Though invisible, the same cadaverous
presence given fictional form in *Thomas the Obscure*,[2] and theorized in
The Space of Literature,[3] weighs down on the language in which he seeks
to live on, twisting and distorting it at the turning-point at which he finds
both himself and the world, and subjecting it, at crucial moments, to the
cataleptic spasms of its inertia. To the extent that he is now obliged to
speak in the language of the world, the sole voice he can offer it is one
that has been dead for two decades. In May 1968, as I have suggested,
the revolutionary tone of his anonymous writings rings ominously with
the sound of that dead voice.

Yet although his return to the world and to politics puts a brutal stop
to the processes gradually developing in his fiction (he published no more
narrative fiction for ten years), the work being done at that level does not
stop. Within the world for which he has left the 'world' of literature, the
often distorted language I have described is nevertheless the vehicle for a
reflection on an entirely new mode of language – what he will eventually
call the *fragment* – which intermittently, then with greater frequency, will
itself become an instance of the new mode it evokes. As early as 1960, in
the preparatory documents for the 'International Review',[4] political action and the responsibility it entails will be defined exclusively in terms
of the activity of the writer:

> The sense of the review is to seek to prepare a new possibility, one
> which could allow the writer to *say* the 'world' and everything that
> takes place in the world, but as a writer and with the responsibility
> which comes solely from the truth of being a writer: a form of
> responsibility which is quite different, therefore, (though no less
> essential) than that which brutally marked the relationship between

literature and public life from 1945 onwards, known by the simplistic name of 'Sartrean commitment'. (p. 185)

Though he has emerged from the 'world' of literature and back into a
world he left to its fate in the late 1930s, it is noteworthy that Blanchot's
return is nevertheless so much that of the writer he has become, that for
him it is the world to which he has returned that must be written 'world'.
As he began to argue in **The Great Hoax**, literature remains for him 'a
very special sort of power . . . (*a power without power*)' (p. 182); it is 'an
experience which must be subjected to no restriction, no dogmatic
surveillance' (p. 183); and he goes on:

> What results from this would seem to be an irreducible difference,
> not to say a discordance, between political responsibility, which is
> simultaneously both global and concrete, accepting Marxism as
> natural and the dialectic as a method for truth – and literary
> responsibility, one which is a response to an exigency which can
> only take on form in and through literature.
>
> This discordance has no need to be reduced at the outset. It is
> a given; it exists as a problem, not a frivolous problem but one
> that must be borne with difficulty; one that is all the more difficult
> in so far as each of its discordant terms requires our absolute
> commitment, and their discordance, in a sense, is also what we
> are committed to. (p. 183)

It is clear from this that, at the turning-point he has identified in **On a
Change of Epoch** (1960), and which he reaffirms at the outset in
these preparatory documents,[5] Blanchot is lucidly aware of the changes
that are required in his own thought and writing. In the impoverished
space of the language of political activism, his voice may as yet ring
hollow; while his ability to locate and accommodate in his writing
the new 'beyond' to which he is becoming responsive may still be erratic.
At the same time, he has the measure of the problem, he has located
the unstable borderline where world becomes 'world', reversibly and
uncontrollably, rendering subjectivity in language absolutely uncertain.
At one level, the measure he proposes could itself ring rather hollow,
echoing as it does a position first adopted by the Surrealists fifty
years earlier.[6] At another, however, the perspective opening up in
these preparatory documents looks forward to something totally original. This is first of all a question of space: the path between the two
'worlds' of literature and politics – which for him is one between two
worlds each of which, in its way, does not exist – can now only be an
indirect one:

> The search for the 'indirect' is one of the major tasks of the review,
> it being clearly understood that an 'indirect' critique, by way of the
> detour, does not signify a merely allusive or elliptical critique, but a
> more radical critique, going straight to the hidden sense of what lies
> at the 'root'. (p. 185)

The space that has hitherto been solely that of literature is here extended,
in its essentially extra-literary curvature,[7] to what lies outside literature.
But it is extended in such a way that this outside, raised to categoric
status as *le Dehors* for a period in Blanchot's writing (and analysed by
Foucault),[8] and serving, through the pathos of its associations and the
phantasmatic power of its topology, to deflect the call of *Autrui* encountered through Levinas, is now the space of an active intervention, or
rather, a *collective interaction* between writers, each of whom, in writing,
is taken subjectively beyond the subjectivity of the Self, and a world
which, its course having entered a radical turn, has definitively gone off
course, manifesting itself henceforth in a mode of dangerous and divisive
intermittence.

Corresponding to this new spatiality, and providing it with a medium
and a mode which are indispensable to it, in that, as the outcome of an
experience of language (literature), its viability depends entirely upon
language,[9] is the *fragment*. The interface between writers and events
provided by the review will be a rubric entitled 'the Course of Things' (*le
Cours des choses*). *Structurally*, this rubric will run throughout each number, interrupted from time to time by other texts but, in its discontinuity,
providing a continuum within which the new collective interaction being
projected can find the space it requires. *Formally*:

> The aim will be, under this rubric, to experiment with a *short form*
> (in the sense given to this term in music today). What we mean by
> that is that each text will be not only short (from a half-page to two
> to four pages), but will constitute as it were a *fragment*, not neces-
> sarily having all its meaning in itself, but open rather onto a more
> general meaning that is yet to come, or else accepting the exigency
> of an essential *discontinuity*. (pp. 185–6)

The fragment, as a literary form, had been attracting Blanchot's attention increasingly throughout the 1950s, be it in Proust,[10] Henry
James,[11] Broch[12] or Virginia Woolf,[13] not to mention Kafka and
Mallarmé, whose 'fragmentary stops' (*arrêts fragmentaires*) he cites
in 1957.[14] And as early as 1953, in **The Disappearance of Literature**,
he associates the form with a particular disposition on the part of the
writer:

the writer often wishes to accomplish almost nothing, leaving in a fragmentary state a hundred tales whose interest has been to lead him to a certain point, and which he has to abandon in order to try to go beyond that point. (p. 140)

At the same time, fragmentation is the form being taken on by the writer's experience, both of the world (in 1951 he speaks of ' "those outmoded objects, fragmented, unusable, almost incomprehensible, perverse" which André Breton loved'),[15] and of his own being (his 1955 essay on Broch refers to man as 'scattered and fragmented', faced with the task of constructing a world based 'on the dislocated, discordant and fragmented character of being').[16] At this early stage, Blanchot is still a long way from making the changes to his own language which would conform to this experience of fragmentation. The mobile hiatus between 'worlds' that will generate the fragment remains the static margin from where the world of forms is contested in the name of the subjectivity of literature. Evoking the 'fearsome transformation' caused by the collapse of the world and the disappearance of the self, he is able, in **The Pursuit of the Zero Point**, merely to disqualify existing forms of language as means of accommodating the hiatus or 'leap' which is the sole space left for writing to take place:

> To seek to recover the innocence or the naturalness of the spoken language . . . is to maintain that this transformation could be calculated in the manner of *an index of refraction*, as if we were dealing with a phenomenon fixed in the world of things, whereas it is in fact the very void of this world, a call one only hears if one is oneself changed, a decision which consigns anyone who takes it on to the realm of the undecided. (p. 149; my italics)

Yet indirectly, with the notion of *an index of refraction*, the fragmentary nature of the refractory space in which writing takes place is already being recognized. With the decade, 'the innocence and naturalness of spoken language', which, as I began by saying, proved the final barrier to Blanchot's development as a writer, will gradually be displaced, both in theory and in practice. That the process is gradual, even cautious, is clear from an article Blanchot devoted to Lucien Goldmann's *The Hidden God* in 1956. In a concluding note, having observed that Goldmann proposes the *fragment* as the form best suited to tragic thought in its paradoxical development, he replies:

> And why should not completion [*l'accomplissement*] also be the form in which tragic thought – which is always simultaneously complete

and incomplete – could be affirmed, not appropriately, but in that
coherence without propriety that is its necessity?

Significantly, this section was omitted from the article when it was
included in *The Infinite Conversation* in 1969.[17] For by then, in articles
such as 'Nietzsche and Fragmentary Writing' (1966–7)[18] and **The
Exigency of Return**, a section added to **On a Change of Epoch** when
it was included in *The Infinite Conversation*,[19] Blanchot's own writing had
moved entirely into the fragmentary mode which he began to define in
1960.

Part IV of the *Reader* begins with two examples of the writing destined
to appear under the rubric 'The Course of Things' in the first number of
Gulliver, as the 'International Review' would have been called, had it got
off the ground. Eventually only the first number was published, in
Italian, in Elio Vittorini's journal *Il Menabò*.[20] **The Name Berlin**[21]
evokes 'the problem of division – of fracture' posed by the construction
of the Wall in August 1961, 'a problem which we cannot formulate
adequately, in its *complete* reality, unless we decide to formulate it *fragmentarily*' (pp. 266–7). **The Conquest of Space** is a response to the first
manned space flight, undertaken by Yuri Gagarin in April of the same
year. In it Blanchot clearly revises his category of the *Outside* in accordance with the new interactive spatiality linking writer and world. Now,
rather than deflecting the call of *Autrui* by means of an Outside without
living human reality, he argues that 'it is . . . necessary, up there, for the
man from Outside to speak, and to speak continually' (p. 271). In a
footnote, he indicates his indebtedness to Levinas for part of what he is
saying, proving once again that, in this period, every limitation affecting
his thinking is also the site of radical transformation.[22]

This search for a language of the fragment, both in theory and in
practice, though worked out in the new, politically oriented field of
relations which opened up for Blanchot after 1958, is pursued more
substantially in the writing that he continued to produce, more or less on
a monthly basis, throughout the decade. At this level, an important
transformation occurs, which determines the course taken by the reversal
of the original relationship between literary and non-literary language
that Blanchot effects in *The Space of Literature*. On the one hand, as I have
already indicated, he ceased to write narrative works (*récits*) after 1957.
On the other, the language of literary criticism, to which his non-literary
writing has always roughly conformed, became more and more concerned with philosophy, its authors and its concepts.

It would be wrong, however, to see this as a simplification of his project
as a writer, an *Aufhebung* in the direction of speculative abstraction. The
move had a necessity deriving directly from Blanchot's concrete situation

as a writer since the later 1930s. From then until the late 1950s, Blanchot spanned the divide between literature and criticism by practising the latter as a systematic refusal of false versions of literature, from within the 'world' of his own experience as a writer. In short, criticism did no more than police the border between the language of his 'world' and the language of the world. With his return to the world of politics, and the accompanying loss of distinction between it and the 'world' of literature he had long inhabited, the original divide (which was a static margin) could only disappear, to be replaced, at one level, by that separating a 'world' living on oppressively and the world, or at least the community, of 'the exigency of Communism'. But one thing remains to link this new divide, and the refusal that spans it, with the original one: despite the re-emergence of activism after 1958, the divide runs, before and after, through language: it is, whether between worlds or within the world, a conflict between two forms of language.

To see the disappearance of anything recognizable as 'literature' and the emergence of philosophy as a simple move would entail a neglect of this continuity of opposition between languages in Blanchot's writing. If anything, the disappearance of the conventional divide between literature and criticism intensifies the power of refusal exerted in the name of one form of language against the other. After 1958, as the two 'worlds' to which language gives form become indistinguishable, language as a whole, in Blanchot's writing, is subject, from within, to the full force of a refusal which, in the literary and the political domains considered separately, only affects it partially. If Blanchot begins to write 'philosophically' therefore, it is to the extent that it is philosophy that is the guardian of 'language as a whole'. On the other hand, if Blanchot's refusal of dead forms extends to 'language as a whole' from this time on, it is to the extent that his return to politics and to the world it governs is motivated by his discovery, in that world, of what he has already discovered in the 'world' provided by literature: the obligation endlessly to put a stop, in language, to language in order to be responsive, and show responsibility, to the Other. In short, both the disappearance of literature and the emergence of philosophy, taken at face value, are no more than illusions of perspective, the product of a generalization of Blanchot's relationship to language taking in language as a whole, in a search for a new fragmentary mode.

That 'literature' is not simply superseded by this new mode is made quite clear by Blanchot in the preparatory documents of 1960, where, in by far the longest of four definitions of the fragment, he describes:

a literature of fragment located outside of everything, either because it supposes everything as already realized (all literature is literature of the end of time), or because, alongside the forms of language in which everything is constructed and spoken, a language [*parole*] of knowledge, work and salvation, it has the presentiment of another language [*parole*] altogether, which would free thought from being solely thought with a view to unity, in other words one demanding an essential discontinuity. In that sense, all literature is the fragment, be it brief or infinite, on condition that it designate a space of language in which each moment would have as its meaning and function the task of rendering all the others indeterminate, or else (this is its other surface) in which some affirmation irreducible to any unifying process is at work. (p. 188)

If he can speak so confidently of such a new literary form, it is because he had already begun to experiment with it. In advance of the 'conversation' form inaugurated in 1960 with **On a Change of Epoch,** and pointing beyond its limitations, **Waiting** essays a form of discontinuous writing of far greater complexity. This experiment will continue, as it were clandestinely, until the publication in 1962 of *L'Attente l'Oubli*, a work which, in its fragmented construction, bringing together what appear to be narrative passages and passages of philosophical analysis, points forward to the writing which Blanchot started to produce after 1969.

As an example of 'a *literature* of fragment', **Waiting** also epitomizes the new relationship to philosophy I have referred to, in that it was published in a *Festschrift* to mark Martin Heidegger's seventieth birthday. Blanchot's attentiveness to Heidegger dates back to the 1930s, when, in an extraordinary volte-face, he refers to him in one year as part of 'the dregs of German philosophy',[23] only to salute his work the following year, in **The Beginnings of a Novel**, as part of 'a philosophical movement . . . of the utmost importance' (p. 34). From then on, his preoccupation with Heidegger becomes more and more intense, as he discovers in the latter's explorations of the relationship between philosophy and art an undertaking which cuts across the field of his own experience and research, distorting it intimately (not least for political reasons). With *The Space of Literature*, Blanchot sets about shedding the influence of Heidegger's thinking upon his writing in the early 1950s (as the variants of this work show). In a highly original move, as I have indicated, he composed the volume so as to make it an *instance* of the space of literature which Heidegger sought to define philosophically (for example in 'The Origin of the Work of Art'), but in a way which to Blanchot remains, precisely, merely philosophical: cut off from the experience of literature.

What amounts to a veritable struggle, with and against Heidegger in the 1950s, marks everything Blanchot wrote at that time, in whatever field. The differences between him and Levinas, particularly in the sensitive area of the nature and status of *Autrui*, are conditioned in part by the very different ways in which each of them frames his opposition to Heidegger, a difference in which difficult issues of politics and history are in play. In order eventually to overcome Heidegger, it is to another philosopher that Blanchot turns: namely Nietzsche. Significantly, his return to the world of politics in 1958 was also marked by a turn to philosophy by way of Nietzsche, in two articles ('Nietzsche, today' and 'Crossing the Line') in which all of the uncertainties affecting his return are reflected.[24] Indeed, it can be said that it is in the company of Nietzsche that Blanchot makes the ultimate transition to the 'step (not) beyond' whose in-junction will provide him, after 1969, with both the space and the language for a fragmentary mode of writing unhindered by the dead weight of what in May 1968 he calls 'words that are themselves already destroyed' (p. 202). The two pieces entitled **The Exigency of Return** included here exemplify this closeness to Nietzsche, but also – more significantly – illustrate the change that took place between the completion of *The Infinite Conversation* in 1969 and the new turn that Blanchot's writing entered in 1970, now that it was in effect liberated from the field of writing contained in *the Infinite Conversation*. The first passage is essentially a *description* of Nietzsche's experience in so far as it affects his writing, and central to it is a recognition of the essentially contradictory nature of the subjectivity that Blanchot encounters in Nietzsche's writing:

> The revelation at Sils Maria not only frees Nietzsche from his limited singularity by repeating him indefinitely . . . the revelation at the same time commits Nietzsche to that singularity without which what would come would not already be a return. (p. 282)

The tension in language evoked here, between singularity (the need to speak as 'I') and an experience of repetition and dispersal arising out of the silencing of 'I', is as much that of Blanchot as it is Nietzsche's: since his return to the world in 1958, his language had been caught at this point of conflict and tension, owing to the impossibility of articulating a language that is free of the 'unifying process' of the first person singular. But the brink on which he has been poised for so long is about to be transformed: not crossed, but dislodged from its marginal stasis and rendered mobile. In the opening pages of *The Infinite Conversation*, originally written in 1963, Blanchot traces a genealogy of 'the discontinuity of a literature of fragments' which concludes: 'Pascal, Nietzsche, Georges Bataille and René Char demonstrate its essential persistence.' But whereas the 1963 text ends there, *The Infinite Conversation* adds in 1969: 'even more, the decision that is in preparation there'.[25] That 'decision' is what, in 1969, will allow Blanchot to initiate *le pas au-delà* or 'step (not) beyond' in its fragmentary mobility, leaving Nietzsche and others as it were behind, in so far as their example can at most be described for its limitations and, having broken the bounds of their 'limit experience' which for so long, as in the case of madness, he could only essentialize, enter the breach which they sought to occupy.

That is the sense of the 'Introit' that opens the second text entitled **The Exigency of Return** and is echoed at the opening of *Le pas au-delà* in 1973: 'Let us go into this relationship' (p. 290). Though still referring to Nietzsche, the writing in this text responds rather to a sign coming from him, transmitted by Pierre Klossowski, but which, as with the graffiti of May 1968, is 'written elsewhere, in a world without publication', a stop [*arrêt*] having been put both to history and to the book, so that Blanchot can write, echoing the closing words of *The Madness of the Day* in 1949: 'No more books, never again'[26] (p. 205). Furthermore, instead of simply describing the experience to which, as writing, it aspires, this text practises and explores the repetitive dispersal of singularity that has long been at work in Blanchot's language, putting forward a 'subject' for its discourse (*il*: he/it) that has been in slow gestation since *Thomas the Obscure*.[27] If that subject has at last found a 'voice', though it is one whose speech is the 'plural speech'[28] of writing (*parole d'écriture*), this is because the dead inertia of the language of unified subjectivity, which has so far, in the world and in writing, hindered the reversal and return that Blanchot set in motion in the 1950s, has somehow been dissipated. How has this happened? The answer is: through death. In a process which still requires much delicate exploration, Blanchot ceased in 1969, seemingly at a stroke, to inhabit language in the form and guise of a dead subject living on, with all of the agony and pathos with which this has affected his writing, in every field; and, without eliminating that deadness from his writing (which would be impossible, since historically it affects language as a whole), detached himself from it entirely, which is to say also from any position occupiable by *himself*, and as it were launched off into the space (and time) of what lies between 'I' and the selfsameness of 'He' in language, a dimension with no pre-existing co-ordinates and accessible in its openness and mobility only to a subject that has acceded in advance to his own abolition.

Put simply, Blanchot has now finally taken the plunge, as a subject in language, that the subject of his first novel, Thomas, took three decades before (*il – la mer*). Death in language is thus no longer 'the monumental statue, without gaze, without face, without name: the He or It [*Il*] of sovereign Death'[29] that Blanchot identified in 1947 in Michel Leiris's writing; it is 'the *ease* of dying', which from one angle confines us all to the anonymity of what Paulhan calls 'the single world where we are merged together' (p. 311), but which also, amid the indifference that this imposes and the danger of twofold distraction it presents, commands what Blanchot calls a *vigilance* which he defines as:

> the 'subject' of the experience, the thing which undergoes it, leads it, precipitates it, and holds it back so as to delay it in its moment of imminence, if this experience consists first of all in suppressing itself, or making itself possible through its suppression. (p. 311)

This new subject is original above all in so far as it has abdicated all sovereignty. Revolutionary in its origins, it has come full circle to find that the brink on which it has never ceased to strive towards the unity it desired is uncrossable. The break that has consistently appeared to promise a resolution of division (either as 'I' or as 'He/It') is now, in its pure division, all that can be hoped for. May 1968, in affirming the break, has revealed that 'writing and the decision to break coincide' (p. 204). It being impossible ever to *make* the break, once and for all, either in language or in the world, vigilance, as the subject of this condition of endless imminence and deferral, thus takes the form of a liberated and libertarian mode of writing, enfolding and unmaking the discourses of analysis and narrative, which it inhabits as a fault-line (or *faux pas*) running through all language.

This vigilance is exerted so to speak from beyond the grave: a postface to *The Infinite Conversation* says of the texts it contains 'I take them to be already posthumous.'[30] And thanks to the new subjectivity it allows him, from 1970 on Blanchot can be said to find a kind of release. In referring back to 1940, **The Ease of Dying** inaugurates a new openness concerning his own personal history, which in recent years, partly under pressure from accusers it must be said, has made a wealth of biographical detail available. If this has been possible, it is quite simply because the 'I' of language has been displaced, as the living centre of his existence, by the posthumous vigilance in writing to which he acceded in 1970. Yet though this displacement means henceforth that he somehow lives on outside life – with all that that implies for relations of friendship – it is far from being a solitary survival. In echoing Beckett's **Oh All to End,** he is not echoing the 'have done with it' with which he began: as **Thanks (Be Given) to Jacques Derrida** clearly reveals, his vigilance is at the same time a *Gelassenheit* which, unlike Heidegger's, derives from the new relation to *Autrui* (the Other of Judaism) that his writing has disengaged from what lay athwart it, and to which it has given primacy. Henceforth, what **The Exigency of Return** of 1969 refers to as 'an "ethical" discourse, beyond Good and Evil' (p. 288) will emerge in Blanchot's writing, taking it beyond 'ethics' (condemned in 1969, as the speech-marks suggest, to be superseded) towards the question of *community*, which today founds a philosophical mode of enquiry subsuming all of the issues hitherto addressed in politics, ethics and writing.

Notes

1 The interchange happens, and happens repeatedly during a time-lag or delay which is the sole time-scale, not to say the sole space, of *Le Dernier homme*. See the closing lines of the *récit*: 'Later, he asked himself how he had entered the calm. He could not talk about it to himself. But what strange joy to feel oneself in relation with the words: "Later, he . . ." ' (p. 157).

2 See *Thomas the Obscure*, chapter V: 'There was, then, henceforth, in all the sepulchres where he might have been able to take his place, in all the feelings which are also tombs for the dead, in this annihilation through which he was dying without permitting himself to be thought dead, there was another dead person who was there first, and who, identical with himself, drove the ambiguity of Thomas's life and death to the extreme limit.' (pp. 35–6)

3 See 'The Two Versions of the Imaginary' in *The Space of Literature*, pp. 254–63.

4 See 'Le Dossier de "La Revue Internationale", 1960–1964', in *Lignes*, 11 (September 1990), pp. 161–301. All translations are my own. Page references to this volume will be given in the main body of the text.

5 'We are all aware that we are approaching an extreme movement in time, what I shall call a change of times.' (*Lignes*, p. 179)

6 For documentary examples of this, see Maurice Nadeau, *Documents surréalistes* (Paris, Editions du Seuil, 1949).

7 Literature is described as 'a search [*recherche*] for searching itself in which perhaps something other than literature alone speaks. (Literature, even when called pure, is *more* than literature; why? what is this "more"? why does literature not accomplish itself through the necessary illusion of being more than itself, as the affirmation of an extra-literary "truth"? (p. 183)

8 Michel Foucault, 'The Thought from Outside' in *Foucault, Blanchot*, trans. Brian Massumi (New York, Zone Books, 1987), pp. 7–58.

9 In an article written in 1963 and forming the first chapter of *The Infinite Conversation* ('Thought and the Exigency of Discontinuity'), Blanchot reflects on this need for a language that will accommodate a new relational space as follows:

The speech relation in which the unknown articulates itself is a relation of infinity. Hence it follows that the form in which this relation is realized must in one way or another have an index of 'curvature' such that the relations of A to B will never be direct, symmetrical or reversible, will not form a whole, and will not take place in the same time; they will be, then, neither contemporaneous nor commensurable. One can see which solutions will prove inappropriate to such a problem: a language of assertion and answer, for example, or a linear language of simple development, that is to say, *a language where language itself would not be at stake*. (p. 6)

10 'L'Expérience de Proust [Proust's Experience]', in *Le Livre à venir* (Paris, Gallimard, 1959), collection 'Idées' edition, pp. 20–42 (p. 34).

11 'Le Tour d'écrou [The Turn of the Screw]', ibid., pp. 186–97 (p. 186).

12 'Broch', ibid., pp. 163–85 (p. 165).

13 'L'Echec du démon: la vocation [The Failure of the Demon: the Vocation]', ibid., pp. 144–56 (pp. 148, 150).
14 'Le Livre à venir [The Book to Come]', ibid., pp. 326–58 (p. 335).
15 'The Two Versions of the Imaginary', pp. 254–63 (p. 258).
16 *Le Livre à venir*, p. 165.
17 'Tragic Thought', *The Infinite Conversation*, pp. 96–105. The footnote from which the sentence is omitted is on p. 445.
18 *The Infinite Conversation*, pp. 151–70.
19 The two pieces make up a single section in *The Infinite Conversation*, entitled 'On a Change of Epoch: The Exigency of Return' (pp. 264–81). **The Exigency of Return** is on pp. 271–81. I have separated the two parts the better to reveal the processes at work, both historically and theoretically, during the lengthy period covered by the articles that make up the book.
20 *Il Menabò*, 1 (1964), entitled 'Gulliver Internazionale'. The number also contains pieces by Duras, Genet and Barthes.
21 The existence of this text has become curiously indeterminate. Published in Italian in 1964, the French original was subsequently lost. When the American journal *Semiotext(e)* published a truncated version of it in volume IV, no. 2 (1982), it was based on the Italian text. In 1983, Hélène Jelen and Jean-Luc Nancy undertook to restore the text to its original language, using the Italian and American translations. Maurice Blanchot agreed to sign the resulting text as his own. (See 'Le nom de Berlin', *Café*, 3 (Autumn 1983), pp. 43–6.) Jelen and Nancy point out that the two novels by Uwe Johnson referred to by Blanchot are *The Frontier* and (in all probability, though Blanchot could no longer remember) *The Third Book About Achim*. The translation included here is based on the Italian and French texts.
22 The piece by Levinas which Blanchot refers to, without naming it, is 'Heidegger, Gagarin and Us', in *Difficult Freedom: Essays on Judaism*, trans. Seán Hand (London, Athlone Press, 1990), pp. 231–4. The article in question appeared in *Information Juive* in 1961. Speaking of the paganism of the earth-bound which Blanchot also evokes, Levinas writes: 'Judaism is perhaps no more than the negation of all that' (p. 232).
23 In 'Penser avec les mains [Thinking with your hands]', *L'Insurgé*, 27 January 1937, p. 5.
24 These are included in *The Infinite Conversation*, pp. 136–50.
25 *The Infinite Conversation*, pp. 6–7; translation modified.
26 The closing words of *The Madness of the Day* are 'No stories, never again'. Jacques Derrida provides an extensive analysis of this '*récit*' in 'The law of genre', *Glyph*, 7 (1980), pp. 202–29. See also 'Title (to be specified),' *Sub-stance*, 31 (1981), pp. 5–22. Blanchot's category of 'the absence of the book', which gives its title to the closing chapter of *The Infinite Conversation*, provoked some dissent among the anonymous contributors to *Comité*. A 'Commentary' to 'Tracts, Posters, Bulletins' retorts: 'No more books? But for Revolution (before, during, after), as much as possible of *everything* man can invent is what is needed . . . Millions of people have still not had enough books; enough anything' (*Comité*, 1, October 1968, p. 16). In the postface to *The Infinite Conversation*, it should be said, Blanchot sees the texts it contains as seeking to respond to '*the absence of the book* they designate in vain' (p. 435).
27 Chapter V of the first version of *Thomas the Obscure* begins: 'In the village there lived a man in the form of *He*'.
28 See 'A Plural Speech', in *The Infinite Conversation*, pp. 80–2.
29 'Glances from Beyond the Grave', *Yale French Studies*, 81 (1992), pp. 151–61 (p. 161) (translation modified).
30 *The Infinite Conversation*, p. 435.

23

The Name Berlin (1961)*

For everyone, Berlin poses the problem of division. From a certain angle this is a strictly political problem, for which, let us not forget, there are strictly political solutions. From another angle it is a social and economic problem (and so a political one, but in a wider sense): in Berlin two systems, two socio-economic structures confront each other. From another angle it is a metaphysical problem: Berlin is not only Berlin, it is also the symbol of the division of the world and what is more a 'universal point', the place where reflection on a unity that is simultaneously necessary and impossible happens in each person that lives there, and who, in living there, experiences it not only as a dwelling-place, but also as the absence of a dwelling-place. That is not all. Berlin is not a symbol, it is a real city, where human dramas occur that are unknown to other great cities: division here is called a split. That is not all. Berlin poses, in unusual terms, the problem of two opposing cultures within the same cultural context, of two quite unrelated languages within the same language, and hence calls into question the intellectual security and the possibilities for communication that one imagines are available to human beings who live together, by virtue of sharing the same tongue and the same historical past. That is not all.

To treat or explore the problem of Berlin as the problem of division cannot entail providing as complete a list as possible of the various forms in which we are able to perceive it. As the problem of division, we have to say that Berlin is an indivisible problem. So much so that when we provisionally single out – if only for clarity's sake – such and such a particular aspect of the situation we call 'Berlin', we run the risk of falsifying not only the question considered as a whole, but also the particular aspect in question, which, however, cannot be grasped if it is not considered in its own right.

The problem of division – of fracture – as it is posed by Berlin, not only for Berliners, nor even just for Germans, but in my view for every thinking person – and posed imperiously, which is to say painfully – is a problem which we cannot formulate adequately, in its *complete* reality,

---

* Originally published as 'Il nome Berlino', *Il Menabò*, 7 (1964), pp. 121–5.

unless we decide to formulate it *fragmentarily* (which nevertheless does not mean partially). In other words, each time we find ourselves confronted by a problem of this nature (after all, there are others) we should remember that to speak of it accurately is also to let speak the profound break that exists in our words and our thinking, so as thereby to let speak our incapacity to speak in terms that claim to be definitive. This means (1) that omniscience, even were it possible, would be of no use in this case; the essence of such a situation would be beyond even the grasp of a God supposed to know everything; (2) that it is not possible, in general, to overlook or encompass or take in the problem of division at a single glance, and that, in this case as in others, a panoramic view is not an accurate one; (3) that the deliberate choice of the fragment does not amount to an act of sceptical retreat, nor does it mean that one can no longer be bothered to attempt a complete synthesis (though this could be the case), but is rather a method of enquiry that is both patient and impatient, mobile and immobile, and the affirmation – furthermore – that meaning, meaning in its entirety, cannot be found immediately in us and in what we write, but is always still to come, and that in enquiring into meaning, we take it to be a pure becoming and a pure future of enquiry; (4) which means, in conclusion, that we must repeat ourselves. All language [*parole*] in fragments, all fragmentary reflection require infinite repetition and variation.

I shall add two further (fragmentary) remarks. The insane political abstraction constituted by Berlin found its acutest expression on the day they built the wall, even though this wall is something dramatically concrete. Until 13 August 1961 the absence of any visible sign of separation – even though, well before that date, a series of official and unofficial controls had already served as the enigmatic forerunners of a demarcation line – gave partition an ambiguous character and significance: what was it? A frontier? Certainly: but also something more, because the fact of crossing it did not mean going from one country to another, one language to another, but, within the same country and the same language, going from 'truth' to 'error', 'evil' to 'good', 'life' to 'death', and entailed undergoing, almost unwittingly, a radical metamorphosis (though in order to decide where exactly this 'good' and this 'evil', so brutally opposed to each other, were located, one could rely on no more than partial reflection). The almost instantaneous construction of the wall replaced a still uncertain ambiguity with the violence of decisive separation. Outside Germany, people became aware, more or less intensely, more or less superficially, that this event would usher in dramatic changes, not only to human relations but also in the economic and political domains. But one thing, I believe, went unnoticed (even perhaps by many Germans), namely the fact that this wall, in its reality, was destined to plunge into *abstraction* the unity of a great city full of life, a city which was not and is not, in reality – in fact it is herein that its profound reality lies – either a single city, or two cities, or the capital of a country, or just some city of importance, or the centre of things, nor merely the absence of such a centre. In that way, the wall succeeded in *abstractly concretizing* division, in making it visible and tangible, and so obliging us henceforth to think Berlin, in the very unity of its name, not under the sign of a lost unity any longer, but as the sociological reality constituted by two absolutely different cities.[1] The 'scandal' and the importance of the wall lie in the fact that it is, even given the concrete oppressiveness it represents, essentially abstract, and hence reminds us of what we continually forget: namely that abstraction is not simply an incorrect way of thinking, or a manifestly impoverished form of language: abstraction is our world, the world in which, day after day, we live and think.

There is now available a considerable amount of writing on the situation in Berlin. I am struck by the fact that, among all these texts, it is two novels that provide the non-German at least with the best approach to the situation, two novels that are neither political nor realist in nature. I won't put this down entirely to the talent of Uwe Johnson, but to the truth of literature. It is the very difficulty, or rather the impossibility, faced by the author who seeks to write books such as these, where division is brought into play – and hence the necessity for him to capture that *impossibility* by writing it and in writing – that brings the literary undertaking into line with the singularity of 'Berlin', precisely through the hiatus that it was obliged to leave open, with an obscure and unflagging rigour, between reality and the literary expression of its meaning. An impatient reader or critic might say that, in works of this sort, the relation to the world and to the responsibility of a political decision concerning the world, remains remote and indirect. Indirect yes. But we must ask ourselves, precisely, if in order to gain access to the 'world' through language and especially through writing, the indirect way is not the right way and also the shortest one.

Note

1 The wall claimed to substitute the sociological truth of a situation, its de facto status, for the deeper truth of the situation, which may – by oversimplifying – be called dialectical.

Translated by Michael Holland

24

The Conquest of Space (1961)*

Man does not want to leave his own place (*luogo*). He says that technology is dangerous, that it detracts from our relationship with the world, that true civilizations are those of a stable nature, that the nomad is incapable of acquisition. Who is this man? It is each one of us, at the times we give in to lethargy. This same man suffered a shock the day Gagarin became the first man in space. The event is now almost forgotten; but the experience will be repeated in other forms. In these cases we must pay heed to the man in the street, to the man with no fixed abode. He admired Gagarin, admired him for his courage, for the adventure, and even paid tribute to progress; but one such man gave the right explanation: it is extraordinary, we have left the earth. Herein lies, indeed, the true significance of the experience: man has freed himself from place. He has felt, at least for a moment, the sense of something decisive: far away – in an abstract distance of pure science – removed from the common condition symbolized by the force of gravity, there was a man, no longer in the sky, but in space, in a space which has no being or nature but is the pure and simple reality of a measurable (almost) void. Man, but a man with no horizon. A sacrilegious act. On his return, Gagarin made some jokes in bad taste: he had been to heaven and he had not met God there. The Catholic bodies protested, but wrongly. There is no doubt that it had been a profanity: the old heaven, the heaven of religions and contemplations, the pure and sublime 'up there', had dissolved in a moment, deprived of the privilege of inaccessibility, to be replaced with a new absolute, by the space of the scientists, which is nothing more than a calculable possibility. Despite all this, more than the Christian, the man who was left defeated by Gagarin was the man inside us, who is eternally seduced by paganism, who desires above all to live upon the earth, to take over the earth, to remain, to found, to put down roots, to belong ontologically to the biological race and his ancestry; the possessive man who wants to have land and who has land, who knows how to take possession and how to cling on; the man, who wherever he is found, is eternally encrusted in his tradition, in his truth, in his history,

* Originally published as 'La conquista dello spazio', *Il Menabò*, 7 (1964), pp. 10–13.

and who does not want the sacred seats of his beautiful landscape and great past to be attacked; the melancholy man who consoles himself among the trees over the evil of mankind. Gagarin, for a moment, freed us from such a man and lightened for us the load of his millennial baggage (represented so well by Ionesco in *Le Locataire*). A victory for technology? Certainly. The freedom gained (even though in a still illusory manner) with regard to 'place', this sort of levitation of man as substance, of man as essence obtained by breaking away from 'locality', came to prolong and briefly to conclude the process by which technology upsets sedentary civilizations, destroys human particularisms, makes man leave the utopia of childhood (if it is true that the man-child, in each of us, wishes to return to his place of origin). And how difficult it is to leave these regions and to raise oneself to a formulation of the problems of maturity. We suddenly had occasion to state this, because scarcely had the same Gagarin, escaping originary forces and placing himself in a movement of pure dislocation, begun to become a detached man, than Khruschev hastened to reintegrate him into the species, greeting him in the name of earth, his 'homeland': a surprising intimidatory expression, a memorable refusal to recognize that it could have been pronounced in the same way by statesmen called Kennedy or de Gaulle, men of the same heritage, ready to exalt the advantages of technology for prestige, but unable to accept it, to realize its consequences, namely the breaking down of all sense of belonging and the questioning of place, in all places.

That is all very well. But should it not also be said that, in a way, Gagarin's feat – in its political repercussions and in its mythical ones – gave grounds to the Russians to inhabit Russian land even more staunchly? Moreover, can it not appear to have changed the physical relationship with the Outside in a decisive manner? Naturally it is correct to say this, as it is correct to say that the superstition about place cannot be eradicated in us except by a momentary abandonment to some utopia of non-place.[1] The condition of the cosmonaut is, in some respects, pitiful: a man who is the bearer of the very sense of liberty and who has never found himself a greater prisoner of his own position, free of the force of gravity and weighted down more than any other being, on the way to maturity and all bundled up in his scientific swaddling clothes, like a new-born child of former times, reduced to nourishing himself with a feeding bottle and to wailing more than talking. Still today I listen to that poor speech, which offers only banality when confronted by the unexpected; a speech devoid, moreover, of any guarantee, and which nothing stops us from attributing (as Nixon did) to any mystification one cares to name. And yet, something disturbs us and dismays us in that rambling: it does not stop, it must never stop; the slightest break in the noise would already mean the everlasting void; any gap or interruption introduces something which is much more than death, which is the nothingness outside entered into discourse. It is therefore necessary, up there, for the man from the Outside to speak, and to speak continually, not only to reassure us and to inform us, but because he has no other link with the old place than that unceasing word, which, accompanied by hissing and conflicting with all the harmony of the spheres, says, to whoever is unable to understand it, only some insignificant commonplace, but also says this to him who listens more carefully: that the truth is nomadic.

Note

1 Emmanuel Levinas should be quoted at this point, to whom we are indebted for part of these reflections and who has stated with force: 'Technology is dangerous, but less dangerous than the geniuses of the place.'

Translated by Christopher C. Stevens

25

Waiting (1959)*

X   To be waiting, only waiting.
Since when had he been waiting? Since he had freed himself for waiting by losing the desire for things in particular and even the desire for the end of things. Waiting begins when there is nothing more to wait for, not even the end to this waiting. Waiting is unaware of and abandons what it is waiting for. Waiting is waiting for nothing.
Whatever the importance of the object of waiting, it is always infinitely surpassed by the movement of waiting. Waiting renders all things equally important, equally vain. To wait for the slightest thing we command an infinite power of waiting which seems unable to be exhausted.
Waiting is always a waiting for waiting, resuming the beginning, suspending the end and, inside this interval, opening the interval of another waiting. The night in which there is nothing awaited represents this movement of waiting.
The impossibility of waiting belongs essentially to waiting.

X   In waiting he could not enquire about waiting. What was he waiting for, why was he waiting, what is awaited in waiting? This latter is characterized by its elusiveness to all the forms of question which it renders possible and from which it is exempt. And yet it would imperceptibly change words into a question, bidding him seek in waiting the question that waiting carries within it.
It was not a question he could have found and made his own, nor even a particular manner of enquiry. He says he is seeking, but he is not seeking, and if he enquires, this is perhaps already a betrayal of waiting which neither affirms nor enquires, but waits.

X   When he affirms, he still enquires. It's that he must speak in waiting.

X   Through waiting, each affirmation would open onto an emptiness, and every question was shadowed by another, more silent, which he could have taken by surprise.

* Original published as 'L'Attente', in *Martin Heidegger Zum Siebzigsten Geburtstag* (Pfullingen, Neske, 1959), pp. 217–24.

The question which waiting carries within it – it carries it, but remains distinct from it. It is like a question that could be revealed at the end of waiting, were it not in the nature of waiting, even when coming to an end, to be without end.

The question of waiting: waiting carries a question which is not put. Between one and the other there is a common infinity which is there in the least question as well as in the mildest of waiting. As soon as there is a question, there is no reply that could exhaust that question. He refrained from enquiring, awaiting a reply that would reply to no question.

Astonishment and unease at the reply which replies to no question. It thus replies in vain.

X   He seeks to attain through waiting, without emitting anything that enquires and even less that replies, the measure peculiar to the essence of the reply – not the measure that limits, but the measure that measures while holding the limitless in reserve, while measuring it.

X   He felt that the force of his questions – those he did not utter, those he merely held in reserve – ought not to be drawn directly from his life, that he ought first, by the movement of waiting, as it were to exhaust his life and, with this presence without present, to render clear and tranquil what he avoided saying. But surely he was saying it. Yes: it was thus that he intervened against his saying it. As if the same word could have expressed and yet acted as a barrier to expression.

X   Express that alone which cannot be expressed. Leave it unexpressed.

X   Waiting gives time, takes time, but it is not the same that is given and that is taken. Waiting does not leave him time for waiting.

X   'Am I going to have to endure this for much longer?' – 'For always, if you experience it as duration.'

X   Waiting, what was it that had to be waited for? As soon as we wait for something, we wait a little less.

X   In waiting, time wasted.

There is waiting when time is always superfluous yet when time is lacking in time. This superabundant lack of time is the duration of waiting. In waiting, the time which allows us to wait goes to waste, the better to respond to waiting.

Absence of time makes us wait; time gives us something to wait for.

Waiting, where the pressure of absence of time makes itself felt, borrows from time which does not wait the appearance of this power of waiting, which it seems so easy to command.

In waiting reigns the absence of time where waiting is the impossibility of waiting. Time renders seemingly possible impossible waiting, which is governed by absence of time.

In time, waiting comes to an end without an end being put to waiting.

Waiting which takes place in time opens up time to the absence of time where there is no place for waiting.

In waiting, if time always gives us something to wait for, be it only our own end or the end of time, we are doomed to the absence of time which has always already detached waiting from this end and from every end.

He knows that when time comes to an end, so also does absence of time disperse or escape, far from beginning with this end or revealing itself in it, even as the appearance of what is disappearing.

X Waiting fulfilled by waiting, fulfilled-frustrated by waiting.

X To be waiting, only waiting. Unfamiliar waiting, equal in all its moments, like space in all its points, equal to space, exerting the same continuous pressure, not exerting it.

Solitary waiting, which was in him and has now moved outside, waiting for him without him, leaving him nothing more to wait for.

X Attention is waiting. He does not know if this waiting is his own, cut off from him and waiting outside him. He only remains with it.

The attention that waiting concentrates in him is not destined to secure the realization of what he is waiting for, but to let move aside, through waiting alone, everything that is realizable, so as to approach the unrealizable.

Waiting alone gives attention. Time empty of time, without project, is waiting that gives attention.

Through attention he was not attentive to himself, nor to anything that might have related to anything in particular, but carried by the infinity of waiting to the furthest limit, which cannot be attained.

Waiting gives attention while withdrawing all that is awaited. He commands, through attention, the infinity of waiting which gives him access to the unawaited by carrying him to the furthest limit, which cannot be attained.

Waiting is the disinterestedness of attention which neither concerns itself nor cares, but seeks its bearings, in relation to that which is without relation.

X Mystery: this cannot be the object of attention. Mystery is the centre of attention when attention, being uniform and perfect uniformity with itself, is the absence of all centre.

In attention there disappears the centre of attention, the central point around which ought to be deployed perspective, vision and the order of the internally and externally visible. Attention is unoccupied and uninhabited. Empty, it is the transparency of emptiness.

X Mystery: its essence is always to fall short of attention. And the essence of attention is that it can preserve, in and through itself, that which always falls short of attention and is the source of all waiting: mystery.

Attention, accommodation of that which eludes attention, opening onto the unawaited, waiting which is the unawaited in all waiting.

X Mysterious, that which leaves itself without cover without uncovering itself.

X The secret is a burden to him not because it strives towards utterance – that cannot be – but through the weight that it gives to all other words, including the simplest and the slightest, demanding that, except for itself, everything that can be said, be said. This immense necessity for vain words reduces them all to equal importance, equal insignificance; there is none which counts more than the others; what counts is that they should all equally be spoken, in an equality where they are exhausted, while the possibility of speaking them remains unexhausted.

he did not think that one expression could have more importance than another; each one was more important than all the others; every sentence was the essential sentence, and yet they sought only to group themselves together in one of their number which could then have remained unspoken.

X What is concealed without anything being hidden.

No one likes to remain face to face with what is hidden. Face to face would be simple, but not in an indirect relationship.

X He had believed that the secret counted less than the approach to it. But here the approach was without approach. He was never either nearer to it or further from it. Therefore he must not approach it, but get his bearings through attention.

X In secret in the sight of everyone.

X   He was not sure that he could put up for much longer with such attention. When he speaks even the speech in him is already attentive. Attention never leaves him – in it he is cruelly abandoned.

X   Waiting waits. During waiting, he who waits dies while waiting. He carries waiting into death and seems to make of death a waiting for that which is still awaited when we die.

Death, considered as an awaited event, is not capable of putting an end to waiting. Waiting transforms the fact of dying into something which it is not enough to attain in order to stop waiting. Waiting is that which allows us the knowledge that death cannot be awaited.

He who lives in waiting sees life before him like the emptiness of waiting and waiting like the emptiness of the afterlife. The flickering absence of distinction between these two movements is from that point on the space of waiting. At each step we are here and yet beyond. But as we attain this beyond without attaining it through death, we wait for [*attend*] it but do not attain it; without knowing that its essential feature is that it can only be attained in waiting.

When there is waiting there is waiting for nothing. In the movement of waiting death stops being something that can be awaited. Waiting, in the intimate calm at the heart of which everything that occurs is distracted by waiting, does not let death occur as something that could satisfy waiting, but holds it in suspense, dissolved and at each instant surpassed by the empty uniformity of waiting.

The strange opposition between waiting and death. He waits for death in a waiting which is indifferent to death. In other words, death will not keep him waiting.

X   He had endured waiting. Waiting has rendered him eternal and now it only remains for him to wait eternally.

We ought always, in the presence of each instant, to behave as if it were eternal and waited for us to render it transient again.

Sterile waiting, ever poorer and emptier. Fertile waiting, always the richer for waiting. The one is the other.

X   The decay of waiting, boredom. Stagnant waiting, waiting which has taken itself initially for its object, has developed a complacency towards itself, and finally a hatred towards itself. Always alone in waiting, and always separated from himself by waiting which did not leave him alone. He felt the impression of being at the service of an initial distraction which could only be attained when concealed and dispersed in acts of extreme attention. There waiting, but subservient to that which could not possibly be awaited.

The infinite dispersion of waiting always brought together again by the imminence of the end of waiting.

X   He lives in the imminence of a thought which is no more than the thought of eternal imminence.

X   Narrow the presence, vast the place.

X   For a long time he had been trying to say nothing that might weigh down space, speaking space, exhausting finite limitless space. Here there is no real dialogue. Only waiting maintains between the things that are said a certain relationship, words said so as to keep waiting, waiting for words.
Wishing to and unable to speak; not wishing to and unable to avoid speaking; in that case, speaking-and-not-speaking, in an identical movement which it was his duty to sustain.

X   Even if waiting is linked to the anxiety he experiences, waiting, with its own tranquil anxiety, has already eliminated his long ago. He feels himself liberated by waiting for waiting.

X   Forgetting, waiting. Waiting which brings together, which scatters; forgetting which scatters, which brings together. Waiting, forgetting.
He would forget, if he remembered.
Sometimes he would forget, sometimes he would remember, sometimes remembering forgetting and forgetting everything in this memory. You will not discover the limits of forgetting, however far off you can forget.

X   Forgetting, assent to forgetting in memory which forgets nothing.

X   Keeping watch over the unwatched-over presence.
Knowing that the presence was there, and having forgotten it so perfectly, knowing that it could only be there if forgotten, and himself knowing it, forgetting it.
'Look at it a moment, over your shoulder; cast a half-look in its direction; do not look at it, look; with a half-look, look solely.'

X   The thought of waiting: thought which is waiting for that which cannot be thought of, thought which is carried by waiting and postponed in this waiting. The calm turning aside of thought, returning from itself to itself in waiting. Through waiting, that which turns aside from thought returns to thought become a turning aside from itself.

Waiting, the space of turning aside without digression, of errancy without error.

X   Is it hidden by that which manifests it and makes it manifest?

X   When he looked, he knew that the mystery was entirely manifest in this visible presence which, by the transparency of that which is only visible, formed an obstacle to the darkness of a true night. And yet the presence did not render the mystery present, no more than it illuminated it; he could not have said that this presence was mysterious; it was, on the contrary, so devoid of mystery that it left this latter without cover, but without uncovering it.

X   That which is concealed without anything being hidden, which asserts itself and remains unexpressed, which is there and forgotten: That what was there should have been always and every time a presence, was the surprise within which thought fulfilled itself, unsuspected.

Translated by Michael Holland

26

The Exigency of Return (1969)*

± ± *Ignorance of the future: the end of history: the law of return.* – To speak of the 'end of history' is simply to pose the question of the place of such words, henceforth without content since, as soon as history comes to a close, speech loses the direction and meaning that are only given to it by the possibility of historical accomplishment.

'History is over.' Who can say this when 'the end of history' still belongs to discourse, moreover to the very discourse that this end alone makes possible? The end determines the coherence of the discourse; or rather it is the coherence of discourse that allows us to set down as an acceptable term 'the end of history'.

The fact remains that the 'end of history' belongs also to eschatological language: Christ is only possible because he bears the end of time. The death of God, in the 'Christic' sense, in the Hegelian sense and in the Nietzschean sense, is always a passage to the limit: the transgression that marks the imperceptible divergence by which knowledge, becoming absolute, would reverse itself into a non-knowledge (in an immobile movement such that the 'no', losing its negative character, is simply that which allows a dash [*tiret*] to be inscribed: the mark, in no way oriented, that still permits knowledge to be named while setting it aside). None the less, transgression, the end of history and the death of God are not equivalent terms. But each indicates the moment at which the logos comes to an end, not in negating itself but in affirming itself and always again anew, without novelty, through the obligation – the madness – of repetition.

± ± Whoever asks 'what is transgression?' asks nothing and can only indefinitely repeat in this form or, more surreptitiously in another: what is transgression?

'I too am ready to say it, thus to repeat it and, even more surreptitiously, in repeating it, make of the question a response – if repetition and transgression echo one another.

– Then repetition would be transgression?

– On condition that transgression in this very way is able to repeat itself.

* Originally published as 'L'exigence du retour', *L'Entretien infini* (Paris, Gallimard, 1969), pp. 405–18.

– *But is able only to free repetition, thus making it impossible.*'

Repetition is transgression in so far as transgression displaces transgressive repetition, rendering it impossible.

± ±   The end of history. It is not history that comes to an end with history, but certain principles, questions and formulations that will from now on be prohibited through a decision without justification, and as though with the obstinacy of a game. Let us therefore suppose that we renounce the question of origin, then all that makes of time the power of continuity and mobility – that which surreptitiously makes thought advance in that it also sets speech into motion. Let us suppose we give ourselves (with the obstinacy of a game) the right to a language in which the categories that until now have seemed to support it would lose their power to be valid: unity, identity, the primacy of the Same and the exigency of the Self-subject – categories postulated by their lack, and from the basis of their absence as the promise of their advent in time and through the work of time. Let us suppose that, supposing the end of history, we were to suppose all these categories not abolished, certainly, but realized, comprehended and included, affirmed in the coherence of a discourse from now on absolute. The book now closed again, all questions answered and all answers organized in the whole of a sufficient or founding speech – *now*, writing, there would no longer be any reason or place for writing, except to endure the worklessness of this *now*, the mark of an interruption or a break there where discourse falters, in order, perhaps, to receive the affirmation of the Eternal Return.

± ±   *Affirmation of the Eternal Return* – Through this affirmation, and through the difficulty it proposes, the limit-experience finds itself at grips with what always steals it away from thought. Let us first recall briefly in what ways such an affirmation, one that shakes everything, was received:

First thesis: the affirmation of the Eternal Return testifies to the shattering of a mind already ill, not because the affirmation would be mad, but because of the vertigo of thought that seizes Nietzsche when it declares itself to him. Out of a modesty of thought, better to disregard it. This is the conclusion of the first commentators, and later of many others. Even Bertram, despite his idolatry, speaks of the 'monomania of the Eternal Return, the pseudo-Dionysian mystery of the Solitary One'.

Second thesis: be it as a paradox, the affirmation belongs to what in Nietzsche is most important, either inasmuch as nihilism recognizes itself and confirms itself in it, or, on the contrary, overcomes itself by accomplishing itself therein. Thus Löwith intends to show that Nietzsche's true thought constitutes a system: first, the death of God; then in the middle, its consequence, nihilism; finally the Eternal Return, which is the consequence of nihilism and its overturning.

Third thesis: the Eternal Return and the Will to Power must be thought together. In the series of lectures given in Freiburg from 1936 to 1939, Heidegger meditates on Nietzsche's 'fundamental position', which he delimits by two propositions: the trait of being as a whole: Will to Power; Being: the Eternal Return of the Same. Heidegger says further: the Will to Power is the ultimate fact; the Eternal Return is the thought of thoughts. But in arguing that Nietzsche still belongs to metaphysics, and even completes it by bringing it to its end, Heidegger also introduces the thought of the Eternal Return back into metaphysics: eternity is thought as instant, and the instant is thought as the instancy of presence.

Fourth thesis: I would not want to conclude anything from conversations bearing on the Sils Maria experience, but which left no trace. None the less it seems that Georges Bataille did not feel drawn to such an affirmation: he gave it little emphasis, despite the courteous assent he accorded to the research of certain of his interlocutors. What was important and, to say it more precisely, beyond importance, was not the affirmation itself (which in any case Nietzsche was mistaken in presenting as a doctrine) but the vision at Surlei, a pre-eminently sublime vision by which a sovereignly atheist thought, and by its very atheism, opened onto the most gripping of mystical experiences. In its discursive formulation, the thesis is no more than its laborious translation and debris: as after a great fire, the charred wood of thought. Nietzsche's obstinacy in imposing, and even in scientifically giving proof of, an affirmation escaping all knowledge only testifies, poorly, to what for him had been the untransmissible experience in which, in an instant of empty sovereignty, the whole of being and of thought was attained.

Fifth thesis: nevertheless, how can one not ask of this affirmation whether there might not be some relation between it and the fact that it gave rise to a 'highly mystical experience'? What relation? What possibility of relation? The question was unfolded in all its rigour, its breadth, and its authority by Pierre Klossowski. It is not only Nietzsche who is done a new justice with this questioning; through it, there is determined a change so radical that we are incapable of mastering it, even of undergoing it.

± ± *Affirmation of the Eternal Return.* This is a thought of the highest coherence in so far as coherence itself is thought in it as that which institutes it and such that nothing other than this coherence can ever be thought; none the less also such that this coherence could not but exclude the coherent thought that thinks it; thus always outside the thought that it affirms and in which it is affirmed: the experience of thought as coming from Outside and in this way indicating the point of disjunction, of non-coherence, at which the affirmation of this thought, ever affirming it, already unseats it. Such is the sign – from now on inscribed at night on our walls – to which Pierre Klossowski gave such a dazzling quality: *Circulus vitiosus deus*.[1]

Is Nietzsche, with his affirmation of the Eternal Return, simply struggling with one of those pseudo-thoughts (analogous to those of a dream) under whose attraction, through the evidence that radiates from it, one cannot resist falling as soon as one falls into it? Further, is not the affirmation of the Eternal Return not only one of those pseudo-thoughts (impossible to think and impossible not to think), but also its 'explanation', its 'truth' in the sense that, as a semblance of thought, it denounces in all thought its simulacrum, which alone would make it true?

At this point, the difficulty Nietzsche does not master is perhaps the very one that exalts him. To think, to affirm the Eternal Return – to affirm such an affirmation in making the instant at which it affirms itself the great moment wherein *time turns* – is either to overturn this affirmation by recognizing in the fact that it declares itself, at the same time as it strikes, forgetting the possibility of breaking with the affirmation radically, or else it is to acknowledge the insignificance of this declaration since, having already occurred and having to occur an infinity of times, it does not cease to occur and, henceforth, is struck with insignificance, as it strikes with nullity the one who proclaims it as sovereignly decisive.

But Nietzsche does not shirk from this consequence. A consequence entailing multiple paths: the Sils Maria revelation is not that of Nietzsche, not that of a unique individuality arriving at a unique truth, at a unique site, at an instant of singularity and decision; it is affirmation itself, an affirmation that does no more than affirm, that affirms affirmation and, in the latter, maintains together repetition and difference, forgetting and waiting, eternity and the future. The revelation at Sils Maria not only frees Nietzsche from his limited singularity by repeating him indefinitely, it not only frees the revelation from itself since it reveals nothing that does not reveal itself without end, but the revelation at the same time commits Nietzsche to that singularity without which what would come would not already be a return, just as it condemns the revelation's insignificance to the ridiculous exaltation of its decisive importance.

But let us question this revelation again. What is new (for Nietzsche) at Sils Maria? Well before this hour the thesis had been mentioned both by the Greeks and, in this same century, by Goethe, Schopenhauer and Nietzsche (according to the testimony of Rhode and Overbeck). But it was a thesis: a proposition of thought, not yet related to itself by the aleatory necessity of its declaration. At Sils Maria, the affirmation wherein everything is affirmed disperses as it takes place: the very place of its affirmation, the thought that bears it, the existence that causes it to exist, the unity of the instance of its occurrence, and the still indispensable coherence of its formulation. But at the same time (which time?), while it disperses in affirming itself, not ceasing to defer from itself through the repetition that disavows it, it gathers itself in this difference that can only differ and, in reproducing itself as difference, eternally return, and, in returning, differentiate itself through repetition – in this way distinguishing anew, as unique, Sils Maria, the instant, the thought, the lucidity of an individual perhaps named Nietzsche, but as such already deprived of a name, of memory, and of reason.

So why the 'return' and why the 'same'? If it is the 'same', why must it be thought as *Wiederkunft* (*Wiederkehr*), a turning that repeats itself, a repetition that produces itself through its own detour? And why, if it returns, is it the 'same'? Is it the 'same' because it returns, and through the force of return; or is it the same in any case, therefore without return, therefore a single time and forever the same, thus impossible to recognize as the same since the 'same' must be several times – an infinity of times – the same in order to identify itself as the 'same'? But if it is the 'same' through its return, is it not the return alone that would give rise to the same? And thus it would necessarily happen that the 'same' has deferred through an infinity of rounds and times, only returning to the same by the law of return. Is it therefore not the case that nothing in this same comes back to the same, except *the return itself* (turn, detour, overturning); and is it not the case that the affirmation of return leads to affirming together – but without constituting a whole – the difference and the repetition, thus the non-identity of the same?

But does affirming the return mean to come around, to circulate, to make of the circle an accomplished sovereignty? Clearly not. If only because the eternity of the return – the infinite of the return – does not permit assigning to the figure a centre, even less an infinity of centres, just as the infinite of the repetition cannot be totalized in order to produce the unity of a figure strictly delimited and whose construction would escape the law it figures forth. If the Eternal Return can affirm itself, it affirms neither the return as circle, nor the primacy of the One, nor the Whole, and not even by way of the necessity that through the Eternal Return 'everything returns,' for the circle and the circle of all circles do not give it a figure any more than the Whole can encompass the Eternal Return, or coincide with it. Even if 'everything returns,' it is not the Whole that returns, but rather: it returns, the return returns (as neutral).

± ±   'The end of history.' We should listen carefully to what this limit concept allows to be said: a critical operation, the decision to put totality itself out of play, not by denouncing it but by affirming it, and by considering it as accomplished. The end of history: the total affirmation that cannot be negated since negation is already included in it (just as, on the basis of the discourse that contains its own silence, no silence of this discourse can be attested to, hoped for, or dreaded).

'Saying it differently': what exceeds the whole, what (forever) exceeding the whole, can 'say' itself 'differently'?

'*We know by hypothesis that this – this speech or this non-speech – still belongs to the whole.*

– *Certainly, by hypothesis.*

– *But, by hypothesis, it marks itself off from it.*

– *Yes, by hypothesis.*

– *We therefore have something that is of the whole, that totalizes itself therein, and, as such, marks itself off from it.*'

Is this not what the Eternal Return says (neither hypothetically nor categorically)?

± ±   The Eternal Return is for Nietzsche a mad thought. It is the thought of madness, and he dreads it to the point of fright at the idea that he will have to bear it; to the point also that, in order not to be alone in bearing up under it, he must free himself from it by seeking to express it. A dangerous thought if, in revealing it, he does not succeed in communicating it – in which case he is mad; more dangerous still if he makes it public, for it is the universe that must recognize itself in this madness. But what does this madness of the universe mean if not, first, that this madness could not be universal? On the contrary, it is removed from all general possibility, even if Nietzsche comes to write that such a thought will *little by little* be thought by everyone.

An allegory: the thought of the Eternal Return, a madness of the Universe that Nietzsche, in assuming it as a madness that would be proper to him – that is, in madly deciding to give an account of it – accepts saving the universe from. He thus takes on the role of Christ, but by going further than the Messiah in accepting what Christ could not: not the ignominious though still tragic and finally glorious death on the Cross, but rather a senile death, watched over by the devoted and abusive Saintly Women, mother and sister, and even the atrocious exaltation (his Resurrection) by he who in the twentieth century represented horror itself. The Crucified against Dionysos: Nietzsche crucifies himself on his madness in order that the jubilant dissolution, beyond sense and non-sense, the excess without goal and without rules that finds its sign in Dionysos, may remain just: a pure generosity to which is suited only a thought that sacrifices itself in it while resisting it in order to remain a thought.

± ± Everything is played out in the manner in which the thought of the Eternal Return is communicated. A troubled and troubling game. One could say that Nietzsche undertakes to speak in five ways: (1) through *Zarathustra*; (2) impersonally, in having recourse to a practice of language that imitates that of knowledge; (3) personally, in confiding to friends in the mode of a mute murmuring (Lou, Overbeck); (4) in entrusting this thought to the future by imagining a secret conjuration; (5) in proposing it, apart from all science, all metaphysics, and all historical practice, as the simulacrum of an ethical speech, beyond Good and Evil: would I will it in such a way that I should will it infinitely?

Why does no communication seem able to respond or to correspond to the exigency of the Return? Because all communication already belongs to the exigency and, inasmuch as communication does belong to it, could only break in on it if, in producing itself, communication claims to help it realize itself. The question constantly poses itself to Nietzsche: why this revelation that isolates him from what is revealed? Why such a revelation – the revelation of detour – and such that it turns away from every identity and, by way of this exception, makes either the revelation derisory or he who reveals it mad, because divine? The circle is in any case vicious, being so first inasmuch as it condemns Nietzsche to this exaltation beyond the circle signified by the name of God: *circulus vitiosus deus*. The 'vice', the fault in the circle, lies in the fact that the knowledge that repeats it breaks it, and in this rupture establishes a faulty God. '*Whoever does not believe in the cyclical process of the Whole must believe in an arbitrary God.*'

± ± Nietzsche is there in order to maintain together 'detour' and 'return', and if he speaks of 'the eternal return of the same' it is perhaps so as not to have to speak of the 'perpetual detour of difference' – in relation to which there is never anyone to make remembrance of it, or to make it the centre of a circular affirmation. '*To the paralysing sense of general disintegration and incompleteness I oppose the Eternal Return.*' A formulation that prompts this reading: maintain the law of the Return if you are not capable of entering by way of it into what always turns you away from it, turning you away from yourself as it turns you away from maintaining yourself in it, that is to say, the perpetual neutrality of Detour.

± ± But the law of Return is without exception; it cannot be got beyond, everything repeats itself, everything returns: the limit of thought. To think or to affirm this law is also to speak *at the limit*, there where the speech that affirms affirms speech as that which transgresses every limit: setting down every mark, that is, all writing, on the basis of a line of demarcation that must be gone beyond inasmuch as it is impossible to exceed. 'Saying it differently,' to write in the return, is always already to affirm detour, just as it is to affirm by repetition difference without beginning or end.

± ±   Through *Zarathustra* Nietzsche maintains a zone of silence: everything is said of all there is to say, but with all the precautions and resources of hesitation and deferral that the one writing knows (with a disquieting lucidity) are necessary, if he wants to communicate that which cannot be communicated directly; and if he wants, further (under the accusation of unreason that he foresees), to preserve for himself the alibi of ridiculousness. If, however, between the thought of the Eternal Return and its affirmation, Nietzsche interposes intermediaries always ready to allow themselves to be challenged (the animals, Zarathustra himself, and the indirect character of a discourse that says what it says only by taking it back); if there is this silent density, it is not due simply to ruse, prudence, or fear, but is also because the only meaning of *news* such as this is the exigency to differ and to defer that bears it, and that it bears: as though it could be said only by deferring its saying. The deferral therefore does not mark the waiting for an opportune moment that would be historically right; it marks the untimeliness of every moment since the return is already detour – or better: since we can only affirm the return as detour, making affirmation what turns away from affirming, and making of the detour what hollows out the affirmation and, in this hollowing out, makes it return from the extreme of itself back to the extreme of itself, not in order to coincide with it, but rather to render it again more affirmative at a mobile point of extreme non-coincidence.

± ±   When Nietzsche, ill and drawn by the attraction of a formidable speech that devastates him, confides in Lou or Overbeck, this can be treated as an anecdote; and it is one, however moving it may be. A man in bed who is delirious betrays himself lugubriously without realizing that he is compromising his thought in delirium. That he does not realize it is in fact probable and unimportant. But the relation of the delirium to the thought of the Eternal Return that the delirium communicates is more important and perhaps not anecdotal. Nietzsche can only speak (in that direct–indirect manner, in the mode of a mute murmuring) by forgetting – in forgetting himself, and in this memory that is a forgetting in which he disappears to the point of giving way to the sinister murmuring voice that Overbeck, out of the modesty of friendship, will refuse to remember up to and including the final catastrophe. Overbeck, quite literally, did not hear this voice – it remained without a hearing. The 'delirium' most assuredly does not constitute that deliberate (or non-deliberate) simulation with which later, at the moment of manifest madness, Nietzsche's reason was credited: the 'delirium' is the form of absence in which Nietzsche's identity destroys itself – that Nietzsche who, formulating the *everything returns*, thus opens the circle, marks its point of singularity (the point at which the non-circularity of the circle would be defined) by means of which closure and rupture coincide.

± ±   God, that is to say Nietzsche, that is to say the 'communication' that imperfectly, viciously closes the Circle into a non-circle by the hiatus constituted by this 'communication' or revelation.

± ±   The fragment: *'Do I speak like someone under the sway of revelation? In that case, have only scorn for me and do not listen! Would you be like those who still have need of gods? Does your reason not feel disgust in allowing itself to be nourished in such a gratuitous, mediocre fashion?'* Let us understand, then, better than Overbeck, better than Lou, and better also than ourselves, readers of Nietzsche, that what we call the 'exigency of Return' was not revealed at Sils Maria and could not have been communicated in an experience that would have occurred at a particular moment or for the gain of an individual. Not only because it is not a matter of a religious truth, fallen from above and received through grace in order to be spread abroad by faith, but because this 'thought' cannot but escape every mode of 'knowledge', active or passive: this is its characterizing trait. No passivity whatsoever, no activity whatsoever would be able to receive or grasp it. Then would it be forever outside revelation and outside knowledge. And of what am I speaking when I speak of it? Exactly: it is related to speech if it changes all relations of speech and writing, placing them under the decision of repetitive difference. Each time Nietzsche (to retain this name for him that is just as much our own, that is, the name of no one) has recourse to a particular formulation (lyrical, metaphysical, existential, or practical) it is not in order to privilege the one he momentarily chooses, but to challenge all the others. If he happens to express himself in a mode that appears to be 'scientific', is it not simply to say: I am not speaking like someone who is under the sway of revelation? And if he speaks of this to Overbeck like a lightning-struck prophet, is it not also to warn him: be attentive, remain vigilant, for what is at stake here imperils all reason and modifies the possibilities – indifference, objectivity, unity – of every exercise of thought? It is true, I speak as an unreasonable man, but it is because unreason here is less the lapse of thought than the excess of lack that the exigency of another reason – or of the Other as reason – calls for and desires.

Through the Return we do not only *desire* that which turns us away from every desired, but here there is desire without anyone desiring and by way of a detour from all desire, as from all that is desirable.

± ±   '*If the thought of the eternal return of all things does not subjugate you, this is in no way a failing on your part, just as there would be no merit if all the same you were subjugated by it.*' This means: the infinite of the repetition determines innocence, and for all the more reason, therefore, the thought or the non-thought of repetitive possibility is still innocence. This means then: you are innocent, all the more so as, through this innocence, there is nothing in you that is you; you are therefore not even innocent. That is why you are hereby responsible for what is most weighty: the irresponsibility that comes to you from that which, turning you away from yourself, always (never) makes you come back. That is why, also, to the question of what sort of discourse would befit the enigma of the Return the response, if there must be one, is: an 'ethical' discourse, beyond Good and Evil. Will to live this instant of life in such a way that you can accept having already *desired* it and having always to desire it *again* without beginning or end, even if it be as you yourself, without identity and without reality: the extreme of insignificance. *Will.*

± ±   '*I love my ignorance of the future.*' Now we return to this phrase, responding to it quite differently, for the desire it proposes to us must be set in relation with the thought of the Eternal Return, and called up at this moment when something like 'the end of history' is pronounced. This ignorance does not free us from knowledge, but holds it still in reserve when everything is already known. Ignorance: uncertainty. And in another (posthumous) fragment from *The Gay Science*: '*I love the uncertainty of the future.*' Applied by Nietzsche to Nietzsche, this signifies: do not be impatient to the point of anticipating by a too resolute seeking what is in store for you. Do not simplify. But there is this uncertainty: the ignorance borne by the hazardous trait of the future; the chance that implies either infinite detour through the return or the rebeginning again through the absence of end.

Let us gamble on the future: let us affirm the indeterminate relation with the future as though this indeterminacy, by the affirmation that confirms it, were to render the thought of the Return active. For there is *the future*, the one within the ring that offers itself to repetition as a temporal instance, and there is *the future* itself of 'Everything returns' – the to-come now carried to the greatest power of lack; that to which, in its uncertain non-coming, we who are not in it, being henceforth deprived of ourselves, as of all present possibility, say: welcome to the future that does not come, that neither begins nor ends and whose uncertainty breaks history. But how do we think this rupture? Through forgetting. Forgetting frees the future from time itself. Forgetting is this lack that is lacking to desire, not only so as to permit desire, but in such a way that desire is lacking and forgotten in desire. Forgetting is the manner in which the '*chaos sive natura*' opens, the '*chaos of everything*', which, Nietzsche says, does not contradict the thought of the circular course. But what else does he say? '*Excluding the return*, there is nothing identical.' There is nothing identical except for the fact that everything returns. 'Everything returns' does not belong to the temporality of time. It must be thought outside time, outside Being, and as the Outside itself; this is why it can be named 'eternal' or *aevum*. '*I love my ignorance of the future*': this desire to be ignorant by which ignorance becomes desire is the waiting welcomed by forgetting, is the forgetting traversed by waiting, *annulus aeternitatis*: the desire of the 'Everything returns' that alone makes desire return, without beginning or end.

± ±   The affirmation of the return: an affirmation that is itself without return, excluded from every site of affirmation. Where would this affirmation that is without return be situated? There is no moment – no instance – for the affirmation of all affirmation, any more than for he who would affirm it since its presence means: a lack whose lack no mark could indicate without thereby annulling itself. It therefore never affirms itself. This 'never' is the sole fault in such a thought; it is also its 'verification', the sign of its absolute seriousness, and precisely what makes it impossible, whatever word bears it, not to take seriously – the limit-experience. But of this as well, Nietzsche warns us, so as to have done with it: '*Thus you prepare yourself for the time when you must speak. And then perhaps you will be ashamed to speak.*'

Notes

1 Heiddeger also cites and comments upon this 'sign,' borrowed from fragment 56 of *Beyond Good and Evil*. Pierre Klossowski, *Un si funeste désir* (Paris, Gallimard, 1963), and *Nietzsche et le cercle vicieux* (Paris, Mercure de France, 1969).

2 This fragment of *The Gay Science* is taken from the notes in which Nietzsche questions himself for the first time on the nature of the 'event'.

Translated by Susan Hanson

27

The Exigency of Return (1970)*

For Pierre Klossowski, who has reinscribed on our walls, bringing out its fragmentary value, the sign: Circulosus vitiosus deus, *and in so doing, as if by hand (gently, perfidiously), led us to where, since always and for always, in time and out of time, we would meet without recognizing each other and recognize each other without meeting, accompanied by dead friends, dead and living together with them.*

Let us go into this relation.

◆ Death is something we are unused to.

Death being what we are unused to, we approach it either as the unusual that amazes us, or as the unfamiliar that horrifies us. The thought of death does not help us to think about death, does not give us death as something to be thought. Death, thinking: these are so intimately close that, thinking, we die, if in dying we get out of thinking. So all thinking could be said to be mortal; all thoughts, last thoughts.

◆ The relation to 'it' [*il*]: the plurality contained in 'it' is such that it cannot be marked by some plural sign. Why? 'they' would still indicate a multiple singularity, a set which would be analysable and hence manipulable. 'They' is the manner whereby (it) frees itself from the neuter by borrowing from plurality a possibility for being determined, thereby conveniently returning to indetermination, as if (it) could find there the indicator that would suffice to secure it a place, that fully determined place in which every indeterminate is inscribed.

If I write *it*, denouncing it rather than indicating it, at least I know that, far from giving it a rank, a role or a presence which would raise it above everything that can be designated, it is I who, in so doing, go into the relation where 'I' allows itself to be immobilized in a fictional or functional identity, in order that there should come into play the game of writing in which *it* is then either the partner and (at the same time) the product or gift, or else the bet, the stake which, as such, being the main

---

* Originally published as 'L'exigence du retour', *L'Arche*, 43 (1970), pp. 48–53.

player, plays, changes, is displaced and moves to take the place of change itself, in a move or displacement that is without placement and lies without all placement.

it: if I hold at the edge of writing, paying attention not to bring it in in a capitalized form, paying even greater attention not to make it carry surplus meaning drawn from the fact that what it designates is unknown, this word that I keep, not without a struggle, in the position that moment-arily I assign to it (at the edge of writing), must not only be constantly kept under surveillance by me, but, on the basis of it, by means of an impossible usurpation or fiction, I must also keep watch over the change of place and of configuration that would follow from this for that 'me', given the task from the outset of simultaneously representing the same, and the identity or permanence of signs themselves in and through their written form, while at the same time having no form other than this identifying function or punctuation. *The me is not myself, but what is selfsame in the term myself*: not some identity, personal or impersonal, certain and faltering, but the law or rule that, by convention, guarantees the ideal identity of the terms or notations. The 'me' is thus an abbrevia-tion that can be termed canonical, in a formulation which governs and, one might say, blesses, in the first person, the claim of the Same to primacy. Whence perhaps the sacred character that seems to attach to the self, and which egoism confiscates by making it the privilege of the central point that it occupies, as well as the characteristic trait of every process of assembling, associating, grouping and unifying, not to say (negatively) of disunifying, dissociating or disassembling.

◆   it: at the edge of writing; a transparency which is, as such, opaque; bearing what inscribes it, effacing it, being effaced in its inscription, it is the effacement of the mark by which it is marked; neuter, under the attraction of the neuter, to the point of seeming dangerously to fix it and, were we capable of 'following' it to that edge where what is written has always already disappeared, not in the other of the written [*l'écriture*] but in the neutrality of writing [*écrire*], seeming also dangerously to tempt us to form a relation with what is excluded from all relation, and yet which gives an indication that it is absolute only in the relative mode (that of relation itself, hence multiple).

Whether it be capitalized or not, in the position of a subject, in the situation of a pleonasm, indicating some other or no other or indicating only its own indication, the it without identity; personal? impersonal? not yet and always beyond; and being neither someone nor something, no more than it could in any way correspond to the magic of being or the fascination of non-being. For the moment, the only thing that can be said: it, *a word in excess*, which cunningly we locate at the edge of writing, that is to say the relation of writing to writing, when writing gives an indication of itself at the edge of itself.

◆ Non-present, non-absent; it tempts us in the manner of what we could only encounter in situations where we no longer are: save – save at the limit; situations that are called 'extreme', supposing there are such things.

◆ The relation from me to the other, which is difficult to think (a relation that the it 'relates'): because of the status of the other, in turn and simultaneously the other as term, in turn and simultaneously the other as relation without term, relays needing always to be relayed; then, because of the change it proposes to 'me', requiring this latter to accept not only that it is hypothetical, not to say fictitious, but also that it is a canonical abbreviation, representing the law of the same, fractured in advance (hence once more – beneath the fallacious proposal of this shattered, intimately wounded self – once more a living me, that is to say a full me).

◆ The Eternal Recurrence of the Same: the same, which is to say what is selfsame in myself, in so far as it epitomizes the rule of identity, which is to say the me which is *present*. But the exigency of return, *excluding from time any present mode*, will never free up a now in which the same would amount to the same, to the selfsame in myself.

◆ The Eternal Recurrence of the Same: as if the recurrence, ironically proposed as the law of the Same, in which the Same would be sovereign, did not of necessity make of time an infinite game with two entrances (presented as one but nevertheless never unified): a future always already past, a past always yet to come, from which the third instance, the instant of presence, in excluding itself, would exclude all possibility of the identical.

How would it be possible, under the law of recurrence, where between past and future nothing can combine, to jump from one to the other, when the rule does not allow any passage, even that of a jump? Past, so it is said, is the *same* as future. There would thus be a single modality only, or a dual modality functioning in such a way that identity, in being deferred, would regulate the difference. *But* such could be said to be the exigency of return: '*under the false guise of a present*' the past-future ambiguity invisibly separates future from past.

Either a past, or a future, with nothing that would allow the passage from one to the other, so that the demarcation line would demarcate them all the more for remaining invisible: hope for a past, a future already elapsed. All that would then remain of time would be this line remaining always to be crossed, always already crossed, and yet uncrossable and, in relation to 'me', non-situable. The *impossibility* of situating this line is perhaps all we ever name when we name the 'present'.

The law of recurrence, in supposing that 'everything' might recur, seems to posit time as ended: become the circle, withdrawn from circulation, of all circles; but in so far as it breaks the ring in its middle, it proposes a time that is not unaccomplished, but on the contrary finished and finite [*fini*], except at this present point which we think is all we possess and which, because it is lacking, introduces the breach of infinity, obliging us to live as if in a state of perpetual death.

◆   (Empty) past, (empty) future, by the false light of a present: these are the only episodes to be inscribed in and through the absence of the book.

◆   Let us suppose it: the past is empty, and only the multiple play of reflections, the illusion that there is a present destined to pass and be withheld in the past, could lead one to believe that it is filled with events, a belief which would make it appear less inimical, less frightening: being thus an inhabited past, even if only by ghosts, it would grant the right to live innocently (in the narrative mode) precisely that which nevertheless presents itself as for ever revoked and at the same time irrevocable. Irrevocability would thus be the trait by which the emptiness of the past marks, by presenting them as impossible to relive and thus as having already been lived in an unsituable present, the semblances of events that are there only to cover up emptiness, to beguile it by concealing it, while all the same announcing its existence by using irreversibility as an indicator. In that case, the irrevocable is then in no way, at least not only, the fact that what has taken place took place once and for all: it is perhaps the means – a strange one, I grant – whereby the past alerts us (while making it easy on us) to the fact that it is empty, and that the moment of falling due [*l'échéance*] – the infinite fall – towards which it points, that well of infinite depth into which events, if there were any, would fall one by one, signifies merely the emptiness of the well, the depth of what is a bottomless deep. Yes, it is irrevocable and indelible: ineffaceable, but only because nothing is inscibed there.

◆   Let us assume now that events are only 'real' in the past, which is a machine operating so as to allow us to recollect, by means of a well-ordered memory, though with slight doubt, everything that the future could promise us or make us dread. But is the past not always less rich than the future and always other? Definitely unless, the past being the infinitely empty, and the future the infinitely empty, each were merely the oblique way (the differently inclined screen) by which emptiness offers itself, alternately simulating what is possible–impossible then what is irrevocable–elapsed; and unless, again, the law of Eternal Recurrence did not leave any choice but to live in the past what is future and live the future as past, but without past and future being called upon to alternate with one another according to the circulation of the Same, since, between them, interruption, the *defective lack of presence*, would prevent all communication other than through interruption: an interruption lived either as what is elapsed about the past or what is possible about the future, which is to say precisely as the *unbelievable* utopia of Eternal Recurrence. It is impossible to believe in Eternal Recurrence. That is its sole guarantee, its 'verification'. Such is, over there, what is demanded [*l'exigence*] by the Law.

◆ If, in the 'fearfully ancient', nothing was ever present and if, no sooner has it occurred, than the event, through an absolute fall, immediately falls into it, as the indicator of irrevocability informs us, then (whence our icy foreboding) the event that we thought we had lived was itself never in a relation of presence either, be it with us or with anything whatsoever.

◆ (It is as if he had written in the margin of a book that would only be written much later, at a time when books would only ever be known as something that had disappeared, and evoke merely a fearfully ancient and seemingly speechless past, with no speech other than the murmuring voice of a fearfully ancient past.)

◆ The emptiness of the future [*futur*]: death holds our future [*avenir*] there. The emptiness of the past: there death has its tomb.

In a way, as soon as one has approached the law of return – the Eternal Recurrence of the Same – by the movement that comes from it and which might be said to be the time of writing, if it were not necessary to say also and first of all that writing holds within it the exigency of return, this law – outside law – might lead us to take upon ourselves the temporality of time, in such a way that, by suspending (or making disappear) all present and all presence, this temporality would make disappear (or suspend) the instance and the basis from which it is uttered. That would be the movement of irreversibility, which is as such always reversible (the labyrinth). The revelation at Surlej, revealing that everything returns, turns the present into the gulf where no presence has ever taken place, and in which 'everything returns' has always already been engulfed. The law strikes the present dumb and, through the present, the present yet to come which the ordinary future – a present future – is content to be. So that in the future there will only return what is incapable of being present (the poetic mode), just as in the past what returned was only what in the past never belonged to a present (the narrative mode).

◆ On the one hand, 'everything returns' no longer allows that rhythmic scansion that lightens the relation to time constituted by time itself in its temporality: time is every time 'all' the time, at the 'same' time, without 'all' and 'same' being able to maintain their directive power within it; past, present, future would be 'all one and the same' [*tout un*], were it not precisely that unity, in foundering and going down, had also modified these distinctions by exposing them to naked difference. That is the first thing. But from another angle, 'everything returns' cannot be controlled by means of the extension in every direction which an eternal present, become the commonplace of space, might bring to mind. *Everything returns*, signifying: 'everything will return, everything returned already and once and for all, on condition that it be not, nor ever have been, present', excludes 'everything returns', even if it takes the form of 'nothing perhaps returns.'

◆ The exigency of return could thus be said to be the exigency of a time without present, a time that would also be that of writing itself, a future time, a past time, one which the radical disjunction (in the absence of all present) between one and the other, even were they the same, makes it impossible to identify other than as the difference borne by repetition.

Between past and future, the greatest difference is given in the fact that the one can be said to repeat the other without the common measure of a present: as if between past and future there reigned the absence of present in the simplified form of forgetting.

◆ *In a way*, it is necessary for presence – absolute contentment – to be accomplished through the ending of discourse, in order for Eternal Recurrence to reveal, under cover of forgetting, the exigency of a time without present, that is to say a mode of affirming that is totally other. There is no doubt that Nietzsche can be born before Hegel, and when he actually is born, it is always before Hegel; hence what it is tempting to call his madness: that necessarily premature relation, ever anticipated, ever inactual, therefore lacking anything that could guarantee it by basing it in something actual [*une actualité*] – be this of now, of the past (an origin) or of the future (prophetic). When one is content to say that madness is a reason too advanced for reason, this is to wrong both madness and reason. Even the statement: 'they were mad so that we should no longer need to be,' which Nietzsche could perhaps have accepted, still presupposes simple temporal relations, that are always unifiable and conciliable within a conception of time as essentially unique, itself excluded, as something thought, from its own becoming, since it depends upon the great System. In this light, a mad person is someone who is wise before being so, wise prematurely [*avant de l'être, avant la lettre*]. But the *other* madness – that which has no name in which it can be put away – would be an infinitely multiple relation which, even if dubbed temporal, would elude everything that sought to subject it to time, even as the Outside of time. Madness is named thus only by the language of the Law which, at best, appoints it to be what can be said to precede it, as what would always come before the law, which nevertheless, in itself, is such that it implies the impossibility of anything that could come earlier than it. That is why there is no madness, but there *might be* madness, its existence, considered as a real possibility, needing always to be placed in parentheses and in a conditionless conditional. Which is something 'madness' also permits, for the parenthesis is its madness, into which it seeks to put everything, including itself.

◆   Nietzsche (if his name serves to name the law of Eternal Recurrence) and Hegel (if his name invites us to think presence as everything and everything as presence) allow us to sketch out a mythology: Nietzsche can only come after Hegel, but it is always before and it is always after Hegel that he comes and comes again; before: because, even thought as the absolute, presence has never gathered within itself the completed totality of knowledge; presence knows that it is absolute, but its knowledge remains a relative knowledge, since it has not been fulfilled practically, and so it knows itself only as a present that is practically not satisfied, not reconciled with presence as everything: hence Hegel is still only a pseudo-Hegel. And Nietzsche always comes afterwards, for the law he bears presupposes the accomplishment of time as present and, in this accomplishment, its absolute destruction, so that, as a consequence, Eternal Recurrence, affirming future and past as the only temporal instances and as instances that are identical and without relation, freeing the future of all present and the past of all presence, shatters thought and reduces it to this infinite affirmation: *in the future there will return infinitely what could never and in no form ever become present, just as in the past there infinitely returned what, of the past, never belonged in any form to a present.* That, henceforth, for Nietzsche, is the exigency that must be lived and thought. And writing alone can respond to such an exigency, on condition that discourse, the logos, having been accomplished, deprives it of any basis from which it could declare itself or sustain itself, and exposes it to the threat, to the futile glamour of what no one henceforth would dare to call: *mad writing*.

◆   The madness of '*everything recurs*': its primary trait is a simple one, in that it carries within itself the extravagance of forms or relations that are self-excluding. It formulates in Hegelian language what can only destroy that language; this formulation is not, however, an accidental anachronism; anachronism is its necessity; 'ideological delay' is its appointed time; in the same way, it is only able to destroy what is completed and accomplished in it, and through the rigour of the accomplishment by which it is itself destroyed. '*Everything recurs*': that is the logos of totality; for 'everything' to recur, totality must have received from discourse and praxis both its meaning and the completion of its meaning. And the present must be the sole temporal instance, if totality of presence and as presence is to be affirmed. But '*everything recurs*' is the decision that the infinity of recurrence must not take the form of the circularity of everything; and that no recurrence may be affirmed in the present (whether that present be future or a past present), that is to say may only be affirmed through the exclusion of any possibility and any experience of a presence, or through the affirmation of a time without present: free of all affirmation, even if it concerned a time without present. The thought of *everything recurs* thinks time by destroying it, but, by means of this destruction which seems to reduce it to two temporal instances, thinks it as infinite, the infinity of a breach or the interruption substituting for present eternity an infinite absence.

In saying that, we say almost nothing. We do not have a language in which to affirm recurrence while respecting the indirect exigency that is said to come from it, and language collapsed in Nietzsche, when, with a mortal desire, he desired to raise it to the level of an impossible affirmation.

◆   'You only *remain* a philosopher to the extent that you . . . *keep silent*' (Nietzsche).
Deliver me from too lengthy a speech.

Translated by Michael Holland

28

Oh All to End (1990)*

Let there be no mistake. Our intention is not to pay homage to Samuel Beckett, knowing as we do that the very word, with its inevitable air of glorification, always remained foreign to him. In a way, when *Molloy*, then *Malone Dies* first appeared in France, it was naïve of us (Georges Bataille, Maurice Nadeau and myself) to hope to alert the Prix des Critiques to these texts, even though so many remarkable writers and critics were on that committee, admittedly still as members of the 'literary establishment', when it was clear that even Beckett's early books (which still retained several features that might be termed classical) were foreign to the resources of 'literature'. But does literature need resources? If, as was said once (rightly or wrongly), literature tends towards its essence which is to efface itself or disappear, this exhaustion, which is perhaps profoundly mournful, but can also be a mixture of seriousness and sarcasm, constantly appeals to its own perseverance by making itself heard as a ceaseless, interminable voice. Samuel Beckett was entrusted with this movement of the end that never reaches the end. In his final published text (but not, I think, his very last one), under the title *Stirrings Still*, a wish is formulated which is all the more clearly expressed because it is affirmed in vain: 'only ever fainter oh to end. No matter how no matter where. Time and grief and self so-called. Oh all to end.'[1]

In dying, did Samuel Beckett himself reach the end? Did he leave us with the pain of bearing the burden of what could not achieve completion with him? Or else, by a cunning twist that would hardly be surprising, is he still keeping watch in order to find out what we intend doing with his silence, that silence that still speaks, since, beneath all language, may be heard the obligation to say the 'voice that speaks, knowing that it lies, indifferent to what it says, too old perhaps and too abased ever to succeed in saying the words that would be its last'?[2]

In the obituaries respectfully delivered to mark his passing, the great works of the age have often been mentioned, Proust, Joyce, Musil and even Kafka, these finished–unfinished works, which nevertheless retain, in what one can barely call their failure, 'a form of appearance of truth',

* Originally published as 'Oh tout finir', *Critique*, 519–20 (August–September 1990), pp. 635–7.

including, most of all, a concern to glorify, if not the author, then at least art itself by pushing traditional literature (even if one then calls it modern) to its furthest limit. But compare Sartre and Beckett, both having to contend with the false glory of the Nobel Prize for literature. This prize that, nobly, Sartre refused, one might say he did everything possible to be awarded it by the very act of writing *Words*, a book which, he believed, by the sublime power of its rhetoric, would henceforth make it impossible to hope for a finer work. The dream is a touching but childish one (entirely in keeping with Sartre's own child-like nature). And the punishment for having wanted to write (and publish) a necessarily glorious text followed immediately, in the form of the award of the Nobel Prize, from which he derived additional glory by rejecting it. Nothing of the sort happened to Beckett: he had neither to accept nor refuse a prize that was for no particular work (there is no work in Beckett) but was simply an attempt to keep within the limits of literature that voice or rumble or murmur which is always under threat of silence, 'that undifferentiated speech, spaced without space, affirming beneath all affirmation, impossible to negate, too weak to be silenced, too docile to be constrained, not saying anything, only speaking, speaking without life, without voice, in a voice fainter than any voice: living among the dead, dead among the living, calling to die, to be resurrected in order to die, calling without call'[3] (and I quote – to end – these lines from *L'Attente l'Oubli* because Beckett was willing to recognize himself in that text).

Apart from the texts for the theatre, written when he wants a double, a companion for solitude (there is always or almost always another whom he remembers, if only by forgetting him), it is necessary to cite or recall, so as to contradict the assertion that there is no work in Beckett [*L'affirmation d'absence d'oeuvre*] the astonishing exception of that epic in three cantos entitled *How It Is*, in which, from verse to verse as though from stanza to stanza, the vast stretch of time of his life makes itself heard, from childhood and from even before childhood: there one finds a rhythm, a modulation, a cadence marked by refrains *I hear it my life*, and even the reminiscence of a spiritual world, the eternity of time without sleep: *prayer in vain to sleep I have no right to it yet I haven't yet deserved it prayer for prayer's sake when all fails when I think of the souls in torment . . . twenty years a hundred years not a sound*, with the result that he is left *fallen over on his side tired of waiting forgotten of the hearts where grace abides asleep*. Here, the object of waiting is not Godot, but the intimacy where the grace of sleeping hearts abides. *That is why I was given a companion.* And again the epic tone: *there he is then at last that not one of us . . . this not one of us harping harping mad too with weariness to have done with him*[4] – and, if one may say, for us too, to have done with him. But it is necessary still to wait. Oh all to end.[5]

Notes

1 Translator's note: Samuel Beckett, *As the Story Was Told* (London, John Calder, 1990), p. 128.
2 Translator's note: Samuel Beckett, *Molloy, Malone Dies, The Unnamable* (London, Calder and Boyars, 1959), p. 309.
3 Translator's note: Maurice Blanchot, *L'Attente l'Oubli* (Paris, Gallimard, 1962), pp. 155–6.
4 Translator's note: compare Samuel Beckett, *How It Is* (London, Calder and Boyars, 1964), pp. 7, 40, 27, 26, 151, 157. Throughout this passage, Blanchot is quoting rather loosely from Beckett's text. Blanchot silently runs together sentences that appear in different sections of the book; and on one occasion he changes Beckett's syntax, so that the adjective 'asleep' (in the phrase 'where grace abides asleep'), which, in *How It Is*, must refer to the figure of Belacqua, is now used, by Blanchot, to qualify the word 'grace', then, immediately following, the word 'hearts'.
5 These closing words – *Temps et peine et soi soi-disant*, as Beckett's French text has them – need to be read with care; *soi soi-disant* is not a final stammer or hiccup, but the fact that *soi*, the self, cannot affirm itself alone; if it is self, it is still the speaking self, the self who speaks and calls itself that, and thus (humour, terminal sarcasm) the so-called, the self-styled, would-be self, a simple *soi-disant*.

Translated by Leslie Hill

29

The Ease of Dying (1969)*

I believe that the first letter I received from Jean Paulhan is dated May 10th, 1940. In it he said to me, 'We will remember these days.' Then, eighteen years later, there came a certain May 13th which, because of its consequences, left us in disagreement – then another ten years, and what happened prevented me from learning that Jean Paulhan was beginning to leave us, just when we had planned to see each other again once the spring returned. I wish to begin by recalling this gravity of history: not to use it in trying to evoke, through it, all that was grave – it seems to me – in a relationship without anecdotes; still, since what is not seen is the only important thing, in the end, it remains true that great historical changes are also destined, because of their burden of absolute visibility, and because they allow nothing but these changes themselves to be seen, to better free up the possibility of being understood or misunderstood intimately, and without having to spell things out, the private falling silent so that the public can speak, thus finding its voice. This is also what communism is, this incommensurable communication in which everything public – and in this case everything is public – binds us to the other (to others) through what is closest to us.

** I often observed that his *récits* – which touched me in a way I can better remember now – are almost all written with the war as their backdrop or their medium, even when it is not their main subject. (Sometimes there are brief allusions, as in *Progress in Love on the Slow Side*, and sometimes nothing more than a date, as in *The Crossed Bridge*.) I said to myself, too easily, that this great void into which war displaces us is necessary – depriving us of ourselves and only granting us private happiness, or unhappiness, as a deprivation – so that we should be able to speak of it, or rather, so we should not be able to speak of it. I furthermore thought that Jean Paulhan preferred to publish his books during times of war: but why? Perhaps in order to leave them in the margins of time; but perhaps also because we all need this immense lack which frees us from the usual literary scene, so that the act of

* Originally published as 'La facilité de mourir', *Nouvelle Revue Française*, 197 (May 1969), pp. 743–64.

publishing, even in our own name, in a time outside time, still leaves us anonymous, or allows us, without too much immodesty, to hope to become so.

★★   I almost think (even if this affirmation is somewhat excessive, and yet it is always by carrying it to its limit, where we reduce it to its beyond, that we can affirm it, or simply affirm) that Jean Paulhan wrote nothing but *récits*, or always in the form of a *récit*. Whence this gravity which he would like, discreetly, to lighten for us, this search which never ends, and which is only interrupted in order to begin again in a continuous movement (the movement of narrating), while this continuity only serves to hide the gaps which cannot be seen, but which could still let a certain light through, or even let it disappear, as happens in the phenomenon of transparency. Whence also this feeling of a revelation, as in a dream, where everything is manifest except for the lack which makes the dream possible, ensures it, functions within it and, as soon as one claims to discover it, dissipates it in shifting reflections. If everything is a *récit*, then everything would also be a dream in Jean Paulhan's writing, until one is awoken by darkness, in the same way that writing is like a dream, a dream so precise, so prompt in revealing itself, in solving the enigma, that it never stops reinscribing the enigma into the dream and, consequently, *revealing* itself as enigmatic. Let us recall the first words of *The Crossed Bridge*, or better still, the first paragraph:
    '*No sooner had I made the decision to look for you, than I answered myself with an abundance of dreams. It began the very next night; a dream doesn't have a beginning, but these dreams stopped just when they were about to be resolved in a pure feeling, satisfying to the extent that there was no more need for images.*' With this, everything (starting with that magical story about childhood entitled *Lalie*) is explained.

★★   It is through the movement of the *récit* (the discontinuity of the continuous *récit*) that we can perhaps best understand Jean Paulhan, who distances himself from it, but who also confides in it, because he discovers – and this is one of the first discoveries a writer makes – that one only has to say something for it not to be believed, to point it out for nothing but the finger to be noticed (as is the case with Poe's *The Purloined Letter*, which Jacques Lacan put to such good use). In this there is neither ruse nor perversity, except for the detour proper to writing– reading, this double game which he will henceforth try to account for by recounting it, not only in order to play with it better – one has to realize that the playfulness that is, in Paulhan, consonant with this discovery, and allows him at every moment to mime it, is also for him an invitation to do so – but in order to grasp, within this duplicity, the trace of a single

Truth or the discovery of the secret *as* secret, which would thus be identical to itself, and yet separate, secret in so far as it reveals itself. I would say, with a solemnity which, as certain of his letters show, was indistinguishable from modesty, that few philosophers today have matched his passion for the One, the distracted certainty that a revelation, always deferred, always thwarted so that it could remain faithful to his patience, would not be lacking for him, even if it were in the final failure. But what sort of Unity?

** 'I do not doubt that one day I will discover the thought which will guarantee me, almost at every moment, rapture, the absence of boredom. I have more than one reason to think that this discovery is near.' Rapture: the absence of boredom, or indifference distracted from itself by itself.

** I would like to come back to this idea of a *récit* which goes from one book to the next, in which the writer recounts himself in order to search for himself, and then to search for the movement of the search, in other words, to ask how it is possible to recount, and thus to write. But we ought first to note that the search is made both more difficult and easier because it is always preceded by happiness, or at least an obvious joy, although it is not clearly sensed, the joy of having already found and of constantly finding. The search begins there. Which is why it takes the – deceptive – form of a *récit*: as if, since the thing had happened, there was nothing left to do but to tell how it happened, and in so doing to search for it, but less through memory than in order to be worthy of it and to respond to the promise, always in the future, that it represents; otherwise, it might well never have taken place, and how could one know, if one doesn't keep finding it again – anew? 'Now that I look back at these adventures, which have merged together, I'm surprised that they are so simple. Their greatest quality is, no doubt, the fact that they happened to me; it's also the most difficult one to explain, and this, which is even more to the point: 'Everything happens to me as if I had found a life that was *already* too far along. I would find out about the things that people think are complicated, but I know it's the simplest things I miss, I don't want to cheat. Truly the simplest.'

It is because simplicity is always already given, and consequently lost: the question is, how to find it again at the point of arrival? Or as Hegel would say, as a result, which is thus produced and reproduced by this 'trickery', reason's ruse which I believe Paulhan, so mischievous, was never satisfied with, for his understanding of opposites distanced him very significantly from the process we call dialectical. (This is even one of the most important traits of his search.) Simplicity, which is only simple within the duplicity of writing, must be repeated in order for it to point to itself (which is not to say to recognize itself). It is thus only when it is doubled that it becomes simplified, and in that case how can the first time be made to be already the second time (several times, *all* times – or infinity)? In other words (perhaps): how can we avoid the temptation of death whose intervention is available to us in a way which only frightens us in order to keep us from making too easy a use of it?

** This relationship to death – let us call it illness – plays in the *récit* a role that must not be underestimated. As if, far from disorienting us, and thus instructing us by altering us, being ill taught us all that is strange in the way we normally use our life, which is given back to us by 'recovery'. ('The Severe Recovery,' 'Imaginary Pains' ['Les douleurs imaginaires'], 'Letter to the Doctor' ['Lettre au médecin'], where I find this passage, which disturbs us all profoundly: 'I believe that sometimes I feel several drops of blood losing their way inside me, separating and forming a sort of lake. I can recognize the spot by the discomfort caused there. I hear, with my inner ear, a disquiet settle in . . . As if my body were attempting to give me a sign that I would not be able to hear . . . Usually it is in a dream that I find myself first warned. I immediately wake up. It seems to me that by attending to it quickly enough, I will be able to understand the warning.') I don't therefore need to dwell on the fact that it is through a modesty of vocabulary, which is moreover an effect of the same movement (effacement) that this name 'illness' is proposed, protected by its lack of seriousness (not admitting anything irreversible), instead of the word capable – is it in fact capable? – of ending all words. The narrator (the one who takes upon 'himself' the task of saying 'I' and thus takes refuge in and is deprived of or diminished by a 'me') speaks readily of his indifference, either because he sees in it a reason for his passions (since great efforts of feeling are necessary in order to get out of such a lack of sensibility), or because he responds to it with an untiring curiosity which takes him towards so many things and people, and which would seem to be more a proof of his disinclination for being affected by himself and by others, with the provision that he thus frees himself from a geniality which often embarrasses him (and masks his embarrassment), all the while protecting, through this dispersion, the only movement whose pull he feels: an obstinate relationship to unity – the unity of a single, grand design which also has as its aim the divided relationship to the One. But *indifference*: this is not a character trait. So what is it? Nothing more than the ease of dying from which we are none the less forbidden, awkwardly, by this ease itself, which leads us to suspend it or, to speak more metaphysically, nothing less than indetermination, the reserve of difference, which also leaves undetermined – for the duration of a lifetime – the question of knowing whether we are in the initial indetermination or the final indetermination.

** 'Do I have the same sort of indifference towards her that I'm afraid I have towards myself?' 'I had often been surprised by my indifference . . . I assumed that the failing is a common one. And the most ordinary emotions easily seemed to me in other people to be wilful and artificial.' 'It has twice happened that I have made important discoveries – the kind of discoveries that change one's life. The first time was when I was about ten years old, and it was not an enjoyable discovery, no. It was this: that I was stupid. Stupid, or more precisely empty: thoughts didn't occur to me.' 'It's because I don't stand up for myself enough, through a kind of indifference.' 'And it is certainly true that not many things touch me deeply – but then I also think that not many things *should* touch us these days.' (This last quotation is from a letter to Marcel Arland.)

** The *récit* reveals, but in revealing conceals, a secret: to be more exact, it carries it. This secret is the visible–invisible attraction of every *récit*, just as it has the effect of transforming into a pure *récit* texts which do not seem to belong to the narrative practice. The secret: simply something to be found, which gives several narratives a false appearance of being documents *à clef*; in the end we have the key, a means of opening up the story, of rewarding the wait, of producing meaning by orienting it – with this one difficulty, which we are not always aware of, that the key itself has no key, and the means of explaining, which explains everything, remains unexplained, or else (and this is the source of the most beautiful, the most resistant *récits*) it is nothing more than all the narrative obscurity gathered together, concentrated into a *single* point whose simplicity thus transports us, in the literal sense of the term, because we are in the same moment carried and carried back, from the beginning to the end, from the end to the beginning, possessing everything in a single 'detail', in the unity as it were of a word, but this word only enlightens us because it has *brought together* the obscure dispersion of the different parts, their dis-course: from there it sends us back gloriously to the whole of the *récit*, over which it radiates, until we realize it is the word itself that appears to us to be not only secret but forbidden, excluded from the law that it decrees. We sense then that the secret of the *récit* is also its very possibility, and with this, the possibility of any *récit*; which leads us to these questions: how is something continuous made from something that is discontinuous by elevating both to the level of an absolute, by holding them together, by ensuring their passage? And why this passage, which (atrociously) confuses the necessity of a void and the affirmation of a plenitude, the hiatus which separates, the

306 The Step Beyond

relationship which unifies, the means and the obstacle? Why 'the crossed bridge'?

**   But let us search more patiently. If there is a secret, this secret which makes the course of the *récit* possible because it is the possibility of an impossible movement, the secret is that the *récit* already possesses this secret in advance, but doesn't say it (at least directly), carried as it is by the secret that it carries, and doesn't say it because to say it would be to withdraw it or reverse it. But is not this secret precisely the mysterious 'fact' of reversal, the reversal of for and against, about which Pascal, before Hegel, spoke to us, and about which, in a certain sense, he was wrong to speak to us, if it is true that such an operation would only work on condition that no formulation of it is proposed, since it would only be able to preserve it by cancelling it? This secret is therefore the most common (and because it is too well known, it is happily unknown): it belongs to everyone, the commonplace by which, divided, we communicate as if unaware of it. That Jean Paulhan should have identified it in language, and even with language, to the point of seemingly having made the latter his sole object of study, and of seemingly seeing in this secret only the secret of languages, and not seeing in languages the putting into play of the secret – this we can well understand. We could even say that it is unimportant to speak of the one in the light of the others, or vice versa, because there also the law of reversals comes into play, so that as soon as one has affirmed: language contains that which is secret (and would thus be beyond it), we must add: but the secret is itself beyond language, if it is not only that which language always speaks about without speaking of it, but also that which allows it to speak, on the condition of being itself left outside discourse.

**   Pascal: between Pascal and Jean Paulhan, I would say that the theoretical process, and sometimes its necessity, is the same. There is nothing more striking – or more illuminating – than this rapport of two apparently dissimilar minds. The theoretical process: for Pascal, the point of departure is diversion – equivocation or undecided ambiguity – for Paulhan it is indifference, in which everything is given without distinction; from this ambiguous or indifferent indecision, one must go on to distinguish the differences, then put each term into an oppositional relationship, a contrariness which is so precisely structured that, in language, we constantly come up against something which presents itself as verbal *and* as non-verbal, then meaning *and* non-sense, then still within discourse but already outside it, pure language *and* pure thought, then within thought, the mind *and* the world, then outside thought thus still within it, the world *and* God, light *and* darkness, all this at the same time being endless and necessarily (but this is perhaps what is most extraordinary) not without an end, if, in an experience which is momentarily ultimate or provisionally definitive, we succeed in covering in a single movement, and in grasping in one irreducible term, the mystery of this contrasted alternation, whose rigour is then so great and whose obscurity so violent, so incompatible with the self who undergoes it that the self, escaping as if by surprise, or sinking into the void of a passivity beyond all passivity, gives way to an event at which it is not present but in which it participates (being, in a sense, unknowingly part of it), a pure event whose absolute obscurity is also absolute clarity: that which makes the whole thing clear. Whence, from that point on, this need: to search for the anomaly in order to find the norm, to explain by way of the inexplicable, to think against thought, that is to say 'according to mystery'; a need, it is true, which loses its necessity as soon as the latter is organized into a system, once the obscure part is made to be nothing more than an anticipated way of seeing, or else if one has recourse to incoherence only to emphasize, through its lack, the coherence which has always cancelled it out (assimilated it) in advance, and which is thus reduced to itself.

** I'd like to reflect on the movement which, through contrariness, leads to a hidden God (certain in so far as he is uncertain) and this other movement which brings together, in an experience which is at once unique and banal, illumination and darkness, the law and its transgression. Between the two there is a difference which should not surprise us: it is that the experience that Jean Paulhan initiates is mystical, whereas this is prohibited in Pascal's thought. Mystical, because it is identified by noted experiences of this kind ('so one must return to the mystics, the only ones among all the philosophers who openly put their philosophy to the test and in the end *realize* it'), but above all because this movement is no longer a question of *knowing* but of *being*: 'that which is obscure has become the reason for that which is clear, the problem has become the solution' – 'but on the condition that one is oneself the locus of darkness and of metamorphosis.' Elsewhere there is talk of ecstasy or transport, even if one should add, in a gesture of modesty which is an effect of rigour, that ecstasy is weak and transport renewable. Language itself (but here we are perhaps, in relation to the mystical tradition, in a singular position, since according to this tradition, whether religious or not, the experience could have no relation to the fact of saying, of writing, whereas, in this case, it is saying which would be its first consequence and in a sense its 'centre') is also the place of this ecstasy, inasmuch as there could be no word which does not render compatible the irreconcilable, nor maintain, between the physical and mental aspects, between the

'signifier' and the 'signified', a distance, an interval and something like a
void, a little uncrossable divide, which is none the less distractedly
crossed (but never abolished) at every moment, every time that language
functions and that we perform this mystery by which we know what it
means to speak. It is this void – infinitesimal, infinite – in which, whether
it is a matter of passing from the signifier to the signified, from the
subject to the object, from thought to the world, from the visible to the
invisible, conversion and reversal take place – or, to be more precise, it is
in this void that the contrariness of terms, opposed two by two, is at once
felt as a radical difference, for discontinuity prevents these terms (or
these moments) from following one another, and is consumed as a unity,
if, through the conversion or the reversal which takes place therein, one
can again grasp the certainty that, where there is two, it is none the less
the One which rules: the Single One which would ensure the relationship
of indifference between every different thing. So if we want to try to
understand it, the need or the constraint is such that we must affirm – or
experience – discontinuity, division or sharing, in order to experience –
or affirm – the Unity to which we not only belong, but 'in which we are
merged together' – and each time (it is I who am perhaps overemphasiz-
ing this point), each time discontinuity, division and unity demand to be
thought and carried to the absolute extreme.

** We must therefore not let ourselves be misled by the modesty of
expression: we are asked to witness a formidable experience, which
always fails itself and anyone who claims it as their own. In rare moments, Jean Paulhan agreed to come out from behind his reserve, sometimes in his public texts: he talks of an experience or thoughts 'which one
reaches in a flash and which one cannot sustain, but from which, once
they have appeared, the apparent world with its brightness and its darkness unfolds infinitely,' sometimes in letters (to Marcel Arland): 'It's that
each person inevitably suffers through, in the course of their life, some
almost intolerable experience which they must thereafter accommodate,
if they want to live and to live sanely'[1] – to which he adds, to make clear
his distance from religious experience 'It goes without saying that religious faith is a way of making a compromise with this terrible experience
and, *extending it to all of life*, of taking away its venom: if you like, a way
of diluting the poison.' 'This makes for many adventures, which are not
necessarily joyous ones. How I got out of them, I don't know . . . As long
as it doesn't leave any traces! That is what I sometimes fear, in what I
write.'
   But I would like to indicate another difference between a religious way
of thinking, even if it is mystical, and the one Jean Paulhan suggests to
himself or to us: it is that the former agrees to succeed (rapture and

ecstatic union being the gift and the sign of success), whereas the latter implies, if not its breakdown, at least its failure: the fault, the failing, or the lack by which it allows itself to be taken hold of or by which it takes hold of us, and taking hold of us, lets us go or conceals itself. That is why 'there is no rest.' For this very failing which might be said to belong to the ultimate experience, and which might be said to be its proof (just as, above, it was the incoherence or the lack of meaning by which reason endeavoured to feel completed, and thus justified, recognizing therein something *other* than itself), such a failing, becoming from this point on the promise or the condition of the experience, re- establishes itself as its necessary component, and thus invests itself and affirms itself in this experience, and is immediately lacking in its lack 'like an argument that is all the less convincing for being more so'. Hence, it is certainly true that we can be satisfied with nothing; it is also true that the process is itself marked by the contrariness that it seeks obscurely to bring to light, a patient, obstinate, modest and always clearly and calmly articulated process, just as a scientific argument should be, but which is none the less 'mystical' in so far as it tends towards the inexplicable in order to explain, in so far as it engages us, through the transport of the *récit*, in an experience which is one not of knowing but of being and, more precisely, of feeling the suspense of being, in which some interruption, being put into play, favours reversal and metamorphosis. Or rather, we might say that this method or process is also, being both a scientific and a non-scientific process, the disjunction as it were between the two, and the mind's hesitation between the latter and the former, which is to say, by turns their mutual suspension before jumping, and this leap which alone would allow the forbidden passage from one to the other to be made.

★★ 'The secret we are after could be quite well summed up as follows: none of the differences in the world which you attach such importance to exist. Everything is *one*.'

★★ One should perhaps add that the work of science anticipates this leap, not only by making it easy (by bringing out, for example, this general oppositional structure which the reflexive mind, starting out from indifferent simplicity or ambiguous indecision, comprehends and itself sets in motion), but also by making it difficult, since through interrogation and analysis it succeeds in making apparent, between the terms, the void which interrupts them, and then in *fixing* our attention on the necessity of an impossible passage and, thus arresting the leap while it is being made, in making it almost mortal. So it is as if the experience by which the meaning of this transport is revealed (or, rather than its meaning, its reality as an event), implied its non-completion, or as if we only become aware of the leap when, through our illicit discovery, we prevent it from being made and, in thus aggravating it, we give it its precise import, which is to coincide with the eventuality of a death.

If we are certain that anyone who comes along is able to make this leap thanks to the distraction which allows him, constantly, to cross the divide with giant strides, and if we are certain that such a leap passes through what one would have to name (and how else would we name it?) death itself, we could conclude that it is the 'ease of dying' which, in every life, hides us from death, or makes us neglect or forget to die. How discreet one must therefore remain, not using any words that are too categorical, and this, I think, is one of the reasons which distance Paulhan from any deliberately moving or strong or sombre language: indeed the casualness he sometimes lets himself be suspected of is both a defence against a certain heaviness which inhibits the reversal – the volte-face – and yet is an invitation to jump, and also an insistence upon lightness which seems, by contrast, to warn us, and turns us back towards gravity, but an uncertain gravity which is lacking the guarantee (the security) of seriousness.

Jean Paulhan does not, as I see it, readily agree to mention in such direct terms the necessity of dying which is perhaps constantly at stake in the experience, except, once again, in his letters (still addressed to Marcel Arland): 'I mean: this void which we can hardly *feel*, between us and ourselves, except as a sort of death.' And this confession: 'It seems to me that what I feared, for a very long time, was much less death, than wanting to die (which I felt capable of from one moment to the next). One can scarcely talk about it.' A confession, no doubt, but one which touches the innermost secret of the experience. For as soon as a decisive absence is proposed to us, or as soon as thought is invited to open itself up to its own discontinuity in order to complete itself as thought, it is almost the ease of this movement, the temptation to give in to it immediately (without even having had the 'time' to complete it), which risks intervening and withdrawing this possibility. *The ease of dying*: such would be the danger watching over us.

** Let us take it from another angle: the only way we can be reasonable is not by claiming we are free from all unreason, or even (assuming it were possible) by escaping it, but rather by making this unreason so close, so accessible, so familiar to ourselves, that we never stop passing through it, lightly, without lingering or dwelling on it. Reasonable through a negligent activation of unreason, to the point where the latter would appear invisible: saved, in other words, by the rapidity of the shipwreck.

Yet there still has to be a shipwreck, madness, and this rapid death capable of hiding us from it by turning us away from 'wanting' it. The danger is that it might be easy to die to the point of feeling death's attraction, and to the point, under the influence of this attraction, of dying almost inadvertently: a double danger, since one might either die inattentively or the inattention might let us live because while in it we are unaware that this distraction is the symptom of death itself. But it is also a danger which *keeps watch*: this vigilance is the 'subject' of the experience, the thing which undergoes it, leads it, precipitates it, and holds it back so as to delay it in its moment of imminence, if this experience consists first of all in suppressing itself, or making itself possible through its suppression, since the Unity which is its end only presents itself as such once all the differences which designate it cancel themselves out by cancelling it out. Just as through language, and 'despite appearances, thing, word or thought amount to the same, and are one,' which implies that each of the terms renounces its distinguishing identity and, in renouncing it, destroys this concept of the 'same' on which the harmony of the 'One' seems to be based, so the 'All-One' which disregards differences (according to Jean Paulhan), none the less derives its condition from them, a condition that only works by obstructing these differences.

Whence this essential trait: it is never directly, but obliquely, that this 'single world in which we are merged together' is presented (thus outside presence) – it is by detours that simplicity takes us by surprise and by indirect paths that straightness does; and it is by indifference, the discretion of differences, that another indifference startles us: the indifference where, having been opposed, those differences point to the One in which they vanish (fold back into pure simplicity).

** I would like to go over again, more distinctly, the intentions, the characteristics and the conditions of such a movement within the experience which discovers it.

(1) It is not a question of a personal experience. Jean Paulhan does not claim to discover anything that is his alone. His task is rather, on one hand, to show why and how the knowledge that anyone who comes along possesses fully is lost and divided – into opposing theses – as soon as one turns one's attention to it; and on the other hand, thanks to an attention that is in a sense directed against attention, or as a result of a new movement, his task is to return to the fullness of this knowledge (the initial non-difference), but now richer with the consciousness of the illusions which had destroyed it, and with the recognition of this void – this death – that was for a moment tragically immobilized, and through which it was necessary to pass in order to return. I'd like to emphasize,

then, that this is both a scientific and a non-scientific process, at the intersection of the two and perhaps allowing, if not their reconciliation, then at least a better understanding of the necessity of their opposition. That such a theoretical process is satisfactory to no one, neither to linguists (for example) nor to philosophers, is understandable. Literature, which welcomes everything, is alone ready to welcome it, either academically, taking advantage of the indulgence that is manifested in the concern to reconcile opposites, all the better to deprive a work defined as perfectly literary of its more radical element, or esoterically, in the name of the secret which reveals itself therein as secret, and which it sets in motion without exposing it.

(2) Unity. I again ask the question: what kind of unity? The answer itself could only be ambiguous, diverted from any single possibility. The formula Jean Paulhan uses most readily – it seems to me – is the one I have just mentioned: this 'single world in which we are merged together' or to quote more fully: 'It is a society whose members – all or almost all of us – are able to recognize, or at least suspect in all language the sacred presence of a single world in which we are merged together. If you prefer, of a God that our divisions, our studying, our sciences, tear apart.' This 'single world', divine in its unity, is none the less a world. It is not the One which, as such, would transcend Being, in the same way that Plato invited us to try to think of the Good. (Jean Paulhan does, however, speak in places of a 'transcendent event', which is fairly rare terminology for a work that uses few academic terms.) This single world in which we are merged together is coextensive with us, and thus exceeds us in every way, or rather, is radically foreign to us, being the absolute exteriority of thought, which is an integral part of it. Hence the experience which seems to matter most to Jean Paulhan is the one which would verify 'the reality of the external world', an experience which is, however, only an apparent answer to the traditional problem, since what is affirmed in this case is the overwhelming surprise of the outside itself, overwhelming because it is introduced, as if by chance, into our own coherence, and withdraws us from it, withdraws us from ourselves and, in this withdrawal, relieving us of an 'I which is All', transports us – a pure transport or trance or *trans* – to the One. 'All-One': the formula of supreme duality and of ultimate unity, or of the irreducible duplicity of the One.

(3) The fact remains that Jean Paulhan cannot content himself with a simple affirmation which would restore 'the sacred presence of a single world' making 'our sciences, our studying and our divisions' responsible for tearing it apart. For this would be again to consider as inessential not only this studying and these sciences, but also (beyond knowledge) the demand for discontinuity which holds out, because of the gap and the non-coincidence that thought learns as it is performed, the very

possibility of the One, which is only postulated and discovered in the fleeting glimpse of infinite difference. For it is not only a matter of showing, through the metaphor of the Möbius strip, that there could be a displacement by which, as outside/inside and high/low cancel each other out, infinity would join up with itself: it is also necessary to show that this restored continuity depends on this displacement or reversal, this twisting or recasting which the continuous is unable to account for (and which it is even less able to make possible).

This is to recall, I think, two (inevitable) difficulties: (a) If one is to start out from undecided indifference and to return to recognized non-difference, following the passion of the One, one needs not only to pass through the work of differences, but to decide that the structure of these differences is, as we say, binary and that it is reduced to a rigorous opposition of terms to other terms, which are always disjoined two by two. (Whence this *and*, which is so often made visible by being put in italics in the statements proposed to us: sound *and* meaning, language *and* thought, thought *and* world, time *and* space, with the *and* itself doubling up into an *and/or*, so we have an oppositional alternative which would ultimately coincide with a non-simultaneous simultaneity.) To posit in advance that all plurality, including dispersion, is reducible to an alternating duality – since dispersion, as Heraclitus has already formalized it, would be part of an ordered structure of 'dispersal/gathering together' – is to submit *a priori* to the procedure based on unity which we find again, since it has already been postulated.

(b) This same opposition of discontinuity–continuity (which also has to be presupposed paradoxically, if between the discontinuous and the continuous there needs to be a prior discontinuity) begs the question of whether the void which the *and* covers over and designates is each time the *same*. Let us suppose this continuous chain of discontinuity: sound/meaning, language/thought, thought/world; what would lead us to assume that each time the hiatus between the terms or figures or positions is identical? Why would it be the same gap? And why would the discontinuous, even without being freed from a regulated use, not be such that each time it would take on an *other* function, and through this function, would be distinguished as an always different difference? In other words, are we not already thinking in terms of unity, and according to the principle of the Same, when we think the rupture or the break which supposedly distracts us from it for a time, so that we can hold on, in this play of proximity and distance, to the continuous thread – truly Ariadne's thread – thanks to which we are able, led astray without straying, to get out of the labyrinth of dispersion?

Unless of course this void is implicitly thought or carried to its absolute extreme, and unless the absolute, as such, is necessarily free from all distinction (all plurality). But is not the infinite, except if some demand intervenes which can only be called purely religious, even ethical, indifferent both to the One and the Non-One? In the same way, the break (this break dividing sound/meaning, language/thought, discourse/writing) is perhaps only as decisive as it is because it is infinitesimal, so much so that it might be considered as functionally inoperative, even a supplementary mark of unity, and yet it is (like any infinitesimal) unidentifiable, thus foreign to identification and unification alike. Such that only the infinitely small break – or disjunction – would guarantee the radical non-rapport which the One could never concern itself with, even as a lack, if it is a matter of indifference whether the One controls this non-rapport or not. And such that in the presence of the reunified God, unity would ultimately only be prevented by the division which does not divide – the parcelling out which leaves (him) undivided and, in this indivision, always already divided, with no relation to presence and/or absence.

** 'As if our world were side by side with some other world, which is normally invisible, but whose intervention, at decisive moments, was alone able to save it from collapse.'

'But how can we succeed in seeing at first sight things for the second time?'

'. . . and I abandoned myself to the pleasures of a death, which my body had sensed first of all.'

'This life of waiting and of assent.'

'Whoever thinks I am wrong, I am attracted by. Whoever thinks I am right, I believe to have misunderstood me; I don't stand up for myself willingly. As if I were waiting, in order to be satisfied, to be both other people and myself.'

'Here my despair as a writer begins.'

** The *récit* alone provides the space, while taking it away, for the experience which is contrary to itself, for all of its moments and all of its levels, including in this attraction of the One that it undergoes, and which it obstinately points to as the obsession that turns it against itself, to the point where it could no longer be a question of an experience – as in something having taken place, or possibly taking place – but rather of a non-experience, and almost of a call to manifest itself by suspending (deferring) its manifestation. This is what is at stake in the *récit*, the unendingness that it carries with it and which, preventing it from being realized, leads it, so it can better respond to the demand for incompletion, towards this formal perfection which is, in Jean Paulhan, its painful denial. Easy death remains, then, in the particularly clear expression which circumscribes this 'perfectly' subversive proposition, the secret's evidence, through which we are always questioned, for want of knowing that at every moment in our writing–reading we are forming an answer to it. Easy death, from which we believe we are protected, whereas it is always already too late to escape from it, is thus the manner in which transgression – this step beyond and belonging to the outside – is proposed, given the failure of the Law; it surpasses the Law, in so far as the Law cannot be surpassed, or more enigmatically, it produces it only through its infraction, as if the limit – an *impossible* limit to transgress – could only be marked by the decision which has already breached it with its 'maybe'. This is what writing announces to us, writing which is bound to the desireless attraction of 'easy death': that there is no 'law' except through transgression, and certainly no transgression except in the eyes of the 'law', but with no reciprocity or symmetrical relationship between the two; since just as for the law, any transgression is not only in reference to the law, but confirms it, so for the step which trans-gresses, that is to say attains its beyond (thereby pointing to the unknown), the only space that prohibition can find to lay down the law in is one of adventure, the future of the unknown which has always 'mocked' that which is forbidden.

Transgression points to the limit from its far side or beyond; the law points to the limit from its near side, and between the two, in an interval of irregularity, this supposed limit rules, the same but never the same, a caesura that is all the more decisive in that it is apparently nothing, or infinite (depending neither on affirmation nor on negation), since, from the point of view of the law, the limit is the absolute delimitation (unsurpassable even if it is surpassed) and, from transgression's absence of perspective, the limit is only the 'as if' (as it happens, a turn of phrase whose power to transport Jean Paulhan has reinvented) which is used to measure, by making it incommensurable, what has been accomplished, by the violence of the unaccomplished. It is, then, a line of demarcation which has a 'nothing' marking the distance travelled from one indetermination to another, a nothing, or that which cannot be determined, separating nothing from nothing (and yet nothing non-existent, since the law, as if in advance, is always founded on it only to dissociate itself from it). 'It is impossible,' the Law indeed says. 'Impossible,' says transgression – each impossible, each time, being pronounced in the first place. The radical difference, in their absolute identity, of the the two terms, the one tending to mark the extreme limit of what is possible, the other, the indeterminate space of non-possibility, this difference in identity, or this non-identity of the same (the invisible fissure of unity) belongs to writing, which carries death, 'easy death'.

** 'And for my initial awkwardness in defending myself against the ease which one takes in dying.'

** Easy death. Let us remind ourselves one last time of the constraint of this double word, simplicity itself. (1) Death: the prohibition which is cancelled out or suspended by the ease of dying. (2) But this ease, far from cancelling it out, heightens what is most scandalous in the scandal *par excellence* of mortal violence: dying – impossibility – is easy. (3) Forbidden and indiscreet death, the one borne by, and which bears writing, is restored to the secret of discretion by innocent, happy, *easy* reading. (4) 'The ease which one *takes* in dying': an ease, the power to do, the pure power of producing, which however comes to us, through a violent *possession*, from the predisposition given to us from within what we have to undergo absolutely, the passivity of the most passive; but also the singularity of writing, which is a unique form of 'doing', and which only reading, in its repetition, can cause to be done and undone; and since repetition is the very mode of mortal absence, reading, through its ease, holds in its turn, but reversed, the power of death that writing, as the sole form of violence, concealed in the detour of this death. Thus the reversal is carried out, through the duplicity of easy death, a reversal whose possibility Jean Paulhan for one moment held on to and mastered, at the cost of the patience of his life, and a possibility which had one time, and always over again, been revealed to him, like an inexhaustible secret, by *reading–writing*, the play of the necessity of an indifferent difference.

Notes

1 *La Vocation transparente de Jean Paulhan* (Paris, Gallimard, 1961), p. 152.

Translated by Michael Syrotinski

30

Thanks (Be Given) to Jacques Derrida (1990)*

After such a long silence (perhaps hundreds and hundreds of years) I shall begin to write again, not on Derrida (how pretentious!), but with his help, and convinced that I shall betray him immediately. Here is a question: is there one Torah or two? Answer: there are two, because necessarily there is only one. That one, unique and yet double (there are two Tables standing facing each other), is written, and written with the finger of 'God' (we name him thus by our incapacity to name him). Moses could have taken it down, like a faithful scribe, under dictation, by copying out what the Voice told him. Admittedly, he still hears the Voice: he has the 'right' to hear, but not to see (except once from behind, seeing a non-presence, and in disguise as well).

But this is not the case. The Torah is written, not only in order for it to be preserved (held in memory), but because 'God' perhaps privileges writing, revealing himself as the first and last writer. (Nobody other than he has the power to write.) 'And by what right are you now writing here?' – 'But I am not writing.' What happens next is well known, while still not being properly known (known only in the form of a story). As Moses did not return (forty days and forty nights of absence – the time in years of the days and nights spent in the wilderness), the people doubted and demanded other Gods or another guide. Here I am no doubt putting forward an incorrect interpretation. Aaron, Moses' brother, the Aaron who had the gift of speech his brother lacked (to which we shall return later), had recourse to a ruse (ruses play a large part in the history of the Hebrews as well as the Greeks: paths are not straight, which is a great misfortune, a misfortune that enjoins us to seek rectitude freely). Aaron asks each and every man and woman to give up their precious personal jewellery: their earrings, necklaces, rings, etc.; in a word, he strips them naked, and with their belongings he fashions some thing, an object, a form, which was not theirs. What was Aaron's mistake in this adroit ruse by which he met his end? He became an artist, he falsely claimed the

* Originally published as 'Grâce (soit rendue) à Jacques Derrida', *Revue Philosophique*, 2 (1990), pp. 167–73.

power of creation for himself, even if the image he made ought to have aroused his admirers' suspicions (a calf, a golden calf). In other words, the Hebrews were reverting to the gods of Egypt where they had been kept in slavery (the calf is perhaps a reference to Anubis, with its jackal's head, or Apis the bull). Despite their misfortune, their supreme misfortune in that land, they still yearned for it; though now free, they felt unable to bear the weight of that freedom, its burden and responsibility.

It seems that Moses, lost in the hills, together with the Tables on which there was the sovereign, original writing, suspected nothing. 'God' had to warn him: go down, go down, below is catastrophe. Moses goes down with the Tables and sees disaster. Frenzied destruction is what follows: the Egyptian calf is ground to powder, the image disappears, and the precious substance (gold) is cast out and annihilated. But the destruction does not stop there, since Moses destroys the Tables by breaking them. We ask ourselves: how is this possible? How can Moses destroy the indestructible: the writing written not by him, but by the Most High? Does that mean: all is effaced, all must be effaced? It does not seem that 'God' holds it against Moses for committing an act which it would be a mistake to term iconoclastic. On the contrary, his frenzy is beyond all bounds. The people, so often saved before, is now under threat, under threat of annihilation. There is nothing to be done with this people, already reputed (and famed) for the stiffness of their necks (necks that the labour of serfdom did much to stiffen). Once or twice (perhaps more), 'God' is tempted (the temptation is designed to test Moses) to abolish the whole past and start over again just with Moses, who will perpetuate the law and engender a new people (which I grant does not mean that he might be of some other – say, Egyptian – descent, but that he is other because he knows himself to be responsible for all others – ah, the heavy charge).

But Moses, this strange man, made a foreigner by his task and by the fact that he was the one chosen to carry it out (why did he take as his wife a foreigner, a Cushite woman born of a non-Hebrew family, probably a black Ethiopian, who, for that very reason, was given a hostile reception by the already somewhat racist Aaron and Miriam, a 'woman who', it is true, 'will later become a convert, together with her father'? thus giving us to understand that conversion, according to some religious customs, is right, even though it is not to be recommended). Yes, Moses is essentially a humble man (this is his kenosis), he does not wish to found a blood-line to lord it over this unfortunate people, which is all the more unfortunate because it has committed a sin and is guilty of impatience; and this impatience, which is the virtue and sin of those who cannot wait and for whom salvation (the Messiah) must come immediately, will lead to punishment, but not annihilation. At which point, everything begins again: Moses going up the mountain, his absence, the frustration and expiation of the forty days and forty nights, the submission to the task of finding and hewing (as in some kind of primitive art) the two symmetrical stone Tables, upon which the finger of 'God' writes again, for the second time, the Law (what the Greek refers to as the Decalogue or Ten Commandments). That, too, is God's humility, yet this is the mystery of writing. If God's humility is what grants the possibility of beginning again, the fact remains that, through the fault of man, it is as though there was no first writing; all first writing is already second, is its own second-ariness. Whence the endless debate about the two Torahs (not the broken and the unbroken Torah, that particular quest is the temptation of mysticism, and its danger), but the Written and the Oral Torah: is one superior to the other, the first being white and the second black – white, that is, meaning virginal (like the blank page) and, so to speak, unwritten or rather not subject to reading, beyond reading, made up of a timeless, ageless trace, a mark preceding all time, even creation itself? On the other hand, this mark, this trace, these blanks are cryptic, difficult or impossible to decipher only for the non-student, the pupil without a teacher, or a foolhardy seeker after knowledge (such as myself in this case). Here, it is the Oral Torah that is superior, to the extent that it makes the unreadable readable, uncovers that which is hidden, corres-ponds to its own name which means teaching, the infinite reading that one cannot undertake on one's own, but only under the guidance of a Master, a whole tradition of Masters, all busy 'wringing' new meanings from the text, yet without forgetting the primary rule: you shall add nothing, you shall omit nothing.

If this is true, have we not, then, lapsed back into the debate which Jacques Derrida has made not present to us, but rather warned us against neglecting even while we keep it at a distance?

Before the mystery of the writing of the Tables, Moses, as is well known, wondered about this Voice. For him, speaking is not self-evident. When 'God' commands him to speak to Pharaoh, to ask him to let the Hebrew slaves go (and abolish slavery), Moses is most unhappy for (according to Chouraqui's translation) he knows – and reminds God of it – that he is 'heavy of mouth, heavy of tongue, impure of lips', and thus incapable of using the language of eloquence and rhetoric that is proper to the great men of the world. Whence God's anger. Moses was chosen precisely because he is not a fine speaker, and has difficulty with lan-guage: he has no mastery over the Voice, and is no doubt a stammerer. Moses therefore has his brother Aaron stand in for him, since Aaron is more gifted with social niceties (there are always problems or secrets between Moses and his brothers), but also (and I put this forward with some trepidation) because Moses himself is able to speak only by doubling or repeating words, even the supreme ones, because of his stammer, which is not so much physical as 'metaphysical'.

There follows a proposition that is so daring that I am convinced it is a temptation. When Moses questions 'God', he is careful not to ask his name, which would be a terrible indiscretion, since if he had been given the name, he would in some way have had authority over the Named. What he does ask for, though, he asks for not for himself, not in order to know the unnameable, but in order to be able to say something to his fellow men who will not fail to ask him: where does your revelation come from, in whose name do you speak? The Hebrews, however much they may be slaves, do not obey without being enlightened, they want to know who they are dealing with. And the answer that was given to Moses, but which we know only in the form already passed on by Moses, expressed by virtue of the necessary stammer, will be the subject of endless commentary. I cite it (and recite it) thus: 'I am that is' (according to an ontological interpretation, in which it is Being without being that has primacy and is glorified, a version that Master Eckhart, the dear (or old) Rhenish master, will reject), or, alternatively: 'I am that I am.' This is an answer that may be thought not to be an answer, but more a refusal to answer. The repetition involved may appear sublime or disappointing, but what if – this is my own foolhardy thought – what is heard (or read) is repeated twice over because it is spoken by a stammering Voice, a Voice augmented by that very stammer, so that if Moses had been speaking Latin (why not? he has so many other languages at his disposal), what he would have said would have been: *Sum, Sum.* In the Talmud, without any reference to Moses' particular language difficulty, it is stated: *One word was uttered by God, but I heard two.* But let us return to the question (beyond enquiry, beyond answer) that Moses asks, with no pretensions of finding out the name of God (I am repeating myself in my turn) but only the name to which he lays claim on behalf of the restive people of Israel. And here is another answer (in the translation given by both Meschonnic and Chouraqui): '[I] *will be* (followed by a large blank space as though to mark not only expectancy or uncertainty, but the reference to a non-temporal future, free from all present) *who will be*'[1] (Edmond Fleg offers the same version). God does not constitute himself immediately as a subject, as a blazing 'I', but as acting on behalf of the Hebrew people and dependent on their actions, both their actions towards God and towards others [*autrui*]. This is what, using this time, perhaps wrongly, a Greek word, will be known as kenosis: sovereign humility. But, as we know from Rashi, at the very moment that Moses hears: 'This is my name for ever,' he gives us to understand, by a change of vowel, the words: 'My name must remain hidden,' which confirms the decorum – or propriety – of Moses' discretion. 'God' also says, if my memory serves, 'Even to the patriarchs, I did not make myself known.' Nevertheless, the name released to Moses to arouse Israel is such an important name (so quick to efface itself) that it must not be uttered in vain: it remains non-present even when spoken and addressed as Unknown – *aphonic*, as David Banon puts it, but not *asemic*, the promised God, God of the promise, but also God of the withdrawal of the promise.

God, says Levinas, is not knowledge, nor non-knowledge pure and simple, but the obligation of man towards all other men. As for the name which is only the name of Yahweh, and which, as Chouraqui makes clear, today – in the diaspora – nobody knows how to pronounce, for, Levinas adds, the Tetragrammaton could be uttered only by the High Priest entering into the Holy of Holies, on the Day of Atonement, that is, for post-exilic Judaism, *never* (see his *Beyond the Verse*).

As Jacques Derrida writes, spelling out the demands of the doubling of the Torah, a doubling that is already inscribed in the way in which the Torah is written 'with the finger of God': 'The Torah is written in white fire on black fire.' 'The white fire, a text written in *invisible letters* (designed to remain unseen), may be read in the black fire of the Oral Torah which comes *after the event* to outline the consonants and *punctuate the vowels*: the Law or Fiery Word, Moses says.'

But if the stone Torah is God's inscription, an inscription which as such lays out the commandments, a writing which can be read only as prescriptive, it is also said in Exodus (24: 4), even before the Tables (supposing, of course, which one may well doubt, that there is a before and an after – and thus some narrative order – in such a moment without presence), that 'Moses wrote all the words of the Lord.' Moses therefore has the gift of writing, even if he has not the gift of speech – and he writes because the Ancients of Israel, the Prophets, previously declared: 'All the words which "God" has said will we do.' Perhaps they fail to understand them, or, as in Chouraqui's version, do *not penetrate* their rightness, just like their twists and turns, but the important part is the *doing*, and this promise of accomplishment seals Moses' writing, is made writing through Moses – writing and memorization. Let us note in passing the huge divide that opens up here between Plato and Moses: for one, writing, which is external and alien, is bad because it makes up for the loss of memory and thus encourages the failings of living memory (why bother remembering something since it can be written down?). For Moses, writing assuredly guarantees memorization, but it is also (or primarily) the 'doing', the 'acting', the exteriority which precedes interiority or will institute it – in the same way that Deuteronomy, in which Moses begins the whole story over again in the first person, redoubles and prolongs the difficult Exodus.

At this stage, one can raise an idle question: who is Moses? Let us rule out the answer that says he was an Egyptian prince who betrayed his people to devote himself to another hard-working, unfortunate people held in slavery. Let us also rule out the sublime image given in art: the Superman, the Hebrew equivalent of Solon and Lycurgus. On the contrary (if he does have privileges since he is the only one to 'go up', without growing closer to the heavens), he is shown to be faltering, a poor speaker (heavy of mouth), weary to the point of ruining his own health by the excessive services he does for others (his father-in-law, with characteristic common sense, tells him: don't do everything yourself, don't pass judgement in the little things as well as the big ones, you will not survive – and Moses agrees). He is weary too, when Amalek wages war on the Hebrews, just when they had barely left slavery in Egypt and are a motley band (a disorderly herd or mass) made up mainly of women and children (what Chouraqui translates as a 'brood'). This is what makes Amalek such a nasty figure and shows him up as Evil's chosen one. Moses is not a warrior chief. Yet he is positioned on the top of a hill, as is the case with generals, even Napoleon. But he has to be helped when he gives out apparently simple instructions: he holds up his hand to point to the sky and the Hebrews prevail – but precisely his hands are heavy and he has to be aided in order to carry out his gesture – otherwise his arm will fall to his side (this is not just weariness, but also a lesson), and Amalek wins the day.

Is Moses a mediator? He is mediator to his people, and organizes it into a community and rages against it when it falters. Yet the people do not recognize themselves in him: 'We did not know,' the Hebrews tell Aaron, his own brother, 'who it was leading us.' Moses is other, though he shows brotherly concern, is constantly interceding, and meting out punishment too. Is he God's mediator, whose commandments he passes down? God is without mediation, says Levinas, unless I am mistaken. That is why Moses' responsibility is free and why he has to undergo, in punishment, the excessive words through which he annoyed the Most High, words of invocation and supplication for the fugitives who forget that is what they are and want to 'settle down'.

One may wonder what was Moses' 'fault', the fault that will prevent him from reaching the 'promised land'. There are of course a number of privileged answers. But in the desire to reach his destination and rest there is already one hope too many. He may see, but not have. The rest that is reserved for him is perhaps a higher rest. 'That is one of the mysteries of Elohim' that do not reveal themselves, but require endless teaching. It is sometimes said, in analyses of Deuteronomy, that Moses was incapable of telling the story of his own death, writing it (critical scepticism). Why not? He knows (with knowledge that is never elucidated) that he dies through 'God', 'on God's mouth', thereby carrying out a last, final commandment in which there is all the sweetness of the end – but an end that is hidden from view. The death that is necessarily in life (since Adam) 'here does not take place in life' (Derrida). And God, playing the part of the gravedigger (Levinas), in a proximity that promises no afterlife, buries him in a valley in the land of Moab, in an (atopical) place without place. 'No man knows of his sepulchre unto this day,' which is what allows those who believe in superstitions to doubt his death, just as the death of Jesus will later be doubted too. He is dead, but 'his eye was not dim, nor his natural force abated.' He has a successor, Joshua, but he also has none (no direct heir; he himself refused this kind of transmission). *And there has not yet arisen a prophet since in Israel like unto Moses.* 'Not yet.' The disappearance is without any promise of return. But the disappearance of the 'author' gives even greater necessity to teaching, writing (the trace prior to all text) and speech, to the speech within writing, the speech that does not vivify writing which otherwise would be dead, but on the contrary impels us to go towards others, caring for the distant and the near, without it yet being given to us to know that, before all else, this is the only path towards the Infinite.

Note

1 Translator's note: '*Serai* . . . *qui serai*' in the original French versions by Meschonnic and Chouraqui. (The first-person pronoun is purposely omitted for reasons that are clear from what follows.)

Translated by Leslie Hill

Blanchot in English
by
Peter C. Hoy

(i) Books

Thomas the Obscure, trans. Robert Lamberton (New York, David Lewis, 1973).

Death Sentence, trans. Lydia Davis (Barrytown, NY, Station Hill Press, 1978).

The Gaze of Orpheus, trans. Lydia Davis (Barrytown, NY, Station Hill Press, 1981).

The Madness of the Day, trans. Lydia Davis (Barrytown, NY, Station Hill Press, 1981).

The Space of Literature, trans. Ann Smock (Lincoln, University of Nebraska Press, 1982).

The Sirens' Song, trans. Sacha Rabinovitch (Brighton, Harvester Press, 1982).

Vicious Circles, trans. Paul Auster (Barrytown, NY, Station Hill Press, 1985).

When the Time Comes, trans. Lydia Davis (Barrytown, NY, Station Hill Press, 1985).

The Writing of the Disaster, trans. Ann Smock (Lincoln, University of Nebraska Press, 1986).

Michel Foucault As I Imagine Him, trans. Jeffrey Mehlman, in *Foucault, Blanchot* (New York, Zone Books, 1987).

The Unavowable Community, trans. Pierre Joris (Barrytown, NY, Station Hill Press, 1988).

The Infinite Conversation, trans. Susan Hanson (Minneapolis, University of Minnesota Press, 1992).

The Last Man, trans. Lydia Davis (New York, Columbia University Press, 1987).

The Step (Not) Beyond, trans. Lycette Nelson (New York, SUNY Press, 1992).

The One Who was Standing Apart From Me, trans. Lydia Davis (Barrytown, NY, Station Hill Press, 1993).

(ii) Articles

'Face to face with Sade', *Instead*, 5–6 (Nov. 1948).

—— in *Issues in Abstract Expressionism*, ed. Ann Eden Gibson (Ann Arbor, University of Michigan Press, 1990).

'Adolphe, or the misfortunes of sincerity', *Horizon*, XX (August 1949), pp. 94–110.

'Bergson and Symbolism', *Yale French Studies*, 2 (Fall–Winter 1949), pp. 63–6.

'Marquis de Sade', *Horizon*, XX (Dec. 1949–Jan. 1950), pp. 423–52.

'Adolphe, or the curse of real feelings', *Yale French Studies*, 13 (1954), pp. 62–75.

'René Char' and 'The beast of Lascaux', in *René Char's Poetry* (Rome, De Luca, 1956), pp. 9–26, 27–40.

'The Diaries: the exigency of the work of art', in *Franz Kafka Today*, ed. Angel Flores and Homer Swander (Madison, University of Wisconsin Press, 1958), pp. 195–220.

'Where now? Who now?', *Evergreen Review*, 2 (Winter 1959), pp. 222–4, 226–9.

—— in *On Contemporary Literature*, ed. Richard Kostelanetz (New York, Avon Books, 1964), pp. 249–54.

—— in *On Beckett. Essays and Criticism*, ed. S. E. Gontarski (New York, Grove Press, 1986), pp. 141–8.

—— in *Samuel Beckett's 'Molloy', 'Malone Dies', 'The Unnamable'*, ed. Harold Bloom (New York, Chelsea House, 1988), pp. 23–9.

[et al.] 'Declaration concerning the right of insubordination in the Algerian War', *Evergreen Review*, 4 (Nov.–Dec. 1960), [unpaginated].

'Time, art and the Museum' [abridged], in *Malraux: A Collection of Critical Essays*, ed. R. W. B. Lewis (Englewood Cliffs, NJ, Prentice-Hall, 1964), pp. 147–60.

'The Athenæum', *Art and Literature*, 6 (Autumn 1965), pp. 149–60.

—— *Studies in Romanticism*, 22 (Summer 1983), pp. 163–72.

'Sade', in The Marquis de Sade, *The Complete Justine, Philosophy in the Bedroom and Other Writings*, ed. Richard Seaver and Austryn Wainhouse (New York, Grove Press, 1966), pp. 37–72.

'The main impropriety (excerpts)', *Yale French Studies*, 39 (1967), pp. 50–63.

'Gide and the concept of literature as adventure', in *Gide: A Collection of Critical Essays*, ed. David Littlejohn (Englewood Cliffs, NJ, Prentice-Hall, 1970), pp. 49–62.

'Edmond Jabès's *Book of Questions*', *European Judaism*, 6 (Summer 1972), pp. 34–7.

—— *Montemora*, 6 (1979), pp. 76–81.

'Interruption, as on a Riemann surface', *Literary Supplement*, 4 (March 1973), pp. 13–16.

—— *Montemora*, 6 (1979), pp. 72–6.

—— in *The Sin of the Book: Edmond Jabès*, ed. Eric Gould (Lincoln and London, University of Nebraska Press, 1985), pp. 43–54.

'For Edmond Jabès', *A Range of Curtains*, 6–7 (1973) [unnumbered pages].

'Reading Kafka', in *Twentieth-Century Interpretations of 'The Trial': A Collection of Critical Essays*, ed. James Rolleston (Englewood Cliffs, NJ, Prentice-Hall, 1976), pp. 11–20.

'The limits of experience – nihilism' in *The New Nietzsche*, ed. David Allison (New York, Delta, 1977), pp. 121–7.

'From *The Infinite Conversation*', *Enclitic*, III (Spring 1979), pp. 51–61.

'The look of Orpheus', *Denver Quarterly*, 14 (Fall 1979), pp. 90–5.

'Reading', *Denver Quarterly*, 14 (Winter 1980), pp. 119–25.

'Communication', *Denver Quarterly*, 15 (Spring 1980), pp. 3–11.

'The word Berlin' [abridged], *Semiotext(e)*, VI (1982), pp. 60–5

'Musil', *Scripsi*, 2 (Spring 1983), pp. 15–28.

'Our Clandestine Companion', in *Face to Face with Levinas*, ed. Richard A. Cohen (New York, SUNY Press, 1986), pp. 41–52.

'Marx's three voices', *New Political Science*, 15 (Summer 1986), pp. 17–20.

'Our responsibility', in *Texts for Nelson Mandela*, ed. Jacques Derrida and Mustapha Tilli (New York, Seaver, 1987).

'The last one to speak', *ACTS: A Journal of New Writing*, 5–6 (1988), pp. 228–39.

'Translating', *Sulfur*, 26 (1990), pp. 82–6.

'Enigma', *Yale French Studies*, 79 (1991), pp. 8–10.

'Who?', in *Who Comes After the Subject?*, ed. Eduardo Cadava, Peter Connor and Jean-Luc Nancy (London, Routledge, 1991), pp. 58–60.

'Glances from beyond the grave', *Yale French Studies*, 81 (1992), pp. 151–61.

Index